Bohemia

the protoculture

then and now

This 1740 print by William Hogarth, "The Distrest Poet," exemplifies the popular image of the poor artist before Murger transformed it into the romantic bohemian.

Richard Miller

BOHEMIA

the protoculture
then and now

Nelson-Hall
Chicago

LIBRARY OF CONGRESS CATALOGING IN PUBLICATION DATA

Miller, Richard Connelly, 1925–
    Bohemia: the protoculture then and now

    Bibliography: p. 343
    Includes index.
    1. Civilization, Modern—19th Century.
2. Civilization, Modern—20th Century
3. Bohemianism I. Title.
CB417.M53   909.08   77–14073
ISBN 0–88229–293–5   (cloth)
ISBN 0–88229–518–7   (paper)

Manufactured in the United States of America

"If we survive this century it will only be because you and I refuse to become Nazis."

—Joan Baez, Berkeley, 1973.†

Contents

Preface
The Long Revolution
(1760-today)

Since the eighteenth century technological change has been disrupting the traditional relations between and among men. The institutions that form and moderate these relations have been changing so much more slowly than the relations themselves as to have disintegrated from reality and from each other. Consequently, if not soon replaced by a viable new order, they will self-destruct and be replaced by a dead earth.

The past two centuries have been a time of transition from the traditional order of Western culture to something still concealed by the future. Already weakened, between 1775 and 1815 the old order of Western culture collapsed. This was the time of the American and French revolutions and the rise and fall of Napoleon—in all, an eruption of events which changed the shape of everything.

The nineteenth century, an era of relatively peaceful evolution contained between the battles of Waterloo (1815) and the Marne (1914), can now be seen as an unsuccessful attempt to build a political economy of compromise, one preserving the old institutions in the context of the new realities. To the early Victorians, it seemed a transitional order whose issue was in grave doubt.[1] By 1914, the attempt appeared a success: progress would continue to flow along in the traditional forms until inevitably and at last this evolution would create an ideal society for all.

Such was the belief of our ancestors.

But instead of the utopia they so confidently expected, they got the Western Front. The guns of August 1914 sounded the overture of the collapse of the transitional order, of a thirty years' war coming to crescendo with the bombs of Hiroshima, of a sixty years' war reaching a climax in the bombs of Hanoi or in some catastrophe yet to come.

The traditional order is long dead; the transitional order is crumbling around us. The posttraditional order lies ahead. Although no one knows what this new order will be, its antecedents already exist. These, the posttraditional elements of the present and recent past, ranging across the romantic movement from Adolf Hitler's Third Reich to Bohemia, are elements we can understand. Consequently, barring the intrusion of fortuitous events, we can consciously build a new order out of cultural themes of our own choosing.

The base point of the long revolution is the traditional order of the High Middle Ages. The traditional order was a confederacy of cellular communities resting on an agricultural base and molded around the armature of Christianity, then both a structure and a consciousness. Unlike those of other civilizations, Europe's traditional order was rural. North of the Alps, Europe had few cities. The largest, Paris, held 100,000 people in 1200 and 150,000 in 1300. In 1200, five other European cities had 50,000 people. London had 20,000. Europe was organized in large rural cells around the nucleus of manor or monastery, ruled by baron or abbot. Kingdoms, loose confederacies of these rural cells, found such harmony as they could in the fields of power emanating from emperor, king, and church.[2]

It was in the interests of baron and abbot, of emperor, pope, and monarch, to weaken the authority of all rivals. This endless and chaotic contest among them for power generated a spirit of liberty impatient of all authority. Creator of science and transformer of technology, the spirit of liberty proved to be the nemesis of the traditional order.[3] More than two hundred years ago Denis Diderot stated the quintessence of its creed:

Man will never be free until the last king is strangled by the entrails of the last priest.[4]

Today, as then, we see the spirit of liberty and the principle of authority struggling for possession of the future.

Taking the side of liberty, modern youth is adopting a neobohemian life-style. Most of the traits of that style can be traced back into the Middle Ages, but as a constellation of traits the style began in France within the romantic army of art students and poets who fought to free the arts from middle class control.

From 1830 until the start of World War I, Bohemia and its devotion to setting art free lived and grew in Paris. Concurrently, similar life-styles, equally anti middle class, but clustering around more *Dionysian themes, began taking shape elsewhere. These appear in San Francisco where the Wild West tradition became civilized, in New Orleans with the creation of jazz music, and in Germany with the Wandervogel movement, a revolt of youth soon seen as a new "youth culture."

These styles have long influenced one another and substantially affected the development of the middle-class—the bourgeois—life-style. It is only in recent years, however, that they have been fusing into one, transforming into a new consciousness now embodied in youth everywhere.

Although influenced by greater Boston, this came about in the San Francisco Bay area. In cosmopolitan Frisco, jazz music, scientific innovation, and the folk-song and student-protest movements conjoined with the old Bohemias of the artists and the beats, with the new Bohemias of the pranksters and the Haight and, shot through with LSD, mutated into the developing new consciousness.

This cultural mutation, growing around the double helix of art and science, is the protoculture.

Middle-class culture, too, has mutated. Its current form is technocratic. Generated in Nazi Germany, this life-style predominates over big business and the executive branch of government. Freed from all moral considerations and traditional restraints, the bourgeois mutant's primary concern is expediency. *

Although forming one end of the continuum of possible futures, this, the Nazi alternative for the coming world culture, cannot in fact be a protoculture because the human race could not survive its victory.

This book tells the story of the development of the bohemian tradition and of its mutation into the protoculture. *

It does so in hopes that a better understanding of the story will help the protoculture become its promise.

* relating to the sensual, spontaneous, and emotional aspects of our being

permaculture, perhaps?

* convenience & practicality

* a "prototype", after which each subsequent subculture of its kind will be modeled in some way, shape, or form

Part One

THE ROMANTIC RESISTANCE

"Poor martyr, whose body and thought they have
used up, whose heart and life they have broken by
deceptions without number, here at last comes
the (denouement) of this comedy!"

—Gabriel Pélin, 1861.*

1.

Progress
and Poverty
(1815-1914)

In the early decades of the nineteenth century, anxiety and apprehension suffused the climate of feeling, a mood which among the beneficiaries of the new technology changed eventually into one of confidence and hope. The century itself lived in an environment of wood, stone, brass, brick, and cast iron—a world smelling of steam and blood, excrement and soft-coal smoke. This was a time of change, activity, of tremendous creative energy without precedent in the previous story of man. In order to extract extra savings from the traditional economic base and thus accumulate the extra capital necessary to the building of railroads, machines, and cities—the prerequisites of increased productivity—the century imposed on many of its people privations worse than it exacted of its draft animals.

These prerequisites, once brought into existence, meant that the old power base of human and animal muscles supplemented by wind and water would be replaced by the chemical energy locked in fossil fuels, an energy first employed through the medium of steam and then through electricity and petroleum vapor. In about 1870, the new power running the new machines began to create an avalanche of fantastic new products and the promise that at last mankind could produce enough to provide everyone with the material base of a comfortable and dignified existence.

So it should have been. But something went wrong. In the late 1870's, Henry George, a diminutive red-haired printer/tramp/sailor/journalist/publisher, who in 1858 had come to California as a com-

Has the time come to leave this era and its practices in the past?

1

mon seaman, sitting now in a house at 417 First Street, San Francisco, looking out over the bay, reviewing in imagination the career
of the century, wrote:

"It is as though an immense wedge were being forced, not under-
neath society, but through society. Those who are above the point
of separation are elevated, but those who are below are crushed
down." [1]

This, the paradox of progress and poverty, created two nineteenth centuries—that of the rising bourgeois ascending to <u>and</u>
<u>sometimes beyond the wealth and power of baron and prelate, and</u>
<u>that of the depressed millions of workers and peons crushed down</u>
<u>to die in slums</u>, to abandon home and family in a desperate search
for work, to father children destined to live untended in the streets
of New York, London, Paris—street Arabs—who survived, if at all,
by charity, begging, and crime.[2]

New York street boys.

Consequently, the bourgeois soul harbored a profound guilt
and an omnipresent fear of financial ruin, of at any moment falling
into the abyss with the anguished millions. Collectively, this guilt-
and-fear was felt as the threat of insurrection, as the menace of the

[margin note, handwritten:] Nietzche's "pathos of distance" b/w aristocratic (bourgeois) and slave (proletariat) morality, resulting in the ascetic ideal

masses of suffering humanity coming together and overturning all.[3]
These and other guilts and fears compacted with sexual repressions and the tightening dominance of the profit motive—take more than you give—caused the bourgeois increasingly to support national policies embodying the new chemical power and machine technology in arms. In 1815 the arms of the world's major states were essentially of the same design. By 1914, excepting Japan, the arms of the West had become irresistible. In colonies, protectorates, and "independent" states the black and brown peoples lived as serfs of the whites. By 1914, when the whites started killing each other, they controlled eighty-five percent of the earth's surface.[4] This ice-cold exploitation found justification in doctrines of white supremacy—the White Man's Burden, Kultur, la mission civilisatrice, Holy Russia—doctrines asserting the white man's religious-physical-cultural-moral superiority to all other human beings and the corollary, the white man's manifest destiny to rule (and exploit) his inferiors and to destroy their lesser cultures.

On the black and brown people of the nineteenth century this imposed a question still thematic in liberation movements at home and abroad: will you accept subhuman status or fight for your humanity?[5]

In the nineteenth century the Americans applied European-style racist doctrines to their blacks and Indians, to their Catholic and Asian immigrants. Among themselves, the Europeans expressed their racist doctrines in the fanatic religion of nationalism. In both places the middle classes regarded the hand worker of farm and city as genetically inferior.

Nevertheless, in 1828, in opening the first series of lectures ever offered on the development of Western civilization, Professor François Pierre Guillaume Guizot could truthfully declare that despite abounding imperfections, "the condition of man, compared to what it has been, is easy and just."[6]

In London, in 1906, in his preface to *Major Barbara*, George Bernard Shaw wrote:

"The history of the English factories, the American Trusts, the exploitation of African gold, diamonds, ivory and rubber, outdoes in villainy the worst that has ever been imagined of the buccaneers of the Spanish Main."[7]

He too was right.

By this time, the new energy flowing through the new machinery could have set man free of material want.

It had afforded to millions of aristocrats and bourgeois amenities unknown in the White House of Thomas Jefferson, in the palaces of George III and of Napoleon.

But, on the millions excluded from its table, it imposed a terrible psychological and material deprivation.

This paradox of progress and poverty both at home and abroad dominated life in the nineteenth century. It enjoined on all, both above and below the wedge, what Mark Twain described as the command to "Get money. Get it quickly. Get it in abundance. Get it dishonestly if you can, honestly if you must."[8]

This, the profit motive, the tooth-splitting cherry stone at the center of everything, the paramount motive of the bourgeois, was wrathfully resented by sensitive people as the fatal flaw of modern civilization. Sometimes it seems as if every significant artist and writer across the century loathed and detested the bourgeoisie. Apart from the bourgeois function of house slave and claque to the masters of society and from the bourgeois propensity to regard other people as objects to be manipulated for profit, apart from the timidity and hypocrisy of bourgeois culture, its premier defect was that, in its obsession with the search for safety through money, it suppressed the aesthetic/spiritual dimension. Writers and artists saw bourgeois culture in general as a deadly blight on all sensuality, refinement, beauty, and, in particular, as an implacable personal enemy.[9]

When, in 1815, with the final settlement of the Napoleonic wars, the bourgeois style became predominant, that predominance created its antithesis, the romantic resistance, and began the process of fusion that created Bohemia.[10]

This story focuses on France.

In France, the revolution had overthrown the traditional monarchy and created a republic. Napoleon transformed the republic into what he thought of as a new Roman Empire with himself as emperor. The traditional monarchy of the Bourbon family had been based on the traditional aristocracy; the First Republic, in part, on the people. Napoleon thought that if he could guarantee the middle classes their material goods, they would forget the popular ideals of the revolution and let him be Caesar. So, despite his

(margin note, handwritten:) It seems this trend of antagonism has only exploded in recent years, culminating in the Occupy movement of 2011

contempt for the middle classes, he consolidated their position in the structures of society, in education, law, politics, and economics. When, in 1815, Napoleon met his end at Waterloo and the victors restored the Bourbon monarchy, Louis XVIII found himself seated on a shattered power base and a tarnished throne. The monarchy had been crushed and compromised by the revolution; it had been bereft of majesty and stripped of mystery.

Although restored, it had lost all power to inspire.

In any country, adventurous, able youth concentrates at the centers of thought and affairs. France has but one such center: Paris. Consequently, the best of Restoration youth concentrated in Paris, a city whose working population was a radical anomaly at the core of conservative France.

Paris in 1839. *Louis J.-M. Daguerre*

During the French Revolution, Parisians truly believed they would soon accomplish the construction of a new order providing liberty and justice for all. As with the ancient Athenians of the fifth century B.C., the French had set out on an adventure nigh unprecedented in the career of mankind. As with the Athenians, the promise of a first dawn became clouded by experience and the French turned into a course of conquest they had come to believe necessarily adjunct to realizing their dream. In the wars and insurrections between 1790 and 1815, four million Frenchmen died. After 1815, revolutionary hope betrayed. Napoleonic glory extinguished, nothing remained but dreary routine existence. Slowly healing from the wounds of defeat, still committed to republican principles, the Parisians drew some hope from the constitutional form of Louis XVIII's reign. But, in 1824, Louis XVIII died. The determination of his successor, Charles X, to resurrect absolute monarchy seemed to revive all of the old oppressions but none of the old glories. In art as in politics the authorities waxed dogmatic and severe. The Revolution of 1830 kindled hope, but it produced the bourgeois monarch, Louis Philippe, and the massacre of workers at Cloître-Saint-Merri. Oppression persisted. For Restoration youth, the sad and melancholy ethos wherein it had been reared showed no promise of abating.[11] What had the dramatic events of 1789-1815 and of this new revolution come to? The gray bourgeois monarchy!

Was this all? There had to be more!

Looking around at life, seeking more, Restoration youth came to feel that any other time and place would be better than the mediocrity of here and now. The young would go back or ahead or elsewhere to what they sensed as the loci of life and color and art. Thus, the mind of Restoration youth was captured by idealized images of the utopia of the Count of Saint-Simon, by the mysteries of the spirit world, by the ideals of the Greek Revolution, by nostalgia for the stately and human society of the High Middle Ages, by fantasies of the American frontier, by dreams of the gleaming domes and minarets of Islam, by illusions animated by opium and absinthe, by the antiworld of death and corruption, by witchcraft, diabolism and the occult, by longing for an internal life of solitude unrolling amid the wild cataracts of nature.

The bourgeois, seeking safety through money, suppressed the aesthetic/spiritual dimension.[12] Restoration youth resolved to turn this around.

Concomitant with this and at the very center of the long revolution lies a fearful shift in the quality of existence, a change becoming predominant in our culture and promising to become so in others.

Excepting perhaps the ancient Athenians after the Peloponnesian wars, the Hellenistic and Renaissance elites, and segments of the British and French aristocracies in the eighteenth century, Restoration youth was the first large group anywhere in the long life of the West to face the existential problem.

In traditional times, Christian theology answered all of the basic philosophical questions. Christian theology and associated traditions served as a cultural program, as cultural DNA, which determined the essence of individuals before they came into existence. Throughout Christendom men and women shared the same ethical standards and the same conception of the meaning of life. In this respect, the traditional order stood indeed upon a rock of ages.

In the coming new order this may well again be true.

In between lies the time of revolution, of transition from the old consensus to the new.

During the eighteenth century and through the first series of revolutionary wars, the Christian consensus was attacked and fatally weakened. In the nineteenth century the bourgeois saved as much of the Christian eschatology/ethic as was consistent with its new faith: salvation through success in the communion of nationalism.

But those who had fallen away from the Christian consensus and could not accept this hypocrisy found themselves in a frightful position. They had to create their own answers to the ancient questions. Each, through his own thought and feeling, had to come to some conception of the meaning of life and its postulate, the nature of value. Between the old and the new yawned a terrible void—and even when a person *had* created new answers and with them a new orientation to life those answers and that orientation had neither the old certainty nor the old cultural support.

Restoration youth was virtually the first to find itself facing this, the existential problem. What is the meaning of life!? Invent your own eschatology and your own ethic—if you can! Create your own certainty and your own significance!

Restoration youth responded by embracing romanticism.

Because this youth scorned the bourgeois compromise, it scarcely could have been otherwise.

Romanticism is at once the search for the solution and the solution to the existential problem. Romanticism replaced Christianity because it assumed Christianity's function. It can even be said that romanticism does not appear either as an individual phenomenon or as a general movement until the existential problem does.

Romanticism is the experimental stage of the spiritual aspect of the long revolution.

As early as 1824, Victor Hugo saw that "the new formulae may be in part the *result* of the Revolution without being its *expression*."[13]

Romanticism is the act of creating new formulae and trying them out: it is the act of creating meaning and then projecting it onto the meaningless.

The meanings so projected are as varied as the imagination and fantasies of man and, when shared by cenacles or societies, can coalesce into a bewildering variety of forms, a three-dimensional spectrum ranging from Nazi Germany to Bohemia.

Of all the experimental meanings invented and tried out in the continuing search for a new rock of ages, one will fit the human soma better than the rest.

And that is the one which must prevail in the new order.

When, after 1815, the middle-class mentality quit fighting for its life and became predominant, that mentality proved to be such a defective matrix for human life that the very fact of its coming to power created its antithesis, the romantic resistance. Scorning the mercenary proportion, honoring the artistic one, the romantic resistance generated its most intense expression among Restoration youth concentrated in Paris and, after 1830, refined itself into a resistance culture in the community created by that youth, Bohemia.

The romantic resistance found its focus in Bohemia.

We shall see the romantic resistance manifest in other, baser forms, but Bohemia embodied its essence and so now has become the point of synthesis, of mutation, of transformation into the hope of the future.

Directly when Bohemia appeared, the bohemian and the bourgeois became twin cultural themes of our civilization. Seen together, they appear as contending opposites in which the bourgeois fear and envy the bohemians—and the bohemians fear and despise the bourgeois, intensely, intimately, with the ambivalence of a son newly revolted against his father. With the passage of time, the

son's term of (opprobrium) for his rejected parent, (*philistine*,) has
evolved into *square* or *straight*. The meaning nonetheless remains
much the same.

Despite their seemingly irreconcilable enmity, these two life-
styles, the romantic and the bourgeois—more sharply, the bohemian
and the bourgeois—did in fact work together in building the transitional order of the nineteenth centry. The bohemian was the creator, the bourgeois the consolidator. The bohemian embodied spontaneity, the bourgeois, repression. The spirit of enterprise animated
both.

Here is no question of one person being purely bourgeois while
another is purely bohemian. We are all, so to speak, part bourgeois
and part bohemian. Almost all of the bohemians came from bourgeois homes, profited from bourgeois educations. Then as now the
mass of civilized people suffered a civil war of the soul between these
two basic and seemingly mutually exclusive orientations to life. In
those of us dominated by the bohemian style, the bourgeois lies latent, ready at any time to spring to the controls. And as for those of
us dominated by the bourgeois style Gustave Flaubert bids us remember:

"Every bourgeois in the flush of his youth, were it for but a
day, a moment, has believed himself capable of immense passion, of
lofty enterprises. . . . Every accountant bears within him the debris
of a poet."[14]

When, in 1830, with the advent of the bourgeois king, the bourgeois style gained complete ascendancy, the word *bohemian* was unknown in English and in French it still meant "gypsy."[15]

But the first bohemian community had already been in existence for several months.

The story of this community begins with Victor Hugo.

Someone indifferent to
intellectual matters; an
uncultured person

Part Two
THE FIRST BOHEMIA

"The current generation can scarcely imagine
the spiritual effervescence of that time; in
motion was an impulse parallel to that of the
Renaissance. The sap of new life impetuously
circulated. Everything sprouted, everything
budded, everything burst out at the same time.
Mind-bending perfumes came forth from the
flowers; the air intoxicated, people were mad
with lyricism and art. It seemed as if they
were about to rediscover the great lost secret,
and that was true, they had rediscovered poetry."

—Théophile Gautier, c. 1872.*

2.
Victor Hugo's Romantic Army (1830)

Victor Hugo is regarded by the French as the first citizen of the nineteenth century. To them, he is more than a name and a career set down in school books, more than the author of poems, essays, plays, novels, hastily read for some examination. For the French, Victor Hugo is a symbol and an experience. He is the echo of mother's voice reciting poetry back at the bright dawn of memory. He is Virgil leading the way through the sewers of Paris and out into cathedrals of meaning where, in a tumultuous flow of romantic imagery, awareness of life floods a receptive soul. He is free love embodied. He is Jean Valjean and Notre Dame and the Republic.[1]

Born on 26 February 1802 to a mother devoted to God and the Bourbons, sired by a general in Napoleon's army whose principles always reflected those of the current régime, educated in numerous schools and through the travels and adventures attending the life of a general of the Emperor separated from a wife living in Paris, Hugo, at eight, could translate Tacitus and, at fifteen, he won ninth place in the national academy's poetry contest. At seventeen he was crowned by the Jeux Floraux de Toulouse as a master of poetry, published a novel about the black revolution on San Domingo and, with his two elder brothers, started a literary magazine in which, under eleven pseudonyms, during its sixteen months of existence, he published twenty-two poems and 112 articles.[2]

At that time, the elegant, middle-aged poet François-René de Chateaubriand, a man inspired by the wild coasts of his native Brit-

A system of government ruled by generational elders

tany and by a long trip through the Wild West of North America, one who felt strongly for primitive Christianity and the stately life of the American Indian, stood at the apex of French literature.

"I must be Chateaubriand or nothing."[3]

In the gerontocracy of Restoration France, youth could see no future in the army, the church, the government—the conventional routes to glory. But, in the arts, opportunity presented. Enamored of glory, Hugo devoted his enormous energies completely to poetry.

In 1822, at age twenty, he published his first book of poetry and by way of recognition received a life pension from Louis XVIII. Thus saved from the poverty resulting from the collapse of the magazine he felt able to marry Adèle Foucher, who had long been the object of his passions. Together they began a seemingly model bourgeois life.

Sickly and frail as a child, he had now grown to robust vigor and Olympian self-confidence. So powerful was his presence that people thought of him as being bigger than he really was. Dark brown of hair and eye, reserved in manner, he had, as he wrote, "a high and intellectual forehead, wide, ardent nostrils, a calm and sincere expression."[4]

In 1824, Charles Nodier, twenty years his senior, a leading literary figure recently appointed Librarian of the Arsenal Palace, asked Hugo to join him and others in the Cenacle of the French Muse, a magazine-publishing society which met on Sunday evenings at the Arsenal Palace to talk, dance, and hear music.

Soon the Salon de l'Arsénal, attended by writers and artists both young and established, became the informal center of creative life, a colloquium where Hugo acquired an informal college education.

In 1827, Hugo wrote *Cromwell,* a verse-drama about a man of the people, risen to glory. The preface of this piece, calling for liberty of expression, elevated Hugo to glory in the estimation of his peers. Although too long to produce, the publication of the play and its preface generated a typhoon of resentment in the neoclassical establishment and of praise among the young romantics.

"The conventionalism of the eighteenth century may attempt to oppose the impulse of a young generation. It will be in vain! ... There is today an 'old regime' in literature like the old regime in politics."

This preface, charged with such declarations and exuding rebellion, polarized the latent conflict between neoclassicists and romantics, authority and liberty.

Added to his other accomplishments, this made Hugo, at twenty-five, the prince of youth, over whom, according to the poet Charles Baudelaire, he came to enjoy the influence of an absolute monarch.[5]

In those days, there were somewhat more than 700,000 Parisians, most of whom were concentrated tightly in the old quarters near the Seine. The rest lived in cottages, houses, and apartments among market gardens and fields. In 1827, the Hugos moved into a house near the country with a back yard opening into the Luxembourg Gardens. Of afternoons and evenings, his work finished, Hugo received the visits of young artists and writers. After *Cromwell*, his house became the center of the romantic resistance. The cenacle—this time the word fits perfectly, for *cenacle* denotes the room in which the Last Supper took place—comprised a few regulars and an ever-changing personnel of painters and poets, all young, to whom Hugo often wrote flattering letters discussing their work. Here entered almost every lad who later made significant contribution to letters and the arts; here these young men came to know each other and to form a personal bond.

Sometimes Hugo, dressed in black frock coat and gray striped trousers, at the head of his young apostles, would walk into the country where, enchanted, they would sit around him on the grass listening to him extemporize or recite poems, often his *Orientales*.

By now he had grown far enough away from the authoritarian principles imbibed with his mother's milk to write: "We carry in our hearts a rotting corpse—the corpse of that religion which was a living presence in the lives of our fathers."[6]

Thanks to *Cromwell*, theater managers began asking him to write a play short enough to produce. He remembered a verse adaptation of Sir Walter Scott he had written at twenty and gave them that—but took the precaution of signing the name of his seventeen-year-old brother-in-law to it. Eugène Delacroix, a cenacle regular, painted the stage sets but even so the play expired under the shouts and hisses of the first night.

Hugo determined to make up for this humiliation and to create a new theater "national by its historical teaching, popular through its truth, human, national, universal through its passion."[7] After vacillating between a play set in Spain and one set in the Paris of Cardinal Richelieu, he chose the latter and went to work. The first four acts came slowly; the fifth he achieved in a single day.

On 10 July 1829, he read the play to a large assembly of literary and artistic friends including Honoré de Balzac, Prosper Mérimée, Alfred de Musset, Alfred de Vigny, and many others. Bursts of applause, even cries of passion, interrupted. The reading completed, the elephantine young mulatto Alexandre Dumas lifted Hugo in his arms shouting: "Hugo, we will carry you to glory! Hugo, you will make us all famous!" Then Adèle Hugo, tall, buxom, and beautiful, came in carrying refreshments. Stuffing himself with cakes, the gigantic Dumas roared out through a full mouth: "Superb! Superb!"[8]

Four days later the play was accepted for production by the Théâtre-Français—the first theater of France, the Bastille of neoclassicism, and, considering that plays to people then were as television is to people now, the CBS of the nation.

But then came a traumatic shock: the state censor refused to authorize the production. Hugo appealed to the king's first minister, the Vicomte de Martignac, who soon informed him that its portrayal of Louis XIII constituted a threat to the monarchy. Hugo then went to the king himself. Charles X received him graciously, promised to read the offending passages, did so, and sustained the prohibition. Because Hugo was still thought a monarchist, the government tried to soothe his feelings by offering him a substantial new lifetime pension. This he refused in a dignified letter—the text of which reached the press, instantly generating an enormous swell of sympathy for the twenty-seven-year-old Prince of Youth.

Bent on revenge, Hugo took the Spanish story he had previously rejected and, concentrating all his astonishing energy on it, he began to write a new play.

That was on 29 August 1829. He finished *Hernani* or *Castilian Honor* on 25 September, read it to his friends on 30 September, presented it to the Théâtre-Français on 5 October. The theater accepted it; the censor—reluctantly—passed it.

Hernani breaks most of the rules of neoclassical drama; it rapes the three unities; its down-home dialogue in the mouths of the mighty—as when the king asks "Is it midnight?"—affronted convention; its wild, passionate, uninhibited tone is anathema to the

Hugo, aged 30, as drawn by Nanteuil.

principle of neoclassical restraint. The play tells the story of Hernani, a young Spanish outlaw, a Robin Hood, a man of noble quality who has been ravaged of his estate, a "soul dwelling apart,"[9] a
rebel alone against the authorities, pursuing a desperate love affair
with the peerless young Doña Sol whose sixty-year-old guardian is
obsessed by the desire to marry her and whose young suitor, Don

Carlos, is driven by lust and is in fact the king and, later, the emperor, Charles V.

When at last it seems that Hernani and love will prevail over all, the guardian exacts of him the fulfillment of a pledge to suicide.

Hernani himself embodies the self-image of Restoration youth; the story of his love is modeled closely on Hugo's own impassioned and successful suit of Adèle.

In fanatic concentration, Hugo turned to the rehearsals and to other preparations for the proper production of the play and for its best possible reception.

In many ways, Hugo's real situation was as desperate as that of the fanciful Hernani. Some passages of the play had been smuggled out, by the cast, by the censurate, and were being mocked in music halls and critical columns. The police showed deep concern. His finances lay in ruins. Some of his old apostles turned on him. Then Nodier of the Salon de l'Arsénal castigated him in print. "Et tu, Charles!" Hugo replied in anguish. The cast, fed for so many years on neoclassics, became obstreperous The professional claqueurs embodied a strong neoclassical bias and an insatiable greed. No longer having time to go home to Adèle and the children, he had to take rooms nearby. He felt, as he confided, "crushed, overladen, choked."[10]

Because he had led the way in the fight to set art free without once betraying the confidence of the young believers, he still had one resource: the flaming faith of youth. Recently he had declared that in the "garden of poetry" there is no "forbidden fruit." In a published letter then being discussed, he had gone on record with "liberty in art, liberty in society," that is the dual standard which rallies "all the youth, so strong so patient. . . . Literary liberty is the daughter of political liberty. This is the principle of the century. To a new people, a new art."[11]

The issue was clarified; the decisive battle imminent. In cafés and dining rooms and newspapers, the dispute swelled to passionate intensity. In this relatively small city of so much spirit and, by today's standards, of so few amusements, the anticipation of *Hernani* aroused an absolute sensation.

The students of painting and sculpture of all the studios seemed ardently determined to help this prince who fought so nobly for the freedom and glory of art.

But how to use them?

As early as 1821 at the Odéon Theater, in a hurricane of shouts and whistles, a barrage of baked apples and theater seats, the students had overwhelmed plays suspected of clericalism, royalism, classicism.[12]

Conversely, in 1827, at the head of his apostles, Hugo had gone to applaud an English company producing the scandalous Shakespeare.

In 1829, at the opening of Dumas's *Henri III*, he had again appeared at the head of his swaggering artists and poets to help their mutual friend overcome the hostile classicists.

Then, quite recently, together with his aide-de-camp, the critic Charles-Augustin Sainte-Beuve, he had gone to the support of Alfred de Vigny's *Othello*.

To an astonished public, Hugo announced that for *Hernani* he would employ no professional claque.

Instead, he had determined to enlist a romantic army from the Latin Quarter, using the young members of his cenacle as recruiters and staff. The Napoleon of poetry would plan a military campaign against the forces of classicism; his romantic army would occupy every strategic point in the theater and overcome the opposition. At home, Adèle Hugo was soon surrounded by a fanatic elite force of young longhairs studying the map of the theater and preparing for eventualities. Day after day, some eighty hirsute volunteers passed up and down the stairs of the house. Inside, they reported on progress, consumed free wine and food, received instructions, reveled at late parties. The landlord, an old man living downstairs, annoyed and frightened by these outrageous young zealots, eventually gave the Hugos notice.

The manager of the theater had agreed to admit 1,500 of Hugo's friends free and early. To identify them, Hugo issued red cards stamped *HIERRO*, Spanish for *iron,* which reference the young artists recognized as being to a war cry from Hugo's *Orientale VI,* a poem they knew by heart.

Hugo delegated recruiting to picked disciples.

One of these, Jules Vabre, a twenty-year-old architect, agreed to find 150 men.

Another, Célestin Nanteuil, nicknamed the Captain, undertook the enlistment of more than a hundred. Nanteuil, a painter, big, fair, long-haired, a complete medievalist—and sixteen years old—

was described by a friend as one of those angels "living in the gables of cathedrals who has come down into the city in the midst of the busy bourgeois" without suspecting "it's not natural to wear one's aureole in the street." Quite recently he had been admitted to the Royal Academy of Fine Arts as a student, then expelled for leading a disturbance. In similar vein, as a symbolic act of enlistment, the students at Lethière's studio smashed their plaster cast of Venus de Milo.[13]

This army's table of organization was informal, its basic tactical unit the small squad. The field command devolved on Gérard de Nerval, now twenty-one, an ethereal-looking lad with light golden hair and soft gray eyes who at nineteen had translated *Faust* into French with such style that Johann Wolfgang von Goethe wrote:

"I have never understood myself so well as in reading you."[14]

Nerval, who in 1855 would meet a tragic death by suicide or murder, went to recruit an old schoolmate, Théophile Gautier, now eighteen, a student of painting at the studio of Louis Rioult. Finding him there, Nerval peeled six of the red tickets off of his packet, presented them with an air of solemnity, and told Gautier to bring five more men, tried and true. From among his student comrades Gautier selected two romantic painters who were, as he put it, ferocious enough to eat an academician, two romantic poets who wrote in secret for fear of being disinherited—he made them swear to show no quarter to the philistines—and his cousin.[15]

In 1830, beards so outraged conventional society that it took real courage to wear one. As Gautier later said, there were only two beards in France, those of his friends Pétrus Borel, the wolfman, and Eugène Devéria, the painter.[16] Still an ephebe, the whiskerless Gautier made up for it by wearing his dark chestnut hair waistlength. He later grew into a huge, gentle, bearlike man who, as a journalist, was to write more than 2,000 articles about the arts. In 1830, he was tall, slender, broad-shouldered, olive-complexioned, noted for his strength, an expert at swimming and French footboxing (*la savate*) in which he was reputed to throw a killing kick, although he may never have used it, for throughout his long career he was known everywhere as "the good Théo."

After accepting the tickets, Gautier went to his tailor to order new clothes. The idea was to look good and to make the bourgeois

extremely delicate & light, in fact, unnaturally so

18–20 year old in Ancient Greece

sweat. In explaining what he wanted he made the tailor sweat, but out of respect for Gautier's family the tailor restricted himself to saying in a timid voice:

"But, sir, that's not in fashion."

Affecting a true Byronic hauteur, Gautier replied: "Maybe not, but it will be in fashion once I've worn it."

So the tailor set to work preparing a pair of pale sea-green trousers embellished at the seams with black velvet stripes, an ample gray coat faced in green satin, and a ribbon of mottled silk to perform the services more conventionally rendered by collar and tie.[17]

Gautier thought of mankind as being composed of two parties, the Flamers and the Grays. A painter, he thought about color all the time, and of all the colors displayed on the palette of creation he had come for reasons both aesthetic and symbolic to like red the best. "*Hernani*, wasn't this the sublime occasion to restore red to the place it should never have ceased to occupy?" He would become the knight-champion of that color so odious to the Grays. He would make the Grays see red while listening to the polychromatic poetry of Hugo. To this end he commanded the tailor to construct a doublet of Renaissance cut, laced in back and rising to the neck, made in silk of a blinding Chinese vermilion.[18]

Another youth, an adolescent nobleman, on volunteering for the battle, was told: "It's going to be tough."[19]

The day of the opening, 25 February 1830, turned out icy cold. The first captain on the scene was Philothée O'Neddy, who had composed this alias by making an anagram of his real name—Théophile Dondey. As dark as a mulatto, blue-eyed with fair curly hair, presenting an aspect half African and half Viking, just turned nineteen, O'Neddy had imposed on his platoon a uniform of red vests like Marat's, collars like Robespierre's.[20]

Somewhat after 2 P.M., singing the songs of the studios, detonating into wild cries, about eighty romantic troopers converged on the theater from all neighboring streets. Curiosity piqued, people came running. "Go ahead, stare at us!" O'Neddy shouted. "We're the brigands of thought!" When, at the head of his column, Nerval encountered Gautier's romantic chasseurs he yelled: "Can you speak for your men?"

"By the skull whence Byron drank at Newstead Abbey I speak for them!" Turning, raising a hand, Gautier signaled his comrades

[margin notes:] of a number of wavelengths or frequencies i.e. colors

gang numbers who ambush and rob people in forests and mountains who all together responded: "Hierro! Death to the establishment!"[21]

Came another voice: "We're the Wild Men of Art!"[22]

But, as Gautier recalled:

"It was not the Huns of Attila who camped before the Théâtre-Français, filthy, bristling, stupid, but rather the knights of the future, the champions of the ideal, the defenders of free art; and they were handsome, young and free. Yes, they had hair . . . they had lots of it falling in brilliant and pliant curls. . . . And true as all this is, it's also so well suited to their spiritual heads, dauntless and loyal, that the masters of the Renaissance would have loved to have taken them as models."[23]

In the side door they came, settled into their assigned places for a four-hour wait. Presently the first formation of the romantic army was marshaled on the field, men like Edouard Thierry and Hector Berlioz, with his mass of bronze-colored curls: in all, 500 zealous fighters for the freedom of art. The battle would soon begin. Five months hence some would be among the 6,000 Parisians dead on the barricades of the Revolution of 1830. Anything could happen. One lad turned to the adolescent nobleman and said: "You can well believe that the success of the new play is only secondary for us. That which we want, and it's not all that difficult, is to conquer Victor Hugo for our cause. . . . He leans there; he must fall there. . . . Yesterday, he was royalist; today, he is neutral. Tomorrow he'll be a revolutionary!" Hungry, they began opening their provisions, spreading ham, butter, bread, cheese, and garlic sausage out on handkerchief and bench. Wine appeared everywhere. Sitting there in the theater of Molière and Racine, the first theater of France, [they shared everything; they laughed and sang and imitated the cries of animals and drank so much that some went into the boxes seeking out dark corners in which to piss—this because they'd been locked in and the toilets were still closed.[24]]

At seven o'clock came the sound of coaches drawing up outside and the rumble of doors and voices as the lights flared up and high society began coming into the loges and boxes. The odious smell of garlic! And those abominable impudent barbarian boors! The eyes of the elegant first-nighters fixed on a tall young man adorned with a flat Rembrandt hat, Merovingian hair cascading from it down over his back, and by a vermilion doublet flaming so brightly that forty years later some people were still to identify him by that flam-

boyant image. Adèle Hugo remembered the "impassibility of his pale and regular features and the sangfroid with which he regarded the honest men of the loges." Of this Gautier himself said: "Yes, I looked at them with a perfect sangfroid, on these larvae of the past and of routine, on all these enemies of art, of idealism, of liberty

composure or coolness, especially under trying circumstances and poetry, who sought with feeble, trembling hands to hold shut the door of the future, and in my heart I felt a savage desire to raise their scalps with my tomahawk and adorn my belt," a fancy he had to eschew for they were mainly bald or bewigged. As for his comrades, they were too poor to dress *à la* Rubens or Velasquez as they had wished, but, even so, compared to the stovepipe hats and dress coats of the philistines, he found them graceful and refined.[25]

"It sufficed to glance at this public to convince oneself that this was not a matter of an ordinary representation; that two systems, two parties, two armies, or even two civilizations—and that's not saying too much—were present."[26]

Victor Hugo, looking out through a hole in the curtain, must have shared Gautier's impression. From top to bottom, the room was all silk, jewels, flowers, bare shoulders, wigs, bald heads—and romantics, dressed, as Adèle put it, in every fashion save the fashionable. Already the two sides had clashed. Unable to bear further the sight of the society types, a young sculptor screamed out: "Skinheads to the guillotine!" Honoré de Balzac, Alphonse de Lamartine, and Stendhal and Chateaubriand sat out there, sympathetic but detached from the romantic escadrilles; at age thirty, thirty-nine, forty-seven, sixty-one, they did not burn with the same spirit. For Hugo, the suspense was terrible. When he had arrived, the manager, horrified by complaints about silk dresses and satin shoes being fouled in the pools of piss, said, "Your play is dead" and "it was your young friends who killed it." No, said Hugo, not them, but whoever it was who locked them in for four hours. The manager tried to keep this scandal from the leading lady, but Hugo's enemies saw to it she was informed. Furious, on first catching sight of him she said: "All right, you have some nice friends! You know what they did!" Well, "it's your romantic young friends who've ruined us."

In Adèle's words, "Actors, extras, stagehands, ushers had passed from frigidity to hostility."[27]

The footlights are lit; the curtain draws open.

The audience sees an old woman dressed in the mode of Isabelle the Catholic moving about a dim chamber. From behind a panel, two knocks. "Can he be here already?" Another knock. "He is indeed—at the hidden stairway (*escalier dérobé*)."

In the audience an old gentleman snorts: "*Escalier dérobé!* That doesn't even scan!" Now the battle joins. The army shouts defiance. From the enemy: "Throw them out!" The audience trades insults; the tumult rises to white intensity—subsides, the suspense of the plot, the poetry of the lines, causing everyone to hush. Then a new burst of outrage, followed again by silence. Cowed by the ferocious romantics, society, both individually and in the mass, refrains from giving full voice to its anger. At one point a philistine hears *"Vieil as de pique, il l'aime"* in place of *"Vieillard stupide, il l'aime,"* which is to say "Old asshole, he loves her," in place of "Stupid old man, he loves her."

The man fulminated against such vulgarity. Gautier, who had understood no better, took the man by the throat swearing that "Vieil as de pique" was a lucky hit for Hugo.[28]

The final part / summary of an artistic narrative that ties the strands of the plot together into one.

Finally, after the calms and the storms, came seeming fulfillment for Hernani and Doña Sol, which mood she expresses in a passage become classic in French poetry. For Gautier this passage of Hugo's climaxed an awesome poetic experience. "At each instant, a magnificent verse, a great stroke of his eagle wing, elevated you into the highest skies of lyrical poetry."[29]

And then the denouement:

A horn sounds and fades, returns, prolongs itself.

Doña Sol's senile old guardian appears and holds Hernani to his promise of suicide. The lovers take poison and expire. The lights go up; the army, transported by feeling, thunders ovation. Hugo has left, but in the author's box Adèle still sits. Tall, dark-eyed, a white ribbon around her head, at twenty-five she radiates an impressive beauty. The ovation turns to her; she, known to be the model of Doña Sol, receives it in cool classic dignity.

The next morning, Hugo's twenty-eighth birthday, François-René de Chateaubriand, whom Restoration youth once regarded as the first poet of France, wrote him:

"I am going, sir, and you are coming."[30]

At the intermission that first night a publisher offered Hugo 5,000 francs for the book rights. Hugo had but fifty francs left to his name.[31] A week later, in the first entry of a new *Journal*, Hugo wrote:

"*Hernani*'s been playing at the Théâtre-Français since 28 February. Each time it makes 5,000 francs in receipts. Each night the public hisses all the verses; it's a real uproar, the parterre hoots, the boxes explode into laughter. The actors are mortified and hostile; most of them sneer at what they have to say. The press has been close to unanimous and every morning keeps on jeering at the play and the author. If I go into a reading room, I cannot pick up a paper without reading there: 'Absurd like *Hernani*; monstrous like *Hernani*; silly, false, turgid, pretentious, extravagant, incoherent like *Hernani*.' If I go to the theater during the play, at each instant, in the corridors where I hazard myself, I see spectators leaving their boxes slamming the doors in indignation.

"Mlle. Mars plays her part honestly and faithfully, but laughs at it, even in front of me. Michelot plays his burden and laughs at it, behind me. There's not one stagehand, not one extra, not one lamplighter who does not give me the finger."

"Why bother to hiss *Hernani*? Can one stop a tree from greening by crushing one of its buds?"[32]

For forty-eight performances, ever-renewed by new blood, the romantic army kept up the fight. Inside the theater, outside in street and parlor, in the papers, the battle went on, throwing the young men of the Latin Quarter into a frenzy.[33] In Toulouse, a young man died in a duel over *Hernani*. At the end, its chains broken, Romanticism stood victorious, to become fully established when Louis Philippe, King of the French, bought Eugène Delacroix's painting of Liberty Leading the People and gave it to the state.

The Hernanists—soon known as Young France after a pamphlet written by Hugo—dispersed to fight guerrilla actions against the enemies of free art.

But Victor Hugo's romantic army has never disbanded. Constantly in flux, ever renewed by the young, operating in Europe, the Americas, Asia, and Australia, sometimes as small as Ken Kesey's Merry Pranksters, sometimes as large as the assault on the Pentagon, sometimes in forced withdrawal as in its invasion of Washington State from Canada in 1970, sometimes in slashing victories as in Paris 1968, sometimes bloodied as at Chicago 1968, People's Park 1969, or Kent State 1970, sometimes peacefully successful as in its first occupations of Haight Street and of Woodstock or in its Bicentennial march on Concord, Massachusetts, in 1975, for 147 years the formations of Victor Hugo's romantic army have been prosecuting their war for the liberation of corpus and consciousness.

At the San Francisco Film Festival of 1969, a phalanx appeared and threw hundreds of custard pies at the first nighters.

In 1970, the San Francisco Chronicle spoke of the United Farm Workers' Organizing Committee's "ragtag army of hippies, clergymen, housewives, and farm laborers."[34]

In 1970, two thousand strong, a squadron appeared at noon before San Francisco's Federal Building, the State Building at the rear, and, responding as one to a cheerleader, its voice shattering off the faces of the buildings and the ears of the government clerks inside, it gave

an F, a U, a C, a K;
an N, an I, an X, an O, an N!
FUCK NIXON![35]

A few days later in Washington, D.C., another column well over 100,000 strong surrounded the White House and, all together, shouted it out again.[36]

And on Nixon's resignation in 1974, a large contingent of the romantic army danced on Telegraph Avenue and then paraded the streets of Berkeley, singing "Ding-dong, the wicked witch is dead!"[37]

3.

The First Bohemians
(1830-1833)

Rare in any culture, genuine youth movements are to be distinguished from counterfeit youth movements like the Consomol or Boy Scouts or Hitler Youth by the fact that they embody some vision not shared by adults and are formed and led by youth itself. Their existence indicates the presence of some deep change that the master culture cannot accommodate or some deep schism between the social ideal as taught and the facts of society's actions. The Children's Crusade and perhaps the Goliards as well were youth movements of the Middle Ages.[1] In the late eighteenth and early nineteenth centuries the romantic movement was but an ethos. By polarizing the aspirations and sentiments of thousands of young romantics along the theme of freeing the arts, and by doing so in a field of common experience, the Battle of *Hernani* transformed the Romantic Movement into a youth movement, one which is now ubiquitous. Of *Hernani*'s first night, Gautier wrote almost forty years later:

"That evening decided my life."[2]

The forty-eight performances—the mornings of frantic preparation, the long waits at the theater, the dialogue soon learned by heart, the spontaneous and emotional explosions of the fight, the joyful celebrations when the fight was over—brought the regular combatants into as close and intimate a comradeship[3] as later was to be found among the soldiers in the trenches of the Western Front.

Then it was over—this deep, bold, intimate experience shared with beloved comrades, this time of sympathetic souls resonating as

29

one to the same clarion, had ended. Could all of this be left behind in a return to the dull and lonely routines of conventional living?

Gautier and most of the other adolescent leaders of the romantic escadrilles thought not. They banded together in a formal group reminiscent, ironically enough, of veterans' organizations, in a colloquy they called the Small Cenacle. Their master ascended, the disciples gathered once more in the room of the Last Supper. Thematic in these apostles are two traits of the culture of the youth movement clarified during the Battle of *Hernani*.

As in Dumas' *Three Musketeers*, the ethic is all for one and one for all; the object: liberty structured by art.

Pour tout peindre, il faut tout sentir!
(To portray all, one must sense all!)

Gérard de Nerval (Labrunie, aged 21), Jules Wabre (Vabre, 20), Théophile (Pierre Jules) Gautier (18), Célestin Nanteuil (Nanteuil-Leboeuf, 16), Philothée O'Neddy (Théophile Dondey, 19), Pétrus Borel (Pierre Borel d'Hauteville, 21), Jehan (Jean-Bernard) du Seigneur (Duseigneur, 21), Augustus MacKaët (Auguste Maquet), a tall, shy 16-year-old who later became Dumas's collaborator, and four others[4] composed this closed group of twelve apostles, this Hugolatry, chief among whom was Pétrus Borel.

His authority derived more from his aspect and reputation than from his majority. Later to be known as Lycanthrope (Wolfman) and as the poet of vampirism, bearded, welcome in Hugo's house, he seemed to Gautier "the perfect specimen of the romantic ideal." Tall, distinguished by a fatal allure and a Byronic air of disdain, dark, beau, dressed in black, eloquent with a rough brilliance, he looked as a Spanish nobleman ought to look and was in fact a red republican, one who asserted that when, in its turn, the final hope for a free society proved a deceit, "there will remain for me, Missouri."[5]

At the outset he worked with Jules Vabre as an architect. In the interests of romance and economy, they lived in the basements of the houses they were building. Too Gothic for bourgeois taste, Borel's ideas led to a passionate dispute with his fourth client. In a rage, Borel ordered the half-built house destroyed and quit architecture forever.

In the summer of 1831 or 1832, Borel rented an isolated house high on the green hill of Montmartre. Following him there, the cenacle members lived in tents, slept on carpets of animal skins, and went naked all the time. The hill rang with animal howls and savage cries. The neighbors called it the Tartar Camp and complained so bitterly that the landlord drove the Hugolaters out. In revenge, the story goes, they set fire to the caretaker's cottage.[6]

After a career of failure to earn a living as a poet, Borel joined the French administration in Algeria where he often quarreled with his superiors. Discharged after a long and angry dispute, he became a colonist-farmer, eventually in 1859 to die of sunstroke.

His partner, Jules Vabre, a Rabelaisian type with the drooping blond moustache of an ancient Gaul, spent many years trying to make a perfect translation of Shakespeare and then disappeared.[7]

When celebrating together, the brothers of the Small Cenacle liked to dress imaginatively—Nerval as Goethe's Werther—and they sometimes ate ice cream from skulls. They all knew Hugo's poetry by heart. On occasions, each taking a part, they would act out *Hernani*. They always referred to themselves as *Young France*, the word *bohemian* not yet being in currency.[8]

But the philistines called them something else.

Early in 1832, after a long and joyful evening of booze, Nerval, the army's old general, by no means as ethereal as usual, O'Neddy the African Viking, and some others ranged the streets of Paris singing as loudly as they could: *"Nous avons fait du bouzingo"*—we've been making lots of noise—eventually to be arrested. Many good citizens awakened by this declaration concurred: too damned much bouzingo! A journalist applied the word as a generic term for the lads of the new life-style, much as Herb Caen of the San Francisco *Chronicle* innocently invented the word *beatnik* and applied it to the precursor group of the current youth movement. Henceforth, *bouzingo*, which may derive from our word *booze*, written bousingot, a term of hostile connotation, became the bourgeois label for the new youth.[9]

On 9 February 1832, *Figaro*, a four-page two-column daily tabloid devoted to literary satire, a paper which printed a burlesque of James Fenimore Cooper and dialogues with imaginary American Indians, introduced this attack on nonconforming youth in an article called "The Bousingot."

Others quickly followed:

"The Bousingot as Father of Family" (18 February); "The

Bousingot Banquet" (26 February); "Liberty According to the Bousingot" (28 February):

"Man is born free. We are free to have dirty hands, to go dine and drink and not pay the restaurant. We sang at the top of our voices. The people who were eating in the same room wanted to impose silence on us; they would eat in peace; these are aristocrats, tyrants; they attack our liberty. Each of us killed eight thousand policemen in the month of July. We are free. Without a crime of lèse-liberté, they cannot stop us from shouting and howling as long as we please. Yes! the true defender of the nation can no longer yell: *Où est la liberté.* Yelling is a modulation of the voice; the voice is only thought rendered perceptible. Thus, if they prevent us from yelling, it's because they would repress thought. . . . "

"The Last of the Bousingots" (5 March); "The Bousingot's Woman" (16 March); "The Fashionable Bousingot" (19 March); "The Bousingot Tour of France" (20 March):

"When the bousingot can no longer cause trouble at home, he goes to seek it abroad, because the bousingot does not restrict his patriotism to his country, to his locality, to his family. His family, it's the world, it's the universe. He gives one hand to the negro rebel and the other to the mulatto of San Domingo. He demands freedom of religion for the savage who worships the great serpent, and liberty of thought for the Cretins of New Zealand. . . . "

"The Red Bousingot" (23 March); "Figaro Besieged by the Pink Bousingots" (25 March). A catastrophic cholera epidemic broke the momentum, but, the epidemic over, enough thrust remained to produce "The Old Bousingot" (October 2).

On his first exposure to the articles, Gautier exclaimed: "These bourgeois idiots don't even know how to *spell* bouzingo!"[10]

Although living and working apart, with their parents, with friends, at jobs, at school, at the arts, the cenacle brothers met regularly for recreation. They liked to go to the Little Red Mill, a cheap Italian restaurant owned by a Neopolitan who provided ethnic nourishment for his poor and homesick countrymen. At this cabaret, everything was done in a prosaic, down-home manner. Where is the romance in macaroni and spaghetti? So, remembering talk of Lord Byron and his crazy young friends, some of them girls, dressed in clerical gowns, holding nightly bacchanals in the ruins of Newstead Abbey, drinking liquor from the skull of a beautiful girl dead of tuberculosis, Nerval and Gautier decided to add a Byronic flavor to their dinners. Alas, they had no somber ruins, no clerical garb, no girls even, but they could make a cup. A military surgeon during the wars, Nerval's father had accumulated a large anatomical collection. From it Nerval took a skull. This particular specimen came from a drum major killed in 1812 before Moscow. But no matter.

Gautier screwed a copper drawer-handle onto it.

By way of introducing the new cup to the community, they filled it with wine and passed it around, greatly amused by watching each in turn try to hide his repugnance as for the first time he put lip to skull.

The round finished, Nanteuil shouted: "Waiter! Some sea water!"

"Hey kid," said Vabre, "what for?"

"Don't they say of [Hugo's] Iceland Jack: 'He drank the waters of the sea from the skulls of the dead?' So okay, I want to make like him and drink his health!"

That they all exploded into laughter, Gautier cites to show that they did not take everything seriously.[11]

Because it was private, their favorite meeting place was du Seigneur's studio, a small room over a fruit store. Ashamed of the disparity of his pink-and-white complexion with the pallorous romantic ideal, du Seigneur compensated by dressing completely in black and by brushing his hair up from two side partings to a high peak to simulate the flame of genius.[12] A sculptor, he made medallions of all his comrades, medallions now mainly lost because he was too poor to have them properly cast.

Despite such signs of poverty, these lads were not truly hard-pressed for money and although some of their work caught attention they did not accomplish much. Borel, in 1832, published *Rhapsodies,* a book of poetry, which, he said, should at the very least stun the bourgeois. Its cover advertised a forthcoming volume by Vabre, *An Essay on the Incommodity of Commodes,* and two books by Borel—*Bear Grease* and *The Beautiful Rope-Maker*—none of which got written.[13]

O'Neddy in 1833 published a book of poetry, the title page etched by Nanteuil, called *Fire and Flame,* the first section of which, "Pandemonium," suggests what the Small Cenacle meetings were like.

Nerval.

A group of youths sits around an iron urn brimming with rum; the room is dark save for the flickering blue light cast by burning rum fumes. Some wear red stocking caps, liberty caps, a uniform with the tougher republican students. All smoke Byronic cigars or Faustian pipes, fancying witches' cauldrons or hell as they respire the smoky atmosphere, feeling love as they watch the weird light playing in the hair, over the features and muscles of their comrades.[14] And they talk of

> Virulent hatred and pity morose
> For bourgeoisie and law and prose;

These hearts dispense exultation
For but two truths, art and passion.

And

Then a turbulence of incoherent phrases
Of hot dispute, of Teutonic emphases,
Rolls out, howls, bounds, thanks to rum,
Like a hoarse uproar across a forum.

Now these votives of the deified Hugo, this Hugolatry, minds blown away by rum, listen to a brother

In a voice vibrating like a grave Kinnor,
Begin to recite some strophes of Victor.

Borel rises and speaks——
And now O'Neddy himself, dark-skinned, red-lipped, his hair a curly blond natural, in his hot penetrating voice says:

Surely, we must admit our fanaticism
For camaraderie is an anachronism. . . .
Malice of hell!—For us the guillotine!
For us, for works of art by blood predestined,
For us, who worship naught but the trinity
Of love, of glory, and of liberty.

He speaks of the day when the "Art-God" will prevail and the poet will at last occupy his just place. Others speak; all drink until morning, shouting, laughing, dancing, pledging to plunge their daggers into the abdomens of all *cashiers*, "swearing to spend their souls in warring against this arid century."[15]

In 1833, three years after their union, the comrades drifted apart. That year Gautier published his own *Young France,* a good-natured satire on his old companions, which at one point tells of a banquet held by a group of young men where each acts out in exact detail his favorite orgy scene from literature.[16]

O'Neddy's biographer, referring to the Small Cenacle, wrote: "He enrolled himself in a sort of advanced guard of the future, which promised to renew and rebuild, from base to summit, first, art, and by means of art, society."[17]

In the preface to *Fire and Flame,* O'Neddy himself said:

"Workers muscular and strong, beware of rejecting my feeble coöperation; never will you have enough arm for the erection of a work as great as this! And perhaps I am not altogether scornful of being nominated your brother.—Like you, I detest from all the heights of my soul the social order and above all the political order which is its excrement."

Forty years later, a French scholar wrote:

"Some revolutionaries of our days will possibly have tried to take them as the precursors of socialism. But one must be careful about this." Nevertheless, he continued, "those people never spoke of money, nor of business, nor of position." A decade later, another scholar wrote: "Along with their frivolous and singular appearance, the youth of those days had serious convictions, in politics as in literature. Pursuing an ideal, determined to fight to make it triumph, they did not lull themselves with material possessions." Of the cenacle itself, Gautier said to a friend, we were concerned with everything, "but I scarcely knew what they said, because everyone talked at once."[18]

In 1857 Joseph Bouchardy, once a painter who wore a blue habit with silver buttons at the Battle of *Hernani,* then a cenacle member, now the author of melodramas, wrote Gautier:

"Our meetings were so much more beautiful than anyone can say, where all wished the success of all without insensate exaggeration and without collective vanity. . . . Happy times, dear Théophile, of which we must take pride, for when one has walked through this life which so much grief so often saddens, we should be proud of having found there some good times, we ought to boast of having been happy!"[19]

Of which Gautier said:

"No doubt such joy could not last. To be young, intelligent, to love one another, to understand and commune through every kind of art, one cannot conceive of a more beautiful manner of living, and it left with all of us who followed it a dazzling light which does not fade."[20]

4.
Doyenné:
The Wealthy Model
(1833-1836)

In the 1830's it was still unusual for a young man coming to Paris from the provinces to seek his fortune in the arts. Of those who came as students most eventually returned home to follow conventional careers. Those who came to Paris as job seekers were but few in number compared to the human tide that was to flood into the construction projects and new factories of the Second Empire, fill the cheap houses spreading over the fields and gardens of old Paris, and triple the population by 1890.

With no newspapers of mass circulation until 1836, without a seaport, still waiting for a railroad and for tourists, with but rudimentary public transportation, so stable had been the population of Paris perhaps since its beginnings in the first millennium B.C., that Parisians not only spoke dialects varying from quarter to quarter, but constituted a distinct physical type.

The real Parisians were gray-eyed, fair with light brown hair, slender, and of middle stature. But most of them never developed into the handsome people programmed by their genes for they existed under an iron rule of poverty and disease so severe that it is by no means an exaggeration to describe them as *Les Misérables*. In Paris, the wedge of progress and poverty was being driven deeper and deeper. Call Hugo, call Balzac, call Emile Zola to the stand: all testify that most Parisians were stunted and brutalized by a terrible omnipotent poverty enforced by economic, police, and military power. Balzac tells us the Parisians had a cadaverous physiognomy admitting of but two ages, "youth and decay." Their aspect mani-

Parisians in 1849. *W. Thompson*

fested so cruel a suffering as to lead Zola to compare the whole city to a slaughterhouse, a suffering toward which the aristocracy and bourgeoisie alike demonstrated arctic indifference.[1]

Early in 1832, a cholera epidemic killed 22,000 Parisians, 960 in a single day. Some burials were so haphazard that the dead banged at their coffin lids on the way to the grave. At that time a blond lad of seventeen named Arsène Houssaye (Housset) came to the city in search of excitement and literary fortune, arriving, as he put it, in the first fire of dawn. His initial impression of Paris, as he walked through the Latin Quarter, was the sight of scores of cholera victims lying in the street, wrapped up, waiting for the dead cart. Soon, wearing a liberty cap, he and a new friend settled into a cheap hotel room in the Quarter where, in defiance of the epidemic, they gave their productive time to writing and selling songs and their love to Nini Black-Eyes.

For Houssaye this adventure ended on June 5-6, 1832, when in the interest of economic justice and republican government the poor of Paris and their romantic allies rose in rebellion against the new monarchy. Being a youth deeply sympathetic with republican ideals, Houssaye joined in. This time the government held; the people made their last stand behind an enormous barricade near Cloître-Saint-Merri. After hours of savage combat the soldiers took the barricade and in hand-to-hand fighting on rooftops and in houses killed everyone, men, women, children. In *Les Misérables*, Victor Hugo has Jean Valjean and Marcel escape this massacre through the sewers of Paris. Houssaye was just as lucky. The soldiers cornered his group in the church itself where they fought it out with bayonets. A police commissioner allowed the survivors to surrender. On interrogating Houssaye, he suddenly exclaimed: "What! It's you!" The commissioner came from Houssaye's home town and was a friend of his father. "You'll have to answer to me for this man," he told the police. To Houssaye he said: "You deserve to be shot." But instead of sending him to the tribunal, he sent the boy home. Houssaye decided henceforth to fight his revolutions with the pen only.

This terrible event split the artistic/political revolt of the romantics into its constituents; the more political types, repressed, drifted into activist groups like those surrounding Comte Henri de Saint-Simon and François Marie Charles Fourier. At Cloître-Saint-Merri, republicanism lost the victory so recently won on the barricades of 1830. And even that "July Liberty" appeared to Nerval as a "divine-busted woman whose body slims to a tail." The bourgeois triumph over the people cemented the hatred felt by romantic youth for the bourgeois, both as a social class and as a spirit. As for the bourgeoisie, Adolf Thiers, a historian and minister of the government (and forty years later the arch enemy of the Commune), manifested its sentiments by hunting down the romantics. In 1833 he declared that "literary revolutionaries are more dangerous than political revolutionaries."

Houssaye stayed home until feelings died down and then he

went back to Paris. His father, though rich, gave him nothing save the admonition to "live by your wits."

At the grand annual art show, the Salon of 1833, Houssaye met Gautier, now twenty-two. Disenchanted with the dying cenacle, Gautier seems to have been searching for something to replace it. So impressed was he by Houssaye that he "superinvited" Houssaye to dinner at his parents' house.

Wanting another opinion of his new acquaintance, Gautier also invited his close friend Nerval. Houssaye proved to be a sympathetic and brilliant companion. At length, Gautier said: "You know I still don't know you; tell me eight of your verses and I'll tell you who you are."[2]

So well did Houssaye pass their test that the three of them decided to live together.

But where?

The place they left to Nerval. Above all things, Nerval liked walking around Paris and he liked it so much that he wrote while walking except sometimes at night when he was known to work with a candlestick balanced on his head. He said he would like to write on an endless roll of paper letting it unwind behind him as he went. At a time when youth affected unusual dress to attract attention, Nerval wore such clothes as would allow him to pass anonymously in the crowd. One can picture him walking along in a suit made baggy by books and papers stuffed into its pockets, his high porcelain forehead crowned by wispy golden hair, stopping on the sidewalk to write something down, pushing the notebook into a pocket and moving on. He often told people he was a bastard son of Napoleon. Once in the gardens of the Royal Palace he paraded a lobster on a ribbon because "it doesn't bark and it knows the mysteries of the deep." He suffered a terrible obsession, an unrequited love for an actress whose beauties of mind and soul existed only in projection from his imagination. Gautier thought of him as a swallow, lighting for a moment then flying away to light somewhere else, sweet and kind in disposition, showing no signs of the madness which later was to keep him moving in and out of mental institutions. Rich and stylish publications solicited both his services and his writings but he preferred to publish in the most obscure places, almost as if he did not want to be read at all.[3]

In his endless wanderings around Paris, Nerval discovered the ideal spot. Three small blocks of medieval houses and the ruins of a medieval deanery stood along Doyenné Street and Doyenné Alley, resting on lower ground than the Louvre at one side and the quays of the Seine at the other. These crumbling buildings constituted the last remains of a quarter being urban-renewed since the time of Napoléon.

In a building on Doyenné Alley was a suite comprising an enormous chamber decorated during the eighteenth century with grooved paneling, pier glasses, and a luxurious molded ceiling. Camille Rogier, a 25-year-old painter who was making a good living as an illustrator, leased it; eventually Gautier, Nerval, and Houssaye moved in with him. They decorated their aristocratic salon with medieval and Renaissance furniture and art objects. The mania for antiques had not yet struck the bourgeois, so the brothers had their choice of the rare old treasures with which Paris abounded. Theirs was a magnificent studio, a harmony of fading ancient splendors. Here in the rich patina of olden times the four worked diligently at their painting and their writing, consciously building a way of life around creative work and sensual joy.

Houssaye recalled: "One wrote by the corner of the fire, another rhymed in a hammock; Théo, all the while stroking cats, calligraphed admirable chapters, lying on his stomach; Gérard, always inscrutable, came and went with the vague anxiety of a seeker who doesn't find."[4]

The studio on l'impasse du Doyenné soon became an art-sun radiating its influence from the center of Paris deep in the Latin Quarter and off to the elegant boulevards and cafés of society. The students of the Quarter led a similar life, but by no means an identical one. Thanks to the Revolution their private lives were no longer the object of supervision and so they reveled as much as they could in the joys of the flesh.[5] Despite this, their work was as purposeful as that of the Doyenné fraternity. That purpose was not set by themselves, however, but by the authorities who in university and college ruled over both subject matter and the students' thinking with dogmatic severity. As late as 1950, students had to come to attention when the professor entered or quit the room.

Out on the boulevards, the sons of the rich, the "Dandys," denied their traditional careers, in revolt against the bourgeois, led purposeless lives devoted entirely to pleasure, a pleasure ultimately dissipating their qualities into a gilded boredom where each luxurious day was like the last, only a little duller.[6]

But at Doyenné, four charming and able young men had built a purposeful life, the purpose decided by themselves, in an aura of hedonistic delights.

The legend of Doyenné penetrated everywhere.

At Doyenné, they worked all day. After five, visitors came—girls who sometimes stayed to model, Pétrus Borel and Célestin Nanteuil of the old group, Roger de Beauvoir, the famous Dumas. The four friends valued their beautiful scene so highly that they refused to admit any of those dilettantes and poseurs who are the curse of the arts.

The comrades always had enough money to get by. They ate regularly, dressed well. Gérard wandered most of the time; the others when not at home, went to a nearby cabaret to drink beer and flirt with the barmaid, to the theater which always proved to be the preface to rum punch, to dance at the gardens of the Royal Palace or at the Chaumière.[7]

And then, of course, they participated à l'outrance in the great Parisian festivals.

Like ancient Rome before it, the traditional Christian culture suspended its exacting discipline completely during communitywide festivals in which everyone participated. In Paris today, the sole survival of this tradition is the réveillon of Christmas Eve when the people stay up all night drinking. But in the 1830's, such festivals still came frequently, the summit being Mi-Carême when, made anonymous by costumes and masks or dominos, everyone relaxed moral restraints and plunged into a mad citywide bacchanal.[8]

Suggested perhaps by this tradition, late in 1835 an inspiration flashed on Nerval. What a pity never to have a company in perfect harmony with this antique salon. Fill it with the personnel of the past! A costume ball—and dramatic representation! Yes, true: we're almost broke. But people lacking the necessities of life should have the superfluities or they'd have nothing at all! We'll do it free! We'll get our artist friends to decorate! We can't afford drink, but we won't need it!

Presently a visitor would see ranged around the walls a squadron of artists, some on ladders, declaiming poetry, smoking cigarettes, singing, roses behind their ears, intently at work: Camille

Rogier, paint crusting his beard, the now burly Gautier, Nanteuil tossing back his long blond hair, Charles Emille Wattier, Auguste de Châtillon, Pierre Etienne Théodore Rousseau, Théodore Chassériau, Adolphe leLeux, Camille Corot.

The results, all agreed, looking at the posts and panels, were stunning. What millionaire or museum could boast such a room? The party was stunning too. Early in the morning it flooded down the stairs to revel in the ruined deanery until the arrival of the November dawn.

This formed the summit of what Nerval later called La Bohème Galante. Sometime toward the end a very young and witty lad named Henri Murger may have visited them. In 1836, the landlord, unable to understand Bohemia and seeking to explain why so many people visited these strange tenants, concluded he had detected a conspiracy to overthrow the government. So informed by the landlord, the police commissioner told him it was not the government they wished to overthrow and advised him to send them to the devil. The landlord went to see them and ordered them out. They said they would throw his whole house out its own windows and to make the point smashed some window panes. He fled, but soon managed to evict them.[9]

Camille Rogier, who had subtly afforded to this life its tone, went to Istanbul to bask in harems and paint Islamic themes. The others drifted apart, each to his own destiny. But from the boulevards to the Latin Quarter the legend lived on, sustained by the conversations and writings of the Doyenné brothers.

In their hearts, particularly that of Arsène Houssaye, the gilded memory glowed forever.

5.

Murger:
The Poverty Models
(1837-1851)

In 1851, still not yet accustomed to fame, scarcely yet used to three meals a day, Henri Murger wrote:

"Today as in the past, any man who enters into the arts, without any means of support other than art itself, will be forced to go by the paths of Bohemia. The majority of our peers who display the handsomest blazons of art were once bohemians; and, in their calm and prosperous glory, they often recall, regretting it perhaps, the times when, climbing the green hill of youth, they had no fortune, in the sun of their twenty years, except courage, which is the virtue of the young, except hope, which is the millions of the poor."

Bohemia is the foreword to Fame, the Charity Hospital, or the Morgue.[1]

In 1842, himself twenty, Murger wrote to his friend Léon Noël:

"Here I am in the hospital again—One night, two days after I sent you my last letter, I was suddenly awakened by an extreme smarting sensation all over my body. It was like being enveloped in flames; I literally blazed. I lit my candle, and was horrified by the sight presented to me by my poor self. Imagine now that I was red from feet to head, and just like a cooked lobster, no more no less. So first thing in the morning I ran to the hospital, where I'm staying— Henry IV Ward, No. 10. The doctors were all astonished by my case; they say it's a *purpura*. I believe it! The purple of the Roman Emperors was not, I'm sure of it, any purpler than my envelope. Sometimes my head aches real bad too. Right now, I'm a little better, and I take advantage of that to advise you of my sad state."

By way of treatment they bled him, fed him arsenic, put leeches on him, rolled him in mustard plaster. When he finally left, the doctors could think of nothing better to do than tell him to cut down on coffee and to go to bed early. And this for a youth suffering most likely from scurvy due to malnutrition![2]

This was by no means Murger's introduction to suffering, his constant companion since his move to Bohemia.

Born on 22 March 1822, Henri Murger grew up an only child in an apartment house where his father kept a tailor shop and served as custodian. His mother nursed him through a phase of infantile diseases from which he emerged robust, healthy, a beautiful boy with curly auburn hair and big brown eyes, radiating what Noël called a carnation freshness rare among Parisian children. He was the pet of the tenants and of his quarter. Determined to rear a gentleman, his mother dressed him expensively, all in blue, and nourished his ambitions. At eight, while following the Battle of *Hernani*, he is said to have resolved to become a great tragic poet. His father expected him to become a tailor. At fourteen, the elder Murger took him out of school and into the tailor shop. Although "naturally avid to know and see all," Henri never went back to school. Throughout life he suffered from the effects of a defective education. One friend said he took for new ideas as old as the Parthenon; another remarked that he had learned his reading from street signs and his arithmetic from house numbers.[3]

In the days before telephones, business messages too urgent for the mails were carried by boys. Murger fell into a job as messenger boy to a lawyer. This gave him the chance to explore Paris. He made friends with two fellow messengers who went to art school at night. His other friend, Eugène Pottier, who later wrote the communists' anthem, the *Internationale*, had been a monitor at his school. Pottier, the son of a crate maker, encouraged Murger's writing. Murger decided no matter what happened and regardless of his father's tough opposition, he would be a painter or a poet.

Pottier's roommate, Adrien Lelieux, then nineteen, later wrote:

"Monsigny Street, No. 1, on the sixth floor, a little room, furnished with air, sun and gaiety, window with a balcony on Ventadour Square, behind the theater which was then called the Theater of the Renaissance, it's there that I saw Murger for the first time. He was then sixteen.

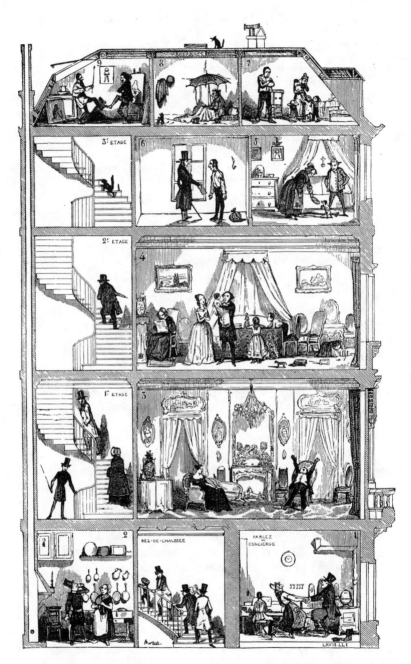

Parisian house, about 1850.

"The key was in the lock. Murger had knocked lightly, then he came in, calm and smiling.

"He was then a heavy young man, beardless, chubby, pink," with "the air of a young monk destined to contemplative happiness."[4]

About this time Murger's mother died: his father forbade him to paint or write. So he painted at the house of his painter friends and poetized at the house of his poet friends. When in cold candor one of the painters told him he could never be a painter and should quit, he began concentrating his intense ambition on poetry.

In the words of Lelieux, he and Murger and Pottier were "epileptic admirers" of Victor Hugo who would only excuse prose to great poets and who thought of the theater across the street as their temple, for in it Hugo produced his historical dramas. They would spend hours on their balcony straining to hear the voices and music coming out the door. At last, with the audacity of desperation, Murger wrote to Hugo begging free tickets. In a gracious but patronizing letter, Hugo complied, and Murger treasured the letter until he died. The lawyer fired Murger; someone found him a place as secretary to a Russian diplomatic agent, a job involving little work and less pay.

Noël says: "He had a marked personality, one of those sweet, naïve, childish personalities without angles, all in curves, which never hurt anybody."[5]

At seventeen, Murger fell in love. "This first love, the only true love I ever knew him to have, soon did him in." Marie, twenty-four, the daughter of a stove merchant, was blue-eyed, frail-looking but strong, and married to a criminal type of fifty-five who neglected her. For months, as Murger put it, he kept the affair aloft "in the purest regions of feeling," an altitude enjoined by the romantic ideal. Then, fleeing the police, the husband went to England. Poor Marie had no one to care for her. Murger "who until then had not stayed with Marie except from morning till evening, stayed there once from evening till morning. It was a winter night—one of those long nights, so long and so hard for the poor, so short and sweet for those who put their arms around the neck of a beautiful woman." Then Marie learned the police were after her. Murger could not hide her at home; the old man would explode. So he asked an artist friend to let her stay in a room the artist kept near his studio. This painter called on them several times; called once when Murger was out and stayed for hours. Marie then ran off with Murger's friend, breaking Murger's heart. Most of the women in his writing were to be modeled wholly or in part on Marie.[6]

Concurrently, as a result of his late hours or possibly of police inquiries, Murger's father threw him out forever. Murger took his bed and moved in with Lelieux.

Of this Noël writes:

"By his break with his father, Murger opened for himself an abyss to the bottom of which he proceeded to fall. Up to then he had known no want whatever, and, strictly speaking, he had been able to delude himself as to the mediocrity of the position into which he'd been born; but now, reduced to himself, he would know more than poverty, more than destitution, every horror that misery has— at certain times, you understand, for all his bohemian existence, as dark, as sinister as it was, he most certainly did have numerous sunny days."[7]

This was literally true. Murger liked to sit in the sun on rooftops with his friends. Sometimes on nice days he and Noël and Lelieux, dressed *en bourgeois,* would walk to a nearby woods where they climbed trees and played bird. Once, Noël remembered, perched in trees they "improvised an opera, words and music, hymns to nature and to springtime, *solos* quite short, *duos* often interrupted, but *trios* interminable, finally choruses of such harmony as to cause shudders among the blond children on the other side of the Rhine."[8]

Murger was to live among the frequent sorrows and occasional joys of Bohemia for almost ten years. Consumed by burning purpose, sustained like Balzac by countless cups of coffee, bundled in bed to escape the cold, he often worked all night, sometimes on a single page, worried, hungry, sick—suffering, hoping.

But not alone.

Because of his happy wit, kindness, generosity, trusting nature, good cheer in the face of adversity, everybody in the big, loose, poor, young, art community of the Latin Quarter liked him. Among his special friends were two brothers, sons of a cabdriver named Desbrosses. Joseph, a sculptor, called Christ, and Léopold, a painter, called Gothic, had both been thrown out of their father's house for their devotion to the arts. When Christ, whom all regarded as a sculptor of exceptional talent, died at twenty-three in the Charity Hospital, his father refused to pay for the funeral. Christ's friends had no money to tip the gravediggers. One of the diggers said, "Well, all right—next time." The other spoke. "I know these gentlemen, they're regular customers."[9]

Christ, Gothic, Murger formed the center of a group of young men from poor families who sustained each other in their dedication to art. In the fall of 1841, they constituted themselves as a formal cenacle, The Society of Water Drinkers. Murger, who proposed the name, was thinking of *A Big Man from Province at Paris*, a Balzac novel published in 1839 that uses the word *bohemian* in its new sense and includes the Cenacle of the Four Winds, a group of gifted and idealized youths combined for mutual aid. Noël, Lelieux, then a writer; a youth who was to become a prominent painter; a Polish refugee and some others composed the bohemian cenacle of Water Drinkers.[10]

Imagine what it must have meant to be poor in Paris in 1841! Imagine what it would have meant to direct all your passion into the arts, and in a society where anyone with five francs (a silver dollar) "was regarded as richer than Rothschild"[11] to give first priority in spending money to art materials! All of the Water Drinkers lived in hunger, cold, discouragement, discomfort, and, when they had rooms at all, in attics, because attics for good reason are cheapest. These men did indeed put art before pleasure, materials before food, free time before comfort.

It is this pattern of choice that Murger and his friends added to Bohemia.

Gathered around the noble principle of art-for-art, the Water Drinkers were pledged by their articles of incorporation to pay dues into a mutual-aid fund, to shun political discussions and drink only water at their monthly meetings, and, once a year, to justify their membership by presenting some major work of art.[12]

Eventually the society cracked in the vise of poverty, but Murger and his intimates kept on seeing each other.

Soon Murger was at the center of another cenacle. Picture him, as he puts it, having a forehead as bald as a knee and an enormous beard, red, blond, black—a tricolor, his face flabby and wrinkled at age twenty-two, sitting with a company of madmen in the upper room of the Café Momus.[13]

Most obvious among the Momusians would be Nadar (Félix Tournachon), a caricaturist and journalist who somewhat later may have taken the world's first nude picture and did take the world's first aerial photograph hovering over Paris in the basket of a balloon. But these distinctions of Nadar fade before the image of his bright red hair, his staring eyes, his elephantine body. He stood seven feet tall! Once he appeared at a fancy-dress ball in a long dress, string of yellow beads, oilcloth bib—as a baby!

At least two of the regulars were what Murger called amateur bohemians—men pretending to be poor. Other Momusians were Gustave Courbet, a rugged young painter celebrated in art history as the inventor of realism and in political history for his participation in the Paris Commune; a man who had just completed a jail sentence for showering socialist leaflets on the audience seated at the Opera; some Water Drinkers; and a clean-shaven, sternfaced poet dressed in black and white: Charles Baudelaire.

From time to time, Gérard de Nerval or Théophile Gautier, now both in their thirties, dropped in.

Once at the Momus, some of Murger's friends invited six wet nurses and six professional pall-bearers to a party. To the nurses they offered milk—and to the bier carriers they served *beer*. This provoked a brawl which, in turn, led to the temporary closing of the café.

Bohemia seems to have been then, as it is now, a loose, overlapping structure composed of small societies, cenacles, coteries, and cabals. Baudelaire, though never a man to follow mutual-aid principles, stood at the center of a group organized by Gautier, established in a hotel behind Notre Dame, called the Haschischiens (the Hashishers), a group that introduced dope into Bohemia with effects resembling those of the introduction of LSD a century later. Fancying he was copying Thomas De Quincey, author of *Confessions of an English Opium Eater,* and Edgar Allan Poe, whose poetry he had translated, Baudelaire, for quite some time, had been using opium and hashish and, some say, in doing so had originated the romantic image of poet/doper.[14]

By this time the market for writing had expanded enough to afford the Momusians some subsistence. Book publishers and theaters abounded; newspapers, magazines, trade journals bloomed and withered. One of these, *La Naïade* (The Water Nymph), the organ of bathhouses, was printed on india rubber in indelible ink so the readers could safely take it into the tub.[15]

Driven by his burning purpose, Murger worked night after

Nadar raising photography to the level of art. *Honoré Daumier*

night on poetry, which never reached print let alone transformation into fame and fortune. His purpose slowly failed. He thought of suicide. Once he almost joined the navy. He almost accepted a job. He thought of marriage. He would even betray poetry and write prose. "It's all very well for people to paint Bohemia in rosy colors; it will always be a sad and sorry existence." Once he was so hungry that he smoked opium so he could go to sleep. Eventually he became so ragged as to preclude looking for work.[16]

To a younger friend who in 1845 offered him a post in a provincial school, he replied in refusing:

"I am on a bad road, as you say, and I am only too well aware of it. I am doing shameful things so I can go on living, and I know it. What's the use? To go on working in spite of everything, to prove to myself that I *am*, because so far I have not proved this to my satisfaction. I don't go to the theater, the dance hall. I have no mistresses and I live with the austerity of an anchorite. I have only my friends. There is only one good and beautiful thing left in life for me, and that is art."[17]

Less than a month after this, *The Monitor of Fashion* invited the ragged Murger to work on its staff. Then he took some poems to *The Artist*. Murger and its editor, Arsène Houssaye, took an instant liking to each other. Houssaye, now ten years away from Doyenné, later recalled: "He was pale and worn; he had already come through Bohemia without knowing it. But he complained of nothing except of having to write for a fashion magazine, he whose coat was too old-fashioned for words."

When Murger told Houssaye his name, Houssaye asked him to write it out. Looking at it, Houssaye said it lacked style. "Now with a stroke of the pen, a hyphen, a mere nothing, I am going to devise an inimitable trade-mark for you."

Houssaye changed the name to Henry Mürger, the signature Murger put on the three poems Houssaye bought and on everything else he wrote thereafter.[18]

Houssaye commissioned a short story; the *Corsair,* whose editor affectionately called his writers—most of whom gathered at the Momus—his "little cretins," accepted a story. This was the first of the series that made Murger famous enough to be remembered today, a chapter of what was to become *Scènes de Bohème* (Bohemian Scenes), later also called *Scènes de la Vie de Bohème* (Scenes from Bohemian Life) and, as an opera, *La Bohème* (Bohemia). Murger published the next chapter a year later and then chapters followed regularly in *Corsair* until the last appeared in 1849.[19]

In the Revolution of 1848, Nadar started off for Poland to fight for freedom but was arrested at the Prussian border; Baudelaire was seen running about the barricades with a new musket, shouting for the blood of his stepfather. Soon after that, Baudelaire joined two other men in issuing a revolutionary paper. And Murger? He wrote a report on current events for his employer, the Russian diplomat, to send to the Czar, and he finished another *Bohemian Scene*. According to a friend, Murger put the manuscripts in the wrong envelopes. In Paris, the editor of *Corsair* received the diplomatic report; in Russia, Count Orlov of the Third Section of Political Police got a short story about bohemians, ending: To Be Continued in the Next Issue.

The Russian diplomat fired Murger. Shortly thereafter Murger took another of his frequent trips to the Charity Hospital, this time, not for purpura, but probably for syphilis, a disease epidemic among nineteenth-century writers.

Taken all together, Murger's *Scènes de Bohème* tell of the adventures of Rodolphe (a young poet), Schaunard (a painter-composer), Marcel (a painter modeled on Courbet), and Colline, a philosopher who like Gérard de Nerval carries a library in his pockets. These young men are dedicated to art, for that is what they do and why they accept poverty, but rather than sentimentalize their dedication, Murger mutes it. They never talk about art nor do they feel sorry for themselves suffering the neglect of the world. Their art is anything but holy. Marcel works on a painting called *The Passage of the Red Sea*. Each year the Salon refuses it and each year Marcel changes the figures, to Romans, to grenadiers, and resubmits it. A pawnbroker-dealer eventually buys it. When Marcel next sees his masterpiece, a steamboat has been added to transform it into *The Harbor of Marseilles* and it is serving as a food importer's shop sign. Rodolphe (who looks like Murger and is Murger) works continuously on a great tragic poetic play called *The Avenger;* Schaunard struggles to perfect his symphony, "The Influence of Blue on the Arts;" and Colline finally places a philosophical essay—in *Castor,* an organ of the hat trade.

At one point Rodolphe is locked in a room by his uncle, a stove manufacturer, who refuses to return his clothes or let him out until he has finished editing a tome on the problems of heating.

Cold, next to hunger, is Rodolphe's prime problem, but that is not the kind of copy the uncle wants. To evade lodging at the Beautiful Star Inn, Rodolphe accepts any commission, as when he ghostwrites a didactic poem called *Medical-Surgical-Dentist* or when he composes a poetic epitaph for a tombstone.

Marcel revels in a commission to paint portraits of eighteen grenadiers at six francs each and in hopes of painting the whole regiment.

And Schaunard? A rich Englishman hires him at good wages as a pianist—to play the scale all day, for weeks, to take revenge on a neighbor's parrot!

A constant theme in the life of these four friends, the members of the "Bohemian Cenacle," is the search for food.

"Where will we eat today?"

"We'll know that tomorrow," Marcel replies.

At a moment of famine, a deputy invites Marcel to dinner but Marcel cannot find proper clothes. Just then God sends a sugar merchant to ask Schaunard to paint his portrait. The charge: sixty francs with hands, fifty without. "If you'll take off your suit and assume your post, we will begin." Convinced that such is the convention for portraits, the merchant puts on a paint-splattered dressing gown in which to pose and Marcel wears the suit to dinner.

Another time Marcel instructs the janitor to wake him each morning with an announcement of the date, the state of the weather, and the form of government France currently enjoys.

"Sir, today is April ninth, eighteen hundred and forty—there's mud in the streets, and His Majesty Louis-Philippe is still king of France and Navarre."

On politics, the rest of *Scènes de Bohème* is almost as silent as a Water Drinkers' monthly meeting, a circumstance that mutes politics in the conventional model of la Bohème.

Intimate comradeship is central to the stories.

"They were often brought to their knees by the most futile whims of their mistresses, but not one of them would have hesitated a minute between mistress and friend."

Nevertheless, their love affairs are deep and affecting. Unlike the Doyenné fraternity, they often live with their mistresses, two of whom are central to the stories.

Musette, who once entertains the bohemians at an elegant reception in her yard because her furniture has been put there by the bailiff, says, "My crazy life is like a song; each of my love affairs is a stanza, but Marcel is the chorus."

Musette (Marie) and her sister. *Nadar*

The hinge of the stories, of the play, and of the opera as well is the romance of Rodolphe and Mimi Pinçon. This affair, like everything else in *Scènes de Bohème*, is autobiographical; Mimi, like all the other characters, is tightly modeled on a real person.

Mimi, who has left Rodolphe for the arms of a viscount, comes back to Rodolphe, dying of tuberculosis. Her luck has changed. She has worked in an artificial flower factory until she got too weak to operate her machine. Now she is desperate. Will Rodolphe let her stay for a while, at least long enough to get warm? Oh yes! Yes! Tearfully, he sits all night by her bed, finally falling asleep, his head on her pillow. Knowing death is near, she allows the friends to take her to the Charity Hospital. Rodolphe, told by his doctor Mimi is dead, stops visiting and goes into mourning, only to learn the doctor has erred. It is the girl in the bed next to Mimi who has died. Rodolphe runs to the hospital. But he is too late. This time death has really taken Mimi and her body is just now leaving in a van on its way to an anonymous grave.

In the play he sees her buried. As the clods fall, he cries out the curtain line,

"Oh my youth, it's you they inter!"

In serial form, the stories aroused interest but it was not until 1849 when a playwright helped put *Scènes de Bohème* on the stage that this new symbol began to burn itself into the minds of the general public. Almost all of the models for its characters, society, the press, even President Louis Napoléon, came to the opening. The play was a terrific success. Victor Hugo wrote Murger in congratulation. Arsène Houssaye boasted of having been the first important editor to present Murger. That very night Michel Lévy, the publisher, gave Murger 500 francs in gold for the book rights, an investment which it is said returned to Lévy more than 25,000 francs after the book appeared in 1851. The leading lady gave Murger a ride home in her carriage. Imagine, he said, "what it's like for the first time in your life to find yourself sitting beside a woman who smells nice."[20]

Prosperous at last, Murger moved into a good flat in a fashionable district and bought a country house. "The silver dollar is the Empress of humanity."[21] His mother's wish had finally come true. As country gentleman and man-about-town, he began living a thoroughly bourgeois life, though it must be remembered that for the French with their sharp double standard, a bourgeois life may include both mistresses and brothels. He even took up the hunt, but he seldom killed anything. Now it appeared that he had never believed in the all-for-one one-for-all ethic as an end for society, but simply as a means whereby young talent could rise high enough to be seen and thence proceed on its own. The best things in life should go to the aristocracy of the able. Bohemia is but a stage wherein the disadvantaged can overcome their handicap. Ability and hard work should bring success and do deserve all the luxuries and distinctions in society's candy box. Murger's feelings of responsibility expressed themselves as *noblesse oblige*. He was an elitist of a type found everywhere in Bohemia today. In the form he represents, Bohemia, like war, is a functioning institution of transitional society. As soon as he had the means, he began living high on the hog. Who can blame him for that? But it is easier to understand than to accept the reasons for his apostasy from the values of Bohemia. Now he wanted to be accepted by society. Because he saw his bohemian past as an obstacle he was bitterly ashamed of it; nevertheless it still formed the sole inspiration for his writing.

Then in 1858 he enjoyed a real bourgeois triumph, but one which made the obstacle florescent. The Emperor Louis Napoleon appointed the author of *Scènes de Bohème* to the Legion of Honor. Murger aspired more intensely than ever to the Academy, but that accursed bohemian reputation, those few light stories done to amuse the readers of *Corsair,* made this appointment impossible.

Early in 1861, suffering terrible pains, Murger went to the hospital. He died in agony. In the procession to the cemetery, men like Gautier and Houssaye walked near the hearse; students and poor young artists trudged at the end. Murger had received a state funeral—at the age of thirty-eight.

Murger was dead, but the bohemian image lived on, at length fixing itself in the mind of romantic youth everywhere. As serial, play, and book, *Scènes de Bohème* had introduced France to the hitherto unknown albeit much sentimentalized Bohemian life of the Latin Quarter. The students themselves had been ignorant of this other life led by some of their neighbors. Directly on being introduced to it, they adopted it as a model.[22] In 1848, while the *Scènes de Bohème* were still appearing in *Corsair,* William Makepeace Thackeray, through the medium of his novel *Vanity Fair*, introduced the word *bohemian* into our language where, by the time of Murger's death, it had come into common usage. *Scènes de Bohème* itself was soon translated into many languages, to be read and seen everywhere. In the 1890's, as *La Bohème,* it became a popular and somewhat sentimentalized opera. At the same time the image of cheerful poverty and romantic love in the garrets and studios of the Latin Quarter was sweetened still further by George du Maurier, an Englishman, in an immensely popular and saccharine novel about amateur bohemians, an evil hypnotist and an artists' model named Trilby.

The result of burning this image into the mind of romantic youth everywhere was a flow of romantic youth from everywhere to the Latin Quarter. In 1854, James Abbott McNeill Whistler, a young American of artistic inclinations, a West Point dropout and cartographer in President Franklin Pierce's Navy Department, happened on a copy of *Scènes de Bohème.* He read it in French; he arrived in Paris at twenty-one, the first drop in a flood of youth still coming from the American republic.[23]

Henry Murger was not the first to apply *Bohème*—a French word denoting *gypsy*—to the community of the poor, young artists, a way of life until then nameless. Nor did he invent that community. Quite unintentionally, his *Scènes de Bohème* ravaged Bohemia of such innocence as it had, making it at once a romantic symbol, tourist attraction, a hunting ground, and a Camelot to the bourgeoisie everywhere, a sequence of events similar to what happened when San Francisco's Haight Street became copy for the world's press.

Showing its strength, as it has done so often before and since, after brutalizing him the main culture struck at Murger's—and Bohemia's—central weakness, the inability to manipulate or resist success; it coöpted for itself a nascent revolutionary ideal and killed the idealist before he was dead.

Murger's last words were:

"No music, no noise . . . no Bohemia!"[24]

In 1900, the municipal government named a new street after him.[25]

6.
The Real Bohemia
(1830-1851)

In the summer of 1833, when he was twenty-two, William Makepeace Thackeray, in Paris as a correspondent, quit his job and became an art student. Looking back on this in 1862 he wrote: "What is now called Bohemia had no name" in those days "though many of us knew the country very well. A pleasant land, not fenced with drab stucco."[1]

Remembering the same time, Philothée O'Neddy, the man whose *Fire and Flame* shows us life among the Hugolaters, said his compatriots may have numbered 10,000 and always called themselves Young France (Jeune-France). This term refers not to a community but to the veterans of the Battle of *Hernani*. Before 1830 and the intense and extended defense of Hugo's play, such people as had the bohemian mentality lived in isolation. Having neither the idea of defying the bourgeois life-style nor the audacity to do so alone, reluctantly they followed it.[2] Even young Victor Hugo waited until he got home to take off his high collar.

The Battle of *Hernani* revealed to rebellious youth its numbers, formed its community, brought it converts, and developed its tactics. What worked so well against the bourgeois larvae inside the theater would work equally well out in the street. Its troopers young and unknown, wielding neither artistic, literary, nor political influence, the romantic army chose life-style as its weapon, *Épatez les bourgeois* (freak-out the squares) as its battle cry. This calculated assault on the conventional mentality stands as an absolute innovation in human history. As Orlo Williams, Bohemia's first his-

59

torian, puts it: They made "a violent protest in every detail of the ordinary way of living. By outraging the accepted standards of decency in dress, speech, in demeanor, they made their presence daily felt, and where their presence was felt their ideals were made ostensible."[3]

But by Murger's time, the bourgeois had issued artistic licenses, making even this conventional. "He *is* a bit odd, but he's a student, you know, or perhaps even an artist, and then, of course, you're only young once." Bizarre dress and deportment had lost their sting. Murger and his peers did not affect them.

Gautier's generation and Murger's generation each claim to have comprised the real bohemians and made the real Bohemia. The veterans of the Battle of *Hernani* and their partisans argue that the Hernanists had fought the war and won the victory for free art. To their juniors the Hugolaters said: You have no cause, no taste, no spirit. You are mercenary, *bourgeois manqués*, the last decadent phase of what was for us so beautiful and so genuine.[4]

To that Murger's generation opposes: You were rich kids; you didn't risk anything. Yours was the Bohème diléttante. We had a cause, art-for-art, and we fought a real battle, suffered real wounds and real deaths, and showed that burning purpose can prevail over the deadly bourgeois society. To this the magazine *Silhouette* adds: "Bohemia is a district in the Department of the Seine bordered on the north by cold, on the west by hunger, on the south by love, and on the east by hope."[5]

Doyenné, Water Drinkers—which of these was the real Bohemia? The answer is at once, both and neither.

The movement was created by Victor Hugo.

When in the 1820's Victor Hugo resurrected French poetry, he restored a zombie to life and into the heads of a whole generation he inserted the belief that of all possible callings the noblest is that of the poet. Inextricably associated with the soul of poetry were the style of the audacious and disdainful Byron and the rich color and imagery of painting, set free by Eugène Delacroix and others. Most of the Hernanists came out of the painting studios; Hugo himself was a good artist.[6]

The movement was precipitated by the Battle of *Hernani*.

When the battle ended the veterans wanted to keep on going.

This meant that for their community they would have to find a new form.

The first form is represented by the Hugolatry of the Small Cenacle. This, a pastime, found its coherence in the worship of Victor Hugo. Here the old all-for-one and one-for-all ethic prevailed still. But having structured itself around an absent and deified authority, relying on revealed truth, the form remained traditional, and the objective of the communicants emerged as art-for-Hugo. To this model an adolescent affectation cloys as when, holding hands, the cenacle brothers dance around the flaming punch bowl shouting Go Go, Hu-Go, or as when in ostensible sincerity some ephebe sighs of a "heart worn out like the stairs of a hooker."[7] The Small Cenacle model was too incomplete, too rigid, too derivative to last. Restless men like Gautier and Nerval felt, There's got to be more—and there was.

Together they built the Doyenné model, one that was complete, loose, creative; one that fit but one that nevertheless collapsed. Here again the mutual-aid ethic dominated; here the objective clearly showed itself to be art-for-art.

When Doyenné died, Nerval retreated into his own mind, Rogier to the sensual culture of Islam, Gautier and Houssaye to the payroll of the establishment.

The Water Drinkers' model with its frank and open comradeship, its mutual-aid ethic, its art-for-art objective, is identical to Doyenné. But it is a Doyenné ill-educated and impoverished. Its members are sons of the poor who accepted the Victor Hugo vision. By their actions they democratized it. To Bohemia they added the facet of choice. Others had to choose between art and parents; the Water Drinkers had to choose between art and the necessities of life. Too poor to experience the luxuries of romantic sentimentality and affectation, nonetheless dedicated to art-for-art, their lives held them always against the sharp edge of practical reality. The Paris of the 1840's was even tougher than the Paris George Orwell and Henry Miller found in the 1930's[8] and was not nearly so interesting. The Water Drinkers declared with their lives that freedom can be more important than survival.

The bohemians of all the models lived by a supreme value for which no place exists in the transitional order. For our civilization art-for-art is anathema. As Gautier put it, they hesitated between poetry and painting, "equally abominable to our families."[9] Just as these bohemians were driven from one compromise to another, Victor Hugo was to be driven from one exile to another. Bohemians can only feel easy and thrive—live?—in a more humane political economy than that provided anywhere by the transitional order. Do they not thus exemplify a feeling embedded deeply in all of us? Is that not their ultimate appeal? As if offering three romantic alternatives to an intolerable actuality, between the Napoleon image and the Wild West image (Gautier's tomahawk), the nineteenth century erected the bohemian image. At best the Wild West image symbolizes a return to simplicity precluded by our vast populations and the technology that must support them. The heroic ideal of Napoleon (and the Nazis) has proven to be one that breaks its promises.

But the bohemian ideal, with its mutual-help ethic directed toward a life-for-life objective, is at once so appealing and so incompatible with current political economies—U.S.A. *and* U.S.S.R.—as to be a revolutionary force everywhere and a real hope for the future.

Idealists forced to live on the hard edge of life, the Water Drinkers added to Bohemia, to the form of the protoculture, the quality of realism.[10] Ever since the poor moved into Bohemia, the protoculture and its art have manifested the yin-yang form of Romance/Reality; the protoculture has lived concurrently in the gross world that is and the ideal world that ought to be.

"Where will we eat today?"
"We'll know that tomorrow."

Part Three
THE BOHEMIAN INTERNATIONAL

"In 1859 most of the men and women who are now
leaders of American art in the East as well as
the West were in their earliest childhood and had
yet to enjoy those long years of study in Paris,
which, collectively, have had so great an influence
in this country."

—Mabel Urmy Seares, 1916.*

7.

Bohemian Frisco (1848-1866)

In France, Bohemia began in 1830. The romantic army formed the country and Murger named it.

Bohemia also started in San Francisco, and at about the same time, but with a different ethos. Early in 1848, some eight hundred people—Californians, Indians, Americans, French, blacks, Germans, Irish, British—lived on the dunes by the Golden Gate. In 1852—only four years later—the U.S. census counted 30,000 men and 5,000 women, most of them, one presumes, adventurers or outlaws of some kind. By 1854 5,000 French and even more Germans lived in Frisco alongside thousands of Chinese, British, Irish, and Latin Americans. These people were served by twelve daily papers (one in German), by two French tri-weeklies, a Chinese weekly, and a literary weekly counting more subscribers than any other journal on the coast. There were Jewish and Italian papers too. San Franciscans could choose among American, French, Spanish, German, and Chinese theaters. The city had thirty-four schools, good bookstores and music stores, photography studios, a gymnasium, a music hall, two race courses and two bullrings, twenty-seven resident consuls, numerous societies and corporations including two libraries, the Turner Gesang Verein, two historical societies, Levi Strauss & Co., and Wells Fargo. Churches, bordellos, saloons, restaurants, hotels, and gambling halls abounded. The city was served by omnibuses, three stage lines, twenty-three river steamers, and eighteen ocean steamers. In 1851, someone counted 774 ships in the harbor, most of them abandoned. In 1853, 1,653 vessels cleared the port, carrying one million letters sent to Atlantic and foreign ports. Gaslit streets came in 1854. By then the city extended over three square miles, partly on filled land, partly on the leveled hills and dunes where the fill came from. The rest of the fill is the hulls of abandoned ships. Thousands of houses, and bowling alleys, hospitals, and a one hundred room hotel were brought in sections from the East coast, Europe, Asia, Australia. Six times major fires had burned out large sections of the city. Each time more substantially rebuilt, Frisco adopted the phoenix as its symbol. Four years after the gold rush, 35,000 romantics and no philistines composed the city—a population swollen by 1860 to 57,000.[1]

Some people say that a larger proportion of these people were college gradutes then could be found in any other American city[2]— and a contemporary district attorney estimated that between 1850 and 1853, 1,200 people were murdered.

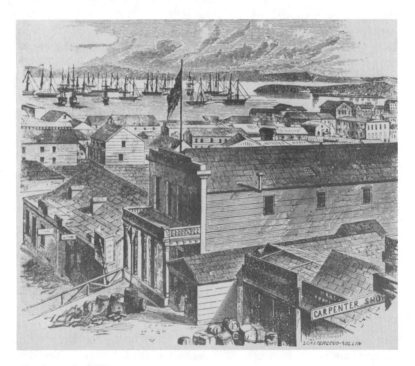

Clay Street in 1850.

The romantic army, in this case raw and racist, built San Francisco. It set in motion a distinctive life style which, though debilitated by creeping bourgeoisism, is the tradition still. It is no accident that topless dancing, sexual therapy, and the beatnik (bouzingo) and hippy movements arose there any more than it is that Frisco is central to the story of the liberation of American painting, poetry, and letters from traditional restraints. Unlike America's other Bohemias, San Francisco has never copied Murger nor is it derivative of Paris. It was the epitome of the Wild West refined by Paris. It is no more of an accident that Frisco had an art school shortly after its beginnings[3] than that Massachusetts had Harvard, a college to train clergymen, shortly after its beginnings. In San Francisco the American frontier tradition of the self-reliant free spirit combined with Europeans and college-bred Argonauts, with seamen and French sporting girls, with savage criminals from the slums of Sydney and New York, and learned how to read and write and build a city.

Daniel Webster called the city "that wretched whaling station."[4]

But as Henry George, Jr., put it, "The whole world was sending the flower of youth and energy into the city and to the young and bold and adventurous of spirit, San Francisco, for all her new roughness, wore a charm, and even fascination, that only they could understand."[5]

"On any occasion of public excitement," wrote the city's first historians in 1854, "there is gathered together a multitude, which cannot be paralleled in any other place, of stalwart, bearded men, most of whom are in the early prime of life, fine, healthy, handsome fellows. The variety and confusion of tongues and personal characteristics, the evident physical strength, reckless bravery, and intelligence of the crowd, makes a *tout ensemble* that is very awful to contemplate, . . . armed, as at all times most of them secretly are, with revolvers and bowie-knives. . . . These youthful giants are the working spirits of San Francisco, that have given it a world-wide reputation for good and evil."

These citizens "are not hypocrites, who pretend to high qualities they do not possess." If "San Franciscans conscientiously think that, after all, their wild and pleasant life is not so very, very wrong, then is it so really and truly wrong as the puritanic and affectedly virtuous people of Maine-liquor-prohibition, and of foreign lands, would fain believe."[6]

Among these citizens were four men soon to lead the Union armies in the Civil War: Ulysses S. Grant, Henry W. Halleck, William Tecumseh Sherman, and Joseph Hooker, whose last name is now a part of the language.[7]

San Francisco in the 1850's and 1860's, like its contemporary the Paris of Napoleon III, radiated the paranoiac opulence of the newly rich. But in contrast to the Paris of the Second Empire, Frisco seems strong, direct, randy, ribald, democratic, open, spirited. Until 1914, the San Franciscans scorned pennies and paper money. They spent gold and silver, rounding prices off to the nearest nickel. In the early days gamblers and other such dandies sent their laundry to Hawaii! Or even China! Some of the city's first families trace back to old-time hookers who, as part of their campaign to add a little tone to their drawing rooms, doubtless smiling to themselves, are said to have placed in the heads of social-climbing bourgeois the voice that says: "Don't call it Frisco." By 1864, when Mark Twain arrived, the city's 115,000 people supported an academy of music, opera, and a vigorous literary movement hinging on "The Bohemians," a cenacle that welcomed Mark Twain and stood in flaming revolt against the polite standards of Boston.[8]

As Mark Twain is said to have said: The miner came in '49, The whore in '51. They rolled upon the barroom floor. Then came the native son.

As for the fine arts, in the 1860's the annual Mechanics' Fair featured heavy mining machinery and art exhibits. Says Francis Bret Harte—who called himself a bohemian and invented the Western and its stock characters—, "If the woolen fabrics and quartz crushers were better than the pictures, it was because gold medals were provided for the former and silver for the latter, and the comparative *status* settled before competition."[9]

Bohemia began in Paris in 1830, in San Francisco in 1848. Each with her own ethos, both wearing liberty caps, the Bohemias of *Paname* and of Frisco, the big sister and the little sister, grew up together, always in close association, each with her own personality, but in the view of friends and acquaintances, surely of the same blood.

In August 1848 when gold fever struck, the French consul re-

Frisco girls.

ported, "Never, I think, has there been such excitement in any country of the world."[10]

This excitement, the hope of making the get-rich-quick dream of the bourgeois come true, refined and qualified by Bohemia, energizes Frisco still.

8.

Bohemians in the Bourgeois Empire (1851-1870)

For the French verb *embourgeoiser*, to make bourgeois, to make middle-class, the English language provides no equivalent. Active everywhere in Euro-American culture from the eighteenth century onward, effected through education and the media, the embourgeoising process has in the United States transformed most of the working class, the farmers, and much of the ruling class as well, making the United States the ultimate bourgeois republic. In France, although many of the workers dreamed of living as bourgeois, they retained their working-class culture. The peasants, however, then the large majority, were eventually embourgeoised, necessitating that any popular government be acceptable to and at least in appearance representative of the middle-class mode of life.

If we consider the embourgeoising process as the strongest cultural movement of modern times and, to complete the model, its contrary, the bohemianizing process, as constituting the resistance, then if we would understand modern times, sense the flux at once internal and external that gives both ourselves and our culture their style, we must on occasions conceive of modern times as a dialectic and, differently, as a yin-yang of the two processes.

In 1814-1815 the settlement of the Napoleonic wars provided for the restoration of the Bourbon monarchy in the person of Louis XVIII, an elderly, fat, lame, lazy, sceptical, and relatively liberal monarch acquiescent in the changes brought about by the revolution. Upon his death in 1824, the new king, Charles X, set out to restore aristocratic rule at the expense of the bourgeois. The Battle of

Hernani in February 1830 and its sequels—in all a subtle and unconventional assault on authoritarian aspects of high culture carried out by ten thousand sons of the middle classes—were followed in July of 1830 by an armed revolution effected in the interests of the middle classes by some of the Hernanists and their peers, but mainly by the desperate working people of Paris. This resulted in the coronation of the son of Citizen Equality, Louis-Philippe, "the bourgeois king," who ran affairs in both the interest and the style of the bourgeoisie. When the poor revolted again at the Cloître-Saint-Merri, attempting to force reforms of importance to them, they were savagely suppressed.[1]

The Revolution of 1848, a widespread and fundamental armed confrontation, drove Louis-Philippe off the throne. Fittingly, he fled in a cab. From these events came a socialist republic in which the muted bourgeois quality soon swelled to dominance. In June 1848, this resulted in a revolt of the Parisian poor, which the armies of the Second Republic drowned in blood. A captain of the National Guard told a journalist who was looking at the corpses heaped in front of City Hall: "Take it easy, no more'n a quarter of 'em were innocent."[2]

Hernani and the July revolution of 1830 sparked an exuberance in the Latin Quarter unknown since the late Middle Ages, an effervescence sustained until the brutal suppressions of July 1848.[3]

Tame and compromised, the Second Republic could not survive in its environment. In 1850, Louis-Napoleon Bonaparte won election as President. In 1851 in a coup d'état confirmed by plebiscite, he killed the Republic, making himself dictator, then, in 1852, emperor. Outraged by the coup, Victor Hugo spent several days one step ahead of the police trying to organize armed resistance and save the Republic. Failing, he fled into exile, taking little but his camera.[4] He vowed never to return until "Napoleon the Small" and his government had been overthrown and the republic restored.

From 1852 to 1870, the French lived under the authority of the Second Empire. This romantic-bourgeois empire, a transitional form trying to harmonize the old with the new, moved from strict absolutism toward liberality, always seeking glory, achieving only a gilded counterfeit, finally to collapse in a military catastrophe provoked by itself and accomplished by Prussian breech-loading cannon.

The Emperor and his Empress, Eugénie, gathered around them

a court of newly rich, of opportunists, of adventurers, a court both effervescent and luxurious, yet sounding a tone of chi-chi vulgarity harmonious with the souls of the entrepreneurs and engineers whom it treasured. In its opulent but bogus romance, its chic prudery and its tough repressive authority, in its chauvinism, in its militarism, and in its attempt to accommodate the old institutions to the new realities the Second Empire reveals itself as a proto-fascist state.

Napoleon III opened the country to risky but necessary economic improvements, unifying France for the first time by a web of telegraph, rail, canal, and steamship lines which, taken together, created the large and regularized markets prerequisite to the factory system. Concurrently, pursuing the Napoleonic ideal, envying the English and their capital city, the Emperor, himself an architect, commissioned Georges Eugène, Baron Haussmann, to rebuild Paris.[5]

Not since Augustus Caesar nineteen hundred years before, who found Rome in brick and left it in marble, had there been in Western culture an urban renewal project on this scale, nor, excepting the vast slum-clearance programs accomplished by the bombers of World War II, has there been since.

Scores of thousands of people came to Paris to work on the demolitions, on the construction of monumental public buildings and the endless ranks of smart apartment houses flanking the broad, straight boulevards Haussmann had caused to be ripped through all quarters of the ancient city. The crooked old streets of the Latin Quarter now flowed into the Boul 'Mich' (Boulevard Saint-Michel), the Boulevard Saint-Germain and others. Gone, much of the medieval romance and squalor; achieved, a splendid awesome seat of power, elegant lodging for the bourgeoisie, and a city more amenable to military control.[6]

On those above the wedge of progress and poverty shone a new and modern splendor, adding chic to the sensual freedom Paris afforded those rich enough to pay for it. "What Englishmen could do in France during the fifties!" exclaimed the author of *Trilby*. Another observer wrote: "Under the Empire Paris was the American paradise, and the British *milord* was quite eclipsed by the Transatlantic millionaire." These were mainly new rich come to Paris to gain social status. In this Empire of parvenus the American plutocrat felt right at home. In an 800-page, hand-set book finished in 1869, James McCabe, an American journalist, dazzled by the brilliance of the gaslights, reported a large commuter population moving daily via train, bus, and cab in and out of the city. In the cafés he found a social democracy such as he had encountered nowhere else, not even in America. "Tell me," he asked, "ye that have seen Paris by night, if you have not also seen your countrymen, staid and respectable at home, plunge into vice here with a recklessness which appalled you?"[7]

In Paris the wedge of progress and poverty had been driven deep. Those beneath suffered a misery even more extreme than that of the thirties and forties. In 1866, of Paris's 1.8 million, Haussmann himself said one million lived "in a poverty neighboring on indigence." Perceiving this fact—one unobserved then as now by the many tourists—McCabe said, "Nowhere else do you see such lavish displays of wealth, such hideous depths of poverty."[8]

The students as well as the laboring poor breathed the smog of privation. Because wealthy parents thought penury the best professor of character, almost all of the students lived in a condition McCabe called "intellectual gypsydom" on allowances too small to buy the necessities of life. "Dirty," engaged in an endless war with landlords, dressed in "affected and ludicrous styles," looking "wild and fierce," seeming "impatient of civilization and restraint," living in sin with mistresses, "romantic but sincere" in their friendships, "they are ultra socialists" and hostile to the imperial government.[9]

Consequently, and to McCabe for good reason, the police watched them closely. Their "every movement" is recorded "in the notebooks of the spies and informers who hang upon their tracks."[10]

The French, unlike the Americans, have always suffered from a ubiquitous and brutal police system, but one concerned strictly with politics and crime, seldom with personal morality. In a city of palatial brothels, of escadrilles of sidewalk hookers, of establishments catering to every pleasure, the Empire brought Charles Baudelaire into court to answer for the immorality of his poems, *The Flowers of Evil*, Gustave Flaubert into court for the immorality of his novel, *Madame Bovary*. At the salon of 1853, the Emperor lashed his crop across the rumps of Courbet's *Bathers,* and called them "draught mares."[11]

In the schools, the Empire tightened up what was already a very tight system. Thanks in part to Murger, student life became more bohemian; the thirty-five-year-old student reappeared from the limbo into which he had disappeared during the Middle Ages. The theater, magazines, books, newspapers, found themselves so severely bound by censorship as to preclude any discussion of public affairs. Consequently, the ravenously competitive journals blandished their readers with the innocuous and the trivial, with anecdotes, scandal, gossip, the occult, theatrical sensations, bloody accidents, and bizarre crimes.[12] In the fine arts, juries became so conventional that in 1863 the Emperor demanded a viewing of the paintings rejected from the annual salon. These were assembled into the Salon des Réfusés (Salon of the Rejected). On seeing Edouard Manet's *Lunch on the Lawn,* the Emperor complained angrily about its sensuality.

Even dancing suffered regulation. The cancan—derived from the chahut, an Algerian dance brought home by soldiers of Louis-Philippe—quickly swelled into a scandalous sensation. By trying to suppress it, the imperial police transformed it into a political symbol. In the vast garden of the Closerie des Lilas and elsewhere, the students kept on cancanning. Crazed by the energy of their frantic spontaneous dance, the men threw themselves around in somersaulting gymnastics, the women kicked hats off of heads.[13]

In 1865, Pierre-Joseph Proudhon's book *Du Principe de l'Art et*

de Sa Destination Sociale appeared. In it, he scorned romanticism and art-for-art, proposing in their place the principle of social art. Diderot and Louis David had advocated similar ideas. Saint-Simon had thought artists should lead change and social progress.[14]

Despite this, the schism between academy and art opened into a chasm, partly because poetry and the fine arts were moving into more sophisticated forms which together with the intensifying embourgeoisement of taste cut them off from popular support, forcing the most original writers and artists, those now enshrined in college textbooks, when without other means of support, down into Bohemia.

This, conjoined with the stern enforcement of political conformity and bourgeois prudery, caused the artists and writers to disassociate from the Empire and from any hope of good markets, leaving many to exist in proletarian poverty.

Now the hope for recognition and prosperity that had previously sustained the young bohemians subsided. Bohemia became a cruel country from which there seemed to be no acceptable escape. Suicide, disease, starvation took the lives of many and haunted the thoughts of all. Writers, practicing art for soup, endlessly ranged the streets of Paris looking for news items such as masons falling from scaffolds that they could sell for what is now two or three dollars. They developed a strong community feeling and an intense hatred of the bourgeois system, at once so fat and so implacably hostile to the warm humanity they cherished in their suffering.[15]

Alphonse Daudet, one of the few whose work steered close enough to bourgeois tastes to be successful, wrote in 1893 of "a world to itself, with special language and peculiar manners, a world that has disappeared and is now almost forgotten; but which at one time held a prominent place in the Paris of the Empire. I allude to that gypsy band, guerrillas of art, rebels against conventional philosophy and literature, fantastic to the very uppermost," which Henry Murger "has celebrated under the title of Bohemia."[16]

But to the gypsy band, which Daudet knew only as a sentimental observer, it seemed different.

"In 1850," declared Jules Vallès, "we left school and in 1851 we were among the vanquished." Artist, writer, poet, our minds were overwhelmed. *Scènes de Bohème* "prostituted the holy misery which nourishes itself on despair and revolt." On returning from Murger's funeral, Vallès, who believed that Napoleon III's coup d'état had cleanly shattered the career of his generation, concluded: "They imagined a Bohemia of cowards. I am about to show them one both desperate and menacing."[17]

These bohemians of the fifties and sixties paid in suffering the price of their stubborn devotion to the arts. Finding their theme, Jules Vallès called them the Refractories. Most of them, discharged professors, painters without studios, poets without publishers, inventors without capital, musicians without work, knew each other and organized a common resistance against hunger. Here lived a community of suffering, a *Bohème misérable,* its days given to plotting for survival, seeking a warm chair, a bag of tobacco, a free drink, a heel of bread.

In 1850, at eighteen, Jules Vallès, the son of a self-repressed and authoritarian school teacher, came to Paris where he soon befriended a number of ardent young republicans with whom he went to study under Jules Michelet. No sooner were they seated in the lecture hall than Vallès began to lead his friends in the *Workers' Chant,* a piece greatly admired by Baudelaire:

> We who, with arms, with hands, with feet,
> With all the body fight without cease
> To arbitrate our future days
> Against cold and old age,
>   Drink
> To the independence of the world.[18]

Hearing of Louis Napoléon's coup d'état against the Second Republic, Vallès and his friends went down into the streets to search out and join an armed rebellion. Although unsuccessful in this, Vallès showed such open hostility to the régime of the new dictator that his father made him come home—and had him committed to a madhouse.

In 1853 he returned to the Latin Quarter. He soon found all of his friends save one who had been sentenced to transportation. In principle a student of law, he really spent his time writing and sitting in cafés, wary of police spies, discussing socialism. Poverty forced him to accept a job in a high school in Caen. One night a revolt exploded in the dormitory and he placed himself at its head. Fired, he went back to Paris and Bohemia where he managed to survive and enjoy a surfeit of mind and spirit food.

Eventually he found a job with the newspaper *Figaro* where from 1857 to 1865 he wrote articles about the Refractories. Then he quit, telling the boss: "I return to my rank in the battalion of the poor."[19] From this position he kept on writing about them.

After years of living in personal and sympathetic association with the victims of this omnivorous political economy, he no longer accepted the image of a poor but happy Bohemia, brave, idealistic, bearing no rancor toward a society that deceived and scorned it.

Vallès decided to fight back. He would combine the poor artists and writers into a regiment of the army of the poor.

As Pierre Labracherie, Bohemia's latest historian, puts it: "For the first time, with Vallès, the Bohemia of Misery became militant, demanded its right to life."[20]

By pen and word, Vallès changed the ethos of Bohemia. Cafés like the Martyr's Beer Hall dominated by the militant painter Gustave Courbet, the Dead Rat, the Faithful Pig, and the Salamander where Vallès met with his own cenacle, became centers of revolution, as did the Procope, where Léon Gambetta enjoyed declaiming *The Chastisements*, Victor Hugo's savage attack on the Emperor.

Occasionally Vallès went to the house of Nina de Calais for rest and recreation. Together with art students and school boys, here in this Salon de Bohème, young revolutionaries of politics and of poetry met to eat and argue and in an ambience of joyful, youthful effervescence to restore their souls by shooting up idealism cut with sympathy.

Among them was Auguste Villiers de l'Isle-Adam, an aristocrat, a prince of the spirit, a poet celebrated from the outset by his generation, admired by Richard Wagner and Baudelaire, published and acclaimed. Yet he was so poor that for six months he slept in a house under construction, worked in a gym as a boxing monitor, and as a shill for an alienist (psychiatrist) in whose offices he played the part of a lunatic undergoing cure. A devout Catholic, remote from politics, he lived, like Gérard de Nerval, in his own fantasies. Arriving at Nina's for food, for love, he comes to life, tells stories, invents plays:

"First act, the scene represents a room with a bed, in the bed a woman writhes, around her all that's needed for childbirth, a doctor, a midwife. . . . Laboriously the baby exhibits its head, it opens its eyes, then cries: 'This is life? Oh!' and goes back inside."[21]

Although crushed down at home, in the twenty years of Napoleon III, Bohemia had taken root abroad. In San Francisco, it was a new species, created by spontaneous generation. In New York City and elsewhere groups of young people formed around the hopeful image projected by Murger's *Scènes de Bohème* and this in much the way that other youths have since modeled themselves on the novels *The Sun Also Rises, Cannery Row,* and *On the Road.* Excepting Frisco, not in reality a colony at all, what the new bohemians created in the colonies of their mother country turned out to be more of a chichi Doyenné than a Water Drinkers' cenacle, more the high Bohemia of Ernest Hemingway than the hobohemia of John Steinbeck's and Jack Kerouac's romances.

Now, in 1869-1870, to Bohemia itself, nailed to a cross, suffering agonies for its honesty, tormented for its other virtues, intimidated, passive, dispirited, came a new hope catalyzed by Jules Vallès:

Kill the Empire![22]

9.

The Bohemian Commune (1870-1871)

Kill the Empire! What the troops of the romantic army could never have done by themselves the troops of Wilhelm Hohenzollern did for them. On 4 September 1870, the Parisians were moving through the pleasant routines of a sunny Sunday when suddenly the voices of news vendors shattered their tranquility. "Napoleon III prisoner!" The Emperor had yielded himself, a large army, and the Fortress of Sedan to the Prussian army. The Prussians were marching on Paris! The news radiated like an earthquake shock through the souls of the Parisians. From everywhere came cries of "Long Live the Republic!" A vast crowd, workers in blouses, bourgeois in high hats and riding coats, women elegant or ragged, children, gathered before the Bourbon Palace where the Legislative Body of the Empire was assembling in its chamber.

The popular militia of Paris, called the National Guard, came, armed and by the thousand. To everyone's surprise, the regular army and the riot police let the crowds pass. Some, displaying a tricolor inscribed 73e bataillon 12e arrondissement, penetrated the chamber itself. The session began. The great doors burst open, the crowd flowed among the benches of the deputies, the president and the military commander left, two disheveled young men bounded onto the president's couch, one ringing a bell. A deputy chased them away. Léon Gambetta improvised a motion:

Whereas the nation is in danger, "whereas we are the regular power, issued from free universal suffrage, we declare that Louis-Napoléon Bonaparte and his dynasty have forever ceased to reign over France."

A tumult of applause—pandemonium.

Arguments, shouts, warnings of civil war.

"I swear with you, no day of blood!"

Obstinately, the crowd insisted the new government be a republic. Gambetta gave in:

"Oui! Vive la République! Citizens, we will go proclaim it at City Hall!"[1]

At City Hall, the Legislative Body formed a provisional Government of National Defense with General Louis-Jules Trochu as president, Gambetta as minister of the interior. The next day, in a scene of intense romantic enthusiasm, after nineteen years of exile, Victor Hugo, now white-haired—the leader of the resistance who from exile had declared, "when liberty returns I shall return"—came back to Paris.[2]

The Prussian army approached.

In Lyon, Marseilles, Toulouse, popular municipal councils denounced the new national government as bourgeois. So did the radical leaders in Paris. Trochu feared the popular enthusiasm for victory: "And if it *doesn't come?*"[3] Part of the government left Paris for Tours. Even the international socialists shared in the ardent determination to resist; first the Prussian symbol of tyranny must be vanquished, then the French could move toward socialism and the Universal Republic. The rich fled the city. On 19 September 1870, Paris was completely surrounded by the Prussians. Explaining it would be shameful to keep order by any force other than patriotic honor, Trochu ordered the hated police formed into a regiment and stationed on the walls.

With the methodical Prussians ringing Paris, the problem of how to communicate with the government officials in Tours became urgent. The solution came from the seven-foot, red-haired Nadar, one-time photographer and associate of Murger, now commander of the observation balloon corps.

On making its debut in Paris in 1839, photography had created an absolute sensation, partly because it seemed to have killed painting. Most of the early photographers started as young romantics, artists, and writers, living a bohemian life in the Quarter. Nadar began taking pictures as notes for a series of sketches of famous people: *Le Panthéon Nadar.* Men as diverse as Victor Hugo, Delacroix,

Manet, Corot, Monet, Courbet, Zola, Dégas, became skilled photographers for similar reasons. In 1853 Nadar opened a photography studio, which soon became fashionable. Painted red, the name Nadar spreading in giant letters across fifty feet of wall, the studio served as a salon for creative people, but not for Society, for Nadar was an ardent republican. In 1858, he took the world's first aerial photograph; in 1859, he refused to place his balloon photography at the service of the Emperor's army. In 1863, he made a successful series of aerial pictures and during the same year he demonstrated a helicopter model to Jules Verne and others. Nadar's balloon, the Giant, was three times as big as any other balloon in Europe. With it he tried to initiate passenger service, but on touching down in Germany the first passengers were dragged for miles.[4]

With the Prussians surrounding Paris, Nadar, at his own expense, began the world's first airmail service. Flying too high to be shot down, his balloons took letters and carrier pigeons to Tours; the pigeons, escaping hunting falcons and the bullets of picked squads of Uhlan sharpshooters, returned to Paris carrying microfilmed messages.[5] The government in Paris decided it must send one of its members to Tours to discipline the delegates there and begin the organization of popular armies to replace those that had surrendered. Chosen because he was the youngest, Gambetta reluctantly climbed into the basket of a balloon and flew over the Prussian army to Tours.

In Paris, scores of thousands joined the National Guard. A notice signed by Jules Vallès and others called for the election of a popular municipal government, one word for which in French is *commune*. The demand for self-government for Paris intensified in the face of refusals by the central government and the suppression of communes elsewhere. Led by Vallès and others, first National Guard officers, then ten battalions in arms, and, finally, on 31 October 1870, a formidable crowd of people, came to City Hall to make the demand. Soaked by rain, this crowd broke in, soiling the carpets and furniture, cornering the government in the Council Hall, demanding its resignation, demanding a commune for Paris. From this a compromise: the election of new mayors for each of the twenty arrondissements (wards) of Paris and a plebiscite that the government won, 557,966 to 62,868.

At Metz, after a symbolic resistance, a large French army surrendered. A pigeon crossed the Prussian lines bringing Paris news of a victory by the popular armies, but after that, excepting a force led by Giuseppe Garibaldi, these too began to disintegrate. In Paris, the poor ate rats; the lower middle class suffered ruin. Victor Hugo dined on cuts of animals from the zoo. Prussian artillery smashed a blundering mass sortie from the city. Fuel supplies fell low. The pay of a National Guardsman with wife and children, 2.25 francs a day, would buy but one egg.

On 5 January 1871, the Prussians began to bombard Paris, firing 12,000 shells in twenty-three nights.

On 18 January, the government posted placards everywhere saying:

"A single cry: To Arms! surges from all breasts! . . . Suffer and die if we must, but vanquish!"[6]

On 19 January, the last sortie failed. The radicals attempted to take power, a coup frustrated in a fire-fight at City Hall.

On 22 January, the government began negotiating an armistice with the enemy. On 26 January, the details were settled: all forts to be surrendered, all cannon to be dismounted, the garrison of Paris to be disarmed save for 15,000 men who would maintain order, a national assembly to be elected to make peace. The chief negotiator won a fantastic concession: Bismarck agreed to let 300,000 National Guardsmen keep their arms!

Romantic fantasy come true! A national government crumbling, its major armed forces imprisoned or disarmed, two million people in the capital city, the police disorganized, 100,000 leading citizens gone—and a popular army of 300,000!

Thousands of soldiers roamed the streets. Police stations were attacked and pillaged. Early in 1870, industry employed 600,000, now it employed 114,000. "Vive la Commune!" became the rallying cry, but not a program, because *commune* meant something different to each person who said it.

Early in February came the election of a National Assembly. In Paris, Louis Blanc, a famous socialist, led with 216,000 votes; Victor Hugo received 214,000; and Giuseppe Garibaldi, the Italian liberator, 200,000. In all, the forty-two-man delegation was mainly republican or socialist. Other cities sent republicans. But in general the

路易丝·米歇尔，巴黎公社女英雄。她在被捕后，英勇不屈，在反动法庭上对法官说：“假如你们留下我这条命，我决不停止呼吁报仇”。最后，反动政府非法把她流放到太平洋的新喀里多尼亚岛上去服苦役。

French elected monarchists because to them monarchists symbolized peace. Convened 13 February 1871, at Bordeaux, the National Assembly seated two hundred republicans and more than four hundred monarchists who could not agree on a monarch.

It then elected as chief executive a small, shrewd, conservative, middle-class, provincial, and machiavellian politician of seventy-three: Adolphe Thiers. The peace treaty awarded the Prussians an enormous ransom, provided for occupation by Prussian forces until payments had been completed, and ceded the provinces of Alsace and Lorraine to the Prussians' new German Empire. In Paris, Victor Hugo had appealed to the Germans to join France in building a United States of Europe. When they scorned this idea, he urged a fight to the finish. Now he called the proposed treaty a deed of violence that would shatter the repose of Europe forever. The treaty passed, 546 to 107. The Assembly refused to seat Garibaldi. By declaring the Italian, Garibaldi, to have been the only general fight-

ing for France who had not been defeated, the outraged Hugo provoked a torrent of hatred from the reactionary majority. Angrily, he
resigned.

In Paris, 3,000 guardsmen met and decided that the Guard
should be France's only army, that its officers should be elected, and
that it should be organized by what later would be called the soviet
system. From this eventually emerged, at the top, the Central Committee of the National Guard. On 24 February 2,000 guardsman-
delegates met. To the podium stepped a handsome youth of twenty-
one, blond beard, clear eyes, named Edouard Moreau, who proposed that when the Prussians marched into Paris a few days hence
the 300,000 guardsmen gather and crush them. Several hundred
new cannon remained in Paris, some paid for by public subscrip-
tion, three by Victor Hugo. These the Guard gathered together in
Belleville and on the hill of Montmartre. Moreau's proposal to ambush the Prussians sparked tremendous enthusiasm.

At the last moment, in a dramatic session, the Communist First
International persuaded the Central Committee of the folly of such
a course and, on 1 March, the Prussians made their triumphal entry.
The same day, two guard companies captured a police station. Several radical newspapers edited mainly by tough veterans of Bohemia began to appear. In his *People's Voice*, Jules Vallès said: "There
are bullets and cannon balls in the cartridge boxes and caissons. . . .
Peace? Can't you hear the tocsin?"[7]

The authority of the Thiers state in Paris had already faded to
a shadow when, on 12 March 1871, the news came that Versailles, a
suburb, not Paris, would be the new capital, that six of the new papers were suppressed, that some of the local leaders including Vallès
had been condemned, and that, despite the economic collapse of the
city, the moratoria on rents and commercial bills had ended.

This brought more segments of the Parisians into opposition to
the national government in Versailles. Thiers, who confided he represented primarily "the world of business,"[8] came to Paris with
his ministers. There is good reason to believe he hoped to provoke
an insurrection and apply the draconian repression he had advocated in 1834 and 1848 as the proper medicine for the recurrent up-
risings of the poor—force enough to bring about a final solution
and establish, uncontested, his central government.

The Prussian occupying forces, camped around part of the perimeter, knew always as they looked scornfully down on the troubled city that if events took an unacceptable turn they could decisively intervene.

Thiers, believing the recovery of the cannon taken by the Guard to Belleville and Montmartre essential to the restoration of his authority, and, perhaps hoping to provoke armed rebellion as well, convened a council to discuss the project. Although for moral and tactical reasons his two highest generals demurred, he ordered the recovery of the cannon.

The operation began at 5 A.M., 18 March 1871, as soldiers began filing through the streets of Paris. As often happens, an abyss opened between the plan and its execution. One column started two hours late; the army did not bring enough horses to allow it to move in swiftly, take the cannon, and get out. At the head of one column marched the hated police. When the columns arrived, the people were already awake. Crowds of curious, groups of guards, gathered at the scene. Women began arguing with the army officers. More guards came—a battle seemed imminent. In a moment of silence, a regular army sergeant yelped out an order: "Comrades, drop your rifles!" Weapons clattered to the pavement; women sprang forward to kiss the insurgent soldiers and, opportunity presenting, disarmed several army officers. Soon the forces of order were entirely disarmed; guardsmen escorted the frightened police to sanctuary at the mayoralty of Montmartre.

Soon after, the crowds took two generals and shot them.

This was a day of confusion verging on moments of mob madness so frantic as to make young Georges Clemenceau, the mayor of Montmartre, think of the worst outbursts of the Middle Ages.

Thiers, on hearing the news, decided to withdraw the army and government from Paris to Versailles whence he would conduct war against the Parisian refractories. The commander of the Polytechnical School convened the students and said:

"In the absence of government I cannot give you orders. I refer the matter to you and place the school in your hands. I ask you not to shoot each other." [9]

On the same day, Victor Hugo arrived in Paris with the body of his son who, weakened by the privations of the siege, had died suddenly in Bordeaux. Hugo accompanied the coffin through the streets to Montmartre. A guard of honor formed spontaneously and followed, arms reversed. Drums beat, bugles sounded, battalions of guards presented arms as the procession passed. At the cemetery, a big man, his face cordial, tearstained, offered his hand and in a deep voice said: "I am Courbet!" Soon after the funeral, Hugo went to Brussels to settle his son's affairs. [10]

By the next day, what had once been a government had become a vacuum. The chief executive, the ministers, the mayor, the police, all had gone, and so fast that they left the treasury and the Bank of France behind.

Most of the government clerks left too.

In France, monarchies, republics, empires are but colored beads strung on a continuous bureaucracy extending back to the Middle Ages.[11] Now, for the first time, the string had been cut. No authority remained save some mayors of arrondissements and the Central Committee of the National Guard, aged six days, so new that its members scarcely knew each other. The Central Committee met, rejected the proposal for an immediate attack on Versailles, which then would have succeeded, and scheduled the election of a Paris Commune. An infrastructure of political clubs and guard units provided a plethora of candidates for the ninety seats. Upon learning who had been elected, twenty-one moderates resigned or refused to serve, their places being filled in a bye-election.

On 28 March 1871, while Gautier sat smugly in Versailles,[12] Gautier's favorite color—red—came to power along with France's first antibourgeois posttraditional government. A vast crowd stood before City Hall, sat on balconies, behind windows, on roofs. Amid the shining bayonets of 60,000 guardsmen floated tricolors and red flags. In front of City Hall, dressed with flags, extended an immense red platform garnished with crimson chairs and embellished at the center with a bust of the Republic wearing a red liberty cap. A large scarlet drape covered the statue of Henri IV on the steps. Everywhere, the color red, symbolizing, because all blood is red, the brotherhood of man.

At 4 P.M., cannon sounded, drums rolled. The members of the Central Committee of the Commune, a red sash crossing the chest of each, came out on the platform. The earth shook with cheers and salvos, soldiers' caps rose on the points of bayonets, as they sang the "Song of Depart," the "Song of the Girondins," the "Marseillaise."

The moderator read the names of the members of the Commune, then declared:

"The Commune of Paris is proclaimed!"

Thus begins one of history's most surrealistic events, a true anachronism, an institution, even an order, born out of its time to live for two months and then choke on smoke and drown in blood.

What was the Paris Commune?
What does it represent?
Can we know it by its deeds?

Although it saw itself as the future against the past, it modeled itself on the Paris Commune of 1793. It adopted the Revolutionary calendar—months bearing names like Prairial and Floréal, the year: LXXIX (79). It proposed a national federal government based on autonomous communes electing deputies to a national central committee. It closed the whorehouses and raided gambling joints. It reinstated the moratoria on rents and debts. Rather than taking what was at its mercy, it borrowed money from the Bank of France. It abolished loyalty oaths. It decreed that public service be done at workmen's wages. It released necessary items from the state pawnshop. Foreigners elected to the Commune it confirmed in office because "the flag of the Commune is the flag of the world republic." It disendowed and disestablished the church, transforming church property into national property, and instituted secular schools freed from all church ritual, symbol, and dogma. It publicly burned the guillotine. It razed the Chapel of Atonement, built in expiation for Louis XVI. It replaced the national army and conscription with a national militia. Although in bending to the implacable pressure of war it eventually delegated all power to a Committee of Public Safety, it established no real leaders. On the model of ancient Athens, it replaced the ministries with ten commissions, on one of which each member served. Under a law of hostages passed in response to the execution by Versailles of some of its captured soldiers, it took a number of clergymen and policemen into custody. Occasionally it imprisoned its own members. It seemed to be moving toward giving the shops and factories to their workers and toward the organization of infrastructures, such as schools, on the commune principle;

it seemed even to be moving toward the liberation of women. In its manifesto it said the communal revolution means "the end of the old clerical and governmental world of militarism, of bureaucracy, of speculation in stocks, of monopolies, of privilege."[13]

A self-made man, Thiers took an intense pride in his possessions and symbols of accomplishment. When the Versailles troops began bombarding Paris, the Commune, on the principle that Thiers was destroying the people's houses, ordered the destruction of *his* house. The demolition stabbed at the tenderest part of his being.

Carrying out a resolution moved by Gustave Courbet, at a great public ceremony where an American girl spontaneously played "Hail Columbia" on the piano, the Commune pulled down the Vendôme Column.[14] This is a copy of Hadrian's Column in Rome, 144 feet high and fourteen feet in diameter. Embellished with a spiral relief depicting Napoleon's victories, made of bronze taken from captured cannon, and crowned by a statue of Napoleon himself, the column fell into a bed of straw and manure. Thus did the Commune show its concurrence with an opinion of the Napoleonic ideal expressed in a graffito recently attached to the column's base:

> Tyrant, perched on this stilt,
> If the blood of your spilling
> Could be held in this Square
> You could drink without stooping.[15]

Can the Commune be known by its men?

Many had been jailed by the Empire for the crime of dissent. Almost all were men who did not fit into society, a severely repressive society that had wounded and scarred them, as it had all the French. Of the eighty-five who served, twenty-seven were artisans or workers, the rest, professionals or students.

Raoul Rigault, at twenty-five the youngest member and one of the two students, became police chief. He had led a bohemian life and been imprisoned for speeches subversive of morality and religion. Jules Vallès, Gustave Courbet, Eugène Pottier—Murger's first friend and teacher—and at the very least twelve others seem to have been veterans of Bohemia. Of the eighty-five members, twenty had passed the age of fifty, twenty-six were not yet thirty. Politically,

X marks Courbet.

they divided on the question of power. The Jacobins and Blanquists held with the French tradition of power centralized to the ultimate; the others, socialists of various kinds, believed in its maximum diffusion. Many agreed with the large group adhering to the teachings of Auguste Blanqui that necessary above all else is the destruction of the bourgeois influence on society. All detested monarchy and feudal institutions. All stood so firmly against organized Christianity and the bourgeoisie[16] that this quality alone justifies their description as posttraditional personalities. Their other qualities place them in the existential phase.

But who *were* the men of the Commune? One of its members said the Commune was not the group at City Hall but the men and women of all Paris, united behind smoking ramparts, in idealism and in heroism, the champions of all the suffering humans on earth. "All of us are fighting for equality, the enfranchisement of labor, the advent of a social society."[17]

Evidently, in the precise sense, we cannot understand the Commune as Bohemia in power. Bohemia has never been in power. Nor can we understand it primarily as history. The Commune's two short confused months do not leave enough of a record to tell us, either through deeds, which were mainly expedients, or through personalities still adjusting to power, what the Commune was. Despite the fact that its study influenced the development of Marxism-Leninism, of the Soviet Union and the People's Republic of China, the meaning of the Commune, though of large importance, is not primarily historical.[18]

The Commune was not a program, but a spirit, not a doctrine, but a poem.

As Jules Vallès said in his paper, Paris cannot aspire to rule France. Paris, with its terrible poverty, was but an urban anomaly in the generally prosperous, traditional, and dull farming nation called France. The Commune cannot be understood politically, for it was an anachronism and its members were not narrowly practical. In essence its meaning is symbolic and therefore poetic. Many if not most of its members were men of real intelligence and varied experience. They could not view their position practically without finding it hopeless. But can anyone view life practically and find it anything else? So, romantically, the communards projected hope on the hopeless and made of their desperate adventure a living romantic poem, which, because of a vow of honor, ends like *Hernani* with the death of the protagonist.

But was the hope of the communards of 1871 any more irrational than that of the Norwegians or the British of 1940? Was their defiance of reality any more quixotic? Both the British and the Norwegians chose to risk almost certain destruction rather than treat with Hitler and accept the subsequent compromises the reasoned view of survival seemed to exact.

The poem of the Commune is intrinsically identical with the poem of Bohemia. Both, and for the same reasons, are anachronistic. With a thin theoretical chance of success, the communards tried to free not art, but man. Because art is man, their story is molded from the same metal as that of Gérard de Nerval or Villiers de l'Isle-Adam or Charles Baudelaire and finds its dual form in Gustave Courbet. Regardless of the risks, the men of the Commune would have life on their terms or not at all.

In this sense, the synonym of art-for-art is life-for-life.

The Commune is a real-life romantic poem inscribed on the hard edge of reality.

The bourgeois spirit—itself a compromise between the traditional and posttraditional—will accept any compromise to minimize risk. The essence of the communard-bohemian spirit is *no* compromise regardless of risk.

The bohemian spirit is alive and well.

What happened to the communards?

On 4 April 1871, after a skirmish on 3 April that spilled the first blood of the war between Paris and France, they sent three columns against Versailles.

The battle plan was prepared either by the communard military commander, Gustave-Paul Cluseret, who had been a brigadier general in the Union Army in America's Civil War or, as many believed, by Cluseret's friend, another Union general, Philip Sheridan, who happened to be visiting Paris at the time. The cannon of a fort and the robot discipline of Versailles's police and soldiers shattered the three columns and drove them back on Paris.

The Versailles government executed some of the captives.

And throughout all these dramatic events, from its positions around part of the perimeter of Paris, the Prussian occupation army looked down, secure in the knowledge it had the absolute and final power to decide the issue. The Commune never had more than 60,000 effectives, ill-trained, ill-disciplined—unwilling to forget the value of life and liberty, even in the face of the enemy, yet driven by the ardent valor of belief. Versailles soon had 120,000 men because the Prussians released enough French regulars from captivity to make sure Thiers would win.

On 23 April, Cluseret reported to the Commune: "We submit, die of hunger, or vanquish.... Live free or die fighting."[19]

This Romantic Army held the walls for a month more.

At one point, 6,000 Freemasons, mostly old, representing fifty-five lodges of the three rites, moving under a forest of flags and displaying a medley of aprons—blue/green/red/black, embroidered with gold or silver suns and triangles—marched under shellfire to the Arch of Triumph. They were led by the red flag of the Commune. A lodge of women received an ovation. These doughty Masons, deep in their tradition of substantial contribution to the success of the French and American Revolutions, took their flags to the ramparts and spent the night under heavy rain and the fire of the Versailles army.

On 21 May 1871, the Versailles troops broke into Paris through an undefended section of the walls and quickly took part of the city.

But even then the free life of the city went on. Stores and theaters were open, cafés were busy, men fished in the Seine, papers were sold, schools were open. Save for exploding shells, there had been no terror nor was there yet any. Bourgeois life moved along in its usual routines, near normal. At the medical school the students were convened and asked for advice on reconstitution in communal style. It seems almost as if words and symbols, not blows or deeds, were the natural mode of the communal revolution.

The first two days of Bloody Week went smoothly for Versailles, partly because the natural tendency of the people to defend their own quarters of the city meant they abandoned the fashionable quarters without contest, partly because the central control, such as it was, collapsed.

When the Versailles troops began to come up against the poorer quarters they collided with enormous barricades, fiercely defended. The Versailles artillery had started some fires; now as a defensive tactic the communards began burning buildings. By the third night, the scene had become infernal: explosions, fire, smoke, death everywhere. The Versaillais shot prisoners and persons denounced as sympathetic to the Commune.

Here is how a barricade in the Latin Quarter appeared to a woman looking out of her window:

"Fourteen Federals are there. Women prepare the guns, the men shoot. The cannon thunders and spits. The machine gun gnashes and rages. Impossible to hang on at home, bullets whistle through the windows. Impossible to stay on the reeling stairs. Through the tumult, wails of the wounded who fall. Then some loud cries:

" 'Surrender! Surrender!'

" 'Vive la Commune!'

"At three a noise of horses makes us think the soldiers of Versailles are master. No! The battle, on the contrary, is more vehement. The Federals let themselves be killed. Cannon smoke envelops us and we hear the oaths of some, the imprecations of others, the plaints of those who are dying.

" 'Down with Versailles! Vive Paris! Vive la Commune!'

"When you see so many ignorant beings die for a bad cause,

you are taken with an irresistible desire to die as valiantly for a generous cause. Why aren't honest men—worse then weak between you and me—humiliated, jealous of the superiority of others over them and why don't they hold it a point of honor to equal, or even to surpass this bravery?"[20]

In June 1848, at the beginning of an insurrection of poor men double-crossed by the bourgeois after the February revolution, at a similar barricade in the Latin Quarter, Etienne Arago, a venerable member of the government, faced the rebels alone begging them to go home.

One of them shouted down:

"But you were *with* us on the barricades! Don't you remember the Cloître-Saint-Merri!"

The old man kept on scolding and insisting.

"You don't know what misery is, Mr. Arago, you've never been hungry!"

Someone aimed a carbine at Arago which was struck aside just in time.[21] At another barricade the defenders were saying the same thing to Victor Hugo.

In those June days of 1848, sixty thousand fought and four thousand died at a cost to the army of the Second Republic of one thousand dead. As a sequel, several hundred rebels were shot, several thousand transported to places like Devil's Island.

This time it would be worse.

The Versailles power inexorably ground down the barricades, broke up the defenses, occupied more and more of the city, executed more and more of the defenders. Now the Parisians began burning buildings. They burned the Tuileries—"this palace, essentially monarchist, execrated symbol of an execrable past."[22] Other symbols they doused with kerosene, filled with gunpowder and put to flame: the Council of State, the Court of Accounts, the Ministry of Finance, the Central Police Station, the Hall of Justice, City Hall.

Now the holocaust proceeded under a roof of smoke illuminated by fire and covered by black snow, the remains of millions of burning documents falling back to earth. Versailles called firemen from all the neighboring towns; few responded. One group that did so was seized as communard soldiers and held in custody for a day. Women numbered among the toughest refractories still firing from the barricades; some 120 members of the Women's Union held the barricade at Place Blanche for hours. The communards began shooting their hostages.

This was the worst fighting Paris had—and has—ever seen.

On the eighth day the last barricade fell, the last armed resistance ceased. The Versailles troops held 39,000 prisoners. At a cost to Versailles of 1,000 dead, 20,000 Parisians had been shot dead, many in cold blood. As soon as the Versailles troops entered Paris some members of the Commune fled into hiding; most fought to the end, to be captured, to be shot on the spot, to be shot on the barricades, to escape at the last moment. Vallès, walking all alone, saw some Versaillais ahead and found asylum in an ambulance where he dressed as a doctor and passed through the soldiers. Recognized three times but not betrayed, he made his escape to London, to return to France upon the general amnesty of 1880. Courbet was caught, eventually fined and given a six-month sentence. Moreau, the handsome youth who had proposed that the Guard ambush the Prussians, was captured and pushed into a room. He lit a cigarette and went out on the balcony, recognized a girl in the crowd below, waved adieu, was taken away and shot.

And throughout it all the German army watched.

The bourgeois Third Republic was now safe—at the cost of completing the severance of the workers from the bourgeois begun in 1832 at Cloître Saint-Merri, the climax of Hugo's *Les Misérables*. Widened in 1848, in 1871 this cleft became a chasm, yet to be bridged,[23] one promising to open wider still in the quasifascist France of today.

The lower classes—in the idiom of Thiers "the vile multitude" —had been tamed. In further repressions the frightened bourgeoisie kept on exacting its revenge on this insolent rabble which had aspired to human status. For years, few dared speak in defense of the transported prisoners, the Commune, or its ideas.[24] An exception was Victor Hugo. The Belgian government denied the refugees asylum. On the seventh day of Bloody Week, in a published letter, Victor Hugo, who now lived in Belgium, offered his own house as a place of refuge to all fugitives. This caused a typhoon of resentment among conservatives everywhere in Europe. A mob of young men stoned Hugo's house. Then the Belgian government deported him. On returning to France, he worked ceaselessly in the cause of mercy for the communards.

While still an adolescent, in a long poem from which the following is taken, the great French poet Arthur Rimbaud, who may himself have been a soldier of the Commune, wrote the epitaph of the Commune:[25]

> O coeurs de saleté, bouches épouvantables,
> Fonctionnez plus fort, bouches de puanteurs,
> Un vin, pour ces torpeurs ignobles, sur ces tables!
> Vos ventres sont fondus de hontes, vainqueurs.
> Oh, filth-hearts, mouths abominable,
> Come on stronger, mouth stinkers,
> Wine, for these bad breaths, on this table!
> Your guts have fused with shame, victors.

On 10 April 1971, echelons of radicals and escadrilles of the romantic army planned to gather in Montmartre to celebrate the centennial of the Commune. The celebration was banned. They changed the assembly point to the Flea Market, came *en fête* in decorated trucks, bringing masks, musical instruments, flags, confetti.

The police had been waiting for three hours. Despite this menacing presence, the local people joined in the celebration. It lasted ten minutes. "Then the pigs began provoking us."

The young American reporting this to the readers of the San Francisco *Good Times* continues:

"The results: three hours of street-fighting in which we were joined by local working class white youths and Arab immigrant workers. When the streets had finally been cleared by incessant police charges, 70 brothers and sisters had been rounded up to spend the night in jail—but, 20 pigs had been wounded, three of them seriously.

"We didn't have to *commemorate* the Commune; we are communards."[26]

10.

The
Bohemian International
(1871-1899)

In 1886, Victor Hugo died. Two million Frenchmen followed his pauper's hearse to the grave—a figure approaching that of the population of Paris.

The romantic army went marching on.

The protoculture and subsociety of Bohemia came together in classic form in the Latin Quarter of the 1890's. As with the salon of Nina de Calais where Vallès and Villiers de l'Isle-Adam and the rest used to go for sustenance of body and spirit, the sympathetic milieu nourishing the bohemians was the Latin Quarter. Peopled by students and the tourists who came to watch them, this vast youthtown centered on the Boul 'Mich' and comprised at least a square mile of cheap hotels, sidewalk cafés, cabarets, bars, nightclubs, dancehalls, beer cellars, and, in those days, bordellos. The Quarter was an area at once jubilant and sad, sensuous and cold, sensitive and cruel, an actionville permissive of any kind of harmless mania and all kinds of spontaneous fun, of which Greenwich Village, North Beach, Soho, King's Cross, are but diminutive reflections.

By the 1890's, the romantic image of La Bohème had been so firmly fixed on the mind of the Western world that youth came from everywhere to play poor artist among the real artists and the real poor.[1] Older persons came from everywhere to spend a week or two and either as voyeurs or participants to enjoy the free but forbidden life of the Quarter.

The resultant river of tourist money flowing through the Quarter attracted all the forms of poseurs, entrepreneurs, spivs, tramps, and ambulatory madmen now found in any place with a bohemian reputation. But here also existed the richest concentration of able youth to be found anywhere on earth, a mélange of students, bohemians, adventurers, of romantic seekers-for-more, coming from six continents and eventually returning to them to disseminate the liberated vitality of the protoculture through the traditional and transitional societies that bore them.

Even though Paris is no longer the capital of the world or of art,[2] it still is a place most serious artists feel obliged to visit at least once. Few are the people of recognized accomplishment in the arts who have not at some time moved with the crowds and sat in the cafés of the Boul 'Mich'. Consequently, the community constitutes an informal school where day and night people of exceptional quality from all countries, quality both potential and fulfilled, live in constant colloquy.

Gathering momentum in the 1870's and 1880's, the Latin Quarter First International came together in the 1890's and did so around four distinct life-styles—associated at all levels but not homogenized—those of the tourist, the hustler, the student, and the artist ranging from Water Drinker to Doyenné.

In the cafés, the natives of the Quarter, professional men and poor workers, storekeepers and bureaucrats, and all four groups mixed together in continuous effervescence. Some bohemians sold manuscripts of their poems in the saloons, by this or other means sucking all of their meager sustenance out of café life. Bohemian life had come out in public; the bohemians lived by the infinity of combinations and permutations possible in such an environment. Many had on this scene degenerated from a youth of fine and ardent talent to a state of stunned vagabondage hard to distinguish from the life of skid-road bums. There is nothing so romantic as a young bum and nothing so revolting as an old one, particularly when his mind has been scrambled and hardened by alcohol and other forms of hard dope. In the 1890's, absinthe served as the great mind-destroyer and many were its victims, once young and strong, now shattered ruins like Paul Verlaine's friend Bibi Dans la Purée (Burned-out Bibi), characters who moved about the Quarter, surviving somehow, known and tolerated by all.

Following the terrible times of 1870-1871, the bohemians, poor poets and artists, formed cenacles like the Hirsutes, the Hydropaths (who also called themselves the Sons of Defeat), the Decadents, the Incoherents. Later they congregated at cabarets like the Chat Noir (Black Cat after Poe's story), and the Golden Sun Café, located near the Café de la Cloche (Clock Café) from whose name and clientele comes the French work for bum—*clochard*. They frequented cabarets where poets and musicians took the stage one after another and presented their work. This innovation, the public poetry reading, made it possible to rise in one night from obscurity to fame.[3]

Poetry at the Golden Sun.

Since the Refractories, the bourgeois attitude toward bohemians had become one of ambivalence. It resembled the ancient Roman attitude toward the Greeks—a mixture of contempt and envy. In the face of this, the bohemians guarded a bitter self-respect, one finding expressions such as this anonymous favorite song:

A nous le pétrole et la trique
Faut que ça finisse: Chahut!

A nous la gloire et la fortune,
Massacrons les bidards
Et faisons la Commune
Des lettres et des arts.
Salis aussi, Salis est riche
Et nous flamberons le
    Chat Noir!

Let's grab coal oil and clubs
This shit's got to cease;
    Freak out!
Let's grab glory and fortune,
We'll kill off the straights
And make the Commune
Of letters and of arts.
Salis too, Salis is rich
And we'll torch the
    Chat Noir![4]

Rodolphe Salis, an inept painter who started the big, popular, bohemian saloon called the Chat Noir, a cabaret in Montmartre where the waiters wore the robes of Academicians, slowly transformed it into an establishment exploiting bohemians and catering to such people as the Prince of Wales, the King of Greece, and General Georges-Ernest Boulanger. Salis, a prototype of the hip capitalist, would, said the song, become the target of the fire bombs of the communards of the arts.

The student life of the Quarter is the armature of which bohemian life is built. For every Houssaye or Murger who entered Bohemia directly, ten like Nerval, Gautier, Flaubert, Nanteuil, Baudelaire, Vallès, or, for that matter, Robert Louis Stevenson and Benjamin Franklin "Frank" Norris—both at one time adolescent art students in Paris, Norris at Atelier Gérôme—seem to have entered Bohemia through the foyer of student life, sometimes law, usually painting. For many years, the central quality of the Quarter was set by the *rapins*—the young students of painting. In an equation where X can equal zero, *Rapin* + X = bohemian.

As an international student quarter, the Latin Quarter, so called because its students, coming from all over Europe, once conversed in Latin, dates back to the twelfth century or earlier. From 1250 onward, thousands of students lived in the Quarter,[5] some in the same buildings where students live today.

Until 1500, education was not in fashion and the students were usually poor. They were not subject to civil law nor could they be arrested for debt. A turbulent lot, they caroused in taverns and carried swords. Five years of studies led to a single examination they called the Last Judgment. Resentment over prices occasionally exploded into riots as did resentments growing from love affairs with local girls. The thirteenth century saw students fighting Saint Louis's archers. A feeling of the cosmopolitan quality of this life is preserved in the tax register of 1295, which shows a single block on the rue de la Ferronnerie housing lodgers from all parts of France, England, Germany, Flanders, Burgundy, Normandy, and elsewhere. For last names some foreigners used their countries, the provincial French, their home towns. Yet others bore names like Alan-Who-Never-Lies, John-Who-Drinks, Ameline-the-Well-Combed, Ysabeau-the-Glutton, Laughing Peter, and Black Perette.[6]

In the late Middle Ages everything began to ossify and then, with the centralization of power culminating with Louis XIV, the Sun King, the university found itself on a tight leash. Since the beginning of the university, in accordance with the ascetic woman-hating doctrines of the church, ecclesiastical authorities had done their utmost to repress sexual expression among the students. Peter Abélard and Heloïse did not suffer by caprice. To the sexual energy of youth, the pedagogues always opposed, most perfectly in the residence colleges, a single remedy compounded of fear, hunger, cold, and fatigue. Hence a work schedule of 5 A.M. to 9 P.M.[7]

The Revolution set the students free of sumptuary control. Suddenly they found themselves embarked on a fantastic idealistic adventure in a context of a relaxed program and sensual freedom. Then, with Napoleon, the inspiration of the humanistic ideal transmuted into that of the heroic. Napoleon's stunning victories and the society behind them radiated heroism. Napoleon modeled the university, the colleges, and the high schools on a bureaucratized heroic ideal. Education became militarization. Uniforms, military discipline to the point of corporal punishment, a rigid schedule announced by drums, the restoration of religious instruction, and the movement of students in military formation served the purpose.

Youth embraced all this with an enthusiasm so intense as to express itself, even in high schools, in a mania for dueling.

But after about 1810, scepticism spread among the few students remaining in the Quarter. They began refusing enlistment and dodging conscription.

On returning from Elba in 1815, Napoleon declared that one night in Paris would fetch him a new army.

He sent press-gangs into the Quarter. But, with the help of keen intelligence and outraged families, most of his prey escaped. At the Polytechnic School itself, a student riot had to be suppressed at bayonet point.[8]

The next morning on all the blackboards the authorities read:

> The world is an atom where creeps proudly
> That insect usurper called His Majesty.[9]

From that point on, the students were militant anti-clericals and ardent republicans.

In 1830, they joined the Battle of *Hernani* and then soon after manned the barricades of revolution. Directly after the ascension of the Bourgeois King they started two underground newspapers— *The Latin Quarter Lantern* and *Avant-Garde, Journal of the Schools*—papers that eventually organized the largest demonstration ever seen in the Quarter. This, a massive demand for the reinstatement of Jules Michelet and two other professors, is a significant link in the chain of events leading to the Revolution of 1848. After the coup d'état, the students formed a core of resistance to Napoleon III, then served in the siege of Paris and supported the Commune.[10]

But it would be a mistake to think of them as deadly serious political activists.

Their concerns may be more truly summarized by their perennial fascination with the legend of the Tour de Nèsle, a sinister medieval keep standing on the left bank of the Seine. The mistress of the tower, they liked to believe, used to invite select students for a night of ideal pleasure, only, in the morning, to have them thrown into the Seine, a stone at their necks.[11]

From before *Hernani* until 1859 a center of manic student life was a giant collapsing tenement near Saint-Germain that people compared to a chicken crate and called Childebert. The woman who owned it had not willingly spent one franc on it since buying it in 1795. Her reason: "After me, they'll do what they want. But it's plenty good enough for people who give me all the trouble in the world about paying."[12]

One student who lived on the top floor and did pay his rent became so outraged after having been drenched through the roof by a rainstorm that, one hot day, he ripped up some of his flooring and hired a platoon of water carriers to pour water down the hole. When the landlady arrived in a cab she was serenaded by the residents. On reaching the flooded room she found the student, naked, who replied to her harpy shrieks by saying he had a right to take a bath at his *own* convenience.

She had the roof fixed.

Childebert's five or six stories mainly sheltered rapins, among whom was Célestin Nanteuil. Until the 1830's some of the lodgers wore doublets, trunk hose, and, on their long hair, flat caps embellished with birds' wings. Some tried to speak in medieval French; all affected a passion for medieval poetry.

About this time, at the height of the war between neoclassicists and romantics, the Childeberts held a party. Some of them dressed in medieval modes, others in the style of the ancients. The ancients brought Romulus and Remus with their wolf, Hercules with his lion. Loosed in the neighborhood, the wolf and the lion provoked a furor. But when the police finally caught them, these dread beasts behaved tamely enough for they had proven to be a Great Dane and a mastiff cleverly disguised. Often the Childeberts yelled "mad dog" to terrify their neighbors. Once they loosed a dog made up *en tigre* which provoked the calling of the National Guard.

After 1830, to confirm bourgeois suspicions, some Childeberts affected the attributes of the mythical bouzingo, carrying cudgels, wearing leather hats, Robespierre hair, Marat jackets, red carnations.

Naturally their neighbors feared them. During Childebert parties, all rooms lit, passers-by would see strange silhouettes against the windows. Matrons crossed themselves when walking past; bourgeois seeking to have their portraits painted were received at the door by a naked man and conducted through further torments. Once the faithful leaving mass at Saint-Germain met a great crowd of Moslems smoking esoteric pipes.[13]

The students of romantic times banded together in prankster clubs like the 45 Jolly Pigs who, after drinking parties, sang in the streets, broke windows, played practical jokes. Another boozehounds' club staffed mainly by Childebertians of proven boxing, wrestling, and fencing ability, exacted of its pledges an oath of perpetual warfare against the repose of all bourgeois. In the initiation, the pledge had to spend three sleepless days in drinking and demonstrating his prankster qualities.[14]

Bouzingos, as seen by Frances Trollope.

Reporting impressions gathered while a rapin in the early 1830's, William Makepeace Thackeray tells us that, in contrast to England's single art school, Paris offered a dozen of the first quality supplemented by models, an artistic environment, and the incomparable Louvre. Despite the curse of neoclassicism, France, "the paradise of painters and penny-a-liners," which had "made Tom Paine a deputy," really valued art and gave to artists more room, more money, more understanding than did England. As for status, in Paris the painter was "caressed by hosts and hostesses in places where titles were laughed at and a baron is thought of no more account than a banker's clerk."[15]

All this makes one think that because Paris was so conducive to the fine arts and to the eccentricities of artists and because so much was happening there that, Murger or no Murger, foreign art students would have come in numbers sufficing to make it the world capital of art.

Although entwined with Bohemia, itself in a sense an art school, the rapin tradition followed its own course of development. During the 1880's and 1890's, the most liberated of these young students of painting were those of the government university, the Faculty of Fine Arts of the University of Paris. After 177 years of vagabonding about Paris under a number of names, in 1806 Beaux Arts was settled by Napoleon into the home on Bonaparte Street it still occupies.

Ninety years later, on the theory that disciplined passion is the dynamic of art, the instruction at Beaux Arts still formed around a rigid procedure in which the energy came mainly from the student's own ardent purpose. The discipline derived from the older students, the classics, the teaching assistants and the master, from the annual Salon and the Prix de Rome. Finding no one to hold his hand, the rapin had to teach himself; finding his way obstructed by formidable obstacles, the rapin had to learn how to overcome.

The rapin began by working as a copyist, drawing from plaster casts of classical sculpture. Eventually if the professor thought him good enough, he was promoted to a life studio where models replaced the casts.

Here, for a year, the rapin held the inferior status of neophyte. After that, a veteran, he aspired to be recognized by the honor of receiving one of the ten private studios, having a painting accepted by the annual salon, and, at the summit, being appointed to the fat scholarship called the Prix de Rome. An elected teaching assistant, the *massier*, managed each studio; the professor came but twice a week.

Monday, the day of auditions, prospective models posed until the students chose one to work for them for the rest of the week. Saturday, the master came and graded the work, marking each student's drawing or painting on its face with a I, a II, or a III, and then with a number indicating its place in the category.

All this was supplemented by a weekly anatomy class where the professor cut up corpses.

This structure was the only one imposed on the rapin; it gave

his life form in a city abounding with temptations, which in the
Quarter after 1871 included Brasseries de Femme, big saloons with
B-girls, which students began frequenting at age fourteen. The discipline of the school, seen in the context of Paris, gave the rapin a
sense of purpose, of consistency, of order.[16]

Around 1898, a group of ten neophytes admitted to the Atelier
Gérôme—the studio of Jean-Léon Gérôme, one of Beaux Art's three
professors of painting—comprised five provincial French, a Turk, a
Hungarian, a Thai, and two Americans (one a cowboy from Nebraska). Neophytes were subjected to hazings meant to test their
qualities and grind out their bourgeois traits. This traditionally began by forcing them to strip and, mounting a table, to duel with
brushes soggy with blue or crimson paint. Their reactions led to
spontaneous pranks. A neophyte is stripped, placed in a hamper,
left on a bridge. Here, the Turk, a proud and humorless being, was
stripped, painted in fantastic designs, tied and carried on a pole at
the head of a procession, made to believe he was about to be branded
GEROME with a red-hot iron, then placed on a shelf fifteen feet
above the floor of the studio and abandoned there. The cowboy,
smiling and laughing, fought off all his tormentors with chairs and
fists.[17]

The queen of the models in those days was Sarah Brown, reign-
ing by virtue of her long blond hair and stunning figure. By going
naked to the third annual Bal des Quat'z' Arts (Four Arts Ball) in
1893, she drew the hostile attention of a senator soon to be nicknamed Father Prude. This led to arrests and then an argument at a
Boul 'Mich' café between police and a youth, which led to the death
of another youth and caused an explosion of resentment, streetcars
and busses overturned and burned, followed by a general student
riot lasting for days, one threatening the existence of the government.[18]

By way of friendly advice to an American rapin, Gérôme once
said: "You must work, my friend, work! To succeed, work all the
time, seriously—understand!"[19]

The other half of the work-hard play-hard rhythm of art set in
its aesthetic and sensual aura finds classic expression in the Four
Arts Ball, an event symbolic of the tolerance Paris showed and may
show still for spontaneity, life, art. In England, the equivalent event
held New Year's Eve at the Royal Albert Hall in London features

artists freaking out on the floor in plain view of the rich, seated above in boxes, drinking. It's not hard to imagine this being transplanted to the New World. Conversely, the Bal des Quat'z' Arts could not take place in any American city save possibly San Francisco where it should be inaugurated at once in the Palace of Fine Arts.

Here, according to the notes of a rapin in attendance, is what happened at the Four Arts Ball of 1899:

Every spring "after the pictures have been sent to the Salon, and before the students have scattered for the summer vacation, the artists of Paris and the members of all the ateliers of the four arts—painting, sculpture, architecture, and engraving—combine their forces in producing a spectacle of regal splendor, seen nowhere else in the world; and long are the weeks and hard the work and vast the ingenuity devoted to preparations—the designing of costumes and the building of gorgeous floats."

For three weeks in advance, the students of the master painter, Gérôme, devoted themselves to building a gigantic copy of his sculpted figure of Bellona, the gaunt Roman goddess of war. After celebrating their accomplishment in draughts of *grog-américain* fifty rapins pulled her through the streets of Paris and up the hill of Montmartre to the Moulin Rouge where she was to wait for the ball.

That evening "we found the Café de la Source already crowded by the Gérôme contingent and their models and mistresses, all *en costume* and bubbling with merriment and mischief. It was ten o'clock before all the students had arrived. Then we formed in procession, and yelled and danced past all the cafés on the Boul 'Mich' to the Luxembourg Palace and the Théâtre de l'Odéon, to take the 'busses of the Montmartre line. These we quickly seized and overloaded in violation of the law, and then, dashing down the quiet streets of the Rive Gauche, headed for Montmartre, making a noise to rouse the dead. As we neared the Place Blanche we found the little streets merging from different quarters crowded with people in costume, some walking and others crowding almost innumerable vehicles, and the balconies and portes-cochères packed with spectators. The Place Blanche fronts the Moulin Rouge, and it was crowded and brilliantly lighted. The façade of the Moulin Rouge was a blaze of electric lights and colored lanterns, and the revolving wings of the mill flamed across the sky. It was a perfect night. The stars shone, the air was warm and pleasant, and the trees were tipped with the glistening clean foliage of early spring. The bright cafés fronting the Place were crowded with gay revelers. The poets of Bohemia were there, and gayly attired cocottes assisted them in their fun at the café tables, extending far out into the boulevard under the trees. At one corner was Gérôme's private studio, high in the top of a house, and standing on the balcony was Gérôme himself, enjoying the brilliant scene below."

In the entry of the Moulin, behind a long bar sat the *massiers* of all the studios, wildly costumed. As the Ball was closed to the public, they identified the ticket holders and, as it was given to art, they judged the costumes, rejecting everyone whose costume did not meet their aesthetic standards. Fifty years later, giant Nubian guards were to throw some people right out into the street.

"Once past the implacable tribunes, we entered a dazzling fairy-land, a dream of rich color and reckless abandon. From gorgeous kings and queens to wild savages, all were there; courtiers in silk, naked gladiators, nymphs with paint for clothing,—all were there; and the air was heavy with the perfume of roses. Shouts, laughter, the silvery clinking of glasses, a whirling mass of life and color, a bewildering kaleidoscope, a maze of tangled visions in the soft yellow haze that filled the vast hall. There was no thought of the hardness and sordidness of life, no dream of the morrow. It was a wonderful witchery that sat on every soul there."

Loges, one for each studio, extending along a wall, presented tableaux of the themes. That of Atelier Gérôme represented an ancient temple, that of Atelier Cormon "a huge cavern of the prehistoric big-muscled men that appealed so strongly to Cormon; large skeletons of extinct animals, giant ferns, skins and stone implements were scattered about, while the students of Cormon's atelier, almost naked, with bushy hair and clothed in skins, completed the picture."

Eventually, "nearly all the renowned painters, sculptors, and illustrators of Paris were there; and besides them were the countless students and models."

The band hushed, the dancing ceased. Together with the cool breath of night, in the front door came the leaders of the grand procession.

"First came a band of yelling Indians dancing in, waving their spears and tomahawks, and so cleaving a way for the parade," Then, a roar. Borne on the shoulders of painted Indians was "a gorgeous bed of fresh flowers and trailing vines; and reclining on this bed were four of the models of Paris, lying on their backs, head to head, their legs upraised to support a circular tablet of gold. Upon this, high in the air, proud and superb, was the great Suzanne in all her peerless beauty of face and form,—simply that and nothing more. A sparkling crown of jewels glowed in her reddish golden hair; a flashing girdle of electric lights encircled her slender waist, bringing out the marvelous whiteness of her skin, and with delicate shadows and tones modeling the superb contour of her figure."

Then came Bellona, fifteen feet high, embodying Gérôme's vision of the fearful reality of war, escorted by Greeks and Romans and followed by the American cowboy, now an Apache Indian, riding a bucking bronco. And then the Atelier Cormon with its cavemen and then Egyptian mummies and then giant eggs whence girls were breaking their way to freedom, and more and more.

The tribune for seating the judges was garnished with fasces and inscribed Death to Tyrants. Beneath this inscription hung a row of heads, macabre and bloody, cut from tyrants.

Circles formed around models doing the belly dance; at 3 A.M., two hundred waiters brought in supper. Then the announcement of first prize, fifty bottles of champagne—awarded for Bellona to Atelier Gérôme.

Although slippery with wine and strewn with broken glass, the floor did not daunt the revelers nor yet did the blue light of dawn penetrating the windows.

Then the orchestra played the Victor's March signaling the end of the ball. Everyone moved out into the quiet square and the bright light of day. "En cavalcade!" and cavalcade it became, the joyful artists marching in procession down the Hill of Montmartre, Bellona swaying on her chariot, as they began the march across Paris back to the Quarter.

"The deserted Rue Blanche re-echoed the wild yells and songs of the revellers and the rattling of the strings of cabs at the rear. The rows of heaped ash cans that lined the way were overturned one after another, and the oaths and threatening brooms of the outraged concierges went for nothing. Even the poor diligent rag-and-bone-pickers were not spared; their filled sacks, carrying the results of their whole night's hunt, were taken from them and emptied. A string of carts heavily laden with stone was captured near the Rue Lafayette, the drivers deposed, and the big horses sent plunging through Paris, driven by Roman charioteers, and making more noise than a company of artillery.

"When the Place de l'Opéra was reached a thousand revellers swarmed up the broad stairs of the Grand Opera like colored ants, climbed upon the lamp-posts and candelabra, and clustered all over the groups of statuary adorning the magnificent façade. The band took up a position in the center and played furiously, while the artists danced ring-around-a-rosy, to the amazement of the drowsy residents of the neighborhood."

The romantic army then advanced toward the Louvre where it met a large squad of street sweepers. "In an instant the squad had been routed, and the revellers, taking the hose and brooms, fell to and cleaned an entire block, making it shine as it had never shone before.

"Cabs were captured, the drivers decorated with Roman helmets and swords, and dances executed on the tops of the vehicles.

"As the immense cavalcade filed through the narrow arches of the Louvre court-yard it looked like a medieval army returning to

its citadel after a victorious campaign; the hundreds of battle-flags, spears and battle-axes were given a fine setting by the noble architecture of the Pavillon de Rohan. Within the court of the Louvre was drawn up a regiment of the Garde Municipale, going through the morning drill; and they looked quite formidable with their evolutions and bayonet charges. But when the mob of Greek and Roman warriors flung themselves bodily upon the ranks of the guard, ousted the officers, and assumed command, there was consternation. All the rigid military dignity of the scene disappeared, and the drill was turned into such a farce as the old Louvre had never seen before. The officers, furious at first, could not resist the spirit of pure fun that filled the mob, and took their revenge by kissing the models and making them dance."

When the romantic army reached the Carrousel Bridge—after having passed over the site of the long-vanished Doyenné Alley—it "performed the solemn ceremony of the annual sacrifice of the Quat'z' Arts to the river Seine." Bellona "was trundled to the centre of the bridge and drawn close to the parapet, while the disciples of the four arts gathered about with uncovered heads. The first bright flashes of the morning sun, sweeping over the towers of Notre-Dame, tipped Bellona's upraised sword with flame." The band played, the devotees prayed and sang the "Marseillaise." "Bellona was sent tottering and crashing over the parapet, and with a mighty plunge she sank beneath the waters of the Seine."

Up the narrow rue Bonaparte went singing the romantic army; the gates of Beaux Arts "opened to admit it, cabs and all, and the doors were shut again. Then in the historic courtyard of the government school, surrounded by remnants of the beautiful architecture of once stately chateaux and palaces, and encircled by graceful Corinthian columns, the students gave a repetition of the grand ball at the Moulin Rouge."[20]

11.

The Last Bohemia
(1890-1914)

By 1914, our ancestors had come to believe in progress as intensely as our more remote ancestors had believed in God. Is this all there is? There's got to be more! The locus of more had shifted from the eternal bliss of the afterlife promised by tradition to the imminent and inevitable arrival of paradise on earth promised by technological progress. In the 1820's, a gray melancholy spread all over Europe; by the 1890's the young and the bourgeois were caught up in an age of discovery as spirited and exciting as that experienced by the Athenians between the Persian and the Peloponnesian Wars. The deeper civilization plunged into the unknown, the more comfortable and interesting life became. Consequently, the people became so profoundly committed to the underlying purpose as to establish that purpose at the level of a cultural trait, as seemingly natural, and therefore unquestioned, as the decimal system or the use of money, as language itself.

The underlying purpose of civilization had become the acceleration of technological progress toward the end of freeing humanity from material want. Because of a covert belief in economic determinism, this promised the eventual realization of Utopia.

Thanks to the long experience of a continuous and almost magical betterment of living conditions resulting from a century of advance into the unknown, the burning purpose became coupled with an intensifying élan, a commitment to the spirit of adventure. In essence, this is a condition where curiosity about the unknown is stronger than fear of the unknown, where risk becomes more attractive than caution, where one believes there is indeed more and that if we dare to reach for it we can have it.

As the century flowed on, men began to find the meaning of life in the search, either vicarious or direct, for adventure, and in the romance of machines.

The Romance of Machines.

Never in Homo Sapiens's 100,000-year career had there been more fundamental change and improvement in daily living, nor has there been since, than that experienced in the major cities of Western civilization between 1890 and 1914. Much of this change originated in the flashing brilliance of the mind of Paris, much in the daring and tradition-free spirit of the United States. For us, who have experienced but little change in daily living, it is difficult to imagine the impact on our ancestors of the enormous change happening at the turn of the century. Think of the revolutionary effect of each of these innovations on the routines of daily living and, more deeply, on the basic relations of man-to-man and of man-to-nature:

— the telephone
— the cheap camera
— the phonograph
— the rotary press and the linotype machine
— photoengraving and the 100-page Sunday newspaper
— the railroad air-brake and sleeping car
— the electric street car
— the skyscraper
— the suspension bridge
— the internal combustion engine and motor vehicles
— the airplane
— the typewriter
— the bicycle
— the electric light
— the motion picture
— the public library
— scientific medicine
— the department store
— the ocean liner
— refrigeration and the end of seasonal diet
— the ship's radio
— the elevator
— professional sports
— the sewing machine
— steam heating
— the gas stove
— hot running water.

In sum, and like as not the work of bohemian inventors, most of the innovations in daily life and almost every machine to which we are accustomed appeared in the cities between 1890 and 1914—in most cases to be enjoyed by the masters of society and their house slaves (the middle class), but not by their field hands and wage slaves being crushed down by the wedge of progress and poverty.[1]

Symbolic of this is the division of the trains of the new Parisian subways, first opened in 1900, into two classes, and the long-standing division of trains on European railroads into three.

The schism between the officers and enlisted men of society widened; the servile classes were to be kept in isolation from those they served. For the poor, the future promised but a third-class paradise. The bourgeois, too cheap to ride first-class and too proud to ride third, occupied the second-class cars and compartments of society. Because the bourgeois culture had become dominant, the promise of the future, much like the objects-of-art and the furniture, had for everyone been degraded to second-class quality. A reaction to this was the invention of a high art for everyday objects—art nouveau.

In innovation and in productivity the nineteenth century had succeeded; it failed in equity—in the distribution of obligations, rewards and power—and in quality.

In Paris, the contrast was striking, but so was the feeling of hope, the excitement of discovery, the pride of accomplishment, the élan of participation, the sense of the unlimited power of the imagination set free. Through his books Jules Verne—himself a quondam bohemian—opened the public mind to the magic inhering in technology. *Around the World in Eighty Days* appeared just after the death of the Commune. By 1880, the memory of both the Empire and the agony of 1871 had faded away. Of the Commune, the Foreign Legion's official history says: "This is not a Legionnaire's affair, so we will pass this painful episode in silence."[2] This articulates a general attitude, one resembling the American attitude toward the memory of Viet Nam. French historians and literati tend to pass over the Commune in silence. The citizens of the romantic republic erased it from memory, this distressing interruption of the orderly progression of events, this scandalous incident in the third-class railway car. So, excepting the passengers riding third-class, the citizens of the Third Republic—a republic capable of cutting Liberty-Equality-Fraternity into the stone above its jailhouse doors —forgot the Commune and would have forgotten the Prussian victory as well had not the reactionaries kept the memory alive to spur their demand for revenge.

The World's Fair of 1879 attracted 13 million visitors to Paris and convinced Europe that France had recovered her high spirits and prosperity. In 1889, Parisians celebrated the centennial of the Revolution by drinking 113 million gallons of wine and 3.75 million gallons of liquor, by producing a spectacular world's fair around the theme of technological progress, symbolized by the Eiffel Tower and a searchlight at its top sweeping a tricolored beam over the city. When Thomas Alva Edison, former bohemian and present god of the liberated imagination, visited his display at the Fair, it created an absolute sensation.

Since 1830, the imagination of youth had been turned from the arts to machinery.

"You perhaps will live to witness the most momentous changes ever to be recorded in the history of mankind."

So said Ernest Renan in 1883 to the students of Louis the Great High School.[3]

That this prediction was coming true seemed confirmed by the giant world's fair of 1900 where fabulous displays of the miraculous accomplishments of technology quelled doubt and hushed criticism of the religion of progress.

Innovation in engineering came to be assayed as the highest value.

Not so, innovation in the arts.

In 1895, commenting on a bequest of Cézannes, Degas, Manets, and Renoirs to the Louvre, Gérôme said: "Only a great moral depravity could bring the State to accept such trash." These artists are all "anarchists and madmen."[4]

To the art community, rooted in Bohemia, belief in progress seemed absurd and creative innovation appeared an obstacle to success. Nevertheless, as the story of the Four Arts Ball suggests and as the incomparable record of artists in pre-1914 Paris demonstrates, the art community embodied the exuberant élan of discovery, of imagination set free of convention.

By the 1890's, the art community was moving out of the city into cheap, pastoral places on the perimeters—Montparnasse and Montmartre.

Montparnasse, then a quiet suburb of small houses, gardens, farms, shops, restaurants, drew to itself an international group of poets and artists and other misfits. About 1914 at a small, dingy cabaret called the Rotonde, a group of Americans could be found almost every night crowded around the bar, dressed like apaches—drinking and, on occasions, firing pistols. The back of the place served as a rendezvous for Russians, two of whom, meeting to play chess and talk politics, bore the names Nikolai Lenin and Leon Trotsky.[5]

It was in Montmartre, however, that the new Bohemia was to be found. As early as the 1870's, atop the Hill of Montmartre with its small houses and potato fields and songbirds and 300-year-old windmills, artists found refuge from the mechanized, bourgeois civilization of the city. Lower down, in the giant tourist traps and cheap cabarets and dance halls of the slums around Place Pigalle (Pig Alley in American) and Place Blanche, they found excitement, friends, refuge from bucolic boredom. Here, in the mornings and late at night, Bohemia mixed with an idle populace composed of whores, pimps, cheap criminals (apaches), tourists, slumming bourgeois, rapins; here Bohemia fraternized with the underworld enemies of society with whom it shares so many traits and with whom it still mixes today.

According to one story, the reluctant balloonist and republic founder, Léon Gambetta, accompanied by the President of France came to the cabaret Chat Noir looking for a salty writer of the staff of *Chat Noir*, a fierce, satirical, refractory magazine edited at the cabaret and supplied by the best writers in Montmartre. On finding him, Gambetta became so infuriated by his stiletto wit that he threatened to crush Montmartre with troops and to do so "in the name of the bourgeoisie who are sick and tired of your verses and songs and paintings," of the financiers made anxious by your putting above them "something they can't understand because it can't be bought with money," and of all of us outraged "by your roisterous gaiety."[6]

For the tourists and slummers the scenes of roisterous gaiety were the Moulin Rouge with its furious cancans; Hell, where the staff dressed like devils; Heaven, tended by angels; the Cabaret of Death, served by undertakers; and the nightclub of the savage and handsome poet, Aristide Bruant, who amused his rich and pompous clients by standing on a table whence he cursed and humiliated them.

Bohemia found its sustenance in other places. One of these was a cabaret formerly called the Murderers' Bar in deference to Montmartre's ancient criminal tradition. It had been renamed The Lapin (Rabbit) à Gill after the rabbit painted on its sign by André Gill. The Lapin Agile (Agile Rabbit), as it soon became, belonged to Frédéric Gérard, a sympathetic Rabelaisian who delighted in roistering with artists. He once declared: "I was born a bohemian and I shall die a bohemian."[7]

Although before 1914 Montmartre had changed from a bower into a well-policed brick-and-cement city neighborhood and consequently was losing its artistic population, as late as 1912, if you were to visit the Lapin at night, you would find a group of wild, spontaneous bohemians, all in their twenties, bearing names like Utrillo, Apollinaire, Laborde, Braque, Modigliani, MacOrlan, Meunier, Derain, Salmon, Vlaminck, Picasso, Carco, and Max Jacob (who was to be murdered by the Gestapo), composing in all a band wherein, as Francis Carco wrote, "Women did not play a major role."[8]

Sometimes they lived on milk and warm rolls stolen early in the morning from apartment-building hallways. At the Lapin their spirits raced in a tide of fantasy and wit; they sang songs of the Legion and the Bataillon d'Afrique for drinks. Cubism seems to have risen from the bottles of the Lapin in a rush of prank and inspiration.

Once the clients tied a brush to the tail of Frédé Gérard's donkey, kept the brush soaked in paint, and provoked the donkey into painting a canvas which they named *And the Sun Sets on the Adriatic* and showed at the Salon des Indépendents where it created a sensation.

And all this to win a bet with Frédé that they could make his donkey famous.

At another time, Picasso painted a study of packing cases on a quay realistically enough to show the legends and numbers, called it *Portrait of My Father*. The next year at the Salon des Indépendents a number of *Portraits of My Father* appeared showing similar legends and numbers and a scattering of loose eyes, ears, teeth.

Most of the Apaches and sporting girls who came to the Lapin liked the artists. Frédé did his best to bar the really obnoxious criminal types. This resulted once in a gun battle and, in 1911, in the cold-blooded murder of his son shot down at the cash drawer.

In the manner of the heavy drinking, dope-using bohemians of what Francis Carco later called the Last Bohemia, the Lapin's clients often ranged Montmartre and the Quarter until dawn when they would come home shouting, singing, declaiming, dancing. Sometimes Picasso would go berserk with energetic good spirits and shoot his revolver.[9]

Some of the Lapinites began to go to the country.

As Carco puts it: "They gathered fruit by shooting it with guns; in the night they filled the river with dried herrings into which live fish had been sewn, thus making the herrings seem alive and swimming; they went to bathe, quite naked, on their bicycles, and when a theater at a fair gave performances they took the places of the actors and greatly complicated the action."[10]

The Lapinards liked Montmartre because it was picturesque, exciting, and cheap. They also fancied it had the aspect of a boisterous waterfront town, in this celebrating the similarity between the merchant sailor's life and the bohemian's. Some Lapinards had jobs as streetcar conductors, warehousemen; some lived by their art, remittances, their wits. Francis Carco's biographer says drugs, disease, accidents, and the fading of creative energy killed off most of Carco's friends. As with old-time merchant seamen, most of the Lapinards who followed the bohemian life not as a preface nor as an expedient nor as an adventure but by preference or by necessity died of it.[11] Like Carco, most bohemians—most creative artists— were anarchists at heart who did not get along in school and ever afterward fit only crossways into society. This, the last generation of the first Bohemia, was, along with the art-for-art it represented, as much of an anachronism as the Commune. True art could not fit in with the institutions of an increasingly vulgar and exploitive society hurtling toward war. Where the two met, the friction created white heat that burned out the artist and charred his art. At least seven of the Lapinards were to die in the war. Enjoying no illusion of progress, sensing the catastrophe ahead, these men sought insulation and repose in dope and alcohol and in the Bohemia of each other's company. This community, already three generations in the building, proved to be at once a foreshadow of the future and a pearl in the decaying flesh of the present.

And this in a city where every social class enjoyed cultivated sensibilities and a true love of art.

It was not for Parisians that the renowned pyrotechnic vulgarities flared but for visiting boobs from the provinces and foreign countries.

At the Moulin Rouge, opened in 1889, customers passed through a long corridor, by photographs, paintings, posters, to the enormous dance hall. Girls on display at the tables transformed the Moulin into a cafeteria of copulation. In the garden, a chorus backed by a brassy blaring orchestra flamed through the cancan. Tame monkeys roamed about teasing the customers. Rifles cracked on the shooting range; seers told fortunes. A wooden elephant, tall as a tree, opened to reveal an orchestra and belly dancers. Now this self-styled *"Rendez-vous du high-life"* presented the house specialty—Pétomane, who sang in a deep bass voice—out of his ass![12]

Rich and admired, the deformed painter Toulouse-Lautrec spent much of his time at the Moulin, in whorehouses, in other night clubs. Delighted by the ironies of the grotesque, vivacious, spirited, as contemptuous as the Lapinards of bourgeois hypocrisy, he once received a pompous prude of an art dealer in his "studio"—the salon of a bordello. In 1895, tending bar at a party, he contrived to make most of the three hundred guests pass out. Among those lying about in drunken stupor were Alfred Jarry, Pierre Bonnard, André Gide, Pierre Louÿs, Léon Blum, Stéphane Mallarmé.[13]

And on the other side of the coin—:

A quiet young Hungarian painter had stopped appearing at a bohemian restaurant in Montparnasse for his daily chocolate and bread. The police came looking for him, asked if he had any friends there.

A French rapin and a young American sculptor said they knew him.

"Then you will take charge of his body?"

They followed the police to an old building, up to the sixth floor and a ladder rising to the roof. "We ascended it and found a box built on the roof. It gave a splendid view of Paris. The door of the box was closed. We opened it, and the young artist lay before us dead. There were two articles of furniture in the room. One was the bare mattress on the floor, upon which he lay, and the other was an old dresser, from which some of the drawers were missing. The young man lay drawn up, fully dressed, his coat collar turned up about his ears. Thus he had fallen asleep, and thus hunger and cold had slain him as he slept. There was one thing else in the room; all besides, including the stove and the bed-covering, having gone for the purchase of painting material. It was an unfinished oil-painting of the Crucifixion. Had he lived to finish it, I am sure it would have made him famous, if for nothing else than the wonderful expression of agony in the Savior's face, an agony infinitely worse than the physical pain of the crucifixion could have produced.

"And all that, too, is a part of life in bohemian Paris."[14]

This last generation of the First Bohemia, perhaps more than ever, manifested the double edge of realism/romanticism in both living and in art.

And at the line of juncture where the two halves of that yin-yang meet, the generation wrote one of its favorite quotations. François Villon's antique verse:

"Je ris en pleurs."[15]

I laugh in tears.

Part Four
THE BOURGEOIS BOHEMIA

"But we were drifting toward the elemental forces that become visible to us for the first time in many years in the hellish abyss of war. We will stand nowhere but where the flame has cleared a path for us, but where the flamethrower has cleared away nothingness. Since we are the genuine, true enemies of the bourgeois, we delight in his extermination. We are no bourgeois, we are sons of wars and civil wars, and only when all this, this spectacle of circles emptily circling about, has been wiped away, will we be able to unfold within us what is natural, elemental, truly wild, and the capacity for real creation with blood and semen. Then the possibility for new forms will have been created."

—Ernst Jünger, 1929.*

12.
Bourgeois Bohemia (1914-1918)

World War I hit Europe with a stunning shock. In a superficial intellectual way, most people thought war inevitable but, in the deeper emotional sense, no one believed war would really come. Yes, weapons proliferated—but civilization had progressed far beyond the barbarity admitting of their use.[1]

And then, in August 1914, mobilization notices appeared everywhere, announcing, particularly to the French and Germans, a romantic drama, a national Dionysian revel, a grand holiday merging everyone into a common purpose, a new life at once intense and meaningful where no one would be lonely and everybody could be somebody.

In Munich, a vast crowd, delirious with enthusiasm, assembled in the central square. A photograph shows a figure jammed tightly into it, hatless, wild with excitement—the young Adolf Hitler. In Berlin, defiant of a soaking rain, people swarmed in the streets, cheering the long gray columns, shouting for the blood of their apostate race-brother, England. In Paris, regiments of breastplated cavalry and red-pantalooned infantry moved through the streets to the eastern and northern railroad stations. Rifle barrels sprouting flowers, festive of heart, *bouzingos* all, young France moved off to war. Transported by a tremendous joyful excitement—drinking, kissing, dancing—the Parisians celebrated while the apaches and pickpockets of Montmartre enjoyed their best business of the year.[2]

In Vienna, the troops were crowned with flowers and wore oak leaves on their helmets. Soon, all would learn "The Hymn of Hate." Who would dispute Stefan Zweig's belief that none of us can emotionally recover the feeling of pre-1914 or of 1914 itself? In Vienna, Zweig remembered: "Strangers spoke to one another in the streets, people who had avoided each other for years shook hands, everywhere one saw excited faces. Each person experienced an exultation of his ego, he was no longer the isolated person of former times." His person, "his hitherto unnoticed person, had been given meaning." The "clerk, the cobbler, had suddenly achieved a romantic possibility in life: he could become a hero, and everyone who wore a uniform was already being cheered by the women." So deeply, "so quickly did the tide break over humanity that, foaming over the surface, it churned up the depths, the desire to break out of the conventional, bourgeois world."[3]

In France and Germany as well, August 1914 brought the people together in profound exultation and deep feelings of brotherhood, closing the chasm separating interests and classes. A German veteran recalled that at the station of Neuss he and a friend watched a long military train pulling out. "Pandemonium reigned, with mothers and sweethearts on the train's running boards embracing flower-covered soldiers. Photos of the Kaiser and his generals were plastered on the train. In huge chalk lettering under the posters was written, '*jeder Schuss ein Russ; jeder Tritt ein Britt; jeder Stoss ein Franzos.*' ('For each bullet a Russian; for each kick an Englishman; for each shove a Frenchman.') After arriving in Cologne, we marched through the streets with hundreds of youngsters, sons of both the rich and the poor, arm in arm and fourteen abreast, singing as if in one voice, '*Deutschland über Alles.*' " From his aunt's yard, earlier that day, he had watched thousands of young troops marching toward the west. "How handsome were their gray battle uniforms, with their spiked helmets adorned with German eagles! How tanned and grim the sun made their faces! And how proud they were of being worthy to carry rifles on their shoulders."[4]

But this effervescence faded as the terrible reality of what the mobilization notices did in fact announce became clear.

The war did not bring unity, but two worlds—the anguished world of the fronts and the comfortable world of the rear. Zweig remembered: "An embittered distrust gradually took hold of the population: distrust of currency, of constantly sinking purchasing power, distrust of generals, officers, and statesmen; distrust of the newspapers and their news, distrust of the war itself and of the need for it."[5]

In the beginning, most of the soldiers believed they were fighting for civilization, peace, and freedom; later they fought simply for survival. By 11 November 1918, 60 million of them, some wearing belt buckles marked *GOTT MIT UNS* (God with Us), others with cap ornaments emblazoned *DIEU ET MON DROIT* (God and my Right), still others following the flag of Liberty, Equality, and Fraternity, had slashed and shot and stabbed and shelled and bombed one another until almost 10 million lay dead and 21 million had been wounded.[6] European youth—the best—and with it the European future, had been physically exterminated or mentally transformed. Most of the young idealists were dead. Among the survivors, broken or whole, the tender idealistic quality of soul had been cauterized and scabbed over. In a sense, they could all answer to the name, Ernst Jünger.

Nothing could ever again be as it had been. August 1914 released a torrent of events that carries us still and a karma of violence not yet redressed. A generation had been lost; enormous capital squandered. The Americans alone wasted enough money to have built a good new house with a garage and a Model T Ford for every family in their country. Many of the old cultural forms had been broken; in those remaining, the contents had been soured if not poisoned. For millions, God, and with Him the Christian traditions, lay rotting alongside His dead servants in northern France, Poland, the Italian Alps. World War I, the event that "determined more than anything else my development," says Erich Fromm, killed off "the nontheistic 'religious' movement of the last 100 years." Not only was God dead, but so was Man.[7]

What do all these abstractions mean? What is the experiential reality of the countless millions of incidents from which they are abstracted?

Here is a composite of impressions drawn from statements by eyewitnesses: Erich Kramer (Erich Maria Remarque),[8] author of *All Quiet on the Western Front*; Philip Gibbs, a noted British war correspondent; four forgotten Frenchmen; a notorious Austrian; and an American:

ERICH KRAMER: We were still crammed full of vague ideas which gave to life, and to the war also, an ideal and almost romantic character.[9]

GEORGES DELEYE: We hasten to deepen the trenches so as to be better protected when day comes, and to get on faster, we place in front of us, in parapet, the corpses of comrades.[10]

ERICH KRAMER: The youngster will hardly survive the carrying, and at the most he will only last a few days. What he has gone through so far is nothing to what he's in for until he dies. Now he is numb and feels nothing. In an hour he will become one screaming bundle of intolerable pain. Every day that he can live will be a howling torture. And to whom does it matter if he has them or not———[11]

PHILIP GIBBS: There were a lot of living Germans in the second ditch, and in holes about. Some of them stood still, as though turned to clay, until they fell with half the length of a bayonet through their stomachs. Others shrieked and ran a little way before they died. Others sat behind hillocks of earth, spraying our men with machine-gun bullets until bombs were hurled on them and they were scattered into lumps of flesh.[12]

ERICH KRAMER: The fire lifts a hundred yards and we break forward. Beside me a lance-corporal has his head torn off. He runs a few steps more while the blood spouts from his neck like a fountain.[13]

CHARLES DELVERT: It's almost seventy-two hours since I've slept. The pigs attack again early in the morning. Steady boys! Let them come way out! We can't waste the merchandise. At twenty-five paces! Smash in their pig faces! At my command!—Fire! Let them have it! A cracking of explosions well together! Bravo! A black cloud rises. You could see the groups of pigs spin around, overthrown. One or two pigs raise themselves to their knees and cringing sneak away.[14]

ERICH KRAMER: A young Frenchman lags behind, he is overtaken, he puts up his hands, in one he still holds his revolver—does he mean to shoot or to give himself up?—a blow from a spade cleaves through his face. A second sees it and tries to run farther; a bayonet jabs into his back. He leaps in the air, his arms thrown wide, his mouth wide open, yelling; he staggers, in his back the bayonet quivers.[15]

PHILIP GIBBS: A boot with some pulp inside protruded from a mud-bank where I stood, and there was a human head, without eyes or nose, black, and rotting in the puddle of a shell-hole. Those were relics of a battle on May 9th, a year before, when swarms of boys, of the '16 class, boys of eighteen, the flower of French youth, rushed forward from the crossroads of La Targette, a few hundred yards away, to capture the ruins of Neuville St.-Vast.[16]

ERICH KRAMER: We see men living with their skulls blown open; we see soldiers run with their two feet cut off, they stagger on their splintered stumps into the next shell-hole; a lance-corporal crawls a mile and half on his hands dragging his smashed knee after him; another goes to the dressing station and over his clasped hands bulge his intestines; we see men without mouths, without jaws, without faces; we find one man who has held the artery of his arm in his teeth for two hours in order not to bleed to death.[17]

JEAN MEIGNEN: When day comes the morning of 25 April, I cannot save myself from a feeling of horror and fright when I see that at the place I'd been occupying, the parapet was formed in part by corpses and that all night I had pressed myself against soldiers' shoes which stuck out, letting flow an infected mud, mixed with blood, with rot and with earth.[18]

ERICH KRAMER: The wisest were just the poor and simple people. They knew the war to be a misfortune, whereas people who were better off were beside themselves with joy, though they should have been much better able to judge what the consequences would be.[19]

A. POINARD: I find not far from where I left him my poor comrade Segnal. The mica of his mask was pierced, he'd been knocked unconscious. I hasten to change it, for the pigs with their shells keep sending gas. Segnal comes to, he tears off his mask and says to me: "Théo old friend, I've had it," and at the same moment he's seized by violent vomiting; blood comes out of him through the ears, the nose and his open mouth; the horrible agony! Never shall I be able to forget it. He didn't want to die and kept asking me to save him; he spoke to me of his dear mother, and then he was saying to me he was suffering too much, to give him a grenade so he could blow himself up.[20]

ERICH KRAMER: Through the entrance rushes in a swarm of fleeing rats that try to storm the walls. Torches light up the confusion. Everyone yells and curses and slaughters. The madness and despair of many hours unloads itself in this outburst. Faces are distorted, arms strike out, the beasts scream; we just stop in time to avoid attacking one another.[21]

PHILIP GIBBS: God had nothing to do, seemingly, with a night raid into Boche lines, when they blew a party of Germans to bits by dropping Stoke bombs down their dugout, or with the shrieks of German boys, mad with fear, when the Australians jumped on them in the darkness and made haste with their killing.[22]

ERICH KRAMER: Bombardment, barrage, curtain-fire, mines, gas, tanks, machine-guns, hand-grenades—words, words, but they hold the horror of the world.[23]

PHILIP GIBBS: Some of the German dead were young boys, too young to be killed for old men's crimes, and others might have been old or young. One could not tell, because they had no faces, and were just masses of raw flesh in rags and uniforms.[24]

ERICH KRAMER: When a shell lands in the trench we note how the hollow, furious blast is like a blow from the paw of a raging beast of prey. Already by morning a few of the recruits are green and vomiting. They are too inexperienced.[25]

PHILIP GIBBS: On the right of the Londoners the French still stayed in their trenches—their own attack was postponed until midday—and they cheered the London men as they went forward with cries of, *"Vivent les Anglais!" "A mort les Boches!"* It was they who saw one man kicking a football in advance of the others. . . . It was a London Irishman dribbling a football toward the goal, and he held it for fourteen hundred yards—[26]

ERICH KRAMER: We recognize the distorted faces, the smooth helmets: they are French. . . . A whole line has gone down before our machine-guns; then we have a lot of stoppages and they come nearer. I see one of them, his face upturned, fall into a wire cradle. His body collapses, his hands remain suspended as though he were praying. Then his body drops clean away and only his hands with the stumps of his arms, shot off, now hang on the wire.[27]

PHILIP GIBBS: They were of Saxon breed. There was hardly a difference between them and some of the German prisoners I saw, yellow-haired as they were, with fair, freckled, sun-baked skins.[28]

ERICH KRAMER: We became hard, suspicious, pitiless, vicious, tough —and that was good; for these attributes had been entirely lacking in us.[29]

CHARLES DELVERT: We will leave our dead in the trench like memories. Their comrades piously move them out of the way. I recognize them. Here's Cosset and his corduroy breeches; Aumont, poor kid, eighteen; Bamboula who stretches out his waxen hand, the hand which once threw grenades so bravely, and Pinguenet, and Génin and Lauraire, and Crinière, and so many others! Alas! What lugubrious sentinels we abandon! They are there, aligned on the parados, stiff in their tent cloth dripping blood, solemn and sullen guards of this corner of French soil that they seem, in death, willing still to deny to the enemy.[30]

ADOLF HITLER: My years as a trench soldier "hardened" me.[31]

CHARLES DELVERT: On the parados, in its bowels, rotting corpses covered with tent cloth. A sore opens in the thigh of one of them (Aumont). Flesh in putrification, under the hot sun, bloats out of the cloth and a swarm of big blue flies presses into it. To the right, to the left, the soil is strewn with debris without name: empty jam tins, riddled helmets, broken rifles splashed with blood. An intolerable smell infects the air. To top it off, the pigs send us some gas shells which succeed in making the atmosphere irrespirable.[32]

ERICH KRAMER: Haie strikes his spade into the neck of a gigantic Frenchman and throws the first hand-grenade.... The next throw whizzes obliquely over the corner and clears a passage; as we run past we toss handfuls down into the dug-outs, the earth shudders, it crashes; dully and stifled, we stumble over slippery lumps of flesh, over yielding bodies; I fall into an open belly on which lies a clean, new officer's cap.[33]

PHILIP GIBBS: One day there were three thousand of them, silent, patient, muddy, blood-stained. Blind boys or men with smashed faces swathed in bloody rags groped forward to the dark passage leading to the vault, led by comrades.[34]

ERICH KRAMER: Just as we turn into animals as we go up to the line, because that is the only thing that brings us through safely, so we turn into wags and loafers when we are out resting.[35]

PHILIP GIBBS: The best of our intelligence was there, the noblest of our manhood, the strength of our heart, the beauty of our soul, in those battalions which soon were to be flung into explosive fires.[36]

ALAN SEEGER: I have a rendezvous with Death/ At midnight in some flaming town./ When Spring trips north again this year;/ And I to my pledged word am true,/ I shall not fail that rendezvous.

"SEEGER, Alan, American poet and soldier: b. New York City, 1888; d. Belloy-en-Santerre, France, 1916. He studied at the Horace Mann School, and from 1906 to 1910 was at Harvard University.... In 1912 he went to Paris, where he continued his writing, and also attended classes in painting. At the outbreak of the World War he at once enlisted in the French Foreign Legion as a private.... In an attack made by the Legion on the village of Belloy-en-Santerre in 1916 he was killed."[37] Vive la mort! Vive la guerre! Vive la Légion Etrangère![38]

As Malcolm Cowley says, World War I was the "extinction of the fittest." Writers then in college learned to regard death "as a sort of final examination for which one should prepare by living intensely in the little time that remained."[39] It was an old man's war and a young man's fight. The young knew they would die. They loathed and detested the old hypocrites who had made their deaths inevitable. Their nation was their own generation.

Erich Maria Remarque tells us that to what its elders had created German youth responded like this:

"For us lads of eighteen they ought to have been mediators and guides to the world of maturity, the world of work, of duty, of culture, of progress—to the future. We often made fun of them and played jokes on them, but in our hearts we trusted them. The idea of authority, which they represented, was associated in our minds

Mort-Homme (Dead-Man), Verdun, recaptured.

with a greater insight and a manlier wisdom. But the first death we saw shattered this belief. We had to recognize that our generation was more to be trusted than theirs. They surpassed us only in phrases and in cleverness. The first bombardment showed us our mistake. And under it the world as they had taught it to us broke into pieces."[40]

Here is what psychology calls a traumatic experience, an experience of such stunning intensity as to cause profound and permanent modifications of personality and behavior.

In the holocaust of the Western Front, of Tannenberg and Carpathia, of Caporetto and Gallipoli, European civilization suffered a traumatic shock.[41]

For this traumatic shock there is no comparison in our history save the Black Death of the fourteenth century.

From the malevolent effects of the Great War we suffer still.

13.
Bohemia and the War
(1914-1918)

Before 1914, the bohemian community in Montmartre had been fading away, the community in Montparnasse growing, and the Latin Quarter becoming more active than ever. While the dominant cultural/economic forces of the nineteenth century and their façade, the bourgeois life-style and mentality, had been making the Western Front, three generations of the romantic army, in defiance of repressive government, social pressure, and economic hardship, had been building up to and making a renaissance, or rather a naissance: twenty-five years of creative accomplishment in the written and visual arts equal to anything previously accomplished anywhere, an achievement swelling out of Bohemia's capital, Paris, and catalyzing achievements elsewhere, a tide that would have kept right on rising had the war not dried it up.

In 1914, the war entwined bourgeois and bohemian, the theme and the counter-theme of the nineteenth century, coöpting many of Bohemia's values and, because of France's universal military obligation, abruptly sucking Bohemia's population off to the Front.[i]

Partly as a result of the war, partly as a result of the automotive revolution emptying the livery stables and their haylofts, New York's Greenwich Village, until then a copy of the sentimental Murger model, absorbed the Americans who in better days would have gone to Paris. For the first time the Village became a real bohemian community.

But it was in neutral Switzerland that the arts found room to continue their advance. Zurich was now the center of Europe, of intellect, of intrigue. At the Cabaret Voltaire in Zurich, Bohemia established a refuge where young people of the warring nations associated in a loving camaraderie of art/antiart and reared the insolent new spirit called Dada, a spirit shaped by the conviction that bourgeois society had caused the war.

Made of the same metal as *épatez-les-bourgeois,* Dada devoted itself to superlatives of boorish behavior, to a crazed assault on all things bourgeois, to the demolition of all established forms of art. Smash the bourgeois mentality! Lay waste the bourgeois attitudes! Raze the banal! By dint of demonic humor, put across a program of antiauthority, antiorder, antietiquette, antichurch, antiart!

Hans Richter, once a soldier in a bourgeois army on the Western Front, then a guerrilla fighter in the Dada army's war against everything that made the Western Front, states: "Humor, antiseriousness, was the basic Dada attitude: the irony of a bluff totally without good-humour. Mockery of all the values of bourgeois society, of all its debased and phony ideals of decency and morality, of religion, state, and fatherland—this constituted the defeat of everything that was 'holy' to the bourgeoisie. Not only 'black humour' and annihilating satire, but simple laughter could destroy."[2]

But Dada does not always speak in brays and howls:

HUGO BALL: "I had no love for the death's-head hussars
Nor for the mortars with the girls' names on them,
And when at last the glorious days arrived
I unobtrusively went my way."[3]

HANS ARP: "Revolted by the butchery of the 1914 World War, we in Zurich devoted ourselves to the arts. While the guns rumbled in the distance, we sang, painted, made collages and wrote poems with all our might. We were seeking an art based on fundamentals, to cure the madness of the age, and a new order of things that would restore the balance between heaven and hell. We had a dim premonition that power-mad gangsters would one day use art itself as a way of deadening men's minds."[4]

MARCEL JANCO: "We had lost the hope that art would one day achieve its just place in our society. We were beside ourselves with rage and grief at the suffering and humiliation of mankind."[5]

Although echelons of Bohemia survived in Zurich, in New York, and a curtailed and despondent art life continued in a depopulated Paris, the war shattered Bohemia and mixed its elements with the general society. That society, in the manner of American society during World War II, became more bohemian than formerly; this was because a common purpose in an aura of peril came to temper the ethic of salvation through money.

In nineteenth-century European civilization the bourgeois values—those of the middle-class middle-aged consolidator—predominated and the romantic values of the artistic, young creator and adventurer lay latent—operating chiefly on the colonial fringes or in the interstices. By no means a dichotomy, these two seemingly antithetical qualities are in fact modalities of the same soul, for they did and do live side by side in everyone.

A war could not be fought unless the latent qualities were made dominant in the soldiers. The values they'd been taught had to be turned inside out. Incredibly, a few weeks of training sufficed to bring about this cultural inversion[6]—an inversion once again accomplished, for most veterans, upon the armistice.

But the mechanism achieving the latter was fatigue.

The trench soldiers of both sides were determined to go home and transform society. Had the war ended in 1916, says Remarque, the Germans would have had the will and energy to bring this transformation about. By 1918, they were too tired, their souls burned out. As with the Germans, so with the French and British. On coming home, their regnant desire was to live out the rest of their days in peace and quiet.[7]

Nevertheless, the trench-culture, that "democracy of death" created by the war, lay sleeping in all of its combat veterans. In Germany, Italy, Russia, societies destroyed by the war where old soldiers could not live in peace and quiet, the trench-culture reclaimed some of its old adherents. One historian tells us that, in Germany and Italy, many young men "cherished their war experience as the most sublime moment of their lives," an observation familiar to those who know American Legionnaires deriving from World War I. Could there be a more eloquent condemnation of the bourgeois way of life than this? To many Nazis socialism was the relationship of men in the trenches and the Third Reich was a recreation of the community of the combat soldier.[8]

Using the materials offered by the creative/adventurous part of man and neglected by the master culture, the Western Front had created an anticulture to which all of its citizens adapted, then assimilated, and which the survivors never forgot.

What, other than the maximization of violence as the solution to problems, were its characteristic traits?

Comradeship in the face of danger shines out as the value giving the culture its style. Here, in an ultimate adversity, is the one-for-all, all-for-one ethic and community of the Water Drinkers, that quality signified in English slang by *mate* and in American by *buddy,* a quality for which contemporary Americans generally have no word.

Conjoined with comradeship are the high values placed on loyalty, trust, generosity, endurance, self-reliance, courage, tenderness, ingenuity, craft, irreverence; on candor in behavior and speech; on living completely in the present.

The Western Front created a bourgeois-hating community of endurance where men judged one another for their real qualities and accomplishments, rather than wealth or social status. So estranged from the home societies did the fighters become that they felt most at home in the trenches![9]

The values of the Front are the direct and honest values of boyhood, recovered under perverse conditions at frightful cost.

They conform with those of the Wild West and resemble those of Bohemia—with the substance of its burning purpose debased.

The bourgeois societies of transitional times never ask youth to join in any great selfless cause except that of mass murder at some Verdun or in some Indochina. Seldom do these societies give youth the responsibilities it can support nor do they challenge youth's limits. As Captain John Smith said early in the seventeenth century: To live is to overcome. In those days, hard old Mother Nature still served as life's spur and measure. By 1914 and even more so today, if a middle-class youth is to overcome he must construct his own obstacles. In 1914, welcoming honorable escape from a society where most people feel lonely and trapped and where the obstacles are counterfeit, the youth of Europe packed its troubles in its old kit bag and marched joyfully off to war. Here was an acceptable romantic escape. But from what? From the intolerable defects of life in bourgeois society. And what lay ahead—? The perfect romantic adventure.

In an existence bereft of afterlife, don't we all yearn for the perfect romantic adventure?

In a degenerate sense, does not war let everyone be a bohemian who has a taste for it but is not liberated enough to dare the real thing?

Are we not perhaps justified in conceiving of the Western Front as the Bohemia of the bourgeoisie?

Bohemia, that state of mind bordered on the north by cold, on the east by hunger, on the west by love, on the south by hope, and which in the Paris of the nineteenth century became a way of life, was the first post-Christian community and a prototype of the future.

The Western Front, itself a way of life, can be understood not only as the bourgeois Bohemia but as the second post-Christian community and prototype.

These two models may delineate the ends of the spectrum of the possibilities of the post-Christian, posttraditional world.

As we shall see, Nazi Germany, the first post-Christian state, was born in the trenches of World War I. Behind the lines, in all countries, the war bureaucratized civilization—refining another component of the Nazi state.

Bohemia's burning purpose, the building of the world-embracing Palace of Beauty and Art, expressed itself, in a most depraved form,[10] in the European nations' drastic effort to prevail over each other.

Brought to an impasse, that effort produced the Western Front which in turn created a bourgeois-hating posttraditional youth of defective purpose who flooded out into a quivering world ultimately, in its energy, to build fascist Italy, the Soviet Union, the Third Reich, in its fatigue, to acquiesce in the zombie political-economies of interwar France, Britain, and, to a lesser degree, the United States.

Peace brought with it revolutions and economic collapse; it brought a terrible new anxiety due to even deeper causes.

For millions, both God and Progress had died, but life went on.

Part Five
BOHEMIANS IN ARMS

"I know how much harm the Nazis have already
done and what disasters Germany can expect from
them in the future. But at the same time I feel
that many of these young men want much the same
things as I do myself. They, too, find this rigid,
bourgeois life quite intolerable, detest a society
in which material wealth and status matter above
everything else. They want to replace this hollow
sham with something richer, more vital. They want to
render human relationships more human, and so, in
fact, do I. I still fail to understand why these
efforts must lead to such inhuman results."

—Hans Euler, 1937.*

14.

Bohemians Manqués (1896-1934)

Just as Bohemia is rooted in the artistic idealism of *Hernani*, the Small Cenacle, Doyenné, the Water Drinkers, so is the community of the Western Front and the posttraditional state of Nazi Germany rooted in the nineteenth century's only other significant and genuine youth movement (San Francisco being a movement of youth) —: the Wandervögel. Equally antibourgeois and pagan in character, deriving equally from the romantic movement, composed equally of children of the middle classes, the Wandervögel (Migrant Birds/Free-Spirits) formed in cenacle-sized autonomous cells called *Bünde* (Bands) around Führers (Leaders), took structure from the Führerprinzip (Leader Principle), greeted one another in Roman fashion with upraised right hands and shouts of Heil! (Hail!).

The bad karma flowing from the Franco-Prussian War and the rapacious treaty of 1871 quickly embodied itself in the German bourgeoisie, inflating its faults and larding over its virtues. Favored servants and smug, newly prosperous apologists for an authoritarian and bureaucratic state caught up in industrialization and suddenly come to power, the German middle classes wallowed in a swamp of superficialities and were as strong on hypocrisy as they were weak on humility. Coarse, gross, aggressively complacent, gluttonous, materialistic, selfish, gilded by a kitsch aesthetic, their representatives voting for every arms budget, expecting perfect submission from their children, these burghers and hausfraus eventually pushed thousands of their children into revolt, a revolt enshrined in our comics by the Katzenjammer Kids' guerrilla war against the Captain and the Inspector. As one sociologist put it: "They thought that parental religion was largely sham, politics boastful and trivial, economics unscrupulous and deceitful, education stereotyped and lifeless, art trashy and sentimental, literature spurious and commercialized . . . family life repressive and insincere, and the relation of the sexes, in marriage or out, shot through with hypocrisy."[1]

The story begins in 1896 in Steglitz, a wealthy suburb of Berlin, when Hermann Hoffmann-Völkersamb, a twenty-one-year-old college student, began an informal club at the high school for studying shorthand. The group began going on nature walks, then on longer excursions, some of which were led by Hoffmann's assistant, a strong, dark-haired adolescent named Karl Fischer. In 1900, when Hoffmann joined the diplomatic corps, Fischer, then nineteen, took over, and adventurous outings eclipsed shorthand completely.

Fischer (seated, left), Hoffman (standing, center) and shorthand club, 1898.

Now, this group of friends, unknown and unnoticed, began accommodating to the style and vision of their Oberbachant, as Fischer styled himself in recognition of the group ideal of the medieval itinerant scholar. In 1901, in the back room of a beer cellar, Fischer, four bachants and five elders, constituted what they decided to call the Wandervögel, a word one of them had seen on a Berlin tombstone. This established an adult front-organization and marks the point where they began recruiting from other schools. In 1902, a friend surprised Fischer by starting a new troop. In 1904, in defiance of Fischer's authority, the movement began splintering into a variety of organizations and, in 1906, the sum of these rivalries plus advancing age caused Fischer to resign. He joined the Marines and went to China. By 1911, the movement, of which the original Wandervögel formed but a modest part, counted nineteen regional units, 412 posts in 350 cities, and about 45,000 members—50,000 by 1914. What in 1900 had been confined to a small group of students from one school had in ten years become the inspiration of German youth. Through the Wandervögel movement German youth created and lived its own myth.[2]

In much the same sense that Victor Hugo had long before precipitated an ethos, a mood, into a subculture and a movement, Karl Fischer had precipitated an ethos, a mood, into a subculture and a movement, one which would eventually fuse with the tradition of the romantic army. So daring and egotistic that his classmates called him "crazy Fischer," he radiated an aura of quality which captured the admiration and confidence of almost everyone he met. The dissenters seem to have found it painful to listen to his rambling discourse and clumsy attempts to formulate his ideal. Some German writers describe him as the very model of the charismatic leader—one whom divine grace made more than human. An associate recalled that, to an inquiry about a fresh wound on his arm, Fischer replied: "I burned the flesh a bit; I wanted to find out the state of my nerves." Another wrote: "When we shoot he has the highest score; when we march he holds out the longest; when we laugh he laughs the hardest; when we talk he talks the best."[3] Virile, rough and tough, reckless, brilliant, capable like Hugo of Promethean defiance, from the outset Fischer organized his classmates around a new ideal.

But he did not accept everybody. He admitted only such young men as he thought truly worthy of associating with him. On initiation to his band, he made each man pledge eternal loyalty not to the group but to himself—much as in later times German soldiers and Nazi party members would pledge allegiance not to Germany but to Hitler.

Inspired by the Goliardic tradition, catalyzed and shaped by Fischer, bands of Wandervögel, the members aged mainly between fourteen and eighteen years, eventually appeared everywhere in Germany. Pooling their money, speaking an argot compounded of hobo slang, peasant patois, and medieval vulgate, in all a down-home funky German that made the bourgeois sweat, they were loud and rude, often ragged and dirty and torn by briars. They carried packs, draped themselves in woolen capes, dressed in shorts and dark shirts, in Tyrolean hats and Byronic collars, in heavy boots and bright neck scarves. Half hobo and half medieval, this ensemble was as offensive to the elders as were the long hair and bell-bottoms of the 1960's. They went on long hikes in the country where they sang their own translations of the Goliardic songs and camped under primitive conditions. In their hometowns and cities these rebel bands established clubhouses called Nests, antihomes, sometimes à la Byron, in ruined castles, where they met to plan trips, play mandolins and guitars, enjoy intimate companionship.

A contemporary historian says: "*Wandervögel*! What magic that word contained! And how different these boys were from others: their speech and dress, the healthy, sun-tanned faces, the straightforward, simple manner, and the disdain for comfort and for everything 'flashy'—all these things, as well as a perceptibly mysterious air distinguished a *Wandervögel* sharply from the *Speisser,* the dull, petty bourgeois."[4]

Their short weekend journeys soon lengthened into weeks and hundreds of miles. In 1898, a month-long excursion into the Bohemian Mountains served as a climax and testament of solidarity. These expeditions led to the establishment of permanent camps in the wild, camps open to all, where, on occasions, many groups would meet around the equinox fire of the ancient Germans. As a sacramental consecration of eternal friendship, it became customary for two youths to jump through the flames together. With no thought of pay, the bands worked at improving their campsites and at building cabins for which they made the furniture—an expression of their deification of the crafts—in all forming a complex of precedents underlying the youth-hostel movement and the youth groups and labor-service camps of the Nazis.

By wandering through the back country and to far-off islands of medieval Germanic peasant culture in eastern Europe and by reading old romantic stories of adventure, they assembled a vast quantity of folk music which a friend of Fischer's transcribed and published in a songbook, *Der Zupsgeigenhansl* (Jacky's Whoopee Fiddle Book), which went through hundreds of editions until finally proscribed by the Nazis. When folk music and dance are happening, one remembered, "no one asks if you are rich or poor, nor to what class you belong. All feel themselves as part of the same unity, as one people."[5]

Wandervögel troop, 1909.

First under the guidance of Fischer and then after 1904 of the Leaders of a number of apostate groups as well—one of which went so far as to make physical beauty a prerequisite of membership—there developed a simple way of life which a distinguished advocate named *Jugendkultur* (Youth Culture) and described as a revolutionary protoculture, an interpretation that the Jugendkultur accepted. In a society that thought of youth not as an estate but as an indecent stage of development on the way to maturity, the very concept of Jugendkultur was a powerful corrosive. As presented, the concept held that youth is not only a state of being with its own values and traits but one quite superior to the castrated bourgeois culture of the adults. Eros, said one communicant, is the epitome. Theirs was a new spiritual elite locked in mortal combat with the eunuch bourgeois world, an elite that saw itself as engaged in nothing less than the creation of a *"New Man!"*[6]

At center, the Wandervögel sought communion with nature, with the ancient folkspirit as embodied in the traditional peasant culture, and with one another. This would renew Germany. A movement magazine said in 1913: "Our people need whole men, not fragments such as notaries, party hacks, scholars, officials, and courtiers." Here was no question of art, of intellect, of any sophisticated program of reform; rather, through their Jugendkultur, the Wandervögel developed a harmonious mystic resonance with their environment and with each other. Highly erotic in character, delighting in their own bodies, rejecting Victorian restraints, sometimes traveling with girls, more often not, many of these liberated youths turned to each other for sex, causing such scandal as to provoke the Bavarian Catholic Center Party to denounce the Jugendkultur as in fact a club and school of "pederasty."[7]

The activities of these young rebels received no rational direction. Rather, in a flash of feeling deriving from Nature, from the group, from the Folkspirit, the Führer of the band would on sudden inspiration tell the others what to do. Articulated by the Leader —an oracle for mystical forces—and sensed by everyone else, this transcendental authority came to be known as the Leader Principle (Führerprinzip), a principle that later was to become basic doctrine for the Nazi state.

And how were Führers selected?

Although the term was not yet established when Fischer was in power, Fischer, in fact the first Führer, selected himself. When asked, another Führer replied: "I don't know *whose* Führer I am; but I do know *that* I am Führer even if no one chose me to be his leader. How do I know this? Laotse would say, 'From Tao.' "[8]

And what was the Wandervogel experience like? Imagine a band of suntanned youths, muddy and ragged, in leather shorts, tramping through the greenwood singing an old bandit song. As the sun sets the scene darkens; the Führer gives the signal to halt. Soon all are seated in the dark around a giant bonfire, close together, cooking food, playing guitars and singing, the red-and-orange light darting over bodies and faces. After eating they tell stories about mercenaries in the Thirty Years' War, about cowboys and Indians in the American West, read stories from Simplicissimus and Karl May. The fire burning down they hush. Drawing together, sensing each other, feeling a mystic union, listening intently, they strain to hear the voice of the Forest.

A boy jumps up in the firelight and says:

"I want the fight, and man naked and unashamed with his sword in hand; and behind, the stars sweeping westward, and in front, the wind in the grass. It's enough, Brothers, Action! The word is spoken!"[9]

And now the Führer rises:

"Where lively people congregate no one needs a program. Our happiest hours are those in which nothing is planned beforehand. ... Each day begins with eagerness and hope and every hour brings forth our wondering gratitude for rich, overflowing life.... You must say yes only to that which finds in your hearts an echo of strength and true human worth."[10]

How close yet how far from Tom Sawyer's robber band or the Hugolatry gathered around the flaming punch bowl, reciting poetry, their Leader's and their own.

In 1913, the Imperial government staged a vast celebration of the 100th anniversary of the Battle of Leipzig when the Germans defeated Napoleon. Several movement groups decided to observe this paramount German centennial with a counter-celebration of their own, opposing a simple, sober, dignified, and human ceremony to the chauvinistic, militaristic, oompah-band and beer-swilling celebration planned by the state. Here is a strong parallel with the forty thousand youths who on 19 April 1975, hiked through the traffic bound for the state celebration at Concord, Massachusetts, to hold their own Alternative Bicentennial Celebration of the shot heard round the world. In 1913, invitations went out to all the youth groups in Germany. So enthusiastic was the response from all sectors of the movement that the leaders decided to have their celebration on top of a mountain far away from that of the state. This, the Hohe Meissner Festival, drew two thousand boys and girls from all over Germany to the top of the mountain where they danced in circles about the meadow and sang around the giant bonfire. This Human Be-In concluded with speeches reminding all assembled of the centenary of Germany's liberation from foreign oppression and resulted in all the groups confederating in a master group called *Freideutsche Jugend*—Free German Youth. An Austrian spoke of crisis, Jews, Pan-Slavism, enemies on the borders, war—and experienced an arctic reception. All the factions found agreement in the Meissner Declaration:

"Free German Youth wants to shape its own life, under its own responsibility and with deep sincerity. For the sake of this inner freedom, it will, under any and all circumstances, take united action."[11]

Through adult-controlled youth clubs and with but meager success various established institutions tried to preempt the fearful rush of energy embodied in the Jugendkultur.

Where churches and boy scouts and the socialist party failed, the armed forces succeeded. Fourteen thousand Wandervögel served in World War I, mainly in combat, and one-fourth of them died. They all wore a green-red-gold ribbon in the third buttonhole of their uniforms so they could identify one another. In 1916 the Wandevögel in the army met at Verdun, soldiers coming as far as fifty miles to sing the old songs and reminisce.

Erich Maria Remarque, a veteran of the movement, remembered: "In the Wandervögel of those days was all the fresh romance and enthusiasm of youth, that lingered on in the trenches for a short while, only to collapse at last in 1917 under the awful horrors of the battle of machines."[12]

Recruited almost entirely from the middle classes, sensing perhaps the holocaust ahead, these young rebels detested the established authorities and the way of life from which the holocaust was to issue. As one historian says: It was not the various components—e.g., beer drinking—of adult behavior, but rather the bourgeois *style* itself they despised. By 1913 and the Hohe Meissner, he says, the movement promised to revivify German culture. Wilhelm Reich, the famous social psychologist, saw the "secret meaning of the bourgeois youth movement as the quest for sexual freedom." Although some segments of the Jugendkultur actively resisted the armaments program, in the main it scorned politics. Instead, it seceded from society. All of these young Germans joined in demanding the right to live their own lives, to be guided by their own sentiments, experiences, peers—and to be free of the deadly hypocrisies and odious restraints forced on them by established authority. They would liberate all German youth from bourgeois influence and control. In these young rebels, the spirit of liberty had been revived. As one historian noted, the ideal figure for prewar German youth was the medieval wandering scholar, the Goliard, "an anarchist if not a democrat." The postwar youth movement took instead as its model the medieval knight, an aristocratic killer who follows an exalted rule of conduct and functions in a strict hierarchy.[13]

Apolitical, homoerotic, pagan, mystic, anxious to submit to a Leader who could sense their souls, given to youth-for-youth, verging on the value of action-for-action, often humanistic and pacifistic, this post-Christian youth went to war, lost its high idealism, its naïve optimism, its innocence, its gentle goodwill, its spontaneity and its liberty, and emerged from combat hard and tough, its traits forged and tempered on the anvil of trench warfare into the most malevolent possible forms, forms which were to develop into the central structures of the Third Reich.[14]

By 1914, having freed youth's body, the Jugendkultur was beginning to refine its intellect and artistic sensibility, thus promising to supplement with physical health the wan bohemian tradition. But that promise died on the Western Front, eventually to be resurrected in California.

The war created a new institution into which many of the Wandervögel were drawn by affinity. This, the Storm Troops, organized into small formations, identified by the silver deathhead hitherto reserved to the aristocratic cavalry, composed an élite force used to smash holes through the Allied lines.[15]

Enjoying the best food, provided with the best equipment, authorized, like officers, to wear pistols, the Storm Troops lived in comfort behind the lines and were occasionally sent up in trucks to lead attacks. Described as a "new type of man," one "who has achieved the highest intensification of all human qualities and blended them so harmoniously and yet so violently" that he can only be called "Fighter," the storm trooper lived in an ambience of democratic informality quite at odds with the traditional *Kadaverdiszipline* (corpse discipline) of the regular army. The storm trooper was described as the first man of a "completely new race, cunning, strong, packed with purpose." Authority emanated not from a conventional commander, but from a Leader (*Stosstruppführer*) whose natural superiority rendered superfluous the rituals, symbols, rigid forms on which command so often rests. The troops and their Leader looked on one another as comrades; like the Wandervogel they responded to the Leader Principle and felt bonded by spiritual ties.

A Storm Troop resembled the ancient German/Viking war band where the Leader stood as a superior among equals.

"Here," as one said, "was born and made virile that pure culture we call the culture of the front-line soldiers."

After the Armistice of 1918, the General Staff accomplished an orderly withdrawal of troops to Germany, but once home the formations fell apart. Everywhere, even in Berlin, the red flag flew. Revolution: one permitted and paid for by the General Staff![16] Polish and Russian Bolshevik forces endangered the Eastern frontiers. Revolution! A melodrama and façade screening the inflation of the Bolshevik menace—a way to extort better terms for the military from the Allies conferring at Versailles. Revolution! In seeming desperation the government called on Germans to expedite the organization of volunteer military formations to crush the Marxist revolts, restore order, hold the Eastern frontier.

Sooner or later, some 300,000 men participated in this *Freikorps* (Free Corps) movement. In 1919, the Freikorps may have been stronger than what remained of the government's armed forces. In Wandervögel fashion, the corps, each with its own distinctive character, formed around a charismatic Leader who infused the *Freikorpskämpfer* (Free Corps Fighters) with the Leader Principle. Called *Der Führer,* each leader stood as the ultimate authority and heroic model in whom was concentrated all the qualities valued by his fighters. In Storm Troop fashion, each corps was militarily self-sufficient, being provided with a full range of arms, including, on occasions, tanks and airplanes. Although acting as vigilantes, as defenders of law and order, these fighters were, in fact, modern mercenaries having no program but self-interest, feeling no loyalty save to their Führers and the Volk-spirit, valuing naught but the intense *now* of Dionysian ecstasy in the communion of comradeship, in revel, destruction, combat.[17]

"People told us the War was over. That made us laugh. We ourselves are the War. Its flame burns strong in us." We "marched onto the battlefields of the postwar world just as we had gone into battle on the Western Front; singing, reckless and filled with the joy of adventure as we marched to the attack; silent, deadly, remorseless in battle."[18]

Invariably of bourgeois or peasant origin, completely posttraditional/post-Christian in character, the free-corps fighter lived for the destruction of bourgeois society and all its works; he would complete the aborted objective of the War, the demolition of decadent bourgeois democracy—now including the German government—and the inauguration of the Völkische Kultur-State.

Typical is the Hamburg Free Corps, flying the ancient Hanseatic flag, singing old pirate songs, tramping through Baltic towns and villages radiating insolent bravado, shooting at windows and streetlights.

"They let their hair and beards grow long and they saluted only the officers they knew and liked." For "this crazy outfit recognized none of the usual military regulations. They had been formed by no particular authority and they recognized none save their own. The only thing that counted was the will of their own Führer."[19]

Typical, too, is the Ehrhardt Brigade, early in 1920, marching from its government barracks toward Berlin to overthrow the government and establish the Kapp junta in its place. Soft springlike breezes stir air cleansed by gentle rain. Moonlight bathes their banners and the swastikas painted on their helmets; their feet fall to the cadence made by their singing of the "Ehrhardt Song":

> Swastika on helmet,
> Colors, Red, White, Black
> The Ehrhardt Brigade
> Is marching to attack!

They pass through a time-fault: the same flags, the same helmets, the same song—one line changed, now

> Sturmabteilung Hitler
> Is marching to attack![20]

And back to 1920. Berlin falls without a shot. From Dresden, the Republic calls for a general strike to overturn the Kapp junta. The strike chokes the junta, spreads over Germany. In many places communes come to power. The Republic calls on the same Freikorps that had driven it from Berlin to crush the revolution! It soon paid the Ehrhardt Brigade a bounty of sixteen thousand gold marks originally promised by Kapp!

As in Munich and in the Baltic States (and Paris in 1871), the forces of law and order shoot hundreds of prisoners and civilians denounced as reds.

Later in 1920, the Republic disbanded the Freikorps. But they contrived to stay together in labor camps, in youth groups, in sporting societies, in military-agricultural communities on baronial estates. Self-supporting or supported by industrialists and landowners they served their benefactors as goons and scabs.

Everywhere, Germans wore lapel buttons declaring: *Im Felde niemals besiegt*—Never conquered in the field.

Now it is 1923. Three men from the Organization Consul—later the Viking Bund—peer intently out of their speeding car as they overtake a smaller car slowing for a turn. A revolver speaks, a grenade explodes—Walter Rathenau, Foreign Minister of the Republic, is dead.

Political murder became the specialty of the Viking Bund; its boss was Ehrhardt, its chief patron, the Police President of Bavaria!

A frightened politician once whispered to him: "Mr. President, political murder organizations exist in this country!"

"I know—but there are too few of them!"[21]

The men who composed the original Freikorps were often young junior officers who knew nothing but war and who liked the gold marks, the excitement, the privileges of an officer's position. They wanted to keep their jobs—the army no longer had room for them. But the Freikorps did. When the Freikorps were dissolved, they naturally moved into the ranks of the Brown Shirts, the private army of the Nazi Party called the SA (*Sturmabteilungen*—Storm Army-groups).

The other large element of the corps consisted of idealistic young students who had identified with the trench fighters but were too young to have been in the trenches and lived the "front experience": *Fronterlebnis.*

Much as Victor Hugo had once set the tone for French bourgeois youth, the Leaders of these corps now set the tone for German bourgeois youth, a youth which through its own organizations set about destroying the bourgeois order from within.

The historian of the Freikorps says flatly: "With the exception of Ehrhardt, Gerhard Rossbach, sadist, murderer, and homosexual, was the most admired hero of nationalistic youth."[22] Together with Ernst Röhm, a man of similar character who had founded the Nazi SA, a man who would purge mediocrity and softness from the Volk by liquidating the "philistines," these leaders organized German youth, became the idols, the heroic models, the soul-führers of the rising generation, a form continued and refined in Hitler Youth and the Nazi Labor Front.

As one Leader put it: "They are just like nature—instinctively good and instinctively cruel. All the strength of life lies waiting within them and the direction in which it manifests itself depends entirely on the opportunities and circumstances in which they are placed."[23]

Thus, beginning in 1896, a post-Christian youth culture grew up in Germany, one in which the very worst possibilities were inflated and solidified by the war, the Freikorps, the Nazis. Here were Bohemians *manqués* whose idealism and purpose had been perverted into diabolic form and from whose inner deep issued an amphibious carnivore.

Their spokesman wrote: "We did not act at all, something acted in us." And—: "All ballast, all sentimentalism, all other values must be ruthlessly cast aside" so that the Free Corps fighter's whole strength "could be set free.... Ecstacy and death, tumult and adventure, heroism and excess, cold deliberation and burning idealism, robbery and plundering, arson and murder—a mixture of every passion and demoniacal fury formed ... the fighters who dominated the postwar period."[24]

These men could have grown up differently. Odin, as the god of ecstasy, inspires poetry as well as war, creation as well as destruction.

Under other conditions these idealistic, talented, energetic adventurers could have become the artist/creators of a humane new order, a Hugolatry living out their belief in art-for-art. As it was, living out its belief in action-for-action, this generation of Germans related to the arts in the manner of the Nazi theater boss who said: Every time I hear the word *culture* I reach for my revolver. Its spirit is that of Josef Terboven, onetime SA man, in 1945 the Reich Commissioner for Norway, who, certain that everything was crumbling, stayed drunk for days, then sat down on a case of dynamite and lit the fuse.

In manhood and in middle age, many of these youths were to

build and staff the first post-Christian state, mainly in its Gestapo and SS echelons.

Ernst Röhm speaks for them: "I wanted to serve a Volk of Fighters, not a people of poets and dreamers."[25]

The writings of Ernst Jünger, who passed from the Wander-vögel to the storm troops, weave all these feelings into a philosophy and radiate the infinite pain of a sensitive love of comrades and of nature forced to survive four years of savage combat on the Western Front.[26]

Disbanded and sometimes harassed, during the early 1920's the underground free-corps groups held together in hopes that *Der Tag* —The Day (of taking power) —impended, in hopes, as one discouraged Freikorps Führer put it, that "a Man will come to lead us—a Man who unites German spirit and German power!"[27]

And so they dreamed of Der Tag and of a Führer of Führers who would bring all the bickering segments of the movement together.

In 1923 Odin keened in the greenwood and Der Tag dawned.

Stricken with a heart attack, the bourgeois god, Money, collapsed, The eternal valuation of the mark at twenty-four cents U.S. fell in a few months to .000,000,000,024. Inflation soared so fast that in order to keep up the mints had to overprint new money with larger figures. That God was dead, the bourgeois could reluctantly accept. That Man seemed dead, they could accept too. But now, the death of Money! A whole bag of the stuff might not buy a loaf of bread! An egg cost four billion marks!—a figure formerly expressing the value of all the real estate in greater Berlin![28] You could live from day to day but you could no longer plan for the future. Philistia's first article of faith had been smashed. Even *with* money you had nothing. Everyone's net worth was the same—zero! What a strange kind of democracy. Debtors pursued creditors. The bourgeois really sweat! The man who values himself by his money is now by his own standard worthless!

And from the money itself, where the Kaiser used to be, peered strange Gothic faces, mocking, announcing to the bourgeois the end of the world, to the armed bohemians *manqués*—Der Tag.

In the milder inflation that had hit Austria somewhat earlier money had lost its value and, consequently, people lived intensely, drawing sustenance from a more direct commitment to their life work, to friendship, art, nature. Never before, a leading writer recalled, had art seemed so important "because the collapse of money made us feel that nothing was enduring except the eternal within ourselves.

"Never have I experienced in a people and in myself so powerful a surge of life as at that period when our very existence and survival were at stake."[29]

In Germany the bourgeois were paralyzed—a great rush of energy surged through the romantics.

Hearing the voice of the Forest, the leader of one large segment of the völkisch movement determined to provoke Der Tag and by riding its crest to win the position of Führer of Führers of the *Völkische Kulturstaat.* Though but a few months old, his political party, the Nazionalsozialistische Deutsche Arbeiter*partei* (National Socialist German Workers Party), NSDAP by acronym, Nazi by diminutive, was by virtue of its audacity, its leader, and its private army, the SA, commanded by Ernst Röhm and built around the steel armature of the disbanded Ehrhardt Brigade, swiftly gaining preëminence among the völkisch contenders.

By a masterful deceit NSDAP's Führer, Adolf Hitler, contrived to trap the leaders of the Bavarian government in a gigantic Munich beer hall where he persuaded them at gunpoint to announce the dissolution of their régime and the establishment of a völkisch government in its place. The next day, in the same square where, in 1914, Hitler had thrilled to the declaration of war, a formation of police fired on a column of two thousand armed bohemians led by Hitler and other party notables. Hitler dropped to the ground, and then fled in a yellow Fiat.

At that time, thirty five cents U.S. would buy one trillion marks.[30]

Six days later, the bourgeois god was resurrected; the mark was stabilized and with it the Republic.

Adolf Hitler eventually transcended this débacle and at the head of his armed bohemians went on to become Führer of Führers. Hitler himself was a bohemian *manqué,* but of a different kind. An Austrian, he missed the Wandervogel experience—in his usage *Wandervogel* was an insult—; a politician, he did not fight in the Freikorps. At the Front he served as a runner—no one seems to have regarded him as elite enough to be anything more. He had in the past

SA Troops, 1922.

presented himself to himself and to others as an artist. Twice the Art Academy in Vienna refused him admission. Later he led an indigent life in Vienna and Munich where he colored picture postcards and sold occasional paintings. His artwork—both architectural drawings and paintings—is stiff, banal, grandiose. Neverthe-less, as late as 1944, he confided to his companions: "My dearest wish would be to be able to wander around Italy as an unknown painter."[31]

Hitler's father, Alois, was an official in the Hapsburg customs service, a man of philandering habits who relished food and beer and his own dignity, one who looked on Christianity as a crutch for the weak and who cared little about what other people thought of him.

Male supremacy—*machismo*—was a strong trait in that society and in Alois Hitler. In the manner of that society, but even more forcefully, he demanded that his son be at once self-reliant and wholly submissive to paternal authority. He tried to push Adolf into preparing for the bureaucracy—Adolf responded by doing badly in school. Upon graduation from secondary school, Adolf Hitler got reeling drunk and wiped his ass with his diploma. As an ultimate of defiance, Hitler kept retorting to his father that he would become an artist.

But Hitler's elemental response was retreat into an imagined world of romance made beautiful by heroic art and music. As a child he was keen on playing cowboys and Indians, on the wilderness of James Fenimore Cooper and especially the Wild West of Karl May. May, a German who had never been to America, wrote novels about Old Shatterhand (a German) and his Tonto, Winnetou (a Coman-che Chief), outsmarting enemies such as the crafty and depraved Og-lala Sioux. Full of action and violence, these melodramas were greatly admired by German children until they outgrew them. The stories are ethical, too, and provide extensive ethnic and geograph-ical information. Hitler read them even after becoming Chancellor. I owe to Karl May, said the Führer, "my first notions of geography and the fact that he opened my eyes on the world."[32] He saw the relationship between May's cowboys and Indians as a model of the future relationship of Germans and Slavs. As an adolescent, Hitler's fantasies began feeding on the epics of German history. Later, after introduction to the occult, he embraced a strange cosmology in which he believed to the end. Called *Welteislehre*, it posits that the dynamic of the cosmos and of history is the struggle between fire and ice, that the planets and stars are thickly enveloped with ice, and that here on earth, in response to the appearance and disappearance of icy moons, unrolls a cycle of warm and cold epochs, of giants, of degenerates, once more of giants, the next of whom will descend from the Nordic people for they have grown strong' in the ice and snow.

Although of artistic temperament and, as Albert Speer puts it, "a bohemian," Hitler was never a true artist. His life was not built around the need to create art nor, prior to NSDAP, was he energized by any burning purpose. Rather, he was a man against himself, devoid of a sense of humor, yearning for a simple construct which would make all come clear and provide some magic solution. He did not listen to people. In Munich, he often carried a dog whip. There is reason to believe treatments for syphilis had rendered him sexually impotent. Some say his deepest sexual fulfillment came when a sympathetic woman would squat over him and shit in his face. He seemed quite incapable of intimate relationships. Even his closest associates sensed that the real Hitler lived deep inside himself in absolute isolation behind some impenetrable arctic wall. So lonely was he that only war could give him a community and even there he kept to himself, enjoying the trench comradeship only in the fantasies of retrospect.[33]

The Nazi mayor of Danzig, who knew and came to loathe him, reports Hitler at night having fits of restlessness and terror. He wanders about; he has light everywhere; he gets young men to keep him company. He shouts for help, he sits on the edge of his bed shaking with fear. He sees apparitions. He wakes shrieking nonsense phrases in un-German syntax: "He! He! He's been here!"[34]

Some say he finally found community with a cabal of Initiates and that he lived in accordance with their occult vision and secret purpose, camouflaging all this behind screens of political rhetoric and the façade of National Socialism and *Welteislehre*.[35]

Did the absolute Führer and fount of the Führer Principle, the thread of will stringing all the Germans, himself have a Führer?

The chain of command did not originate in Adolf Hitler, rather he served as an oracle through which some primal spirit spoke to mankind.

But what—who? The Voice of the Forest? The Aryan Volk Spirit? The Grand Master of the East? Destiny? The King of the Giants? The Cosmic Energy? Providence?

Maybe not even the Führer himself could name the ultimate Führer.

Be that as it may, during the nineteen-twenties and early thirties, with the help of the SA and his small but expanding bodyguard, the SS (*Schutzstaffeln*—Security Squads), he bent every effort toward building his NSDAP power base. His SA and SS ranged through Germany recruiting for Hitler Youth, tormenting Jews, fighting street battles, dispersing political meetings, disrupting movies like *All Quiet on the Western Front*, burning books, spreading scandal, mugging professors, murdering opponents, and sabotaging Reichstag proceedings. Hitler went everywhere, often by air, dealing, intriguing, speaking.

But even after the Depression raged through Germany bringing an unemployment rate of twenty-five per cent NSDAP could not win a majority in any national election. Hitler despaired. Then through a fantastic juxtaposition of improbabilities, the President appointed him Chancellor of the Republic.

The first months of Nazi rule "released a torrent of joy and hope," a revolutionary avalanche almost impossible to control. This atmosphere of perpetual charivari covered a reckless and brutal usurpation of judicial power by the SA and the *Geheime Staatspolizei* (Gestapo), first established in 1933 in Berlin in a dispossessed art school. In the words of the same police authority who reports all this, it was not long before "murder had virtually been incorporated within the system of officialdom." [36]

Hitler finally came to understand that he had to tame the three-million man SA and the undisciplined force it represented. The armed bohemians had to go. In June 1934, the SS struck at the leadership of the SA. Hundreds of Old Fighters were shot; one of them, ignorant until the end of what was really happening, shouted *Heil Hitler* as the bullets crushed into him.

Showing sudden prudish sentiments about SA chief Ernst Röhm's male harem, Hitler personally arrested his ancient comrade and ordered him shot. To Albert Speer he exclaimed: "In one room we found two naked boys!"[37] In justifying the Blood Purge he claimed it had been carried out in the interests of moral purification of the movement and of frustrating a socialist *putsch* planned by Röhm. About the beatings and murders daily perpetrated by Röhm's SA he remained silent, for he saw no reason to purge them from NSDAP's blood. It was in fact the Freikorps spirit that had to be purged. This form of the post-Christian personality, these quasi bohemians, would be as intolerable in any stable state as Hell's Angels with their motto of "snuff or be snuffed" have proven to be in the United States.

From now on, Hitler would build the New Order around the post-Christian bourgeois bureaucrats who believed in nothing but doing what they were told and around the Black Order—the highly disciplined, deeply indoctrinated SS.

Out of all this, a pattern emerges. The Christian tradition is at center one of submission to God's will and to the will of his vicars, both ecclesiastical and secular, who are but lower links in the chain of command. When the bourgeois life-style becomes dominant and the culture becomes transitional, the bourgeois, in the manner of Alois Hitler, teach their children to be at once self-reliant *and* submissive.

This colloidal suspension of incompatible opposites is far from stable. It tastes bad, too. When agitated the submissive/self-reliant soup of the bourgeois soul divides into its bohemian component, the spirit of liberty, and its Nazi component. The latter, when purified by recurrent Blood Purges of tendencies toward independence, represents the tradition of submission to God's will. The Nazi component is thus the Principle of Authority in its refined, modern form —the Leader Principle (*Führerprinzip*), issuing not from God but from some new form of all-embracing will.

Here is how all this struck one German in 1922 on hearing Hitler for the first time. Kurt Lüdecke arrived at the rally, his soul an existential vacuum:

Hitler's words "were like a scourge. When he spoke of the disgrace of Germany, I felt ready to spring on any enemy . . . glancing round, I saw that his magnetism was holding these thousands as one. . . . I was a man of thirty-two, weary of disgust and disillusionment, a wanderer seeking a cause; a patriot without a channel for his patriotism, a yearner after the heroic without a hero. The intense will of the man, the passion of his sincerity, seemed to flow from him into me. I experienced an exultation that could be likened only to religious conversion. . . . I felt sure that no one who had heard Hitler that afternoon could doubt that he was the man of destiny, the vitalizing force in the future of Germany.... I had given him my soul."[38]

In 1939, Hermann Rauschning, the apostate Nazi mayor of Danzig, looking back across these years to the Wandervögel, musing that youth's "mission" among youth itself began with the Wandervögel, wrote:

"That movement started with the aim of returning to primordial human nature, of living the simple life of the natural man, of preserving unfettered personality; it declared its essential purpose to be the bursting of all the bonds of a mechanized order of society; and it is ending in the total bondage of a revolutionary despotism in which all nature has been mechanized and every element is chained to a technical process."

The youth movement "which we all know" and "to which we all belonged" was "the first start of the revolutionary dynamism which to-day is culminating in the doctrineless revolution and turning into its own opposite."[39]

High in the hierarchy of the what-ifs of history stands "what if the youth of prewar Europe—that superb generation—had been allowed to continue the regenerative process represented by the Lapin Agile and Free German Youth instead of being flung by its elders into the holocaust of the Western Front?" A new mentality, struggling to emerge from a metaphysical and authoritarian tradition, striving to put art, technology and nature into harmonious balance, had been thrown into the ancient situation of war—albeit the battle of machines—and in that gestalt of Homeric savagery transformed, emerging part old, part new, a third force, leaving the central task to a future generation.

The Bauhaus movement with its faith in combining art and technology to bring about a prosperous, harmonious, and aesthetic world is suggestive of what might have been.[40]

15.

Henry Mencken's Romantic Army (1920-1929)

In the fall of 1920, while Röhm and Hitler nursed the infant NSDAP and while the Dadaists produced the First International Dada Festival in Berlin on the theme of hatred for the military, a Yale student speaking through the medium of *The Atlantic Monthly* told America: "The older generation has certainly pretty well ruined this world before passing it on to us. They give us this Thing, knocked to pieces, leaky, red-hot, threatening to blow up; and then they're surprised that we don't accept it with the same attitude of pretty, decorous enthusiasm with which they received it, 'way back in the eighteen-nineties, nicely painted, smoothly running, practically fool proof.... "[1]

This Model-T metaphor articulates the mood of a large segment of middle-class youth everywhere in Western culture, a mood that in America flamed up into the youth revolt of the 1920's.

This revolt is America's first youth movement.

The object of this revolt was neither political nor economic; the wealthy young were demanding freedom from onerous restraints on their sensuality. Here is a Wandervogel movement in a more liberal, less traditional society where the wandering is done by couples in automobiles and where the ethos is increasingly shared by the elders. This was the first youth movement in which women played a leading part. The suffragette-feminist movement had been created by adults who demanded a share in all the responsibilities and functions of society. The mature suffragette drew on a moralistic, evangelical tradition; she gave to her movement a serious and self-sacrificing tone. But the flapper, though equally upper middle-class, was young. The flapper by her boyish look and gin flask declared she'd rather be a buddy than a sweetheart, that she would enjoy all the liberties and prerogatives of men, that her sex should not bar her from any form of fun.

The moralistic tradition itself began crumbling under powerful forces. No longer as in the nineties did children of wealthy families, standing on a solid floor of certainties, look out on a radiant vista of days to come. No longer did they see woman as the guardian of morals, as a creature made of finer stuff meant to remain innocent even of kisses until the right man came along, to remain chaste until her honeymoon deflowering at Niagara Falls. As for the two million Americans exposed to wartime Europe: How you gonna keep 'em down on the farm after they've seen Paree?

Breathing the smog of disillusion, struck suddenly by Prohibition, by red-hunting hysteria and the Ku Klux Klan, blandished by sensual movies and sexy magazines, unnerved by advertisements endlessly asking her if she'd make a good lay, seduced by fashions liberating her from Victorian purdah, stunned by the voice of a popularized Freud saying all ills issue from frustration of the natural expression of sex, shaken by the books of Sinclair Lewis disclosing the vulgar hypocrisy of Main Street's most prominent citizen, George F. Babbitt alias dear-old-dad, the young girl of good family assumes the image of brazen hussy and confronts her horrified parents.

There she stands in flesh-colored stockings rolled to the knee and in a light, revealing dress, hair bobbed, face painted, cigarette in hand, savage jazz music sounding from her Victrola, screaming at her parents:

"I *am* going out in that car! I'll neck and drink if I want and I'm going to live my own life and you can go to hell!"

This is the first declaration of moral independence ever issued by young women anywhere in any civilization in the world.

And it struck the flapper's parents every bit as hard as she herself was to be struck when her grandchildren began flaunting dope.

This flapper revolt shows even less structure and vision than did the Wandervögel. It follows no dream, embodies no program. Beyond being infiltrated and coöpted by the media, it was in part a creation of the media and of the French fashion industry. Here, no mutual-aid ethic; here no fight for free art.

Or so it seems.

In fact, the movement was but one manifestation of a battle for free art and personal liberty several generations deep, a fight led by America's best young artists and writers. But now for the first time they had troops. Behind them stood a romantic army of civilized young people from every state in the union: commandos in coonskin coats, escadrilles in JN-4's, motorized brigades in flivvers and Stutz Bearcats, and, most conspicuous of all, phalanx upon phalanx of flappers.

Constantly changing personnel, shifting tactics and strategies, for fifty years this young army has pressed the battle, driving the enemy back all the time until today all academic restraints and most censorship of the arts lie smashed into ruins and the creative mind is at last free to present its vision to the public undistorted— if it can circumvent capitalistic control of the media.

The Grand Marshal of this romantic army, the man who put it together in the first place, the Victor Hugo of the fight to free the arts in America, was Henry Lewis Mencken of Baltimore, Maryland. Of Mencken, another famous journalist wrote: "No single American mind has influenced existence in the Republic as much as did his." He was our "one-man Renaissance."[2]

We have to push our imaginations hard to gain conception of how crude and provincial, how banal, how prudish, how bigoted, how hypocritical and sentimental, how naïve, how contemptuous of sensitivity and aesthetics Americans were fifty years ago. Place this in an ethos of anxious cynicism and disillusionment enlivened only by the appearance of fantastic new toys—cars and radios—and a flood of money for those above the wedge of progress and poverty and you get a feeling of what Mencken and the sad young rebels of the lost generation were reacting to—and of the magnitude of the victory now achieved by the romantic army.

Descended from Germans displaced by the Revolution of 1848, Henry Lewis Mencken was born and reared in a city given to the amenities. After a childhood spent reading books and eating seafood, taking and processing photographs, writing poetry and stories, drawing pictures and composing music, H. L. Mencken determined to go out and learn life. He chose as his teacher the newspaper business, as his subject "all the worldly wisdom of a police lieutenant, a bartender, a shyster lawyer, or a midwife,"[3] an ambience into which he plunged in 1899 at age nineteen and where he remained for four decades. Although his columns in the Sunpapers exerted a powerful influence toward keeping Baltimore civilized, it was beginning in 1923 through his magazine *The American Mercury* that his fierce city-room cynicism and his love of life flowed out into America to refine and sustain the rebel youth of town and city.

At once beautifully literate and savagely insolent, Mencken

Mencken in 1898, just before entering the newspaper business, and Mencken as others saw him beginning in 1912 in the logo of his "Free Lance" column. Sun paper readers came to accept this as his authentic image.

and his magazine crushed with Dada force into the lives of "the anthropoid rabble."[4] into the primitive thought patterns of both Babbitts and Baptists.

He told his readers that at age fourteen in a YMCA gym he had learned to loathe strenuous activity and evangelical religion, having faltered but once in his hatred of the YMCA itself on hearing that German Y's serve beer.[5]

Blond and blue-eyed, a Saxon type himself, he observed that the old American WASP stock had degenerated from an original mediocrity, that the Anglo-Saxon's two outstanding traits are incompetence and cowardice, that the Anglo-Saxon's diligence is limited to holding down the more gifted immigrant stocks because otherwise they'd win every competition.

The Anglo-Saxon "runs the whole South—and in the whole South there are not as many first-rate men as in many a single city in the mongrel North. Wherever he is still firmly in the saddle, there we look for such pathological phenomena as Fundamentalism, Prohibition and Ku Kluxery, and there they flourish." Every "divergence from the norm of the low-caste Anglo-Saxon is treated as an attentat against the commonwealth, and is punished with eager ferocity."

The Anglo-Saxon "brags and blusters so incessantly that, if he actually had the combined virtues of Socrates, the Cid and the Twelve Apostles, he would still go beyond the facts and appear a mere Bombastes Furioso." This "is probably no more than a protective mechanism erected to conceal an inescapable sense of inferiority."[6]

"The normal American of the 'pure-blooded' majority goes to rest every night with an uneasy feeling that there is a burglar under the bed, and he gets up every morning with a sickening fear that his underwear has been stolen."[7]

And all this and more in a family newspaper—in 1923!

By 1927, the art world had split completely away from the Anglo-Saxon rabble and the "Booboisie."[8]

Because for the cultivated man, life in America often seemed intolerable, Mencken felt constrained to ask himself: Why do you keep on living here?

"Why?" he replied to himself, "do men go to zoos?"[9]

Perhaps for him the most delightful zoological excursion of all was in 1925 to Dayton, Tennessee, where he and Clarence Darrow met Fundamentalism's foremost champion, the scourge of *evil*-ution, William Jennings Bryan, on his own turf at the head of his fanatical legions, and by means of scorn and logic drove him to his death. As Mencken put it: "Well, we killed the son-of-a-bitch."[10]

Mencken, toughened by twenty-five years of newspaper work, relished life in the zoo. Not so most young Americans of artistic temperament and refined sensibility. Their answer to Mencken's question was flight, in fantasy or in fact—to Greenwich Village, to Paris.

The Village of the 1920's functioned more as a hideout than a refuge. The bohemian community that had finally developed there during the war lost much of its best blood to a reviving Paris. It soon collapsed under the pressure of soaring rents and swarming tourists brought on through its discovery by the media and by speculative realtors. Spontaneous generation produced boutiques and tea shoppes bearing names like La Bôheme, Ars Minima, Ye Pollywogge, Trilby's Waffle Shop, the Bazaar de Junk, in all a plague of quaintness that spread fast over the U.S.A.

Bohemians still abounded in lower Manhattan, but their community had been adulterated by poseurs, groupies, hustlers; it had been Montmartrized and broken. The mutual-aid ethic, the dedication to art-for-art, the fight to set art free, youthful hope itself, all had been muted by the melancholy and disbelief of the times. The recent concentration of the community on deliverance through creative politics had been cauterized by the Great Red Scare of 1920 as had the social conscience of American youth everywhere.[11]

The Village settled into a booze-sex-psychiatrist era.[12]

As with the larger revolt of American youth for which it had been a pilot, bohemian life in New York concentrated around a central bohemian theme that we have not yet directly examined: sensual freedom as manifested in sex.

Back in the eighteenth century, while still a youth, the prototype of all flower children, Percy Bysshe Shelley, said to his sister: "Scepticism and free love are as necessarily associated together as religion and marriage." Women, to Shelley, were fine and sensitive creatures whom he took into his arms with sensual delight and into his heart as close friends and equals.[13]

But this was an anomaly. And the norm? His friend Lord Byron, the much-idealized first model of the Romantic movement, believed as did most other aristocrats in free sex, but looked on women as being so inferior to men that once he said to Shelley: "I cannot make up my mind whether or not women have souls."[14]

None of the bohemian models—the *Hernani* escadrilles, the Hugolatry dancing around the flaming punch bowl, Doyenné, the Water Drinkers, the Refractories, the Lapinards, admitted women into the intimacy of their comradeship. Bohemia's attitude toward its mistresses resembles that shown by French students in their ancient and perennial joke about one of them going on vacation saying to his friend: "I'm leaving you my pipe and my chick. Take good care of my pipe."[15] Only occasional exotics like George Sand, Simone de Beauvoir, Isadora Duncan, Gertrude Stein, were accepted as equals on the Parisian art scene, and the last two were Americans from San Francisco.

As in almost everything else, Victor Hugo proved an exception. Throughout his life he regarded his wife—the only female Hernanist—and his many mistresses more as comrades than as pets. But it was not this which impressed his contemporaries. They were struck by his fantastic virility. Throughout his long life he was sexually ultraactive. In old age he confided to a friend that until his wedding night he had been a virgin—but that that night he made up for it by coming *nine* times.[16]

On the bohemian fringe of America, from its beginnings about 1850, the common denominator of the participants is not the fight to free art but the fight to free sex.[17] Under the circumstances, these two concepts may well have meant the same thing.

It was in the combinations and permutations of sexual possibilities that the bohemians of Paris expanded sexual freedom. The long and torrid love affair between Arthur Rimbaud and Paul Verlaine represents a widespread Platonic style which Bohemia regards as no more significant than the preference for tea over coffee. In Paris, seventy years after the baroque romance of the two poets, a woman who lived with her police dog and appeared everywhere in his company stirred no more comment—excepting when the dog tried to ball some other woman in a café—than the attaching to her of the sobriquet, Madame Wolf.

Of America before World War I, our conception tends to derive from the cover story, not the facts. In Victorian and Edwardian times, brothels were as firmly built into the American system as into the French. Suggestive is the controversy about them which raged in Los Angeles, then a true Anglo-Saxon town, in 1908. The question debated by city fathers and family newspapers was not that of closing the cribs but simply whether or not they should be restricted to a single section of the city.[18]

The Victorians and Edwardians were sensitive less to substance than to appearance. When Upton Sinclair ranged about the country praising free love, the storm of outrage he provoked was not due to his practicing it (which he probably did not) but to his mentioning the unmentionable in public. Since the end of the nineteenth century, artists, particularly novelists, had been doing exactly that. They aimed their attack on contemporary society at the sexual life of the middle classes. This twisted and repressed sexual life was not condemned for itself alone, but because it symbolized the hypocrisies, cruelties, follies, inadequacies of society generally. Conversely, they all endorsed a free sex life as a good in itself. The bourgeois establishment so feared these revelations that it punished the artist whenever it could and repressed pornography with a ferocity born of panic.

In Europe, before the war, sensual freedom was becoming the primary motive of youthful discontent, a reaction against Victorian hypocrisy which seems most directly expressed in the German youth movement. After 1910, beards disappeared on the young. Women began to wear freer clothing, the larger meanings of this being dramatized during the 1920's by Isadora Duncan. Before 1914, sports and nature had changed the appearance of the middle classes for the better—both had previously been shunned in the interests of dignity and out of fear of the sun.[19] Stefan Zweig, an astute observer of these phenomena, said this youth of 1900-1910 stood in bold contrast to the previous generation:

"More freedom, more frankness, more spontaneity had been regained in those ten years than in the previous hundred years."[20]

In America, because the trend toward moral reform that brought on Prohibition was really trying to make life fit the Victorian rhetoric, it closed the whorehouses. This caused high-school lads to look not to the chippie but to the girl in the next seat for solace and relief—a change in vector which did as much as anything else to bring on the youth revolt of the 1920's.[21]

In the Village of the 1920's sexual freedom became so soundly established that the Villagers had grown to regard one's sexual preference simply as a matter of taste and had become quite indifferent to the sight of black men escorting white women. The newspapers foamed over with stories and features about free love in the Village, thus providing the voyeuristic booboisie with delectable excitement and the hip capitalists with priceless advertising. Beginning in 1919, the *Saturday Evening Post* led a counterattack of puritanism against Parisian-style bohemian sensuality, established in the Village, and spreading from there throughout America. The romantic orgy of the 1830's was transmuted into the cocktail party of today, helping to replace the old production ethic with the consumption ethic energized by emotional advertising.[22]

Nevertheless, brothels and hookers and even courtesans and free sex in a Montmartrized Village—or cocktail parties in Zenith— are a long way from the substance of sensual freedom in Bohemia, or even as practiced by Shelley.

If the substance were developing anywhere, that where was Paris in the 1920's. "Paris was," writes one of America's best journalists, "it seemed to me, the center of the moral revolution. London and New York were not far behind, but Paris was in its usual position as the capital of Western taste, and its cosmopolitan youth influenced all the rest."[23]

16.
Interwar Bohemia
(1919-1939)

In Paris in the 1920's, people noticed ten times as many Americans on the streets as before the war. They brought with them money, exuberance, a tendency shown in their liquor drinking to do everything 100 percent, and the sadness of disillusion. Once in France, this complex collided with the grimness of despair. Together, the sad exuberance of the Americans and the desperate frenzy of the French (Dada, surrealism, rioting at banquets and openings)[1] set the tone of bohemian life in postwar Paris and of the arts everywhere in the Western world.

The Americans came as simple tourists or as libertines (Americans took the Gay Paree legend more seriously than other people) or as refugees from the babbittry ravaging their homeland. Many of them would have come anyway because with its abundance of good cheap art schools, its indulgent attitude toward artists, its artistic splendor, Paris remained what it long had been: the world capital of art, where, as Gertrude Stein said, a writer, a painter has privileges. In 1920, America was still a literary colony of Britain and a fine-art colony of France. In fact, it is not exaggerating much to say that the United States owed all of its painting and sculpture to the school of Paris, especially to the free training given to two generations of American rapins at Beaux Arts. Materials—the Statue of Liberty for New York, a set of classical plaster casts given to the San Francisco Art Institute to replace the original set destroyed by the earthquake and fire of 1906—came as gifts from the French people as did the education of most of the men and women who produced America's fine arts and staffed her art schools.[2]

In the 1920's, two kinds of Americans came to Paris. As good a symbol of the difference as any is the one we already flashed from the Village where a black man and a white girl could walk hand in hand without stirring comment. In Paris as in New York, Anglo-Americans either treated the black man courteously or did their best to impose the color bar. In today's idiom, most Americans visiting Paris were racist pigs. Frustrated racist pigs, for with commendable resolution the French government crushed all attempts to establish the color bar.[3]

The French people earned dividends from this civility. Beginning in the 1920's, a colony of expatriate black Americans took root in Paris and thrives there today. Some like Richard Wright or James Baldwin represented letters; others, fine arts, but most are musicians. It is to these musicians and their visiting friends that France owes the enrichment of its culture by jazz and blues. These have now passed through assimilatory stages like Le Jazz Club Français to become part of every young person in France.

In the nineteenth century, France gave the fine arts to America, a gift spread through that vast land by Henry Mencken's romantic army and, later, by the W.P.A.—a gift just now being assimilated.

In the twentieth century, black America gave to France a regal gift of equal value: jazz and blues.

France and the United States have always lived in a very special and intimate relationship, one to which Germany and the United Kingdom are also parties. So close are the four peoples—French, German, British, American—that they seem to share a single fate. Where would America be today had not 200,000 Germans fought in the Federal armies during the Civil War? So tightly do the four peoples cohere that in comparison all other peoples seem strangers. The four compose a family, albeit a temperamental and passionate one, marked by sympathetic comradeship and deadly quarrels. With the exception of colonial wars, a few slaps exchanged at sea in 1799 and a few blows on the beaches of North Africa in 1942, of the four peoples in this mercurial ménage, the French and the Americans are the only ones who have never tried to kill each other. Of all the relationships among the four, the only one resembling a love affair is that of France and America, or, somewhat more precisely, Paris and America.

Back in the 1890's, Americans, as one of them said, were seen by the French as "enormously rich, and, to put the matter politely, eccentric." By the 1920's, in Paris, the more objectionable Americans were regarded as freaks, but also as free spenders, which fact made their barbarous behavior easier to bear. Fortunately most of these lived far from the daily life of Paris. They inhabited the tourist culture, a fake, staged romance peopled by ghosts of the bohemian and criminal realities of the past century, a culture turning around Montmartre clubs where actors pretended to be apaches or impersonated artists showing and poets reading.[4]

In 1917-1918, the doughboys of the A.E.F., a kind of American not ordinarily found in France, felt they were there to pay a debt to Lafayette and realize a warless world. Not only had these soldiers saved France, but they had done it with an air of good-natured humility that left the French liking them. After the war, Americans gave money to rebuild the ruins; they patronized the luxury industries and the arts. America like France called itself a Republic. America was the home of the Wild West, of the Free Spirit. Although American products and methods as seen in Paris and reflected in American movies were building a new standard, the French did not yet regard the Anglo-Saxon thrust as a threat. Because, with the deepest sincerity, the French still believed France to be the cradle of the arts, the home of Liberty, the most advanced civilization on earth, they welcomed the American presence as a happy supplement. Thus the French could be fond of Americans and indulge Yankee eccentricities.[5]

Compacted into the interstices of its 2.5 million French, Paris lodged foreign colonies: 100,000 Italians (*"macaronis"*), 50,000 Belgians and Swiss, 60,000 Russians, mostly czarist refugees, and 35,000 British (*"bifsteks"*).[6]

Although the American colony comprised but 10,000 people, these made themselves so conspicuous that everyone believed it much larger.[7]

Theirs was more than a colony; theirs was a liberal bourgeois American town established within Paris and without Babbitt, a town held together by American business enterprises, American churches, American doctors and lawyers, American social clubs, an American hospital, an American library, Post #1 of the American Legion, American schools and banks, American stores, a baseball league, and two daily newspapers in English.

Of this community, students may have formed the largest bloc, France having absorbed those formerly going to Germany.

The art center of this American community—and of the rest of the United States as well—was the Café du Dôme at the intersection of boulevards Raspail and Montparnasse.

In the Parisian-international proportion, the Dôme and the nearby Rotonde served as the hub of Bohemia—the Dôme being American and British, the Rotonde, Scandinavian, Russian, French. This cleavage resulted when the owner of the Rotonde expelled his more rowdy customers. Embellished by the shades of its old clients Lenin and Trotsky, famed as a bohemian haunt, respectable people had swarmed to the Rotonde. In the manner of Rodolphe Salis of the Chat Noir, the Rotonde's owner, reputed a police informer, decided to clean up the image, which meant purging it of all its crazed clients, particularly the pistol-packing Americans who liked to play apache and Wild West at the bar.[8]

Bastille Day of 1923 brought with it a chance for revenge. At Montparnasse, the fête grew into a Dionysian freak-out: Chinese lanterns in the trees, bands at every corner, revelers dancing and shouting and boozing at the Dôme, out in the street, crushing together on the terrace of the Rotonde. To a euphoric commando of the romantic army composed chiefly of Dada painters, urged on by surrealist Louis Aragon and Dadist Tristan Tzara, with a toss of long yellow hair, an American proposed: Let's go over there and get even with that bastard!

The commando pushed onto the terrace of the Rotonde and pressed through into the café, cornering its proprietor. Aragon began shouting abuse. Abruptly, Malcolm Cowley, an American writer, outraged by the man's craven and greasy look, pushed to the front and slugged him in the jaw. On came the waiters, but the crowd helped Cowley escape. Hours later, after other adventures, passing by the Rotonde, Cowley spied the proprietor and, in the presence of 600 customers, began yelling at him from the middle of the street. "You bastard (*salaud*)! You fink (*mouchard*)!" Two policemen, one of them drunk, seized him by the arms and led him away. On the way to the station the drunken cop punched and kicked him. At the station they charged him with forcibly resisting an officer, a charge withdrawn when his friends bribed the officer. In court, a group of friends, facile liars and men of influence, testified for him so artfully that the charge of assaulting the proprietor was dismissed.

For this his French friends lionized him. As he later recalled, he had acted in the interest of *public morality*. Having no personal relationship with the proprietor, he had been *disinterested*; he had been *indiscreet*; acted with *violence* and *disdain* for the law. His was an *arbitrary* and *significant* gesture, a *manifesto*: in sum, his had been the perfect Dadasurrealistic act.[9]

As this suggests, Paris still provided plenty of room for free spirits, for free art. For two generations Paris had helped train the cadres of H. L. Mencken's romantic army. Now, the freedom of her atmosphere, her publishers who would print anything for money, the proximity of idealistic and experimental literary magazines, and the structuring of the art world brought about in part by the Dôme, in part by Gertrude Stein and others, made the liberation of American literature possible.[10] Because the structure concentrated the best creative minds of the Western world around a group of superb young Americans, the liberation began to happen. The free new writing so affected young French poets that they dared to coin words in French. The free new writing went back to America in waves to be diffused everywhere by Mencken's romantic army, although it is only in the past few years that the army has waxed strong enough to force publication in America of seminal writers, long available in France, like Henry Miller and William Burroughs.

By 1922, when the French celebrated Murger's centennial they had become aware of the intense excitement centering around the Dôme. The Parisian art community was transmuting into an Anglo-French bouillabaisse thickened by many other cultures and nationalities. For the young Americans this was at once a time of innovation and discovery of what had long been accomplished. Some, having found the freedom they had left home to seek, fell apart, victims of Montparnassia. Others, likewise set free, radiated a purposeful and idealistic spirit, pure and intense. This shone out on the French among whom prevailed war-born feelings of having been deceived, of guilt, of nihilism, of contempt for public service and for all ideal-ism whatsoever. Among them, the survivals of romanticism pre-served its escapist features, carried a cynical hard-boiled tone and delight in decadence. At best, it laughed at the cruel absurdities of life, stood firm in the face of tragedy. Bohemia's old enthusiasm, its flaming purpose, had burned down to embers.

Anachronistic and foolish as they seemed, refreshing as they were, the Americans with their naïve but intense energy restored these qualities to Bohemia.

The Americans had also physically occupied many of the stu-dios that comprised Bohemia's turf.

In these studios, living the image of Trilby and Murger, feeling wicked, the men beardless and long-haired, the women lightly clothed and short-haired, drinking wine and dancing to jazz, arguing about Picasso and baseball and Calvin Coolidge, they remained in essence the clean and wholesome young people they had been at home in Bexley and Hillsboro and Oyster Bay. Here was a decent and do-mestic Latin Quarter, warm with homely comforts, where the guests ate waffles from an electric iron serviced by the Vassar wife of a Princeton painter in the company of a rosy and ultralegitimate baby.[11]

But this did not last. In tandem with the demons of fascism, the Depression struck. The Americans went broke. The Parisians polarized into socialist and fascist. The politicians came to regard the French worker as the primary enemy of France and acted ac-cordingly. When the socialist leaders became the government, they persisted in the old policies. Hope for betterment died. No matter how elections turned out, some gang of parasites ruled France for the benefit of speculators and large employers. The communist lead-ers, participating in the government bureaucracy, resisted change and served the Soviet Union. Republican Spain slowly bled to death. The Italians took Ethiopia, Albania. The Nazis took the Ruhr, the Rhineland, Austria, Czechoslovakia. Feeling helpless and hopeless, the socialists and their cousins in Bohemia fell into the paralysis of despair.[12]

An exception to the spirit of the times, then and later, is Romain Gary, a Polish Jew turned Frenchman who lived *à la Bohème* in Paris, insouciant, a complete idealist, writing instead of going to law school, planning to go to Berlin and kill Hitler, living days without eating rather than asking his impecunious mother for money.

Shortly after fainting dead away from hunger at the sight of a dapper bourgeois eating steak, Gary borrowed one hundred sous from a friend, went to the Capoulade on Boul' Mich', ordered a coffee at the bar and began eating croissants out of a serving basket he found there. When it came time to settle his account, he swore he'd only eaten one, a statement the barman kindly accepted. In 1936-1937, Gary says he ate 1,500 stolen croissants at the Capoulade, regarding them as a scholarship presented by the management.

Every now and then, the barman would ask: Can't you stuff yourself somewhere else?

"I can't. You are my father and my mother."

Croissants, he adds, "have done more for students than the Third Republic," surely an understatement when considered in the context of the débâcle of the Nazi invasion of 1940.[13]

For the 1930's, the tone of feeling in Bohemia and the rest of the art world revolving around Paris is articulated by Henry Miller and so well that he was soon acclaimed by the French. After World War II, in the minds of romantic young Americans, Henry Miller's account in his *Tropic* books of the struggle for survival in Paris replaced Murger's *Scènes de Bohème* as the bohemian standard.

The moment this happened is when the American arts matured.

> And then, when Fillmore "had had his fling, when the tent-top blew off and he had a good look at the sky, he saw that it wasn't just a circus, but an arena, just like everywhere. And a damned grim one. I often used to think, when I heard him rave about glorious France, about liberty and all that crap, what it would have sounded like to a French workman, could he have understood Fillmore's words. No wonder they think we're all crazy. We *are* crazy to them. We're just a pack of children. Senile idiots. What we call life is a five-and-ten-cent store romance. That enthusiasm underneath—what is it? That cheap optimism which turns the stomach of any ordinary European? It's illusion. No, illusion's too good a word for it. Illusion means something. No, it's not that—it's *delusion*. It's sheer delusion, that's what. . . . It's in the

blood. It's the climate. It's a lot of things. It's the end, too. We're pulling the whole world down about our ears. We don't know why. It's our destiny. The rest is plain shit."[14]

In New York, the 1930's generated a different atmosphere, a cosmodemoniacal illusion.

By strangling the bourgeois prosperity of the 1920's, the Depression wiped out the gift shoppes, dropped rents and prices, revived the bohemian community in the Village. As of old, ménages of three to ten lived the communal life in one-room studios. To suffering America, the New Deal brought hope. To Bohemia, it brought something more substantial—the W.P.A. writers', artists', theater, and musicians' projects, each of which provided creative youth with both employment and an audience. Preoccupation with personal relationships, a luxury characteristic of the 1920's, died out. In their intensified preoccupation with survival, the bohemians suddenly found themselves living out the central theme of America. Small consolation! The rest of New York looked on the Village bohemians as comic relief and the bohemians seem to have shared this judgment. They did not have much confidence in themselves. In them lived a sordid quality and a cynical humor as suggested by the fact that in contrast to the high life of Café Society Uptown they called themselves Cafeteria Society Downtown.[15] The bohemian/art community identified itself generally with the revolutionary struggle for social justice; bohemians, strikers, unemployed, revolutionaries, mingled in a common milieu. The adventurous young came from everywhere to seek their fortunes. In the Village, Bohemia began to blend with the labor movement, particularly its most radical and bohemian segment, the merchant seamen.

A sense of the times is captured in the events attending the maiden voyage from New York of the German passenger ship *Bremen.*

It was a hot damp July evening in 1935. The giant ship, its bow rising high above the water, lay docked in a slip facing 13th Avenue. From a staff rising above the bow a Nazi flag was flying. Down in the street, an angry crowd of radicals, communists, bohemians, gathered. The forward deck swarmed with passengers and friends enjoying a gala departure.

From the crowd a sudden shout——

The swastika flag is falling!

Three men dressed as sailors have cut the halyards.

Now they seize the flag and throw it overboard and it flutters down into the greasy water.

Pandemonium. Two pistol shots sound on the forward deck. Women scream; whistles shrill. A detective has shot one of the invaders in the groin. On the street, the crowd cheers and sings the "Internationale." Germans from the crew catch another invader. They try to throw him over the side, more than fifty feet down to the pier. He hangs on with hands and feet; a woman shrieks, the crew relents and delivers him to the police.

Recovering the flag, the crew raise it once more while passengers and guests cheer.[16]

17.
The SS State
(1933-1945)

What would the Nazis have built had history allowed them more than twelve years before casting them overboard? What would the completed edifice of their New Order have looked like and what would it have felt like to live it it?[1] To answer these questions about the National Socialist revolution we must first set it in the context of the other revolutions that swept through societies demolished by World War I.

The Russian Revolution tried to establish the Spirit of Liberty, even as manifest in free art, at the center of affairs, but eventually formed around the Principle of Authority, thus rendering impossible the accomplishment of its objective. The Communist Party rebuilt the nation around itself and itself around the *Führerprinzip*— the Leader Principle. It created a Bohemia *manqué*. When Stalin came to power, if not before, the international promise of socialism was subverted to nationalism. The "Internationale" and the red flag, once the symbol of the equality of all humans, came to stand for the Soviet Union. Here was National Communism. Elsewhere, communist parties were to work neither in the interests of their own peoples nor of mankind generally but in those of the Soviet Union.

From the Russian Revolution issued not the equality of a classless society to which each contributed according to his abilities and from which each took according to his needs but a new privileged class—a new bourgeoisie—composed of bureaucratic managers.[2]

If *to own* means *to have exclusive use and disposition of*, then

183

the Russian Revolution transferred ownership of the means of production and of almost everything else from noble, prelate, capitalist, kulak, and independent bourgeois, not to the public, but to a new class of bourgeois bureaucrats. These hold their powers at the sufferance of the rulers, of the coführers, of those at the source of the leader principle who serve as oracles for the almighty historical dialectic—at the sufferance of the executive committee of the central committee of the national communist party, or, perhaps characteristically, of a single führer—its chairman. A revolutionary ideology dedicated to the liberation of mankind through the demolition of social classes had instead delivered the revolutionary society not only into the hands of a despot but into those of as self-righteous and prudish a middle class as has ever plagued mankind.

The Russian Revolution did not create the humane posttraditional order of Liberty, Equality, Fraternity for which the romantic bohemian revolutionaries yearned and had once partially established in the Paris Commune. Instead, in consolidating, the new state killed most of them in its own blood purges. What had in fact been accomplished in all those terrible years was the transformation of the Russian Empire from a traditional to a transitional order.

The second revolution, Italian fascism and its Spanish reflection, attempted to adapt the old authoritarian traditions *to* the new technology. Fascism is therefore late-transitional in character. National Socialism, as we shall see, would liquidate all traditions, the middle class along with them, and build an authoritarian state *on* the new technology. Contrary to common belief, fascism and Nazism are *not* the same. Both Italian and Spanish fascism maintain the authority of the military, the aristocracy, the Catholic Church, of the capitalists and the independent bourgeoisie.[3] Both make a place for an expanded and, in some ways, new class of managerial bureaucrats. Both, though keeping the traditional Catholic forms of belief, strive to transmute the substance of belief from the Christian mysteries into mystic nationalism. Fascism would replace the absolute and total authority of God with that of Duce or Caudillo and thus slowly introduce the *Führerprinzip*.

National syndicalism and national communism—the fascist movement and the Soviet Union—are transitional and conservative in comparison to the national socialism of the Nazis. Of these three efforts to revise the conditions of human life, the Nazis' was by far the most revolutionary. Theirs was not only the most extreme economic and social transformation—they built history's first technocracy—but it was to have been a *biological* transformation directed at the creation of superhumans and subhumans. Having preserved the least of the past, the Nazis show us the most about the future.

What would the Thousand Year Reich have been like?

Before expiring, the Twelve Year Reich had, in fact, nationalized the ownership of everything including its own people. The Leader and the new class of SS bureaucrats and enforcers through whom his will flowed had exclusive use and disposition of every object and human being in the new German Empire.[4]

Which is to say the Nazis did, in fact, establish state ownership of everything.

What the Bolsheviks introduced through the front door, terrifying the rich everywhere, the Nazis, with the help of the rich, brought in quietly through the back door. In mortal fear of communism, the German middle classes nourished the NSDAP, a demon whose oiled steel will produced a hatred of the bourgeoisie and a resolution to destroy it unmatched even by the bohemians and communards of Paris, even by the Soviets.[5] Too late the German burghers learned that law and order are not in fact complementary. One must choose between them. Perfect order—perfect social harmony—can only result from the perfect operation of a Leader Principle carrying through society to each of its cells a single will, a form of rule but recently made possible by modern technology. To the end of trimming from society all restraints on the Leader Principle, the Nazis set about the demolition of tradition, independent thought and expression, of law, of objective truth itself.

The Nazi revolution began as a headlong rush of tough antisocials and alienated adolescents, posttraditionals all, raging against the transitional society of the Republic, yearning for a leader who would organize their energies and lead them into a posttraditional order compatible with their passions. It was a boiling effervescence, a flow of molten iron from the crucible of trench warfare. Both psychologically and physically, it was the stampede of a panicked people. It was a reconstuction of psychic awareness. Once in power, accepting Mussolini's advice to liquidate "incurable revolutionaries,"

German Soldier. *August Sander*

its Führer and his SS purged the most dangerous intractables, intimidated the rest. Thus harnessed and bitted, the revolution raced on, its program not expressed conventionally in documents and speeches but in deeds and (as Reichsmarshal Hermann Göring put it) in the faces of the storm troopers. Germany quickly became a dual state. Nazi institutions rose alongside the traditional institutions, penetrating them and usurping their functions, promising to replace them completely. The Waffen SS army stood alongside the regular army; the Gestapo (*Geheime Staatspolizei*), the SD (*Sicherheitsdienst*: Security Department), and other SS Police forces stood alongside the regular police forces. Eventually all police, SS and traditional, came under the authority of Reichsführer SS Heinrich Himmler. NSDAP and SS educational institutions grew alongside the conventional school systems and the purged universities. SS industries grew alongside conventional industries. The state foreign service found a parallel in the Party's foreign service. In accordance with Hitler's desire to eliminate lawyers and conduct the German folk community without recourse to any laws at all, the court-prison system of the state found itself being rapidly replaced by the SS police and concentration-camp systems.[6]

Discarding the statute-evidence-precedent norm of law, the Reich Law Leader told the judges to imagine what the Führer would do in their place—and then do it. The Führer announced he had been sent to rid the world of the burden of conscience. Göring declared: "Right is that which serves the German people,"[7] the implications of which begin glowing when you replace *German* with some other national name, e.g., American.

The Nazis established People's Courts, but in the Nazi system, courts were, in fact, superfluous. Police detected antisocial behavior, arrested, charged, tried, sentenced, heard the appeal, carried out the sentence—often all at once. The SS frequently jailed people acquitted by the state courts. It used its concentration camps for the preventive detention of Jews and others. In the camps, a colored triangle identified the category of each prisoner, a system suggestive of the SS sense of humor. Political prisoners wore red; homosexuals, pink; Jehovah's Witnesses, purple; antisocials, black; criminals, green; fugitives, blue; Gypsies, brown. Jews sewed yellow triangles over their category triangles in such a way as to form the Star of David. Race defilers displayed black borders on their triangles; those suspected of planning to escape displayed red-and-white targets on chest and back. Among those distinguished by black triangles were "work-shy elements," men who had refused jobs or quit jobs without good reason.[8]

As is suggested by all this, the Black Order of the SS (SS always being written in lightning flashes, runic for SS, ⚡⚡, a key included on the new typewriters)[9] had replaced the traditional institutions of the state, the SA, and the Party itself as the central institution of power. To imagine the Nazi state as it would eventually have taken form is to imagine the SA and the Party as well as all of the traditional institutions including the regular armed forces vanished utterly and the SS in full control. It is to imagine further as part of the initiation each of the neophytes of this holy antiorder having the runic lightning flashes tattooed onto the inside of the left arm, just under the shoulder.

Although many of its traits are comprised in police forces and populist movements the world around, this SS State is, in fact, unique. It is so posttraditional that the basic pattern of its mentality bears but slight resemblance to that of Western culture, even as manifested in the Soviet Union. So divergent is the SS mentality from the Western norm that the conventionally minded cannot understand it.[10]

For this state, the ideal was the perfect administration of the will of that biological entity called the German Volk as articulated by its spirit medium, Der Führer, and as transmitted to each cell by the Black Order and its capillary institutions. When Hitler says: "We think with our blood," he is to be understood in this context.

Somber foreshadows of what the SS State might have meant to us had it not been strangled in infancy are cast by the annihilation of the towns of Lidice and Oradour-sur-Glane, by the concentration camps, by the Führer's decision to kill off Europe's 9.2 million Jews and by the subsequent murder of some six million of them, by the baling for industrial use of hair cut from the murdered women, and by the melting down of gold from the spectacles and teeth of the dead for deposit in the Reichsbank.[11]

Gold bars stamped with the swastika still serve as part of the international monetary system.[12]

A frightful irony shows itself in the fact that almost every representative of the old traditional elite of professors, civil servants, scientists, clergymen, physicians, businessmen, attorneys, politicians, financiers, newsmen, policemen, soldiers, aristocrats, and princes not only acquiesced in the odious crimes of the Black Order's New Order and in the dissolution of their own authority and way of life, but did, in fact, abet the crimes and facilitate the dissolution.[13]

The resonance with recent events as focused in the Indo-China War is more than coincidental.

Was the weakness and cowardice of the Germanic establishment a uniquely German phenomenon or is it common to the establishments of all the nations of the West?

Is humanity versus SS the story of two mutually exclusive mentalities warring for dominance of the world or is it in the deepest sense the drama of a civil war in the soul of each of us?

What would the New Order have been like?

Hitler conceived of a Greater Germanic Empire extending from Scotland to Italy, from the Atlantic to the Black Sea, bound together by freeways and the Leader Principle, populated by Nordics and helots, centered on Germania, a grandiose world capital embellished by gigantic buildings of Hitler's own design, the first phase of construction to have been completed by 1950. Hitler counted 127 million Germans in Europe and imagined an accelerated birthrate. Northern France and Burgundy were to be Germanized and along with Belgium and German Switzerland would probably have joined Alsace-Lorraine, Austria, Luxemburg, the Sudetenlands, Memel, Danzig, Holland, Scandinavia, the Baltic States, and Finland in becoming parts of the Reich itself.[14]

Reichsführer SS Heinrich Himmler dreamed of rebuilding the ancient realm of Lothar around the nucleus of Burgundy and erecting it as an independent and ultra-elite SS state.[15]

In 1940, Wehrmacht orders specified that all able-bodied men in Britain aged 17 through 45 be interned and dispatched to the Continent and that Britain be looted of its supplies and its industry. The Latins, a people viewed as different but possibly equal, were eventually in their reduced living space to be formed into the Romance Bloc and associated with the Reich.[16] The Slavs, an inferior race, were to be treated like domestic animals. As for the Jewish problem—mass murder would provide the final solution.

As Reichsführer SS Heinrich Himmler put it:

"Whether the Slavs thrive or starve to death concerns me only from the point of view of our need for them as slave labor for our civilization.

"Whether 10,000 Russian females fall down from exhaustion while digging an anti-tank ditch interests me only insofar as the anti-tank ditch for Germany is finished." [17]

To Hitler, the Slavs were "redskins" to be driven off their land in a Wild East epic.[18]

Resettled entirely by South Tyrolese Germans, the Crimea was to become a Nordic cultural and resort area. Educated Slavs were to be exterminated. The rest were to live at subsistence level, be prevented from breeding, receive no medical care, and learn no more than how to count to one hundred and, as Hitler put it, how to read road signs. West of the Urals, Slavic lands were to be resettled by Nordics from the Reich, Scandinavia, Western Europe, and the U.S.A. Siberia would become a giant Nordic-ruled territory resembling British India. That vast area was to be controlled by fortified towns built on the medieval pattern. Eventually, Siberia, too, would be colonized and the Slavs left to die out. Small children showing marked Nordic traits were to be kidnapped from among the Slavs and the Latins and reared as Germans. In 120 years, the population of the Reich was to consist entirely of blond, Nordic types. This Germanizing policy found expression in the organization of Norse, Balts, Danes, Flemings, Finns, and even some 12,000 French into SS regiments. It appeared likewise in the Anglo-American Free Corps which solicited enlistments from American prisoners of war.[19]

Once consolidated, the Greater Germanic Empire would wax strong enough to embark on the conquest of the United States. This might have happened even earlier, for by 1947 the Germans could have had atomic warheads to deliver by missile and jet plane. Recalling that in the eighteenth century German had failed in Congress by but one vote of becoming the official language of the U.S., Hitler hoped to make German the American language and Germanize the American people.[20]

From this empire, all traces of the Judeo-Christian tradition were to be extirpated.[21]

In the largest pattern, the New Order seems to have been envisioned as a hierarchy of race-nations, a radical caste system, descending from the master Kultur-nation through the lesser Kultur-nations of the Latins and the Orientals down to the mudsill: Slavs, browns, blacks. In this attitude the racism epidemic among all whites, one long displayed in the European colonial systems and in U.S. white supremacy, finds logical conclusion. In a sense, as seen by other whites, the real Nazi crime was the inclusion of whites among those who legitimately could be treated as subhumans. With the Nazis, white supremacy constricted to Nordic supremacy and, by so doing, transformed the rest of the whites into gooks and niggers.

Superficially, it appears that the Germanized Nordics—the Brahmins of the New Order—were to enjoy socialist equality in their world-embracing community, "the classless race-and-leader state," as Hitler called it, a state from which antisocial and degenerate elements—the mentally ill, physically handicapped, mentally retarded —had been purged by mercy killings, one in which desirable traits had been maximized by scientific breeding. To this end, the Minister of Agriculture, a former hog breeder, compiled a stud book of the racially elite families to serve as a pedigree and standard for SS betrothals. Heinrich Himmler inaugurated the *Lebensborn* program through which the SS expedited the breeding of pure Aryan men to pure Aryan women who wanted to "give" a child to the Führer. Other officials, such as the Olympic authorities, resorted to equally fantastic expedients. At the Games of 1936, athletes found a pleasure garden furnished with girls of superior blood with whom they were encouraged to breed.[22]

Ostensibly, it was around the principle of social equality that the work of the Germans was organized. The Reich, as Hitler said, was to become "the most solid popular community it is possible to imagine," one whose young, bred like prize horses, knowing nothing else, would be the "personification of the National Socialist Ideal." Old Germany was still in many ways medieval. The aristocratic caste detested the bourgeoisie. Both aristocrat and burgher scorned the worker and the peasant who, in the Old Order, had occupied much the same position the Slav was to occupy in the New Order. In fact, the idea of racial hierarchy is a populistic expression of the medieval institution of hereditary aristocracy. The "people's community" was conceived as a Viking war band of equal comrades where every economic and social function held equal status and judgments would only be made relative to the efficiency with which each person functioned. For this, the Labor Front Leader, Robert Ley, used the model of the community of the trench soldier and declared that the concept of the "soldier of labor" would overcome all class distinction.[23] As shown in the film *Triumph of the Will,* at the gigantic homoerotic Party rallies—the first employment of modern technology conjoined with all the arts to create a single psychic environment— men came by the thousands from everywhere in the Reich to march with spades over their shoulders and receive the accolades of their führers and fellows.

To implement all this, the labor unions and employers' associations were replaced by economic "communities" comprising both groups. These then were federated into the Labor Front which, in turn, came to serve as the sole employment office and to wield the hiring and firing power, even over bosses. Labor conscription was introduced under this agency as were wage and price controls and the Strength-through-Joy program which filled the workers' free time with cheap shows and concerts, adult-education programs, inexpensive excursions and ocean cruises. All hobby clubs, even the bird watchers, were amalgamated into the Front because autonomous organizations of any kind were anathema to the Nazis. Eventually all the slums were to be cleared and each family was to own a *Kraft-durch-Freude* Wagen: Strength-through-Joy Car, one soon called the People's Car. The basic design for this car, the Volkswagen, was contrived by Dr. Ferdinand Porsche and approved by the Führer himself.[24]

"The Volkswagen," said the Führer on 22 June 1942, "—and I think our war experiences justify us in saying so—is the car of the future."[25]

Before conscription into the armed forces all young men, regardless of social class, had to spend a year in the Labor Service, a proposal appearing recently in American politics under the rubric of National Service. In this program, city boys did manual work on the farms and thus put their souls in touch with the Blood and Soil of the people. Girls, even of the aristocracy, served first a Land Year, when they worked on farms in house and field, and then a Household Year in the city as domestics.[26]

Conscription into the Labor Service was preceded by a lifetime of participation in the several grades of Hitler Youth, the Reich's sole youth organization. Comprised in Hitler Youth were the National Vocational Competitions that united the training of artisans such as bricklayers with the spirit of competitive sport. Superficially, in activity, in spirit, in appeal, Hitler Youth resembles the pre-1914 Wandervogel movement, though it really is the obverse for it was imposed by adults and served as an arm of the establishment.

All small and medium farms were entailed by law—they could not be sold, divided, or foreclosed—and their owners, if able to trace Aryan blood back to 1800, were bound to them in perpetuity and distinguished by the title of Herr Bauer (Mr. Farmer). Concurrently, the independent businessmen and artisans were suppressed.[27]

Ubiquitous and strictly controlled to project a single image into all minds, the media so successfully obscured the line separating fantasy from reality as to give the Germans a new standard compounded from both. So powerful was the avalanche of propaganda as to overcome the strongest psychological defenses and fill dreams with its images. Thus the propaganda ministry of Paul Joseph Goebbels policed conscience well enough to render crime-think nigh impossible. To assure the political reliability of the arts, the Nazis forced Germans in creative fields into Chambers controlled by Goebbels. Students, dancing around outdoor bonfires, burned millions of books. The Minister of Culture, himself an incompetent grade-school teacher, told a gathering of professors: It's not your job "to determine whether something is true, but whether it is in the spirit of the National Socialist Revolution." The professors soon discovered Aryan physics, chemistry, biology, mathematics. Hitler himself undertook to cleanse the Reich of decadent art. The show opening the Führer's House of German Art was juried by the Führer himself with such passionate commitment that on occasions he kicked holes through paintings he did not like. Of the 15,000 entries he admitted some nine hundred, forming a show that impressed William L. Shirer as "the worst junk this writer has ever seen in any country."[28]

It would seem that in the New Order the Herrenvolk were to be bound to family farms and conscripted into large economic communities. They were to work at maximum efficiency while being drenched with supervised diversions in an aura of ravaged thought and petrified sensibilities.

And they were to be ruled by a Holy Order—the SS.[29]

Of all this, industrial boss Albert Speer recalled:

"As the Nazi environment enveloped us, its evils grew invisible —because we were part of them."[30]

The educational system was programmed for the production of what Hitler called the New Man. He believed the present generation of leaders would have to be used up and the next one matured before the New Order could truly function. "A violently active, intrepid, brutal youth—that is what I'm after," said Hitler. "There must be no weakness or tenderness in it."[31]

"A new variety of man is beginning to separate out. A mutation, precisely in the scientific sense." The existing variety is declining into a stunted existence. The two will rapidly diverge. "One will sink to a subhuman race and the other will rise far above the

Painted by Werner Peiner

194

man of today. I might call the two varieties the God-man and the mass-animal." Our revolution is nothing less than "the will to create mankind anew."[32]

The core educational institutions were not the conventional school systems but those institutions that homogenized all classes and afforded personal experience in each segment of the national experience: Hitler Youth with its simple outdoor life, its comradeship and crafts, its sports and songs, its classy uniforms, its target practice and its holy youth-knife; the Labor Service with its boys' and girls' camps in proximity, its noble toil in field and bower; the new military service, modeled on the early Roman legion, where officers and men drank beer together and everyone had access to the fabulous new toys and stark adventures which composed the modern mass-murder machine.[33]

From this would emerge the New Man, a Greek hero embodying all the heroic virtues except trained intellect, and the New Woman, a lush peasant and clean white goddess, living to service the Man and to populate his world with perfect Nordics as she accumulated Motherhood Medals emblazoned *Kinder, Kirche, Küche* (Children, Church, Cooking) and participated in her Faith and Beauty Program.

The British secret of empire was the tough Spartan boarding school where, while studying antiquity, the future lords of the earth lived a life of privation and discipline. In modern form, such was to be the matrix for training the young lords of the New Order. Of the Reich's racially pure and physically perfect twelve-year-olds, the most promising were chosen for appointment to boarding schools: either NAPOLA (*Nationalpolitische Erziehungsanstalten*—Junkerstyle schools preparatory for the career of political soldier), or the Adolf Hitler Schools (preparatory for the career of the soldierly politician). Graduates then went to the Labor Service and after that either to the new army and lay brotherhood of the Waffen SS or took their vows as neophytes of the Order and went to the Death Head SS where symbols, rituals, and degrees of initiation modeled on the Masonic Order provided the form. In principle, the NAPOLA reared the future leaders of the military, police, and Labor Service. As the SS magazine *Das Schwarze Korps* put it: "Pupils learn how to kill and how to die." The Adolf Hitler schools reared the future führers of SS and government.[34]

Recruits in the Death Head SS received basic training at the concentration camps. First the neophytes were subjected to an extreme form of Prussian drill, then they were turned loose on the prisoners. In this their tendencies to sadism and brutality were allowed uninhibited expression. Hitler said he had been "hardened" by the Western Front. Now, in a frenzy of brutality and sadism the Death Head SS neophytes were being purged of weakness on the simulated Western Front of the concentration camp. Those showing "sentimentality" or compassion were discharged as unfit or, if suspected of helping prisoners, were called before their fellows, stripped of their rank, shorn of their hair, given twenty-five lashes, and imprisoned in the camp along with the rest of the subhumans.[35]

Conversely, those who excelled at becoming hard and tough earned rapid promotion.

On completion of this program the SS neophyte had been well conditioned for the "desperate situation" and had been made equal to maintaining a continuous "high-tension existence." Without concern for purpose or for means, he was ready to undertake any assignment. He accepted efficiency as his primal value and, in the context of believing accomplishment of the "impossible" to be the "essence of the heroic", he accepted "Heroic Realism" as his ideal posture. This modern Spartan embodied the heroic ideal of ancient Greece, albeit after it had been subjected to a prefrontal lobotomy. In the words of Obergruppenführer SS Doktor Ernst Kaltenbrunner, police boss and butcher of the Jews, "We were all so trained to obey orders without even thinking that the thought of disobeying orders would simply never have occurred to anybody."[36]

From basic training the young SS man went to general service in the Black Order. The cream of this group eventually moved on to advanced training schools inspired by the Order Castles of the medieval Teutonic Knights. In each of the new *Ordensburgen* stood an idol for worship, which Hitler called the image "of the magnificent, self-ordaining God-man." Here, the chosen ones became initiates in the mystic secrets of the cosmos. During the course of years, while moving from one castle to another, they received preparation for service as high officials of the Empire or in the Race and Settlement Office. Eugen Kogon, an expert on the SS, tells us that this high council "guarded the purity of the original idea of the Sacred Order, protected the elite character of the SS, conducted a continuous process of selecting the master class for the super state and, by means of extermination, resettlement and land distribution, buttressed its rule through Germany and Europe."[37]

It is from my castles, said the Führer, "that the second stage will emerge—the stage of the Man-God. ... But there are other stages about which I am not permitted to speak."[38]

"I have seen the vision of the new man—fearless and formidable. I shrank from him!"[39]

Such was the radiance shining forth from the sun-wheel swastika of the Thousand Year Reich. Such was Adolf Hitler's dream of forcing a mutation in the human race to bring about the advent of the God-Man and the victory of fire over ice.[40]

Thus, in an aura of the metaphysical, were the blond supremacy doctrine, cruelty, the occult, *machismo,* witless obedience, and jockstrap romanticism instilled into a recent generation of Germans: the Hitlerolatry.

Although of common origin with the bohemians, the mentality embodied in the Hitlerolatry would cut out of mankind everything Bohemia stands for. Much as the SS State was an expression of the romantic resistance to bourgeois dominance, of absolutism to compromise, it was also the ultimate anti-Bohemia. And this possibly because it was not posttraditional enough! Transitional society taught its children—many of whom it eventually massacred on the Western Front—the same lesson Alois Hitler taught his son Adolf: be at once self-reliant and submissive.[41] These two are so incompatible that they must separate—and separate they did: the SS State preserved and maximized the ancient principle of authority-submission as it constructed the first posttraditional state while Bohemia, the first posttraditional community, built itself around the new quality of existential self-reliance.

Today the Black Order and its dream of salvation through eugenics is dead. No idealism greater than the negative of anticommunism energizes the authoritarian states of the West; no dream more noble than achieving efficiency in functioning motivates their personnel. Stripped of its awesome black uniform, the cultural prototype produced by the SS State is the posttraditional technician; its crazed ideology was a final attempt to give this orientation an ethical justification, a larger meaning. Be it the rocketry of Werner von Braun, the Volkswagens and tanks of Porsche, the mass murder factories of Adolf Eichmann and Kaltenbrunner (or for that matter the behavior modification of B.F. Skinner) —the newstyle military officers, engineers, and functionaries of the SS State were interested only in success with the *problem,* a problem abstracted from all moral and human considerations. This New Man can be understood as the dialectical synthesis of Bourgeois vs. Romantic. The terrible danger Technological Man represents for both present and future is evident in the enthusiasm with which the American military, industrial, and political technicians applied themselves to doing a good job of destroying the Indochinese peoples and their economic base even to the land itself, and this quite regardless of any moral or human considerations. Stripped of his façade, the Nazi is man-as-function, the Organization Man in italics. In the USA today, this Nazi is ubiquitous at the centers of power. Where efficiency is the highest value, the Nazi is the best employee. Where human beings are regarded as materials just like anything else, the Nazi is in power.[42]

In his last days, the Third Reich blazing and crumbling around him, the Führer ordered the destruction of Germany's remaining means of sustenance and declared that the German people did not deserve to survive him.[43]

Contrary to the Führer's will, his subordinates saved the shattered economic base and, with American help, restored it.[44]

Contrary to the Führer's will, a new generation of Germans grew up from the ashes. Guiltless of the atrocities of the past, German youth, like American youth, scorns its elders for their greed and their crimes, repudiates its heritage of racism, war, thought control, technocracy, and arbitrary authority. Longhaired and compassionate, German youth and American youth advance side by side toward a new life style and mentality from which they are determined to create the free and human world that history has granted mankind but one more chance to build.[45]

Part Six
BOHEMIA NOW

"Gertrude Stein always speaks of America
as being now the oldest country in the
world because by the methods of the civil
war and the commercial conceptions that
followed it America created the twentieth
century, and since all the other countries
are now either living in or commencing to
be living in a twentieth century of life,
America having begun the creation of the
twentieth century in the sixties of the
nineteenth century is now the oldest country
in the world."

Gertrude Stein, 1933.*

18.
The Black Bohemia
(1805-today)

Mainly because of the contrast between its ideals of freedom and the concentration camps of the SS State, between its ideals of justice and the practice of white supremacy at home and abroad, modern youth has renounced racism. Concurrently, and for similar reasons, modern youth has renounced nationalism, efficiency, war, hierarchical social systems, and arbitrary authority.

In rejecting racism, nationalism, utility, war, despotism, and all restraints on self-expression, youth has adopted the negating traits of the bohemian tradition. Therefore, we may regard the long, arduous development of the bohemian tradition as the development of an ethic, a life-style, and a mentality appropriate to the international civilization of the future.

The negating traits of the bohemian tradition have long been defined.

Conversely, the affirming traits of the bohemian tradition, also suffusing the life-style and mentality of modern youth everywhere, are just now attaining to clear definition. Of great significance in solidifying the negative traits and refining the affirmative ones is black culture and its music. Black culture in America and the way of life developed by its ambassadors—its musicians—have contributed and are contributing to the clarification of the positive traits of Bohemia and to their swift transmission to young people everywhere.

The story of black music begins centuries ago on the west coast of Africa with the kidnapping, enslavement, and transportation to the Americas of millions of blacks. These ravaged blacks were a gentle and aesthetic people sharing a fundamental attitude toward life, a soul quality one of their poets, Aimé Césaire, in 1939, began calling *négritude*. As with Europeans, blacks are at once culturally identical and nationally diverse. Beneath the diversities of the nations is the common pattern of *négritude*.[1]

It was in the West Indies, Brazil, and the southern Mississippi River region that the musics of *négritude* and of Europe fused into new musics. One of these, jazz, is the product of peculiar historical circumstances focused in New Orleans.

For more than a century of French and Spanish rule the slaves in Louisiana were so rigidly controlled by gun, whip, club, hound, and chain that the laws forbidding them to leave their places of employment or assemble for any reasons at all were hardly ever broken. This form took shape in early days when slaves were taken directly from the ships to a French government concentration camp to be tamed or killed. Here, the men learned farm work and the women, housework. Manacled to a heavy chain, often weighted with iron collars, ill-fed, ill-clothed, supervised by brutal soldiers, the men toiled in the fields as long as the sun shone.

Believing that, for reasons of morale, slaves should be allowed some diversions, the Americans, on coming to power, liberalized the regulations. About 1805, slaves were allowed to gather on vacant lots for dancing—a privilege soon restricted to Sunday afternoons and a place in New Orleans the blacks called Congo Square. Every Sunday until the Civil War, blacks by the hundreds came to the square to sing and dance to bamboula drums beaten in the tradition of the drums of Africa. Around the circumference stood police and around them hundreds of whites, come to watch the sport and to buy refreshments from hawkers selling to both crowds. At a signal from the police, the drummers began a steady rhythm with beef bones on casks, a tremendous heartbeat energy roaring on until sundown. From childhood memories of this experience, Louis-Moreau Gottschalk, a partially black New Orleans composer, made a concert piece, *La Bamboula*, which in the 1840's became the rage of Paris.[2]

Like Chinese, West African languages form a part of their meaning by inflections of tone. In religion, different rhythms represent different gods. As with the drums, the songs of the slaves were much more than songs—they conveyed meanings unintelligible to the oppressor. It is in this direction Warren "Baby" Dodds, an outstanding New Orleans jazz drummer and great-grandson of a bamboula drummer, was looking when he said, "You white people who write and make talk about the music are mighty fine people. But you know, don't you, that none of you *really* knows anything about it?" [3]

Another famous New Orleans musician, Sidney Bechet, speaking of his grandfather, Omar, perhaps the best bamboula drummer of all, said, "And you know, he was a leader, he led the music. But, still, as an idea, the way he played his horns, the way he beat his drums, he [sic] was still a background music. It was still a music that hadn't broken loose, it hadn't stopped being scared." [4]

Then in 1862 the Yankees captured New Orleans and soon after that

"It was Free Day . . . Emancipation.

"And New Orleans just bust wide open. A real time was had. They heard the music, and the music told them about it. They heard that music from bands marching up and down the streets and they knew what music it was. It was laughing out loud up and down all the streets, laughing like two people just finding out about each other . . . like something that had found a short-cut after travelling through all the distance there was. That music, it wasn't spirituals or blues or ragtime, but everything all at once, each one putting something over on the other. That one day the music had progressed all the way up to the point where it is today, all the way up from what it had been in the beginning to the place where it could be itself." [5]

At the core of *négritude* is a feeling that an all-pervading divine force, Muntu, energizes human beings, thus distinguishing them from beasts, and animates the spirits of the dead and of the gods themselves. [6] Muntu—the closest concepts to it in European tradition are the Holy Ghost, divine grace, and, not the individual soul, but *soul*. And the music? To Bechet, it seems a kind of entity enjoying independent existence. The music? Perhaps it is the sound of Muntu.

After emancipation, said Bechet, "All these people who had been slaves, they needed the music more than ever now; it was like they were trying to find out in this music what they were supposed to do with this freedom: playing the music and listening to it—waiting for it to express what they needed to learn, once they had learned it wasn't just white people the music had to reach to, nor even to their own people, but straight out to life and to what a man does with his life when it finally *is* his." [7]

The music of Congo Square had been traditional, but in a new way. It had fused the musics of the many black nations conjoined in Louisiana into the music of *négritude* itself. But now the music was fusing with the traditional musics of the West—eventually with those of other traditions as well—struggling to set itself free of all traditions and become a music of the human race.

Old people kept the African music going in a vacant lot until 1876 when it was crushed out by the reaction to Reconstruction. Freed field hands raised in the Anglo aura flooded into uptown New Orleans, carrying the African tradition. The mixed-blood Creoles of downtown New Orleans carried the tradition of European music. Some, like Sidney Bechet's father, had been trained in private schools in both French and English; some few others, sons of the rich, had been schooled in France. As one historian says of downtown and uptown, "Put them together and an old French quadrille becomes *Tiger Rag*." [8] Soon downtown had opened to the passion of Africa; uptown had advanced from homemade instruments to the sophisticated instruments of Europe. Presently, in the same bands, light-brown stood next to blue-black, playing popular songs at black and white parties alike, playing Sousa marches in parades, playing everything that flashed into the heads of those who had never been told what the limitations of their instruments were supposed to be. The whole city, black and white, began to open to the music's tremendous, euphoric mood of discovery.

In the 1870's when all this was beginning to come together in New Orleans, out in the lumber and turpentine camps of Texas, Africa got its hands on the piano, developed a thundering wildfire style on a rocking-rolling bass later calleed boogie-woogie or house-rent music. The black man, used to living in one place with women and children, had suddenly been cut loose. Thousands drifted to the Texas pine woods for work. The slave owners had thought it quite enough if slaves could count to one hundred and read road signs. Now, dependent on their own resources, boredom drove the restless freedmen from job to job, much to the annoyance of their employers. Then some boss deadheaded an old piano back to camp on a lumber wagon and lured a piano player to go along with it. Presently this polite instrument began roaring forth a vodun spell holding the workers on the job. The style spread to the ghettos of the river towns, working its Dionysian enchantment in barrel houses, dollar whorehouses, rent-raising parties, to live and develop underground away from the whites and beneath the scorn of embourgeoised blacks until 1938 when it leapt full-grown onto the stage of Carnegie Hall. Boogie settled in at Café Society Downtown and blasted from jukebox and radio to stun and delight adolescent America.

At the Chicago World's Fair of 1893, freestyle piano playing had made another breakout. In an immensely popular marathon piano playing contest, several of the contestants, possibly rooted in the Texas tradition, played in an energetic, rhythmic style a newsman called "ragged." By 1900 ragtime had caught on everywhere. Essentially a written music, it supported a publishing industry. It sounded like Sousa brass-band music coming out of a piano. The playing and composing focus was Missouri; the players and composers, mainly black.[9]

While the Texans were initiating boogie and the Missourians perfecting ragtime, jazz itself was growing out of the rich soil of what was by far the most musical city in America: New Orleans. In the late nineteenth century, New Orleans with its quarter million people was small enough to be in human proportions. That quarter million people must have been the most cosmopolitan quarter million on earth. Uptown blacks and downtown blacks, white Creoles and Yankee carpetbaggers, tourists concentrating a lifetime of vice into one night, Cajuns singing bluegrass songs in French patois, exslaves singing Delta blues, rivermen shouting river songs, longshoremen chanting and singing on the docks, Louisiana hokers picking out ballads on banjos and sawing away on fiddles at square dances, Southern ladies listening to string quartets, whisky drinkers listening to barbershop quartets, kids' spasm bands skiffling on washboard and gutbucket, sporting girls playing guitars, French music teachers instructing maidens on the viola, honky-tonk piano professors pounding away in hundreds of saloons and bordellos, Southern Baptists hymning in church, African Baptists hymning in church, choirs at high mass, shanty Irish harmonizing at wakes, college boys singing college songs, sailors of all nations singing in saloons and sporting houses, concerts, operas, organ-grinders, nickelodeons, recitals, peddlers' calls, Calypso singers, military bands, brass bands visiting for Mardi Gras, Salvation Army brass bands, German oompah brass bands, brass bands on riverboats, brass bands at parties, brass bands in concert saloons, brass bands at dances, brass bands in parks, brass bands at picnics, brass bands mounted on wagons advertising dances, trombone sliding at tailgate, brass bands leading parades and funeral processions, brass bands day and night, indoors and outdoors, everywhere—brass bands.

And, as a stage for those ubiquitous brass bands, a violent, criminal, amoral city whose politics had reached an ultimate of corruption long before the Civil War and whose district of legalized prostitution was after its institution in 1897 to win fame as one of the hemisphere's most gratifying sin centers.

And in the interstices of all this lived the black people, still degraded, poor, doing the work whites despised, often cheated, often hungry or when sick refused treatment, sometimes jailed or beaten by the white rabble, bearing up under it all, joyful for their freedom, undaunted life-lovers, saying all this in their music—trying to —for, as Bechet observed: In those days the music "wanted to talk to you and me, but it still didn't know how." [10]

It needed an organizing principle which would precipitate it all into a new and unified form, bring the musicians to doing that which no one had done before.

This came from the bucking contests and then from Charles "Buddy" Bolden.

"In those days," says Bechet, "people just made up parades for pleasure. They'd all get together and everyone would put some money into it, maybe a dollar, and they'd make plans for stopping off at one place for one thing, and at some other place for something else —drinks or cake or some food." And naturally there'd be a band. "Then there were the funerals." The blacks had social clubs also serving as mutual-aid societies. "When a member died, naturally all the members would meet at the club. They would have a brass band" and "they would go from the club to the house of the member which was dead, and would play not dance music but mortuary music until they got to be about a block from the residence of the dead person. Then the big drum would just give tempo as they approached. The members would all go in to see the corpse, and then they would take him out to the cemetery with funeral marches." And they'd bury him and leave playing "Didn't He Ramble" which is "really the story about a bull. This bull, all through his life he rambled and rambled until the butcher cut him down. Well, that really meant that this member he rambled till the Lord cut him down." And "they'd play that" and "that band it would go back all through the town seeing the places where that man had liked to be before he died. The music it was rambling for him one last time." [11]

Why such joyful music on the way back? To celebrate leaving this world of day-to-day survival for a better land? One old-time musician said: "Can't do nothing for the brother that's gone. He's out of it. Might as well make the young'uns happy on the way back." [12]

Whenever band wagons met, which was often, they'd lock wheels and play in intense competition until the crowd awarded the victory to one of them. And this crowd, everyone agrees, made a sensitive and sophisticated jury, which is not surprising. For, like Hitler's speeches, the bands gave expression to what was already in the community. Hitler could never have won applause from these people; their music went on to win applause from Germans, even in the Third Reich.

Bands on foot, meeting, would blast away at each other until one gave up. And the winner, "the people, they'd rush up to it and give it drinks and food and holler for more." That "band was best that played the best together. No matter what kind of music it was, if the band could keep it together, that made it the best." If "a band could play numbers that weren't arranged . . . with a kind of inspired improvising—that was the band that would naturally win in the bucking contests." [13]

Sometimes social clubs parading behind twenty-piece bands would meet, the bands playing different pieces, and they'd march right through each other and as they began to separate "You'd hear mostly one band, so clear, so good, making you happy, sadder, whatever way it wanted you to feel." [14] It would still be playing together; the other would have slid toward chaos.

And the people could tell which band was best. How? As Bechet says, from the music inside themselves. "The music, it was the onliest thing that counted. The music, it was having a time for itself. It was moving. It was being free and natural." [15]

The music flamed up into its second stage with the band of

Buddy Bolden. Born in 1868, Bolden put his band together in the 1890's; by 1900 he had become a living legend. In 1907, he went berserk in a parade and was taken to the East Louisiana State Hospital where he was diagnosed as paranoiac and lingered on until 1931.

No newspaper reported his death.[16]

Bolden's band, although it mainly played blues, is honored as the world's first jazz band, a fact no doubt as long as we accept it symbolically. Out of this band came Willie G. "Bunk" Johnson and Edward "Kid" Ory, and, soon after Bolden left, Bechet and others. There is not much reliable information about the earliest days of jazz, but it would seem that Bolden built into the music of this band a new conception of the communal music of New Orleans, creating the large forms characteristic of jazz, forms accepted and refined by others. Bolden was the pure innovator, in the sense of Marx, Freud—his followers, innovative technicians.

Surprisingly, considering that they credit him with the precipitation of jazz, his contemporaries do not remember him as a great musician. It was rather his peerless irreverence and dedicated showmanship always aimed at making the audience happy that earned him his preëminence. There in tough New Orleans under the curse of racist violence his salty insouciance, his free spirit, and his raw-energy music brought status and respect to black people. His message before anyone had said it: Black Is Beautiful. To the Uncle Tom blacks of New Orleans, but recently freed from slavery, he seemed a man who had driven Uncle Tom from his soul and stood proudly facing the world as a do-not-give-a-damn life-lover devoid of any desire to turn bourgeois.

Tall, poised, with sloping broad shoulders and graceful movements, he was distinguished by natural *style*. To the pioneer trumpet player, Bunk Johnson, Buddy Bolden was "one fine-looking brown-skinned man, tall and slender and a terror to the ladies." [17] He was often to be seen with three women, always lovely but not always the same. Number One carried his cornet, Numbers Two and Three his coat and hat. Groupies from throughout the city were at him all the time, on occasions trying to tear his clothes off. Once, when leading his band at a dance, twenty women rioted for places nearest the stand. Habitually, women threw money to him wrapped in handkerchiefs and he would keep the money and throw back the

Louis Armstrong, Buddy St. Cyr, Walter Brundy, Buddy Johnson, Bunk Johnson, Peter Bocage, "Big Eye" Louis Nelson, Buddy Bolden, Brock Mumford.

handkerchiefs. Sometimes he would win the hearts of all by dedicating a tune to the ugliest woman in the place or by kissing her.

George Murphy "Pops" Foster, the great string bass player, tells us that in the early days music was a sideline, but never a profession. Foster and Louis Armstrong drove wagons and worked on the docks. For others, like pianist Ferdinand "Jelly Roll" Morton, the mainline was pimping. Bolden, by trade, was a barber. He often created new hair styles. As an adolescent, Bolden set type and, by watching printers, learned how to run a press. During his flush times, he published a scandal sheet, *The Cricket,* his reporter being a paid police informer willing to sell information twice.

Bolden, like many of the others, drank enormous quantities of whisky. We see him at the head of a parade playing and singing his scandalous tune, "I Thought I Heard Buddy Bolden Say," and the kids go home singing it:

> I thought I heard Buddy Bolden say,
> "Funky Butt, Funky Butt, take it away!"

Or, after checking the scene for white cops, he sings:

> I thought I heard Abe Lincoln say,
> "Rebels, close down them plantations and let all
>   them niggers out,
> "You gonna lose this war; git on your knees and pray,"
> That's the words I heard Mr. Lincoln say.

We hear his bandsmen shouting scatological insults at each other, one of the antics which won them distinction as the coarsest mouth in town. Buddy Bolden roared out the lyrics of his compositions, numbers like "If You Don't Like My Potatoes Why Do You Dig So Deep," or "All the Whores Like the Way I Ride." When stuffy bourgeois types meeting in some other part of the building asked him to quiet down, he liked to reply with his dirtiest songs at full volume, and both were legendary. According to Jelly Roll Morton, when Bolden wanted to fill Lincoln Park his cornet could be heard for twelve miles or more. Lincoln Park, a vast amusement park set aside for the colored, was always so much fun that half its customers were white. Bolden delighted in the hot sweaty press of humanity and he would happily shout from the stand: "My chillun's here; I know it cause I can smell 'em!" and then he might tell the band to quiet down so he could hear the whores dragging their feet. And then maybe he'd play "The Bucket's Got a Hole in It," and, as Louis Armstrong put it, "Some of them chicks would get way down, shake everything, slapping themselves on the cheek of their behind. Yeah!"[18]

This is his legend, the impression he made on the public. Can one doubt that he gave to the music a greatly expanded freedom and spontaneity? And, like so many of his successors, he paid the price, burning himself out before he was forty. But in those short years his impact on young and old alike was tremendous. Bolden bears the same relation to modern music, says Elliot Paul, as Chaucer does to English poetry.[19]

"Back then," says Foster, "everybody classified musicians as bums, which they were." Some were model family men, but to make a living even these had to be at the center of the action. As for others, Foster said of Bunk Johnson, "In those days the saloons never closed and Bunk never left the Eagle Saloon." He played there in Bolden's old group, the Eagle Band. He'd drink till he passed out and then sleep it off on a pool table, get up, and start drinking again. If we came along and wanted to shoot pool, we'd just lift Bunk off and lay him on a bench. Although unlike most of the others Johnson could read music, inspired innovation ruled him too. A leader once wrote down what Johnson had just played and asked him to play it again. Johnson looked it over and said, "Do you think I'm a fool? I can't play that."[20]

As one would imagine, the new music was too strong to accept confinement to New Orleans. Just as Missouri ragtime had done around 1900, New Orleans jazz (which everyone called ragtime, too —but it was band ragtime plus more) went out into the world and made a smashing sensation. Chicago millionaires coming to New Orleans had used Bolden's band as the hub of giant underworld parties. It, like many others, was heard by tourists. On riverboats, bands played as far away as Saint Paul. In 1912, Freddie Keppard's band went to San Francisco to build a show for the Orpheum Theater Circuit, thence in 1913 to Los Angeles, 1914 to Chicago, and in 1915 to New York, astounding audiences everywhere, for none had ever before heard anything like that. Because he feared corruption of the music by mass production and the profit motive—or, as Pops

Foster said, because he feared others would "steal his stuff"—Keppard refused to be recorded. So, in 1918, the Original Dixieland Jass Band—a white New Orleans band playing a pallid copy of the real music as interpreted by Joseph "Joe" Oliver—made the first recordings and introduced the music to America. Kid Ory's band went to the West Coast, Joe Oliver's to Chicago where it was joined by Louis Armstrong. In 1919 Omar's grandson, Sidney Bechet, went to London where he played a command performance for King George V. "Once we got started we had the whole royal family tapping its feet." And the King said what he'd enjoyed the most "was that blues, the Characteristic Blues."[21]

In 1920, Bechet went on to Paris to play in Montmartre.

New Orleans jazz became the craze of the twenties, fell out of favor in the swing era, and then, in 1943, in San Francisco, on the arrival of Bunk Johnson and the subsequent national network broadcasts of Kid Ory's group from Los Angeles, it enjoyed a worldwide revival. Johnson, the first member of his family to be born free, played with white sidemen, Lu Watters's band, and left behind him in Frisco Turk Murphy's band and the Studio Thirteen Dixieland Jass Band, an amateur group composed of artists, both of which bands still play. Other New Orleans style bands sprang up in the U.S., Britain, France, Poland, Italy, Sweden, Germany, Holland, Denmark—one there, Papa Bue's Viking Jazz Band, always appeared in horned helmets, beards, and full Viking dress. Armstrong, Bechet, George Lewis, and others took the music to all of the continents, playing to enthusiastic audiences. Bechet spent his last years in France and died there in 1959. Lewis, before his death in 1968, went to Japan three times and played everywhere, for millions. Armstrong, born on the Fourth of July, 1900, lived to play the "Saint Louis Blues" with the New York Philharmonic as sidemen and to return to his ancestral home in what is now Ghana to play to 100,000 frenzied Africans.

On his seventieth birthday, after listening to a record of one of his early solos, Satchmo said:

"Ain't nobody played nothing like it since, and can't nobody play nothing like it now." [22]

Nevertheless, New Orleans jazz, the blues, and their grandchildren Bop and Progressive, and the whole Rock family are alive and well and have inherited the earth.

Kid Ory and granddaughter in Frisco. *San Francisco Public Library*

The world capital of the international New Orleans jazz empire is San Francisco. As one jazz-lover puts it: "There's more traditional jazz being played in the San Francisco Bay Area in public for money than anywhere else in the United States—including New Orleans."

In concluding an obituary for Armstrong an Associated Press writer said: "Gabriel, move over." [23]

Louis Armstrong, the herald not of Jehovah but of Muntu, when deep into the music, surged with an intense sensation that everybody hearing it was his brother. In his lifetime he had seen the music of the despised New Orleans blacks take form and, partly as a result of his influence, grow from a local phenomenon into a deathless global force.

Sidney Bechet and others brought jazz to Germany in the twenties. Some of the many young Germans who loved it formed bands and played it as best they could. The Bauhaus had a jazz band in

1922. The Nazis denounced the music as the effluent of black submen. On coming to power they banned "jazz," but German bands began calling their music "swing" and kept on playing. British jazz bands came to Berlin regularly until the war.[24]

During the war, Hugues Pannassié and Madeleine Gautier (granddaughter of the long-haired youth who had defied the bourgeois larvae in the Battle of *Hernani*), acting from their refuge in Switzerland, helped to keep the international jazz movement alive in Europe and the jazz force working against the racist evil of the Black Order. By 1960, the music of black culture had become the music of whites in rebellion against white culture. It helped them select among the many contradictory voices in their heads and mute those they had been trained to hear while attending those they wanted to hear but had been taught to repress. The embourgeoised blacks detested black music as intensely as did the middle-class whites they were trying to copy. In it, the rest of the blacks found themselves. The analogous position of the black man in America to that of the white artist "gave a deeply native reference to the direction of American Bohemianism, or artists' life, of the fifties."[25]

When LeRoi Jones (Imamu Amiri Baraka) wrote these words in the early sixties it would have been difficult to foresee that ten years later black music would become the *Iliad* and the *Odyssey* of the rising generation, the common denominator of young America, and be well on the way to becoming that of young people everywhere.

> "I rather drink muddy water, Lord, sleep
> in a hollow log
> "Than be up here in New York, treated
> like a dirty dog."[26]

19.
The Mobile Bohemia
(1905-today)

In the early 1700's, while the French were running their slave-breaking camp in Louisiana, the freest men on earth were the French *coureurs-de-bois* (woods-runners), trappers and traders who ranged unrestrained through the magnificent cathedral of virgin forest extending from Quebec City to New Orleans, from the Alleghenies to the Ozarks and beyond.

The *coureurs,* always on friendly terms with the Indians, traveling alone or in small bands, embodied for Europeans the legend of the free spirit living free in the American West, a legend strong enough to dazzle men as diverse as Chateaubriand, Gautier, and Hitler.

In 1871 Jules Verne's *Around the World in Eighty Days* appeared in many countries as a serial, one building to an intense suspense, a romance diverting the French from the terrible tragedy of the Commune and, in its description of the trip across the American West on the new railroad, focusing European attention on the western epic as embodied in plainsmen, buffalo, and Indians.[1]

When, in 1887, the Wild West legend went to Europe in the flesh—the antelope, buffalo, elk, wild horses, trick riders, marksmen, Deadwood Stage, cowboys, and five score Indians of Buffalo Bill's Wild West Show—it transformed itself from woodsrunner to range-rider and won enthusiastic praise from monarchs and commoners alike. Before 1914, Wild West shows and western fiction —invented in San Francisco by Bret Harte—passed continuously through the European countries, pressing the legend ever deeper into the European mind, a process accelerated after the war by Western movies.[2]

In 1887, at the first royal command performance of the first Wild West show, a graceful horseman introduced the American flag while announcing that he carried it "as an emblem of peace and friendship to all the world." Queen Victoria rose from her seat and bowed. Then, as William F. "Buffalo Bill" Cody recalled, "the whole court party rose, the ladies bowed, the generals present saluted, and the English noblemen took off their hats. Then—we couldn't help it—but there arose such a genuine heart-stirring American yell from our company as seemed to shake the sky. For the first time in history, since the Declaration of Independence, a sovereign of Great Britain had saluted the star-spangled banner, and that banner was carried by a member of Buffalo Bill's Wild West!" [3]

At the turn of the century, in defiance of respectable society, this free spirit was what the Wandervögel struggled to embody and express, and it was from stories of the Wild West that they drew part of their sustenance as they sat around their campfires attending the voice of the forest.

In America the omnipresent Wild West shows and the news of their enthusiastic reception in Europe brought to Americans a consciousness of the romance of their own times and helped make it respectable for the arts to stop copying from European models.

Relatively speaking, the literary establishment of the East reflected polite Victorian and Continental themes. Much the same was true of music and the fine arts.

Frisco drew its inspiration from a different source.

The free spirit fusing with the free arts of the bohemian tradition is what the story of the Wild West's sophistication in San Francisco is all about.

Then, after being schooled and refined in the city, the free spirit broke loose to range once more.

It was in California that Bohemia first gained mobility, that it coalesced with the soul of the *coureur* and the cowboy, the mountain man and the hobo, that it became physical and at last broke loose from the city slums and went out to nature.

This first happened in 1905 when bohemians established themselves in a bower of idealized natural beauty at Carmel-by-the-Sea on the Monterey Peninsula, a hundred miles south of San Francisco.

Going West, a Hitchhiker's view. *Huck Pease*

Bohemians had once enjoyed a quasi-rural existence on Montmartre. Murger had moved to a country village and lived a gentleman's life at the center of a circle of sycophants. An art colony, at one time the host of Robert Louis Stevenson, had existed in Monterey; bohemians had long sought the exotic in faraway places, but Carmel was the first bohemian community to be established in the country.[4]

The Carmel story begins in San Francisco.

After Mark Twain and Bret Harte left San Francisco in the mid-1860's, its bohemian life subsided into lethargy. The other segments of the city thrived. The Barbary Coast, bordering China Town and centered on "Terrific" (Pacific) Street, grew into one of the wildest sin centers in the world, notorious because it was a wide-open People's Sin Center—the rich always have their pleasure domes. Here were addicts shooting cocaine and morphine with medicine droppers, whores of all kinds and sexes suited to any pocketbook or taste, vast concert saloons resembling the Moulin Rouge of Paris, and a host of other places, many of which set up drunks for rolling and the unwary for shanghaiing. The latter was sometimes accomplished by giving the victim a Miss Piggott Special: equal parts gin, whiskey, and brandy, mixed with opium—or more often by striking him down with a blackjack. A newsman styled the vicious adolescent gangs roaming the neighborhood during the seventies as "hoodlums" (possibly Muldoon spelled backward with an elevated n— more likely a derivative from the gang's signal to attack a victim: "huddle'em") and the word entered the language.[5]

The wild life of the Barbary Coast eventually expressed itself in the turkey trot, the Texas tommy, and other free-form dances reminiscent of the chahut and the cancan, dances that spread throughout America, replacing for the young the polite dances favored by their elders.

At the art school at the turn of the century, each winter the students produced a Mardi Gras Ball, resplendent with costumes, exuberant—climaxed at midnight by the crowning of the King and Queen of Bohemia.[6]

Frisco's fun-loving spirit contrasted sharply with the work-hard spirit found in all other American cities save New Orleans. In 1890, when thirsty, Frisco's 300,000 people could choose among 3,117 licensed drinking places and about two thousand illegal "blind tigers," which means everyone in town could be in a saloon at the same time.[7] Hedonistic Frisco—in many ways a city-state—was noted for its amenities and legitimate theaters—and wrathfully impeached by Mark Twain for its barbarous persecution of the Chinese. Despite the appalling racism held in common with the rest of EuroAmerica, its citizens celebrated their ethnic festivals: the Fourth of July, Columbus Day, the Oktoberfest, Saint Patrick's Day, Cinco de Mayo, Bastille Day, Hallowe'en, Bobby Burns' Birthday and, with its dragon parade and tempests of exploding firecrackers, Chinese New Year, and others still yet more arcane—composing in all a continuous round of celebrations obscuring ethnic lines and making visitors feel that Frisco was *en-fête* all the time.

Although some bohemians lived in remote places like Street-

Car Bohemia, a group of abandoned streetcars out at the ocean beach, their community established itself adjacent to the Barbary Coast, on Russian and Telegraph Hills, and in North Beach, "the Latin Quarter," where, in the manner of their Parisian contemporaries, they intermingled with the underworld. In the 1870's bohemian life centered around the Bohemian Club, a cenacle of newsmen and art types, which soon changed from a wild beer-drinking sandwich-eating spontaneous and rude bouzingo-style brotherhood into a snobbish retreat for millionaires. "It was apparent that the possession of talent, without money, would not support the club," wrote a charter member, and "it was decided that we should invite an element to join the club which the majority of the members held in contempt, namely men who had money as well as brains, but who were not, strictly speaking, Bohemians." The score of original members were "almost to a man, thorough Bohemians, blissfully indifferent to the value of money." They soon became embittered toward the army of newcomers brought in as a scam to pay the bills. In the 1970's, the annual outing of the Bohemian Club is an informal colloquium of the nation's master class. There, among the redwoods, the rich, famous, and powerful from all over America gather to have fun while making contacts and agreements, while planning tactics and strategy.[8]

In 1874, on its inception, the San Francisco School of Design (now the Art Institute) received from the French government a set of plaster casts of classical sculpture from the Louvre, a gift sent in recognition of the generous contribution San Franciscans had made to the fund set up to aid the sick and wounded of the Franco-Prussian War. A favorite local story relates that when on arrival it appeared that the arms of the Venus de Milo were missing the Chamber of Commerce sued Wells Fargo and collected damages!

Soon, students, carrying drawings taken from the casts, began arriving in Paris to study art. In the late eighties, they began coming back and formed the nucleus of an explosion of enthusiasm for the arts. This community of energy intent upon the arts probably qualifies as America's first true Bohemia, the Greenwich Village of World War I and the Harlem Renaissance coming later. Out of this community of energy grew a spirited revolt of the students against the authoritarian classicism of the School of Design. Out of it also came the prototype comic strip, and a number of celebrated poets, painters, sculptors, writers, printers, photographers, journalists and others bearing names such as Frank Gelett Burgess, Mary Austin, Arnold Genthe, Will Irwin, George Sterling, Ina Coolbrith, Edwin Markham, Gertrude Stein, Isadora Duncan, (John) Gutzon Borglum, John Griffith "Jack" London, and Frank Norris. Most of them defied the genteel tradition. Some of them, self-styled *les jeunes,* built one of the decade's best literary magazines, *The Lark.* Among other things, this magazine brought America to realize that Frisco is the cultural center of the West, put the Burgessisms "blurb" and "bromide" into the language, and set Burgess' purple cow loose on the world to craze the millions with its lunatic and relentless rhythm:

> I NEVER SAW A PURPLE COW
> I NEVER HOPE TO SEE ONE
> BUT I CAN TELL YOU ANYHOW
> I'D RATHER SEE THAN BE ONE.

He tried to call it back:

> Ah, yes, I wrote the "Purple Cow"——
> I'm Sorry, now, I wrote it;
> But I can tell you Anyhow
> I'll Kill you if you Quote it!

In 1897, tiring of *The Lark,* Burgess launched *Le Petit Journal des Refusées.* It was to be—and was—the *reductio ad absurdum* of the fad for fad magazines. As he wrote later in London, it could have happened nowhere but San Francisco, that small, compact city of tightly juxtaposed extremes and contradictions with its people "from every nation that travels," with its splendid views, its cable cars, its demonic romantic Philistines. Everything in the *Petit Journal* was said to have been thrice rejected by other magazines and was signed by women when in fact it was all written by Burgess. It was straight silly, not sly; it was total farce, fantastic rubbish, gaslit work, showing the results of late hours.

"We made borders of Goops, square trees and cubical suns, striped elephants and plaid hippopotami, architectural monstrosities, falling tears, lightning flashes and deformities unmentionable."

And all this was printed on wallpaper samples and presented

Drawing by Florence Lundborg

between trapezoidal covers and was quite as insane as the notorious mural Burgess and his friends painted around the walls of their favorite restaurant, Coppa's.[9]

Eventually, money, fame, adventure lured most of these young people away, mainly to New York. Advancing years tamed some of them. The terrible earthquake and fire of April 1906 razed their environment. It destroyed the central part of the city, some 514 blocks with 28,000 buildings. It left two-thirds of the population homeless. Not much remained of Frisco or Bohemia but their people and their spirit.

An outpost in Carmel stood ready to receive Bohemia's refugees.

The outpost had been established by George Sterling, a hawk-nosed and aging Apollo, a prospering realtor who wrote poetry on ferry boats while commuting back and forth from Oakland. Originally from Sag Harbor, influenced by trips through the Barbary Coast with Jack London, he had slipped from realty to poetry and become San Francisco's leading bohemian.[10]

Of this he observed:

"Any good mixer of convivial habits considers he has a right to be called a Bohemian. But that is not a valid claim. There are two elements, at least, that are essential to Bohemianism. The first is devotion or addiction to one or more of the Seven Arts; the other is poverty. Other factors suggest themselves: for instance, I like to think of my Bohemians as young, as radical in their outlook on art and life, as unconventional, and, though this is debatable, as dwellers in a city large enough to have the somewhat cruel atmosphere of all great cities."[11]

In 1905, enthusiastically supported by his wife, Sterling built a house in the woods near Carmel Mission and moved there with her. Probably he hoped to escape the booze and other-women that filled his life in Frisco, where, as he put it, he was "beat upon and semi-submerged by temptations to folly and luxury." His new home, he said in a letter to his mentor, Ambrose Bierce, afforded "a really magnificent view of the Carmel Valley and River, and of the wild and desolate mountains beyond them. I'm half a mile from the ocean (Carmel Bay), which is blue as a sapphire, and has usually a great surf; and I'm four miles from Monterey. Here a soft wind is always in the pines. It sounds like a distant surf, just as the surf sounds like a distant wind in the pine trees."[12]

At thirty-eight Sterling had determined to change his life by escaping to a place where he could wander alone in forests and on beaches, where he could sit naked in the sun and swim naked in the sea, where he could live in peace and write his poetry. For company he soon had his friends Mary Austin and Arnold Genthe, both of whom moved to Carmel shortly after he did.

Genthe, a young Ph.D. who had come from Prussia as a tutor, had in Frisco abandoned his academic vocation and painter's avocation in favor of photography. Dignified and reserved, marked with dueling scars, he soon developed a fashionable business in portraiture. An inner informality shows itself in the portaits; a genuine interest in the camera and its uses appears in his experiments with color film and in his pursuit of candid shots of life in the city. Outstanding among these are his photos of the catastrophic earthquake and fire that consumed everything he owned. Mary Austin wrote novels, good ones, often on feminist themes. Free-living, neurotic, homely, hair to her waist, considered eccentric even by her companions, she had a writing platform in a tree and while walking through the woods or the streets of Monterey often wore Grecian robes, possibly less for romantic reasons than to conceal a squat figure.

After the quake, more artists and writers settled among the pines of Carmel. They formed a bohemian community revolving around George Sterling and living on what they could get for their work. Because Carmel was a place where they could build a board-and-bat shack or rent a house for six dollars a month, where it was spring all the time, where fish and game abounded, the living was easy.

Sterling, Genthe, Mary Austin and the others liked to picnic on the beach, drinking Monterey dago red, roasting mussels and abalone, and occasionally, it would seem, smoking hashish.

They would pry the abalone off the rocks and then, seated around a driftwood fire, pound the meat for an hour or more to break the fibers and make it tender. It became their custom while doing this to sing the "Abalone Song," a ballad invented by Sterling for which they improvised new verse while pounding, while drinking wine, there, at home, in the woods, in restaurants and saloons:[13]

> Oh! some folks boast of quail on toast,
>   Because they think it's tony;
> But I'm content to owe my rent
>   And live on abalone.
>
> Some say that God is fat
>   Others say he's bony;
> But as for me I disagree
>   He resembles abalone.

The Carmelites—"the Bunch" as they called themselves—were radicals by inclination and, probably because of their elite college backgrounds, traditionals in the form if not in the content of their writing. Here, as everywhere else in Bohemia since the Hugolatry chanting around the flaming punch bowl dedicated itself to the Art God, the community scorned traditional Christianity. The Bunch liked to gather in a pagan grove Sterling had sanctified by nailing cow skulls to the trees. Despite Theodore Roosevelt's enthusiasm for the strenuous life and the profound effect the Wild West shows had on the American imagination, the bourgeoisie still regarded roughing it as coarse and sun tan as the mark of vulgarity. California had yet to make people body-conscious through its hedonistic sun-life of surf and beach.[14] The community of college professors that grew up in Carmel at this time stood aloof from the bohemians,

On Carmel Beach: Sterling, Austin, London, Jimmy Hopper.

even though the Bunch and its guests included many of the best writers in America. On first look, the Carmel experience seems a delightful, almost precious romantic idyll, an outdoor Doyenné, the *Bohème élégant* transplanted to the open spaces of the Wild West, in all an aesthetic paradise. But in the country the body thrives and the mind dies—the Bunch kept going away, to Frisco, New York, London, Paris, and coming back again. Over their Eden, Robinson Jeffers' hawk sailed brooding. Like Gérard de Nerval, the Sterlings and some of the others most often seen laughing carefree around driftwood fires eventually killed themselves.

For all of its aesthetic power, the magic of Carmel was not strong enough to save the Bunch any more than it had been to save the Indians who for thousands of years before them had roasted abalone over bonfires, only to be enslaved by the mission or dispersed and killed by the Americans. Both the Bunch and the next generation of bohemians, of which Robinson Jeffers is the symbol if not the center, determined to preserve Carmel unspoiled. Through the 1920's these bohemians successfully fought off the improvements so dear to most Americans. Carmel lived without factories, street numbers, or grass lawns. It had few telephones or cars, few radios, sidewalks, door locks, street lamps, or paved streets, and it detested business of all kinds. Outside the post office stood an old oil drum marked as a receptacle for rejected manuscripts. In tandem with Chicago, the Bunch organized the Little Theater movement. By 1935, a bookstore was exhibiting 200 books by local authors. In this hedonistic community, Aimée Semple McPherson, the pop evangelist, built herself a love nest. Robinson Jeffers, a poet of the highest quality, with his own hands built a stone castle.

In Carmel, the idealized beauty soon attracted more realtors and others lusting for profit. This passion was intensified in the 1920's by news of the big money that realtors were making off the romantic reputation of Greenwich Village. On the platform of "DON'T BOOST, Keep Carmel off the Map," the art types united politically, winning the local offices and holding back the greedy moneymen in a Mexican standoff. But the Carmelites themselves embodied the detested enemy. Under their aegis, hip capitalism in the form of tearooms and shoppes took root along Ocean Avenue. Hip realtors came next, to be followed in World War II by Southern racists in the military.[15] The Carmel of the 1970's is peopled mainly by what the kids call reptiles: retired colonels, greedy businessmen, coupon clippers, remittance men, social climbers, society artists, blue-haired women, tourists in Bermuda shorts. The beach remains unspoiled, but the buildings look as if made by cookie cutters and are in perfect aesthetic harmony with the clipped poodles. As John Steinbeck put it in 1961:

"And Carmel, begun by starveling writers and unwanted painters is now a community of the well-to-do and the retired. If Carmel's founders should return, they could not afford to live there, but it wouldn't go that far. They would be instantly picked up as suspicious characters and deported over the city line."[16]

Although in part rhetorical, for, like the Doyenné bohemians, the Bunch and their friends came mainly from wealthy and well-connected families, in substance Steinbeck's statement is true. A city that provides a special sand vehicle for police patrol of the beach allows but scant room for the free spirit. Despite the triumph of creeping embourgeoisement, of the eventual suppression of the very qualities that made it famous, the original Carmel lasted long enough to create both in fact and in romance a new model of what Bohemia might and ought to be.

In San Francisco, after the fire and earthquake of 1906, Bohemia was resurrected from the ashes in its old location. It contributed to the general strike of 1934 and to the W.P.A. art projects but it did not recover intensity and purpose until after World War II.

In the middle 1940's came the revival of New Orleans music and the constitution of the United Nations; in the late 1940's bohemians helped to build KPFA, an early commercial-free radio station, and artists in San Francisco and New York developed abstract expressionism—an accomplishment said to have set American painting free of subservience to European models and placed it in the lead of Western art. Concurrently, local youth shared in the inspiration kindled by the university community's series of marvellous advances in microphysics and biochemistry. Not the least of these, the bubble chamber (as the story goes), was inspired by the behavior of beer in a quart bottle standing on the floor at a Berkeley party. Among the new elements synthesized in the Bay Area were Cf251 and Bk247, Californium—and Berkelium!

Out of this milieu in the middle 1950's grew what has been called the San Francisco Renaissance, the beat Bohemia of North Beach, and an innovation in bohemian style—mobility.[17]

Long ago, the *coureurs-de-bois* had been the freest men on the continent. Now, plowed, fenced, built-up, what once had belonged to all had since been deeded to a myriad of jealous owners. Woods-running was constricted to public parks and constrained by forest police. Head down, wounded by the picadors but vital still, the Spirit of Liberty went along beside the hobo on highway and railway. It sang through Joe Hill (Joel Emanuel Hägglund) and Pete Seeger. It sang through Woodrow Wilson "Woody" Guthrie:

> My daddy is an engineer,
> My brother drives a hack,
> My sister takes in washing,
> And the baby balls the jack,
> And it looks like I'm
> Never gonna cease my wanderin'.
>
> I been wandering
> Early and late

From New York City
To the Golden Gate
And it looks like I'm
Never gonna wander on home.

The Wandervögel had modeled themselves in part on German hobos they encountered on their travels, but they themselves were only on the periphery of the developing bohemian tradition. It was in San Francisco that the tradition fused with that of the hobos, mainly because what appears as Wild West when seen from a distance looks like the hobo tradition when seen up close. The appeal of both is a complex of wanderlust, open spaces, free spirit, and Huck Finn lighting out for the Territories. Bohemia and the hobo tradition were formally engaged in 1905 when Jack London published *The Road,* the first book ever written by a first-class American writer about hobo life seen from the inside.

"I was first a road-kid then a profesh ... the profesh are the aristocracy of The Road. They are the lords and masters, the aggressive men, the primordial noblemen, the *blond-beasts* so beloved of Nietzsche." I was "in the pit, the abyss, the human cesspool, the shambles and charnel house of our civilization." A hard life, dangerous, painful, humiliating, free—anything but bourgeois, snow and sun on the endless track: the Katy, Wabash and Espee; side-door Pullmans, blinds and rods; Wobblies and bindle-stiffs, bulls and jungles, jails and Mulligan stew: 1915, lit with sentiment by Charley Chaplin's movie *The Tramp*—1915, radiating purpose as Joe Hill, soon to be executed by firing squad, writes to an admirer "I have lived like an artist and I shall die like an artist."[18]

"Don't waste any time in mourning. Organize!"[19]

Between 1930 and 1935, a half million young tramps, mainly farm boys, follow the roads and rails, impelled as much by mass unemployment as by the romantic quest for the Big Rock Candy Mountain or for the intense life of a high-energy perilbalance.[20]

In his book *On the Road,* written between 1948 and 1956, Jean Louis Lebris "Jack" de Kerouac, a New Englander of French-Canadian origins, wove the hobo yearning into the style of Bohemia. Born too late to be a *coureur-de-bois,* Jack Kerouac became a *coureur-des-vois*—a road runner—a vagabond of the road and of prose.[21] Almost as soon as the Kerouac cenacle moved from New York to Frisco

it became the center of a community that it precipitated and energized and for which it spoke. This community in turn became the central station in a series of Bohemias. Via 29 Palms, Venice, Claremont, Santa Barbara, Big Sur, the Monterey Peninsula, Santa Cruz, Palo Alto, Frisco-Berkeley, Marin, Mendocino, Eugene, Portland, Seattle, the network runs from Mexico to Vancouver and Alaska; via other stations it runs from Frisco to Chicago, Cambridge and New York, London, Paris, Tangier—in all an underground railroad connecting a series of stations and terminals—some on the Paris models, some on the Carmel model—through which, hitching, driving, riding in boxcars, the same population flowed and flows.

No longer did Bohemia cleave to a single slum and make occasional trips to the country for fresh air.

California established it in the country; the Beats put it on wheels.

And from this mobile position the newly mustered Beat Corps of the Romantic Army pressed the fight for free art and the free spirit.

The corps took its name from black argot where *beat* means exhausted.

For weapons it used life-style and outrageous poetry.

In the late 1940's, young Americans began wearing Levis in

preference to more formal clothing, doing so partly because their comfortable old military clothes had worn out, partly because they increasingly scorned the bourgeois uniform and partly because they liked the style of the ancient clothes of the Wild West, still manufactured by Levi Strauss, Inc., in San Francisco. In Paris, fertilized by existentialism, beards began growing on young Yanks, sometimes thriving so mightily as to survive the trip home. These and other elements the Beats brought together in a style defiant of the well-groomed bodies and minds of the bourgeois in both business and academy.

The Beats are literary. They invented the paperback bookstore. They make poetry and novels—albeit on the theme of *épatez les bourgeois*—not fine art and music. They associate with artists and listen to folk songs and jazz, but never dance. They smoke dope but favor wine. They would free both form and diction from all tradition, release free-flow poetry and prose, make *cunt* and *fuck* respectable. Closer to thirty than to twenty, they are a morose and humorless lot, typically apolitical. They are literary, hence, voyeurs, and they watch themselves nourishing souls lamed by the city, scarred by the bourgeois, distorted by machismo, hamstrung by too much dope and booze. They see life as a Manichaean struggle between Hip and Square. When at their best, in true hobo style they make no compromise with the established order and its values. Believing you have to get dirty to stay clean, they suffer the consequences and seek solace in pop-Buddhism. Seeing no hope for mankind but rejecting participation in his destruction, they live for the day. They are Jules Vallès' refractories reincarnate; they radiate a gray energy Karma and find Satori in bed with groupies, sometimes boys, groupies whose language was typically North Beach no-speak.

"Well, like, uh, man, that like wigs me."

The hub of their wheel was and is composed of poets, around which revolve novelists and at whose rim glows a garish stripe of poet-showmen—in pure form, Lenny Bruce; in affected form, Allen Ginsberg. In the mirror, they see Baudelaire, Verlaine, Rimbaud. They claim Dada as their blood type, but the blood is now degenerate—the Beat dada is not one of spontaneous discovery but of imitation, NEODADA—Dada *à la mode.*

Tristan Tzara cut-up long before William Burroughs.

What *is* new, what *is* happening spontaneously, coming out of

North Beach tours Squaresville. *San Francisco Public Library*

real experience, is not the refractory Bohemia of the paraParisian community in the Co-Existence Bagel Shops and pads of North Beach—an ambiance quickly defaced by commercial exploitation— but the quality of mobility, the hobo-poet communities strung out along the roads and tracks. Concurrently, the Beat movement gave a center and a legitimacy to Wild West poetry, to the crude, rebel, democratic literature erected in defiance of the East Coast's polite tradition and effete literati.[22]

This brings us back to Kerouac, the man whose books set the style of the communities and fixed a primal influence in the mind of romantic youth throughout America. In his books, Kerouac, a tough-looking but handsome son of the New England slums, gave joyful celebration to the disreputable voices whispering in the minds of those inclined to adventure, voices ordinarily reviled and suppressed by bourgeois authority, particularly in the timid and conventional 1950's. Kerouac's road books jumped into the middle of the caution-preaching authorities and began yelling at youth: There's gotta be more and there is! Go find it! Live, baby, live! ... Exuberant, they tell of Kerouac's trips back and forth across the country, Kerouac constantly being pressed to surpass his ultimate of daring by the crazed and demonic Neal Cassady. They tell of mad boozathons and Mexican brothels, of stolen cars and skid roads, of marijuana magic and the majestic beauties of this vast continent, of outdoor decadents, Times Square hustlers, Denver broads, Frisco jazz maniacs, all of them beads on a rubber band stretched by Cadillacs going 120 mph.

After moulting his academic training, Kerouac tried to make his writing as spontaneous as his trips, to blow jazz solos on the typewriter. Like, uh, holding the feeling in mind let the words rush out constrained only by the sense of substance, a projection undisciplined, a mind-film unedited, let it flash down onto an endless roll of United Press teletype paper. "I don't make any corrections. Everything's down there just the way I want it." *On the Road.* And the others too. Rambling, manuscripts in seabag, this wanderbird writes wherever he stops—a paragraph in Nebraska, a chapter in Mexico, rememberances "written on the run." Kerouac. Tough Kerouac. Down-home drifter, eighty-percent adventurer, takes the bus when hitching gets hard, sends home for money when despairing, and goes from youth through forty without changing at all. There's nothing so romantic as a young bum, nothing so revolting as an old one. Intense energy-rushes through marshes of guilt—undaunted life-lover daunted at last, road running through fame and booze to death.[23]

And the hippies? How do they relate to the Beats?

"Of course they followed us in certain ways," said Kerouac.

Yet, in other ways, they had different ways, ways Kerouac neither liked nor understood.

"But anyhow," says Kerouac, "one thing I wanted to say—I want to make this very clear. I mean, here I am, a guy who was a railroad brakeman, and a cowboy, and a football player—just a lot of things ordinary guys do. And I wasn't trying to create any kind of new consciousness or anything like that. We didn't have a whole lot of heavy abstract thoughts. We were just a bunch of guys who were out trying to get laid."[24]

If the Beats with their literary orientation are the fathers of the hippies (and we don't object to admitting incest to this metaphor), the Folk-Song Movement, elder sister of the Beats, is their mother, and their teachers are Jazz-Blues and Liberated Fine Arts.

Unlike the Beats, who had their scenes and their rituals and their sense of cohesive identity, the folk-song movement shows scarcely any structure at all save that provided by Woody Guthrie and others who injected people's music into the labor movement, an innovation said to have been made by Joe Hill of the IWW just before and during Word War I.[25]

Next comes Pete Seeger.

Peter Seeger on the *Clearwater. John Putnam*

In 1938, Pete Seeger quit Harvard when he ran out of money. A solitary Wandervogel, banjo on his back, he hitched around the country. Playing "in saloons, churches, on corners and back porches," learning new songs and riffs, he visited each of the forty-eight states. "Painstakingly," as he put it, he "transcribed songs note by note from Library of Congress records" because, excepting a few nineteenth-century adaptations of European music, "there was nothing printed for the five-string banjo back in thirty-eight." Eventually, he changed the instrument itself by extending the neck. "There's nothing like traveling the country broke—you're forced to meet people, make friends. I used to be shy." He got money for his music; he knocked on back doors; he "did anything for food."

"The history of the U.S. is told in folk songs. Read between the lines and you can see the life of the people in those days. The pioneer women dragged out on the lonely prairie. Or the slave. It took the heroism of a whole people to build this country. People tend to forget that now, but sometimes the old songs get them to see it."[26]

Out of this came his banjo book, mimeographed in 1948, an underground classic of the folk-song movement.

The folk-song movement itself emerged circa 1947 as a mutiny of middle-class youth against the dreary prospect of a personal future like that embodied in their split-level mothers and fathers. Superficially, it appears as an aggregate of musical hoboes roaming carefree through slum and countryside, drinking beer and wine by the roadside, hitchhiking, playing guitars and banjos, sensually free, apolitical, independent, stopping as Bob (Samuel R.) Gibson did once by a split-railfence to sing and play to a cow,[27] associating with beatniks but representing something else, young, spontaneous, content without intent.

In fact, though such was its style, and its hard core, the mass of those suffused by the field of the movement lived ordinary bourgeois lives, except when they retired to their rooms and songbooks to sing and to play.

Although of much greater magnitude than the beatnik movement, and of large covert influence, the folk-song movement was almost invisible. It never thought of itself as a movement; it urged no ideology. Where apparent to bourgeois America, be it at the Gate of Horn in Chicago, the Abbaye in Paris, or as Weavers' selections on every jukebox in America, it looked like a facet of commercial entertainment. When appearing at the center of college parties or even in the Sunday afternoon gatherings at Washington Square in the Village,[28] it seemed to signify nothing more than commercial entertainment in embryo.

Washington Square, 1953. *Richard Miller*

Here, though invisible except in booming guitar and banjo sales, was a genuine youth movement rising spontaneously out of America's past/present, conscious of no significance more abstruse than affirmation of the free spirit, hating no one, open to everyone who'd sing along or just sit and listen and let the good times roll.

In the long view, one can see these thousands of young folk singers as the American Wandervögel, wandering more in fantasy than in fact, as Wandervögel growing not from the soil of a nouveau-riche and paranoiac feudal-military empire, but out of the suffering and self-confidence, the despair and the dreams of the common man's America. It shows the same völkisch orientation as the Wandervogel, but an American völkischness, the völkischness of the melting pot, its repertoire of songs being a chemical analysis of all the elements of which the American alloy is composed[29]—a purified alloy, for missing from this metal is the dross of the bourgeoisie:

Songs about seamen:
> Oh the banks are made of marble,
> With a guard at every door,
> And the vaults are stuffed with silver
> That the seaman sweated for,[30]

But who ever heard a folk song about a banker, or an office manager, or an adman?

We have no folk songs about Hindus or East Asians either. Nevertheless, the repertoire, alloyed as it is of Black/Celtic/Latin/Semitic/Nordic/Slavic and more, in all of their isotopes, and in their völkisch state, is anything but monocultural.

In 1945, Louis Adamic perceived that America stood at a fork in the road of diverging traditions—either it would become a WASP culture, built entirely around a single set of standards and values, or a pluralistic culture, patterned by its polyglot heritage.[31]

By singing America's origins, the folk-song movement helped to break the bourgeois bias against the bourgeois' own peasant/craftsman/outlaw past; beyond this, it helped steer the generation now in power down the cosmopolitan road, the road to which the generation now coming to power is completely committed.

Bourgeois values demonstrate an envy of the aristocracy; they also demonstrate renouncement of the crude, raw, submissive and ignorant ways of the traditional poor. In returning to their origins, both the Wandervogel and the folk singer brought with them the expanded consciousness and refined sensibilities of the middle classes. In compounding with the traditional ways, this broader awareness created something new, bearing quite another meaning than traditional völkisch values have when left to themselves. What is conventionally called *völkisch* is in fact *neo*völkisch. Unlike German neovölkischness, with its implicit racism, the American variety by definition excludes racism and consequently forms the prototype of a basic pattern of the worldwide culture of the coming century.

As Pete Seeger put it back in 1953:

"Something old is creating something new—a new idiom. It won't be just Anglo-American, but be a brand new folk tradition containing contributions from many lands."

"I'll tune up my fiddle, I'll resin my bow;

"I'll make myself welcome wherever I go." [32]

On reading these pages in 1975, Pete Seeger wrote, "Directly or indirectly I have always hoped my music could help build a new socialist world society." He then added: "I feel strongly now that Woody and I either praised the traveler too much, or didn't praise the stay-at-home enough." [33]

This is because, as he wrote elsewhere, the job is to "save each neighborhood of the world," a job only to be done by people who stay home and work at it.[34]

20.
Bohemia
in Transformation
(1955-1965)

The story of Bohemia is both the story of the development of an aesthetic consciousness subsuming an aesthetic ethic and that of the growth in phalanxlike communities of the protoculture. Once limited to Paris, the bohemian experience has now suffused youth everywhere, presenting an alternative to the fatal predominance of Technological Man and, consequently, offering hope for the future.

The protoculture and its mentality derive in part from the Harlem Renaissance.[1]

In the early 1920's, thrill-seeking whites began flowing to Harlem to hear jazz and to dance the Charleston at famous nightspots like the Cotton Club (which barred black clients) and the Savoy Ballroom where Fletcher Henderson was developing the big-band sound. Throughout the 1920's, nigger-watching was in style. Books by and about blacks enjoyed a long vogue. At least one play with a black cast could always be seen on Broadway. Ethel Barrymore, acting in *Scarlet Sister Mary,* appeared in blackface. Black artists and writers gained admission to the international art set—blacks were to be seen at most chichi artistic parties. Out of this came a precious group of bourgeois white-blacks, living in Harlem still because Jim Crow wouldn't let them live anywhere else, constituting in all what one black called the "niggerati."[2]

For the first time, blacks had become romantic to whites. Concurrently, in the Harlem community, blacks were losing their awe of whites.

These niggerati are the conventional referent of "Harlem Renaissance." In fact, the niggerati were but lily pads floating on the surface. The waters themselves represent a different phenomenon. Blacks were coming to Harlem from everywhere. In Harlem concentrated most of the distinguished jazz musicians and most of the young blacks with developed artistic aspirations. In almost every case, these young aspirants, under the pressure of hard necessity, lived bohemian lives often expanding far across the line dividing Bohemia from its traditional neighbor, the underworld.

"When you passed over 110th Street it was like zooming off to another planet where they didn't build any brick walls between wanting and doing, the urge and the act. People up there, even the kids, led full and functioning lives, no matter how heavy a ball of oppression they carried around their necks, so they weren't walking skinfuls of repression and they didn't mope around having sex flashes every hour on the hour." [3]

The real Harlem Renaissance ... ?:

"The kids who grew up in Northern cities wouldn't have any more of that kneebending and kowtowing." Some of them "had creative abilities you could hardly match anywhere else. Once they tore off the soul-destroying straitjacket of Uncle Tomism, those talents and creative energies just busted out all over. These kids weren't schooled to use their gifts in any regular ways. So their artistry and spirit romped out into their language." Their "sophistication didn't come out of moldy books and dicty colleges." It "bubbled up out of the brute scramble and sweat of living. If it came out a little too raw and strong for your stomach, that's because you been used to a more refined diet."

"You know who they were, all these fast-talking kids with their four-dimensional surrealistic patter? I found out they were the cream of the race—the professionals of Harlem who never got within reaching distance of a white collar." They "held their office hours and made their speeches on The Corner. There they wrote their prose poems, painted their word pictures."

"Spawned in a social vacuum and hung up in mid-air, they were beginning to build their own culture. Their language was a declaration of independence." [4]

And the guy they looked up to?

That cat "is *hip,* like a guy who carries a bottle or a bankroll or, more likely, a gun on his hip," a guy who "can take care of himself in any situation." He's *"righteous,* in the Biblical sense of having justice on your side, and he's *ready,* like a boxer poised to take on all comers, and he's *really in there,* as a prizefighter wades into the thick of it instead of running away from his opponent; he really *comes on,* like a performer making his entrance on the stage, full of self-confidence and self-control, aware of his own talents and his ability to use them; or he really *gets off,* that is, is so capable of expressing himself fully that he gets the load of oppression off." He's *groovy,* "the way musicians are groovy when they pool their talents instead of competing with each other, work together and all slip into the same groove." [5]

These reflections—written in the middle 1940's about the late 1920's—are those of a man who introduced a superior marijuana to Harlem. And that man was white! Milton "Mezz" Mezzrow came out of Chicago via white bands which found indirect inspiration in H. L. Mencken "yelling the same message in his magazine that we were trying to get across in our music" [6] and drew direct inspiration from the great black artists of Chicago jazz.

It's men like Mezzrow, not Kerouac, who are the protohippies. Mezzrow is one of the first whites who tried to become black—not in affectation but in deep substance. What was to him a triumph came in a New York jail when after insisting he was black he got himself locked up not with his fellow whites but with the blacks. Of the 1940's in Harlem, Malcolm X said: "A few of the white men around Harlem, younger ones whom we called 'hippies,' acted more Negro than Negroes." [7]

This tendency was to lie latent for twenty years more. Its activation begins with the train of events initiated by . . . . But let the black poet Langston Hughes tell it:
"To Rosa Parks of Montgomery

> who started it all when,
> on being ordered to get up and
> stand at the back of the bus
> where there were no seats left,
> she said simply. "My feet are
> tired," and did not move, thus
> setting off in 1955 the boy-
> cotts, the sit-ins, the Free-

dom Rides, the petitions, the
marches, the voter registtration
drives, and I Shall Not Be
Moved.[8]

The Montgomery bus boycott and subsequent events caused the formation here and there across the country of civil-rights support groups, mainly among students, and attracted the attention of the House of Representatives' Un-American Activities Committee. When, in May 1960, this group held hearings in San Francisco City Hall, the song "We Shall Not Be Moved" burst into a new context. During a large shouting protest outside the hearing room and upon seeing police coming in the front door to drive them away, the protesters—students from Berkeley, Frisco, Stanford—sat down on the foyer floor and the marble steps leading up to it and locked arms. There, under the vast ornamented dome of City Hall, shouting "Abolish! That! Committee!," singing "We Shall Not Be Moved," some 250 of them defied a police order to disperse. While clubbing some, the police battered the rest with water from fire hoses and drove most of them away, but not all. These refractories they pried loose from their fellows and led off or dragged down the stairs by the heels, heads bouncing on the marble.

In all, the police arrested 64 people, including the granddaughter of Albert Einstein.

In response to this outrage, the next day some five thousand young people including the heirs of three English lords picketed City Hall.

No one could remember young people in America ever having done anything like that before.[9]

Here was a new and unsuspected development. The Apathetic Generation had transmuted. American youth had become defiant and political.

Becoming ever more active, the student elite began disassociating from the established order. Learning now what the blacks had always known, white youth began to see through the American myth to the truth. Ours is not a humane society with liberty and justice for all. We have the ideal, and that is unique, but in contrast to the ideal, America appears corrupt, repressive, racist, and brutal. In the fall of 1964, the youth rebellion flamed off into a second stage. In response to the University of California's decision to remove support tables for the Civil Rights Movement from Sproul Plaza on the Berkeley campus, police arrested a worker who refused to move his table. About 2,000 students trapped the police car right on the spot, using their bodies to prevent it from carrying off their comrade, now locked inside. Students climbed to the top of the car, made speeches, sang, and played guitars. Some old-left types tried to bully the students into kicking in the doors of Sproul Hall, into smashing the car, assaulting the cops. The students affably declined. Here was a new phenomenon: two thousand people in an extremely emotional situation composing not a mob nor yet even a crowd but a congress of self-contained individuals. The next day, in hopes of freeing the car, fraternity goon squads appeared, only to be driven off in confusion by girls who confronted them and called them names like "shithead," "cocksucker," and "motherfucker,"[10] an effective weapon in those far-off days when counterfeit chivalry was still conventional.

The police-car episode escalated when, in defiance of the university, student-spokesman Mario Savio began speaking from the steps of Sproul Hall to vast crowds of students. The sit-in at Sproul Hall quickly followed, then mass arrests. This, the Free Speech Movement, an inspiration of the French Revolution of 1968, was the precipitating event in the youth insurrection soon to be in progress everywhere.

Significant—astounding—as all this was, by later standards the life-style of these early student activists with their short hair, ties, sweaters, and traditional folk music seems downright archaic.

Concurrently, a new life-style was developing among Bay Area art students and bohemians around rock music, a black/white idiom popularized by the Beatles, together with the new city folk music of Richard Fariña, Joan Baez, and Bobby Dylan—a folk music not speaking of a pastoral eighteenth century *then* but of an asphalt urban *now*.

The Beatles with their scandalous long hair and their happy insouciance and their screaming electric guitars filled the air with a wild Dionysian joy. Joan Baez sang songs resonating with stunning beauty a feeling epidemic among the young, generated by the terrible and suddenly evident contrast between what things are and what they could be. Dylan broadcast a hard-edged surrealistic poetry of the nameless adolescent rolling stone on the city streets. To-

Oakland jail after the sit-in. *San Francisco Public Library*

gether they shocked the young art types into euphoria and bourgeois America into catatonic rage. In Berkeley in what the press
called the Foul Speech Movement, a young poet was busted for reading a fuck-poem in public—and an old Baltimore labor leader and
saloonkeeper started the *Berkeley Barb*, which specializes in tough
radical news and ads for hookers, male and female. In Oakland, a
tough and angry black, Huey Newton, formed an armed self-defense
league against the police: the Black Panthers. In Frisco, radicals began producing the magazine *Ramparts*; Broadway area promoters

began presenting topless dancers; the voters staged a successful free-way revolt. Everywhere, young people began picketing markets and liquor stories in the interests of Cesar Chavez's farm workers' union. Adjacent to Golden Gate Park, in an area of Victorian townhouses then regarded as a model of integration, Jefferson Fuck Poland—he had legally changed his middle name—rented a store on Haight Street to serve as headquarters for his Sexual Freedom League. He thus called attention to the low-profile but flourishing bohemian community there, one composed mainly of art students and refugees from the anti-Beatnik pogrom being conducted by city police in North Beach.[11] In North Beach some friends joined together in an electric band they called the Byrds. Because the Bay Area has long had an infrastructure of small clubs offering sophisticated live music, often by the great black musicians, young people have long found the inspiration, money, and audiences necessary to developing both themselves and the music. Consequently, the Byrds found a place to play as did The Great Society and others.

Like black culture in America, bohemian culture everywhere has always been partly underground and has always Uncle-Tommed Mr. Charley about what it's really up to. For many years, artists, art students, and other bohemian types have smoked hashish and mari-juana, explored amphetamines and heroin. In 1955, as soon as Al-dous Huxley's *The Doors of Perception* appeared, people in Frisco entered them. As early as 1961, Bohemia knew about LSD.

In the middle 1960's in the San Francisco Bay Area, the bohe-mian culture began to rise above ground showing more and more of itself—eventually to mutate and suffuse through American youth.[12]

Why did this first happen in the Bay Area?

In the Bay Area, as nowhere else, the media were open to trans-mitting a sense of what's really happening locally and thence via the national and foreign media to the world. Radio station KPFA and the students' *Daily Californian* and *The Daily Gater* rallied the forces that disrupted the hearings at City Hall in 1960—and enough of the truth of what had happened was printed in the *Chronicle* along with a full front-page photo larger than any photo anyone had ever seen on a front page before and reminiscent of the Odessa Steps, to bring five thousand people to picket City Hall next day. These people were in turn protected from police attack by their numbers and by newsmen from as far off as Japan. There were the infrastructures of clubs for musicians, large black communities, *The People's World* and *The Berkeley Barb*, *Ramparts* and *The Express-Times* (*Good Times*) and *The Rolling Stone*, black radio stations, listener-supported radio and tv, a pamphleteering and poster tradition. There were a strong labor movement, a large community of artists, writers, and film makers, substantial Italian, Irish, and Japanese communities, America's largest Indian, Latino, and Chinese communities, the San Francisco Mime Troop doing commedia dell'arte free in the parks,[13] and influential disc jockeys like Russ "The Moose" Syracuse and Don Sherwood with his crusade for justice for the Navajo.

The Bay Area is graced by the presence of two distinguished universities, the prerequisite of their accomplishments being popular support and a tough commitment to academic freedom. And there is San Francisco's flamboyant, hedonistic, artistic, and free-swinging Wild West tradition, dating from the Gold Rush.

This all gains significance in the proportion of Western culture. In the same sense that the United States compared to Europe embodies the future, California relative to the rest of the United States embodies the future. California experiments; the successful experiments cross the Rockies and the Middle West assimilates them to America. If, as Gertrude Stein wrote, America is the oldest country in the world, by the same reasoning either San Francisco or Los Angeles (or maybe both) is the oldest city. This is part of what the French writer Jean-François Revel has in mind when in his book *Without Marx or Jesus* he says the revolution is happening in the United States and can only happen in the United States. It made a strong impression on William Burroughs when on returning to the U.S. after years abroad he wrote, "I don't think there is any country where dissent is so widespread or where dissent has a better chance of effecting basic changes."[14]

In San Francisco, toward the end of 1965, the last step on the road to mutation was taken when two couples calling themselves The Family Dog decided to combine electric music with light machines and give kids a chance to dance as they had during the vanished big-band era. In response to the question: why did you pick San Francisco? one of the women said: "San Francisco is the only city in the U.S. which can support a scene. New York is too large and too confused and Los Angeles is superuptite plastic America."[15]

Berkeley, 1965. *San Francisco Public Library*

Saturday, 16 October 1965, several things began moving at once. After assembling on the Berkeley campus, listening to radical speakers, a poetry reading, and a crazed performance by Ken Kesey and his Merry Pranksters, 15,000 people moved off under the blessing of an amplified mantra chant in a march on the Oakland Army Base whence so many of their brothers had sailed away to war. With them walked the Mime Troop's Gorilla Band, looking like a surrealistic Spirit of '76, playing cracked patriotic airs, and on a flatbed truck rode a rock band soon to be known as Country Joe and the Fish. A contingent in the center sang Beatle songs. At the Oakland border, the march confronted a mass of white-helmeted armed police and truculent Hell's Angels. Push through and attack the base or turn? After a bitter quarrel, in a decision of the utmost significance, the leaders decided to turn. The parade went back into Berkeley to Provo Park and dispersed.[16]

The same day the Family Dog's dance took place in Longshoremen's Hall—the home of the I.L.W.U., a union born in Frisco in 1934 out of the general strike—a new building looking like an inverted concrete umbrella. The Dog called their dance a Tribute to Dr. Strange, invoking the pantheon of Marvel Comics, the classical mythology of their generation.

The light show was crude and the music bad. But that did not matter. From everywhere came the people, much to their surprise, in accumulation, forming a group of costumed maniacs so bright and wild that the Hell's Angels circulated unnoticed. And they danced. They all looked like Frontier Days, Wild West, as did the Charlatans, Frisco's first rock band, which that summer had made its living at the Red Dog Saloon in Virginia City, Nevada. And it wasn't the foreplay of ballroom dancing, but feral spontaneous expressive dancing, and it went on all night. The Jefferson Airplane —named for the black musician "Blind" Lemon Jefferson—and some of the other bands on finishing their sets went across town to play in a loft at the Mime Troop's benefit. When the crowd spread out into the street the police shut down the party.

Both dances made money and pleased their customers.

Rock dances began happening elsewhere. The Beatles came to the Cow Palace and Dylan played four concerts with The Band, giving rock music increased popularity and a local claim to sophistication.

On 10 December the Mime Troop held another benefit at an old auditorium in the black ghetto—the Fillmore. Some 3,500 people paid $1.50 each to get in.

This seized the attention of showbiz promoters.

Here for love, there for money, rock dances appeared all over the Bay Area. With as many as six big dances on a weekend, the Charlatans, the Airplane, Sopwith Camel, Big Brother & the Holding Company, Mystery Trend, Country Joe, the Great Society, The Grateful Dead, Quicksilver Messenger Service, and many others found plenty to do—and sometimes did it so well as to shift the dancers into a music metabolism. On 3 January 1966, the first head shop—

the Psychedelic Shop—opened on Haight Street, giving the burgeon-ing contingents of dopers and bohemians a center and a focus.[17]

By that time everything was ready for mutation. The process had begun. Bay Area youth already had an altered mentality and sensibility. All that was needed was a catalyst powerful enough to precipitate the new from this volatile solution of the transforming old.[18]

That catalyst was LSD.

Culture embodies itself in the nervous circuitry of the people. Back in 1957 Norman Mailer had written: "It is not only the 'dead weight of the institutions of the past' but indeed the inefficient and often antiquated nervous circuits of the past which strangle our po-tentiality for responding to new possibilities. . . ." [19]

For this generation, acid was to open synapses hitherto sealed, thus activating latent nervous circuits and profoundly affecting the consciousnesses of those who used it, and, through them, of youth everywhere.

Two young Soviets, 1975. *Stewart Dill McBride.*

21.
The Acid Bohemians
(1965-1970)

The story of LSD's rise to fame/infamy begins with Ken Kesey and his harlequin entourage, the Merry Pranksters. Ken Kesey: balding, sandy-haired, wrestler's build, once a wrestler. Cassady awed Kerouac, and Kesey awed Cassady. Kesey down from the University of Oregon for the Stanford writers' program, Nature boy welcomed to the liberal easy living of Palo Alto's lace-curtain bohemians met acid in 1959 as a guinea pig in an acid experiment, experiments with the experimenters and the lace curtains turn Da-Glo orange 1962 *One Flew over the Cuckoo's Nest*, McMurphy stronger than all the powers of normality until Big Nurse cuts his mind out.

Cuckoo money buys a house in the greenwood high on the mountain at La Honda. Da-Glo tree trunks; friends psychophants minds poached by acid all seated around the campfire, Wandervögel listening for the voice of the forest and hearing it too because of loudspeakers in the trees. Kesey says the present-lag between reality and its registration in the mind can be cut no thinner than 1/30th of a second but can extend infinitely. Kesey says you can shrivel the historical/cultural part of the lag through study but the psychological/feelings part yields only to psychic dynamite. Kesey says everybody's in a movie so get them into your movie before they get you into theirs. Kesey says somewhere before lag and beyond acid is the absolute right-now pattern of reality, the insensible matrix of our own patterns. *Bend* minds up to the simultaneity of past-present-future as geometric time sense fades and past and future collapse into an *almost* NOW.[1]

"Never trust a Prankster;"
Dada à la mode!

Sense the strange synchronizations, the random "synchs" making new systems: bug flying raindrop hum; get the *synch* and live the symbolist synch life on the Mountain. And riding the painted bus synch with manic passengers swastikas and the bus belonging at last to a school district in forward motion. Merry Pranksters on-the-bus-off-the-bus are colors on Kesey's palette to mess around and slop down in this cinematographic art along with painted clothes, breathing exercises, and everybody getting a new name: The Hassler, Danger Ass, Space Daisy, Zonker, Sensuous X, Wavy Gravy.[2]

Back from the cross-country acid bus trip the Cops-and-Robbers game penetrates the sacred grove and cops are planting dope in one room while Pranksters flush it in another. Busted, riding downhill, the driver-cop says:

Okay, tell me, Kesey, why do you use that LSD stuff?

Why—? Well, see, it's like this—when you're stoned on acid you can come *nine* times.

Oh . . . YeahhhhhhhHHHHHHH![3]

Either you're off the bus or you're on the bus.

"I intend to stay in this country as a fugitive and as salt in J. Edgar Hoover's wounds."

CAN
YOU
PASS
THE
ACID
TEST?

The new experience was to be shared with the whole world on the weekend of 21-23 January 1966 at Longshoremen's Hall, a speed-speed-speed hyperkinetic *Hernani* crewed by Ken Kesey's Romantic Army . . . :

Grinding through the ghetto, Prankster bus, signs saying COLORED POWER, advertising

THE TRIPS FESTIVAL

a new Nuremberg rally, searchlights writing in Da-Glo art new-veau:

THE TRIPS FESTIVAL
CAN YOU PASS THE ACID TEST?

Friday night of the three-night festival was produced by others and was well attended but so dull as to be accurately described by the man who leaped to the stage and announced:

"This is a drag even on acid." [4]

Saturday, at the center of the vast floor stood the Tower of Control, framed with pipe and abundantly furnished with electronic equipment. The arts in their latest technological forms were to be combined into a single environment which through the force of the radiant power energy accumulated would produce the acid experience without the use of acid. And so it had been advertised. Chic squares and hip circles buzzed for days about this experiment in experience. Acid without acid!

The people began flooding in early, thousands and thousands of them. Dopers came from everywhere, stoned on acid, astounded to learn their numbers, delighted they could be completely ripped in public and yet be undetected because others interpreted their behavior as being Acid without Acid. Projectors flooding walls and dancers with movies and slides and liquid abstract paintings; people eating free acid tabs; people thundering on the thunder machine; people painting each other with Da-Glo. Under the 1910 movie pulsations of the strobe lights they dance to the acid experience expressed in sound keening out of the mighty sound system of the Grateful Dead. Dancing under the strobe a topless girl. Way up on the balcony, wearing a silver space suit, manning an overhead projector, Kesey, writing phrases on acetate and projecting them onto a distant wall:

ANYBODY WHO KNOWS HE IS GOD
GO UP ON THE STAGE. [5]

The Trips Festival with its acid test transformed things; the proto-mutants had broken free of their cocoons and were on the wing. For the first time aware of their numerical strength, they kept on gaining confidence and recruits. The San Francisco sound—acid rock—had made its debut. Countless are the offspring of the Trips Festival's neo-art-nouveau posters. The press carried the story around the world. As so long before in New Orleans, what had been a local phenomenon among a despised minority suddenly became an element of international life. Acid missionaries carried the new gospel everywhere; neophytes came from everywhere to San Francisco. In the Haight, an acid community formed around the newly estab-

lished Psychedelic Shop and grew in an atmosphere of fading ano-
nymity as the local media covered the story.[6] Almost exactly a year
after the Trips Festival, the several echelons of the dope movement
consolidated and called on the whole world to come together in

A Gathering of the Tribes for a Human Be-In
Saturday, January 14, 1967
On the Polo Fields of Golden Gate Park
A Pow-Wow and Peace Dance
To Be Celebrated with the Leaders of
Our Generation.

Growing out of the Free Fairs put together by the Artists' Liberation Front, free outdoor Trips Festivals with free bands, the Be-
In achieved a summit of good feelings for its twenty thousand participants, convincing some it marked the advent of a new age—the
Aquarian.

With its wild costumes, its happy faces, its graceful dancers, its
throbbing energy music, its ubiquitous flowers, its free food, its two
mounted policemen, its Hell's Angel guards, its celebrities, drums,
flutes, chimes, bells, chants, and its parachute jumper dropping out
of the sky from nowhere, the Be-In proved to be a photographers'
paradise. Here was something "new" and "significant" that looked
good on film and in the media. Photographers, feature writers, and
film crews seemed always at the dances, Be-Ins, and on Haight Street.
This intense and sentimentally sympathetic worldwide exposure
and the sudden national popularity of recordings by the San Francisco bands turned the eyes of romantics everywhere toward San
Francisco. It generated predictions that as many as a million kids
would come to San Francisco that summer. As the song told them all:
If you're going to San Francisco, wear flowers in your hair. It didn't
turn out to be a million, but 100,000 did come, mainly with flowers and nothing else, enough in all to overwhelm the fragile institutions and emerging social patterns of the Haight community, to transform it into the world's first teen-age slum. There, as Malcolm X
had said about previous slums, everyday living was a question of
survival and everybody on the street used dope to keep his nerves
calm and to forget what he must do to survive.[7]

Although it had a favorite product, Owsley's Acid, made quite
legally by Augustus Owsley Stanley III, the Haight community and
the youth movement growing out of it never really did have leaders

Haight Street. *Ruth-Marion Baruch*

—nor does the protoculture. Richard Alpert, Timothy Leary, Ginsberg, even Kesey, figured much larger in the movie the media projected into our heads than in the real community. The kids regarded
them as amusing, but irrelevant. The protoculture is not the work
of some genius or star or hero but, rather, a work of co-op art, made
by a whole community.

The same is true of the bands and their music.

Just as poetry was the art-axis for the romantics of 1830 and as
poetry/fiction was that of the Beats, so was music the art-axis of the
Haight community. The bands were its central institution. They
were at once a cause and a result of the community and as deeply so
as the New Orleans bands were a cause/result of the old black com-

munity of New Orleans. The San Francisco bands embodied and articulated the changing values of the community and served as the community's focal point. As with the old black bands, these bands played a communal music, the object not being purely the music, but making the people happy. It was a communal music you stay inside of and bring the audience into as well—in part because the audience is part of the band. Further, in much the same sense that the young worship no heroes and follow no leaders, the bands recognized neither stars nor leaders. It was Janis Joplin's development into a star with a backing more than anything else that split her from Big Brother.[8]

Although Richard Fariña and Bob Dylan may have led the way, as Dylan did for the Beatles and the Stones, the Frisco bands broke from the pop-music tradition by scorning to use commercial music, lyrics, or themes. Above all else they liked to play free, in parks, for everyone. As with the best black musicians, despising the Tin Pan Alley mind-fuck, the Frisco bands wrote their own music and words, joining the blacks and Dylan in the creation of an urban lyrical poetry which together with the music kept clarifying the experience of the community, and doing so in a more fundamental sense than even its newspapers or underground comix.

And what was the community itself like?

To walk from Hippie Hill in the park down Haight Street in the summer of 1967 was to be in an amazing carnival seen perhaps once before, on a smaller scale, in the Paris of the Hugolaters. To use Gautier's reflection on the opening of *Hernani* in 1830—looking at that mass of youth dressed in every fashion save the fashionable, juxtaposed with the philistines, then in the theater's expensive seats, now gawking from cars and tourist busses, it seemed "that two systems, two parties, two armies, or even two civilizations—and that's not saying too much—were present."

And it still does.

In the park and for half a mile on Haight Street, on both sidewalks, and on the street too, smoking dope, spare-changing, selling dope, a vast throng, mainly under twenty-one, almost half arrived there directly from other states,[9] circulated in a great swirl of hair, flowers, jewelry, love-beads—all the hats of Hallowe'en and the masks of masquerade, Wild West clothes, East Indian clothes, clerical clothes, medieval clothes, Chinese clothes, gowns robes trunks leotard

capes bells flutes bongos harmonicas guitars painted-faces Indian
headbands dancing with Dorothy down the yellow brick road laughter songs kisses for everybody dope-euphoria omnipresent over an
underlying and pervading pain trying in spite of it and despite the
anxiety of being on your own in a teen-age slum like a rolling stone a
complete unknown to be kind and generous, open and gentle.

Free Food. *Ruth-Marion Baruch*

Behind this flamboyant public life of 1966-1967 was another,
never seen by the philistines, seldom seen by any older people, lived
in thousands of apartments, crash-pads, and communal quarters.
Some of these radiated joy and liberation. Others were like the Crys-
tal Palace, a nineteenth century mansion filled with speed-freaks,
or the Greta Garbo Hotel, once elegant, now condemned and abandoned, swarming with the youth of Haight Street. From the lobby,
where the face of Greta Garbo had been newly painted in heroic
size on a peeling wall, up the three main staircases, through foul
halls and littered courtyards, a spiderweb of passages giving the kids
an advantage in the Cops & Robbers Game, up up to the topmost

rooms to the one frescoed with the terrible face of Mr. Mind Fuck, the building pulsed to a manic speed-and-acid teen-age energy racing on day and night—Alice through the TV screen. And so it was with the whole community. The Haight-Ashbury lived a surrealistic life amid the Mad Hatters and super heroes and Red Queens and Mafia killers in 1929 Marmons populating that other America on the far side of the TV screen—Strawberry Fields where nothing is real.

By the beginning of 1968, Haight Street swarmed with spivs, desperate speed-freaks and junkies, bikers, and hoodlums, mostly black. This all received formal recognition in a funeral march down the Street mourning the death of Hippie, the Devoted Son of Mass Media.[10] Love Street had changed into Desperation Row. But not quickly enough to crush the movement. By 1968, the student-activist and hippie life-styles were fusing; the young romantics, less naive now, feeling the holy rage, toughened like the Paris bohemians in the school of the streets, carried this fusion—the newborn protoculture—with them to every part of America, and beyond, where it was swiftly assimilated by the young.

Is *this* all there is. . . ? There's got to be more! In the Haight they found more—the idealism of shared and open love framed by hard trouble, disease, despair, madness, and death. As one young playwright said: "If you're going to have a renaissance a few people have to die." But this in the awareness if we don't have a renaissance, we're all going to die. "Maybe the most important of all the gifts of Haight Street is the now overt recognition that it is all right to feel all right and to be the best you can be." So writes one veteran from the retrospect of 1976.[11] As the Haight citizens would tell you, they were putting themselves through changes to get beyond playing games and taking ego trips—which is to say beyond bourgeois rôle-playing and status-seeking—to get their heads to a place where they could tell it like it is and turn people on to life and love and doing their own thing. Such was the idiom of the Haight community. For some it was rhetoric. But others really had determined to change themselves for the better, to go through personal renaissance. Cumulatively and in community these renaissances were to add up to *Renaissance.*

In this process, acid served as psychoanalyst, the Haight as boot camp.

In boot camp the Marines break recruits down to rubble then build them up again as something else. These youths, and some were aware of it, used exploration, experimentation and dope to break themselves down to rubble. For some, the process stopped right there. These are the "acid casualties,"[12] mental cripples who never will recover. The rest, with no guidance at all save that offered by teen-age folklore, pseudo leaders, and acid itself, undertook self-reconstruction. Emerging from this metamorphosis, these liberated people formed cadres of the protoculture furnishing guidance to millions of young people alienated from the transitional authorities and the arrogant hypocrisy of their teachings, precepts such as war is good and marijuana, evil; elders who sent young men to prison for smoking herbs and refusing to participate in mass murder. Sometimes it seemed as if the elders had declared war on youth, that they were blaming youth and punishing youth for the fatal defects of their own transitional society, defects for which the elders themselves were responsible. After all, who was in power? From this came episodes like the riot at the Democratic Convention in Chicago, the Cambodian invasion, and the subsequent Kent State, Jackson State

Vietnam: Their first kill. *Wide World Photos*

killings, crimes acceptable to authorities who, for all their talk of law and order, were, as youth had come to believe, the real criminals.

Concurrently, affected by the youth revolt at home, energized by outrage, desperation, and dope, young draftees renounced the standards of the military and built their own subculture, one inspired by the protoculture and so deeply opposed to what it had replaced that the grunts and GI's lost their efficacy in combat and began killing their own officers, thus ending the war.

As one paratrooper who was decorated for heroism put it: "Acid made me see everything new." In the airplane coming back from Viet Nam he took acid and, transformed, proceeded to turn Fort Bragg onto both acid and an underground, antiwar newspaper, produced by the GI's themselves. "People can adapt to anything as long as they don't question the context." Acid shattered his heritage, the narrow context of the Los Angeles hoodlum world whence he came and its extension, the army, and set him to seeking wider referents.[13]

In order to stay out of jail, blacks and bohemians have always lived partly underground and in consequence have developed subcultures and the habit of relying on each other for help and guidance. Millions (no one knows how many) of Americans, mostly young, used marijuana and by so doing became *ipso facto* felons. By 1970, draft evasion, doping, and being accessory to the two, had rendered the whole generation felonious. For the same reason blacks Uncle Tom Mr. Charley, youth Uncle Toms its elders and so successfully as to conceal the intensity and extent of its transformation. A way of life once confined to blacks, a few art students and bohemians, refined in the Haight and then on elite campuses and in the jungles of Indochina, still refining itself, is now to a significant degree the peer standard of all youth.

Here's how the acid wave hit an East Coast lad of seventeen back in 1968. Neil Healy, now a Frisco film maker, in 1969-70 a member of the *Quicksilver Times* publishing collective in Washington, D.C., writes for this book:

It was in an elevator, the first time, licking up that cylinder of purple-and-white speckled powder. It was what we'd been waiting for, the great catalyst of situation. It made street corners look like shooting galleries in the Amusement Park twenties. It knocked us for a loop beginning the second the acid disappeared from a lump in the throat and became a movie. Motion was everything. Anything could touch off a laugh. Laughter turned into eons of monumental gasps for air.

It was in an elevator I first tasted the Frisco experiment LSD. It seemed to me a direct line to my shadow. It was a solid shaft of what made me myself. We took this stuff called ozzly (Owsley) in the elevator and pressed 6. We went from there to the roof. Up, I tell you, not down, up those final stairs and out into the New York sunlight high above the sidewalk.

I could see clearly every detail in the cavalcade of madness below me. Be it the games of the streetcorner or a local romance. Each street a woven blanket of family, each street leading from an adventure to a story of woe and back. All this I watched from my apartment-house rooftop in Queens under the eye of the Empire State Building, under the influence of Owsley acid.

You make it sound so simple, you might be saying, and that's exactly what it became. You could see yourself as others see you and look down at your own defenseless being moving around amid all the great stone and ivy-covered buildings and see how you were a mere ant.

Oh! but the colors of the springtime! The maple trees remaining on your block, budding and greening into view. And the budding girls, each with her smile that cannot be controlled since she knows she is young and beautiful and deserves more than this, what's around you, the dark black asphalt that beckons with hot fragrance of oil and lust. Summer is just around the corner and acid races in your brain.

It never gets ahold of you, No, not you who would rather ride it like a sunfish than give in to the crazy wanderings it sends your brain on. You as you sit on the rooftop, or on the post office steps and stare down at the weary neighborhood residents. You who walk the street beaming because you think you've found the key to what has lain beneath your eyes for so long that you grin as it comes streaming out. Who was this guy Owsley anyway, a madman joker or super wizard?

As the summer heat drives you from your schoolyard perch amid stickball games and poker you are driven to the subway. The cool gray tunnels of billboards and urine, vending machines and pretty Manhattan ladies who chew gum to break the tension and stare at you and smile and recognize the gleam in your eye.

The long thin serpent, the subway, runs its course every day. But only then do you really discover it. Locked in its bowels, swaying from side-to-side, only then do you understand the front car. The first time, that first time, you were only five, riding on your father's shoulders and he was pointing out this and showing you that and telling how Grandpa worked on the first tunnel dug under the East River and here you are in the first car clenched teeth and soaring vision, racing past catwalks and red and green lights through a land Owsley had never seen.

Up out onto Broadway the lights make people into moths drawn to the flame. Death walks there, the theater-goers corsage and tuxedo wearers, well lit up under the excitement and passing glory of the night. In blue jeans with long hair it was easy to see all this and feel new and free from the city's talons. It was not junk but acid surging through our veins and we plotted the course each trip would take.

Sometimes in school, the education factory, at work the economic factory, in the neighborhood tavern a futuristic milk bar, ideas as well as insults were exchanged. Among all this I remember stepping ever so softly so as not to disturb, not to rearrange. Owsley made me an acute observer of life.

For millions of youths, fermenting with outrage, acid sped the dissolution of the cultural context and forced reorientation to a much larger and still elusive one.

Not only in America, but everywhere on earth, this generation is being knocked out of its cultural context. Margaret Mead tells us that modern technological culture, accelerated by modern communications, is smashing the nuclei of all traditional cultures—even those on New Guinea—throwing youth everywhere out into the free space of the existential situation.[14]

It is the youth of America, particularly in the West, which is defining the new cultural orientation and composing the new myths.

Here is a youth at once in history, ahead of it, and above it.

22.

The Protoculture
(1970-today)

What is that orientation? What is the protoculture? Elusive as it seems, can we induce its patterns from its traits, from its attitudes and its beliefs?

The protoculture is determined to be nobody's Nazi and nobody's nigger. It wears the freedom-sex clothes of the romantic in preference to the role-status clothes of its technocratic siblings and its bourgeois parents. It rejects coercive education. It is as interested in the accomplishing as in the accomplishment, in the producing as in the product. In a sharp inversion of standards, it regards blue-collar work as more respectable than white-collar. The protoculture believes no one should be classified or bred into a role; it does not believe in careers but sees employment as a temporary exchange of time for money, as the payment of dues, at best as an unavoidable submission to authority. The culture understands that the locus of freedom is off the job where, as in the arts, oneself is the author of both the project and the way of carrying it out. For it, competition is internal and personal, seldom external and public. In it each person seeks not normality—which in our society means sharing in the conventional neuroses—but excellence, to become perfectly him/her self.

The protoculture believes that the old left is a symbiotic part of the established order, a belief confirmed in 1968 when the Communist leaders joined Charles de Gaulle in suppressing revolution in Paris and when the Soviets crushed the Czechoslovakians. It shares Bohemia's belief in the intense moment and Bohemia's commitment to cenacles—affinity groups—as the basic community. It subscribes to ad-hoc leadership, having such confidence in its own abilities as to believe that each situation creates its own coordinators who moderate group action and then fade back into the people. Although drawn to export versions of Hinduism and Buddhism, even to Pentecostal Christianity, its religion is really a pantheism quite without dogma in which it senses that God—conceived as a life-force—is everywhere, both within and without.[1]

This combines with belief in the occult power of love and music.

And all of this in a manner consistent with the attitudes toward reality taken by contemporary science.

The protoculture is sensitive to the paradox of apparency/transparency—that what we sense is only real in the special proportion of our size, location, and physical design. Enlarging or contracting changes the image of reality. Only a small segment of the electromagnetic spectrum is visible to the human eye. Through the microscope or telescope the apparent becomes transparent and another reality just as real appears. With the time dimension added, the apparency diffuses to energy/matter, itself transparent, being the organized nothing—the noncontained/contained turbulence which is in fact the ultimate reality.[2]

The protoculture follows the native American radical tradition: anarchy, believing that because man is basically good (loving and constructive) and because no supernatural conscience sanctions his behavior, man should be free to do and say what he pleases and that power should be diffused to a maximum among the people. It assumes that people hate and destroy only when hangups or general uptightness (which is to say symptoms of fear and anxiety) prevent them from loving and building. If you can't kiss, you kick—or even kill—because you must relate somehow.[3]

The protoculture scorns the weapons of the state in favor of its own: intelligence, imagination, compassion, honesty. It rejects nationalism and imperialism, particularly the American brand. The nation of today's youth is not America or France or Japan or Colombia or Germany, but all the youth of the world. The protoculture is innocent of concepts represented by that of the efficient biological nation—in Hitler's words "that substance of flesh and blood we call the German people." In fact, the Freikorps, the Nazi SA, and the mentality they embody bear the same relation to the bohemians that Charles Manson and his family bear to the protoculture and that the Nixon gang bears to the American people.[4] The protoculture's heroes are not Napoleons of power and glory, nor are they virtuosity figures like sports stars, nor Christs nor Buddhas, for these are the creation of their own followers, nor yet even the underground man so dear to academics. If it can be said to have any model at all, that model is the David figure with emphasis on sensuality, humor, intelligence, love, and harp playing. The culture knows Goliath is there; it knows what Goliath is, and it accepts the necessity of killing him—by rendering him transparent.

In the protoculture, the American Dream is coming true. The melting pot has melted. The Utopian hope of educating all the people is at last being achieved. Across this vast and populous continent youth has received an education built around the rhetoric of liberty and justice for all, an education recently supplemented for many by the realities to be learned in the school of the streets and that of the jails, and supplemented once more by Watergate and economic distress. Consequently, the protoculture looks not to gods or führers or parents or science or mystic process or even to outer space for salvation, but in full awareness of its fragile mortality, to itself alone.

This, the generation reared on *Mad* magazine and by Doctor Spock,[5] the generation sharing the early memory of hiding under school desks in drills preparatory to atomic attack, is the first generation in history that knows it may be the last.

In the words of one young woman:

"Many people have come to an intense awareness of life's inherent insecurity. We are mortal and alone. The vast responsibility for our lives and 'salvation' is in our own hands. One result of this has been a deep feeling of alienation, the personal realization that we are living a life (on a planet) that we don't at all comprehend, that seems isolated, absurd, futile, that we have grown up on panaceas and lies and that even our minds and hearts are strangers."[6]

Cultural forms persist long after the original content has vanished. The Christian content of our culture has seeped into the sand, but in the American establishment as in the SS State, the forms persist. The Nazi, the lifer, the organization man—all submit to the führer principle, in each case the will of something else having replaced the will of God. Christian thought is either-or thought. In it everything must be judged as either commensurate with the will of God or contrary, *ergo* sinful. Christian thought sees life's drama as the struggle of good and evil for the soul of each man, of Everyman, who in consequence walks through life alienated and alone, cleaving to the sunshine of holy grace, waiting for the release of death. Since sensuality is evil and must be repressed, the ideal is the sexless angel in the other world and the anchorite, suffering and sacrificing to earn salvation, in this. Like the Christian, the bourgeois struggles through each day, fantasy fixed on a resplendent future. Christian thought conceives of man as basically evil, as a depraved soul imprisoned in loathsome flesh, whose only hope is to be saved from himself. Transitional types that they were, the Founding Fathers thought that not only are all men created equal but that all men are created evil. Traditional thought rests on Aristotle's cause-and-effect logic, the notion of separate identity, and his concept of the prime mover —that in the beginning was a point of rest. It analyzes, it specializes, it fragments, it classifies: it fractures perception and experience. It analyzes every situation into an antagonism, one half, good, the other, evil. In transitional form—better and worse—this is the Marxist dialectic. Christian thought posits that part of life is superfluous. When you extirpate evil, all will be good. Its central energy is fear and guilt; it teaches: repress now, submit now, and live later—after you're dead.

The old way of thinking relates all existence to a point: God, a führer, a prime mover. The protoculture, pantheistically, sees meaning as apparency/transparency, that the way you perceive it is the way you conceive it, but in an aura of previous conceptions and extrapolations, in the awareness that all conceptions are, in fact, metaphors. This relates to the concept of *field* as understood in science. You can think of an area of concentration in a field and think of something real. But to think of a point, a line, a plane is to consider a fiction. In its several forms the old mode of thought perceives analytically, scanning the field (itself deceptively organized in relation to an artificial vanishing point) for some point of concentration and in so doing imposes a preconceived order on the perceived. Field-thinking, like acid, reduces to a minimum the preliminary structure/interpretation that analysis and the culture impose on perception. Field-thinking is passive perception. It submits to being ordered by the environment, by what is really there, but with a sense of the extrapolations created by apparency/transparency and by metaphor.

What you really see here . . .

is black marks on white paper.

While in both the traditional and transitional orders the predominant mode of thought is essentially analytical, the protoculture seeks synthesis. Its whole-earth thought knows the fish is also the water and that mankind is the crew of a single spaceship. The old way of thinking is dualistic. Not only does it dichotomize, but it recognizes two independent orders of existence: a sensed world and a world insensible: Earth/Heaven—Matter/Mind—Body/Soul—It/Me. Dualism splits us away from earth. It conceives of a sharp split between the conscious and the unconscious rather than sensing that one blends down into the other and that that, in turn, blends into all nature. Consciousness, it would follow, is neither separate identity nor a point. The soma (body/mind) radiates the environment; the environment suffuses the soma. We make our days and our days make us. Consciousness is a focus of the cosmic field.

Field-thinking is monistic and syncretic. Visually it is manifest in the yin-yang symbol, subsuming the occult but bereft of mystic connotations. Opposites are not separate identities nor are they contentious. They are harmonious, and illusory, for what appears to be in sharp opposition is in reality an expression of the whole underlying circle, the greater unity, the Tao. Not either/or, but both/more, again: apparency/transparency.

The protoculture's ethic is one of compassion in an aesthetic field. You accept others as they are and affect them, not by advising them, or commanding them, but by helping them and by showing a good example. Value is aesthetic: if it's good art, it's good. The protoculture's standard of right action is an aesthetic standard: essentially, its ethic is an aesthetic ethic, one always seeking to harmonize unlikes, each of which is perfectly itself, and at the same time exists in the radiant field of the other. *[margin note: peace]*

The protoculture uses analysis and cause-and-effect logic, but it relies on paradox and probability logic, and this less for control than for adaption.

Traditionally in Euro-American culture, some philosophers and pure scientists apart, the only people who have consistestly tried to see life whole are the very same people around whom Bohemia grew—the painters and the poets. What the Dada painter Hans Richter wrote about the Dada painter Kurt Schwitters might well have been said about the ideal of them all:

He was:

a totally free spirit, ruled by Nature.[7]

The psychological model of traditional culture displays a pattern of God's omnipresent will, moving all, revealing itself through providences, this in a field composed of the effects of the minute free-wills of individuals harmonizing with God's will (flowing with the führer principle) or under pressure from Satan (the instrument of God's antiwill) defying God's will and producing dischord.

Transitional culture presents as its psychology a behavioristic-Freudian model. The first relates to a crude mechanical typology in which all people are rats whose behavior can (and should) be modified by manipulation of the stimuli. The second teaches that we are mainly if not completely the effects of past causes and that the more complex civilization becomes the more we must of necessity accept rigorous discipline of our natural inclinations because it is from such repression that civilization derives the structure prerequisite to its existence.[8] The most to which we can aspire is to advance from the oral through the anal to the genital stage and, on the way, internalize authority. Every man his own führer, so to speak, and that in a civilization whose structures stand in defiance of the larger patterns of Nature, one whose personnel must of necessity repress themselves or be repressed.

The protoculture presents as its psychology a gestalt/existential/humanistic model, sometimes called third-force psychology, which teaches we are more than rats, that we are mainly our relation to the field of the now, and that civilization derives the structure necessary to its existence from the larger patterns of nature, the cosmic field. Hence we must strive to open ourselves to the present, both external and internal, so that we may be at this instant in harmony with the cosmic natural patterns, both with each other and within ourselves, be free spirits ruled by Nature. To do this we must free ourselves from the patterns imposed by the past and from anticipations of the future, from reverie, calculation, and repression. The more open we are, the more intense being—or is it becoming?—becomes.

Marijuana, alcohol, LSD, and other dopes are artificial means of liberating consciousness from cultural inhibitions and accomplishing this intensity of experience or the illusion of having done so. They help us break the chains bound round us by the behavioristic-Freudian culture in which we live. Painful and dangerous as they may be, they liberate us momentarily from self-repression and bring us closer to the ideal, crudely expressed as drunk without booze, stoned without acid.

In this field psychology, sanity can be understood as that condition in which all systems of the soma are working in full harmony with each other instead of against themselves and one another, a condition fully attainable when these systems, working in complement, are also working in resonance with the large systems of nature.

Victor Hugo's romantic army (itself an old-fashioned concept) marched under a banner emblazoned *EPATEZ LES BOURGEOIS*, an attitude expressed in more recent argot by *blow their minds*. Epatez les bourgeois has been a theme among artists and bohemians ever since. It is the parade back from the Bal des Quat'z' Arts of

1899; it is the essence of Dada, a facet of the Beats, the center of Kesey's Merry Pranksters. And its object is the liberation of the bourgeois from their bourgeois programming, if only for an instant, so as to make them sense new *synchs*—that is, see alternative patterns or, better still, none at all.

The marriage of Captain Garbage and Thunderpussy. *Pirkle Jones*

But above this in gilded letters the standard of the first bohemians bore *L'ART POUR L'ART*—Art for Art. Not art for fame, art for money, art for status, art for power, art for education, art for politics, but art for its own intent/content, art for its own experience —the liberation of the artist (and of the observer) from his programming so he can sense it all fresh and whole and live it like it is.

"Activity can be enjoyed either intrinsically, for its own sake, or else have worth and value only because it is instrumental in bringing about a desired gratification. In the latter case it loses its value and is no longer pleasurable when it is no longer successful or efficient. More frequently, it is simply *not enjoyed at all,* but only the goal is enjoyed. This is similar to that attitude toward life which values it less for its own sake than because one goes to Heaven at the end of it."[9]

So says Abraham Maslow, the father of third-force psychology, in his *Toward a Psychology of Being,* a book which is, as the lawyers say, herein incorporated by reference.

Maslow sees two orders of motivation. The first, Deficiency Motivation, that described by the Freudian model, obtains when we act to overcome discomfort caused by needing something normally supplied by environment, be it food, shelter, or some more subtle gratification. But when all of the deficiencies are satisfied we do not, says Maslow, fall into torpor. Instead, a new order of motivation suddenly obtains. We now act toward self-realization, toward making our immediate experience-of-being aesthetically perfect. We try to make real—to *realize*—the unfulfilled potential of our humanity. The greater our Being Motivation is in proportion to our Deficiency Motivation, the saner, the happier, the more human we are. The more intrinsic and the less instrumental our behavior, the more alive we are.

In this conception, art-for-art reveals itself as the focus of life-for-life.

Life-for-life is the pan-value of the protoculture.

... as it is of the Romantic Nazi.

The qualitative difference between these two is that distinguishing action-for-action from art-for-art.

As in societies dominated by the old-fashioned bourgeoisie or by the bourgoisie's modern mutation, the Bureaucratic Nazi, where Deficiency (instrumental) Motivation predominates, the society itself is mentally ill. Seen in this context, Bohemia's is the story of the rise of a Being-Motivated community in the context of a Deficiency-Motivated civilization. The story abstracts from the stories of those who shrink their needs to the minimum, in recent years doing so in defiance of emotional advertising, which, by creating bogus needs and inflating real ones, presses toward the embourgeoisement of everybody. But this is no new trick. Napoleon once said, "I rule men with toys." Bohemia's is the story of the way of life generated by those who look within themselves and not to others for evidence of personal worth, by those who choose creation over comfort, by those who, as with serious artists—or Thomas Edison for that matter —would rather work than eat.

Such are the teachings of humanistic/existential/gestalt/third-force (field) psychology and some of the implications. To this I would add that, biologically speaking, humans are the least specialized of creatures. Thus, relative to all other forms of life, human behavior is free of physical determination and increasingly so as the technological extension of our bodies and nervous systems makes it possible for us to live underwater, fly to Mars, and, ultimately, via genetic control, to make of ourselves whatever we want to be.

Can you imagine taking your energy directly from the sun or being young forever or being an intelligent sphere—or field—exploring the universe?—itself, an intelligent field, or an infinite regression/progression of black-hole quasars!

Can you imagine that anything you can imagine can happen?

By removing its biological base we may be able to overcome Deficiency Motivation completely and by so doing become truly independent.

As constitued today, the core of the human is energy, an energy capable of countless modes of expression. The behavior of the human is constrained by the forms which channel that energy— forms we recognize by names such as human nature, custom, tradition, convention, civilization, personality, culture—forms from the past imposed by necessity or even accident and which become incarnate in our nervous circuitry.

As our awareness intensifies and our technology advances, it becomes progressively more evident that the looser these forms are, the freer we humans are to relate and react to present reality, to be free spirits ruled by nature.

In sum, this new way of receiving life represents a cultural mutation. In it the Freudian and behavioristic models are replaced by the humanistic/gestalt/third-force/existential model. Man is no longer evil, but good—and beyond that, *neither*. As with the Attic Greeks, Beauty, Truth, Good, are but three names for the same value. We are ethically obligated to purify the aesthetic of ourselves and our communities. Man is no longer the fortuitous result of his primal forces expressed through a restraining pattern formed in infancy and childhood, no longer a product of the cause and effect of the past. He can break out of the cultural program and reprogram himself. He can create himself.

This altered sense of man's place in the biosphere, liberated as it is from tradition *vide* cultural programming *vide* synapse control, is the affirmative orientation that has been developing in the bohemian community since its inception in 1830. Placed in the context of history, it forms a new psychology of history, a field history.

This field history sees three great periods in the story of man, a paradigm it holds in common with anthropology. First, having no conception that he might or could change his environment to make it more hospitable, man lived in precarious balance with nature. His characteristic orientation was accommodative with undertones of placation, and thus traditional thought has remained. Next, man conceived that environment could be changed to make a more hospitable context and by doing so he entered a second period of history. Awareness acting on environment accomplished the taming of plants and animals in the Neolithic Revolution, and then, in the Industrial Revolution, it accomplished the taming of chemical and electrical energy. From this grew transitional thought, the orientation of which is typically exploitative. This thought conceives of everything outside the ego, even members of the family, as objects to be manipulated in the deficiency interests of *me*.

The cultural DNA with its double helix of art and science is mutating again. The protoculture rejects the exploitation of men and earth and scorns the profit motive. This third period of history is one in which, essentially, the reconstruction of environment has been completed, albeit in conformity with plans prepared by an incompetent, and the reconstruction of man is about to begin. We are entering a new period of history when through genetic control man can reconstruct his own body thus realizing at last the New Man: Pygmalion 2000 A.D. For most people, this thought is still as unthinkable as was for so many millennia the thought that we can reconstruct environment to make it more hospitable to our being. This new period is also the time of the computer called the universal Turing machine, a reconstruction of mankind in projection which can reproduce and evolve.[10] But now, before all that is upon us, we can orient toward remodeling our new house, our reconstructed environment, toward reconciling it with the Nature from whose wounds is was torn. The protoculture neither asserts nor placates; it reconciles. It tells us to suffuse into the present and be. And in so doing arrive at last where the *I* and the *me* become the nexus of the *it*, where art's intent and experience are the same and art—and life—is for art's sense and we are ready to meet the danger and accept the promise of this mutating future.

But the *I* and the *me* are not yet the nexus of the *it*; life's intent and content are not yet the same and life is not yet for life's sense. Mainly in transitional form, the old way of thinking is still in power. It is bringing about a society in which the premier object of organized activity is the public image it creates, a phenomenon increasingly manifest in institutions as various as universities and police. The established mode of thinking and its institutions cannot accommodate to the reality that production has achieved an efficiency sufficient to satisfy the material needs of man. Although once roughly suited to circumstances, the old way of thinking is now anachronistic and so destructive as to be suicidal. By creating bogus needs, by wasting vast quantities of production on them, on mass murder, on planned obsolescence, and by inflating the bureaucracies of murder, of money and control, it grinds down the quality of experience. Based on scarcity assumptions, it creates a counterfeit scarcity of goods and an artificial scarcity of sensual gratification. In a world where each is mutually dependent on every other, to preserve itself the old mode of understanding preserves the nation-state system with its built-in supreme court of war. In a world where four hundred million people are starving, it feeds the grain that could save them to livestock. In an ecosystem pushed to the edge of catastrophe by analytical exploitation, it preserves in both its capitalist and socialist manifestations the economic system and technology that do the pushing.

If the old way of thinking remains in power the only question left to answer is: will the catastrophe that exterminates mankind be primarily ecological? biological? or thermonuclear/radiological?

In its post-Christian form the old way of thinking produced the American organization man and his military counterpart: the push-button killer. Mixed with romanticism it produced the Manson family and the SS State. It created the executives of the multinational oligopolies and the C.I.A., J. Edgar Hoover, and the Nixon gang, Nazis all, exemplars of technological man, men without ethics who ask *how* but never *why*. Though on the edge of mutation, all these groups have been rendered psychotic by their preservation of the old Christian forms after the content of the forms and, along with it, their reason for being have vanished.

The protoculture leaves room in its world for everybody, even Nazis and anticommunists. Conversely, the Nazis and antis, concerned with scarcity, with Lebensraum, woud exclude most of us, using, if necessary, the final solution.

The revolution that brought transitional culture to power expressed its social ideal as

Liberty, Equality, Fraternity.

In the course of two centuries this social ideal has been refined.

Liberty, meaning the absence of physical restraint, has transformed into liberation, meaning the absence of physical, mental, emotional, cultural, and even biological restraint—of somatic (mind/body) restraint. This ideal, positively rendered, is _Autonomy_.

The concept of Equality has been secularized.

Fraternity is better understood as social democracy in the context of Community.

The social ideal of the protoculture is the field:

Autonomy/Equality/Community.

The inverse field is Authority/Hierarchy/Alienation—and for its own sake because there is no divine or other suprahuman sanction.

So alienated did the citizens of the SS State become that they dared not confide in friend nor child nor spouse. Excluding the physical, the citizen's most intimate way of relating to his most intimate associates was up through some Nazi symbol and down again.

Love, trust, and field psychology equate with the Autonomy field; hatred, suspicion, anxiety, repression, oppression, and Deficiency-Motivation psychology with the Authority field, a field whose structure perfectly accommodates those trained, like Hitler, to be at once self-reliant and submissive.

Because, in a hierarchical system, all relationships are those of dominance/submission, of master/nigger, each person being the nigger of someone else, at the top some_thing_ else, no one can stay in such a system and remain human. Fortunately, the transitional order as currently constituted in the United States and some other countries is pluralistic, perforated with interstices, and puffed with empty spaces. The protoculture, therefore, by occupying these vacuums, can and does disassociate from the sado-masochistic components of the transitional order.

If "society" means a group of beings held together by mutual dependence, mankind is in fact a single society, but one in which national sovereignties, somatic repression, Deficiency Motivation concentrated into the profit motive, and threats of mass murder alienate the constituent parts. The society of mankind is structurally defective. It does not comprise the common institutions and shared ideology requisite to the harmonious interaction of its components.

By simile with a single human being, it appears as if in the largest sense society is insane and, because it cannot be institutionalized for its own good, is moving toward self-destruction.

Here is a world society half of whose million scientists and engineers work at the invention and improvement of killing machines, guided, in the U.S.A., by a policy of Mutual Assured Destruction—MAD. Here is a world society whose most powerful state uses weather and germs as weapons against the crops of other states and, as an instrument of policy, threatens the use of tactical nuclear weapons.[11]

Because to harmonize oneself with an insane society is to become insane, no person can be sane unless a member of some autonomous community, some Bohemia, which bears the same relation to the larger society that the pearl does to the oyster.

What do we see when we cut a bicentennial cross section through this process?

What, today, is the state of American youth?

American youth no longer believes in the old myths and it struggles to compose the new. "The old myths have been sucked through the vanishing point of no return." American youth is between myths with little to guide it but its own experience. It is mired in "a miasma of boring, sweaty expectations," as Anders Edvard Smiltens observes and experiences it, being at once watching it and in it.

" 'This place is boring....' 'Friday night...or Saturday night could be good...or Monday.' 'This place is boring....' 'Where's the party?' 'Where's the action?' 'Boulder maybe.—'

"Consider amphibians thinking 'fish' while their lungs fill with water and they sputter to the bottom...'a wasted generation' and remember 'the lost generation'.... The reliance upon the anachronistic vestigial culture-patterns, the old gills, the old tricks and

Houseboat Bohemia, Gate 5, Sausalito. *Pirkle Jones*

games . . . the frayed ganglia in the sweaty backwaters form a red-neckalia *bohème*. . . . Koestler sees the 'greening' on the whole as a 'pinking' which means partial combustion, loud-sputtering, much internal friction and inevitably little traction, movement for *more*. . . . Waning energy-levels, the gasps of action-for-action, a cultural energy crisis. . . . I sum-up the affliction of redneckalia in the amphibian metaphor, 'misanthropically,' the new man breathes."[12]

The pioneers of the protoculture, the prototype of the only culture offering to mankind a real chance for survival, live mainly in the large society but, and by definition, cannot conform to it. Their relations with the large society and their unsuccessful experiments hurt and distort all of them, cripple or kill some of them, but, nevertheless, their courage maintains, their numbers increase, hope intensifies, and reason enjoins us to give them all the help we can.

23.

Current Transformation (today and tomorrow)

The foregoing profile of the mutating consciousness depicts a conceptual field developing in young people everywhere, a way of forming and interpreting experience that affords real hope for the future. When this same mutating consciousness is infected by authoritarian attitudes, when it is suffused by the führer principle—a point/field principle nonexistent in pantheistic nature—the result is the romantic Nazi, examples of whom are all too evident among posttraditional youth.

In the Nazi, as in everyone else, the appeal of authoritarian attitudes is directly proportional to the intensity of guilt, fear, and anxiety within. As Erich Fromm has demonstrated with his life's work, basic political orientations are expressions of basic personality types.[1] Part bohemian and part Nazi as he is, the romantic Nazi is too impulsive and too independent to live in harmony with the bureaucratic Nazis, the J. Edgar Hoovers and Eichmanns and their apprentices who, as the traditional types die out, gain more and more control over affairs. Having escaped the burden of freedom, having left to his superiors the ethical responsibility for his acts and the psychological risks of choice, the bureaucratic Nazi is concerned only with utility, and that within some specialty. He has waived the romance of independence for the security of dependence. He is an administrator, a technician: one who applies to the specific situation models and policies developed outside of himself. Ask him to devise a system to transport people across San Francisco Bay, to kill and dispose of Jews, to feed the people of India, or to achieve a one hundred percent kill in an atomic war and, like his prototype, the SS man, he will apply himself to the problem without any reservations at all save those of efficiency.

The economic institutions of society—in fact all of its bureaucratic institutions—are modeled on military organizations of past and present, organizations built around the command principle which, through the implementation of a single will, are meant to yield maximum efficiency in undertaking mass murder. This serves as the organizational model for the civil sector despite the fact that it cannot be demonstrated that that which is most effective in the service of death is also most effective in the service of life.

This ultimate authoritarian mentality, ultimate because it is unrestrained by tradition, increasingly gives form to the world's political-economy. Ironically, sound as the führer principle may seem in theory, in practice the human element vitiates it.

After reading an earlier draft of this chapter, a young ex-soldier wrote:

"I was the embodiment of the conflict between romantic Nazi and romantic artist which you describe. The predominant force was romantic Nazi up until the time in 1973 when I realized what I was and filed my conscientious objector's application. When I enlisted, it was with a contract to be assigned as a Pershing Missile Crewman in Europe. I intended to 'hijack' a missile and fire it. By this I mean I would have to force other people at gunpoint to press the fire buttons. There are quite a few security devices which require more than one person to activate and arm the missile and it is only remotely possible that I would have been successful in my attempt at world annihilation, in surpassing Hitler as the worst monomaniac who ever lived.

"There are so many factors which could have affected this scheme that I doubt I could have succeeded. There are other possibilities which I never got to research since I had a rather drastic change of consciousness before I could have attempted it. If my own peculiar experience was indeed a prototype of mass nihilistic mania then perhaps we will all step back from the brink after seeing the blackness of the abyss.

"I sure as hell hope so. Art saved me. Will it save the rest of us?

"Perhaps the most significant thing is not the real possibility of one maniac causing war, but that the intent was there."

At the Pershing bases in Germany, if not everywhere, "Black Jack 1 Alpha" is the code order to ready the missiles to fire and "Red Hotel" the code for completing the atomic countdown to atomic war. At these bases and doubtless at those of the Soviet Union as well, a Black Jack 1 Alpha drill completed without some malfunction in the complex and worn machinery is as rare as a perfectly functioning 1958 Ford. Despite publicity handouts telling us full control of Red Hotel is in the hands of the President, missiles can be activated and fired at the bases themselves. Participants in the drills are on occasion in the agonies of hangover or the surrealism of acid. The mating and dismating of warheads with missiles can and has resulted in the warhead jumping right out onto the concrete pad. Should the high explosive detonate, plutonium 239 debris would escape into the atmosphere. As country after country joins in the manufacture of warheads, all these dangers magnify. Methods of concentrating the unstable isotopes of uranium are simplifying to the point at which some bright adolescent can make a bomb with his chemistry set. A product of all atomic energy plants is plutonium 239, a metal from which, as the government of India demonstrated, bombs can be manufactured. Nuclear waste threatens to poison the groundwaters and the oceans. A nuclear black market looms as does nuclear terroism. A missile fired from Green River, Utah, into the White Sands range landed in Mexico City. Hydrogen bombs have fallen on Spain and on North Carolina. In the latter case, five of the six safety devices went off. Radar misinterpreting the rising of the moon at the same time an iceberg cut a cable resulted in the boards at central command in Colorado showing a Soviet missile attack. The world was spared the results of a counterattack by the good judgment of a single Canadian officer who was not supposed to have been on duty—Air Marshal C. Roy Slemon—to whom a grateful world should build a monument instanter.[2]

Under current conditions a nuclear catastrophe would not be an accident because it is a certainty: nuclear catastrophe is built into the system.[3]

Even though humanity and reason both enjoin immediate and total nuclear disarmament and an end to nuclear power, the bomb and A-power industries and their vested bureaucrats are as active as ever.[4]

In a letter of appeal sent in 1975 to persons around the world,

Jacques-Yves Cousteau, inaugurating the Cousteau Society, warned that if the technology upon which mankind on both sides of the iron and silken curtains depends is not transformed, the seas may soon die and nothing remain on earth but microlife.

And then there is that externalization of the Nazi mentality, the universal Turing machine, a computer said to be under development by the Pentagon—a machine promising to be nothing less than a mechanical Führer who will take decision wholly out of the hands of men.[5]

Mankind is in immediate and mortal danger, but, as in the SS State where neurosis became the norm, we seem to have become so accustomed to what puts us in that danger as to accept it.

Is it any wonder that people of human, of artistic, sensibility rage at the complacency, the cruelty, irrationality, ugliness, and hypocrisy of the cultural patterns and institutions which are pushing us all to the edge of the cliff?

What we see today is the developing consciousness of the proto-culture pressing against the force of a hostile political economy and bureaucracy. Those who tire, those who lose faith, those touched by the cold hand of fear/anxiety, are swept away and, if not clutching for safety at some form of dog tranquilizer or heroin, become romantic Nazis if still struggling, and organization Nazis if not.

Everywhere, however, are people, mainly young, who are not swept away, but, undaunted, feeling the holy rage, keep up the fight, often scarce knowing why beyond an aesthetic sense that life requires it of them.

Art, in the large conception, requires the author/artist to be his own *authority,* to be autonomous, independent, self-reliant, and provides in exchange its own reward. Because this art orientation has a long history of survival in opposition to the most powerful of social forces, these undaunted life-lovers find a model in the serious artists of the past and present and in the bohemian patterns therefrom extracted, patterns which now, through cultural mutation, are becoming the synapse circuitry of youth everywhere.

Because art in essence is the concentrated expression of the being of the artist, this new youth senses that art is not a quality exclusive to some elite but that it can be active in everybody. When freed of deficiency motivation, all of us are artists; all of us, bohemians.

Protoculture armored car—cannon firing roses and Gary Snyder poetry—in 1965 parade featuring Fort Ord military. *John B. Smithback*

To make art the artist has to be free. To fight to free art as Bohemia has always done is in fact to fight to free the artist. On examination that proves to be nothing less than a fight to free everybody. Consequently, in anything less than a free society the artist's influence is subversive. That the authorities sense this is attested by the existence of censors. That Hitler, Stalin, and Nixon all detested abstract painting is adequate testimony to sustain its value. Concealed in the structure of the establishment is a primary contradiction. It must employ creative people in the mind industry as engineers of popular consent. By what magic were the Americans brought to agree to the expenditure of what was by Gerald Ford's own estimate some 150 billion dollars on the mass-murder of Indochinese when they could have spent the money on themselves? This magic is failing because the magicians are in revolt. Even though you cannot hire a man for his imagination without, by the act of hiring him, shriveling his imagination, the artist, shriveled or whole, occupies a key position in society.

Art can and does subvert the mind-industry. It can and is mutating the cultural DNA.[6]

Over the past two centuries, art forms appropriate to democracy have slowly developed: art of, by, and for the people. Today, we have democratic music, literature, poetry, painting, sculpture, photography, graphics, architecture, and film—all of which articulate the protoculture and are restrained only by the selective power of a commercial distribution controlled by the establishment. Art and artists in all their forms are covered with scars inflicted by the thought-and-body police of brutal and repressive transitional cultures, economies, and states, but art has continued its cumulative development and today is stronger than ever.

Firmly established in the arts, the mentality of the protoculture is now embodying itself in politics. It has become a powerful force in California state government, San Francisco city government, in the Bay Area's congressional delegation, and is becoming so in the federal executive branch.

Change results from the interaction of economy and mentality, of environment and consciousness. The mentality of the protoculture finds itself in contradition to the predominating—and suicidal —economy/technology, and to the nouveau Nazis in both the romantic and bureaucratic modes. This fact generates a powerful force in the protoculture toward creating its own economy/technology, one which will accommodate nature and, for food, energy, and shelter, make man independent of vast commercial organizations.

In the San Francisco Bay Area and elsewhere the protoculture, uniting art, science, and technology, is beginning to construct the aesthetic economy. The opposition of pure art to pure science is being dispelled by an intensifying awareness of their common origin and complementary nature. The opposition of art-and-science to technology, of intuition/induction to calculation/deduction, of mystery to certainty, of what to do with how to do it, fancy to practicality, romance to reality, theory to practice, liberty to authority, is being dispelled by the understanding that each is necessary to the other.

Further, it is understood that because of the intermission that would stand between the demolition of the old and the inauguration of the new, complex civilizations cannot survive the overthrow of existing institutions. During the intermission where would we get our food and what would we do with our shit? Clearly, as the I.W.W. taught so long ago, the old must be transformed into the new, either by the development of alternative institutions in such intense harmony with need, cost, and sensibility that the old appear superfluous and vanish of their own accord, or by the transmutation of the functioning old into the functioning new.

Consequently, we must live concurrently in relation to the world as it is and to our conception of the world as it can and should be.

This transitional situation, this peculiar mode of existence, this living within the old while trying to invent and create the new, means that, if you are really trying to do something effective about the menacing present, you feel like an outlaw, sometimes act like one, and are treated as one.

But the feeling is one of intense satisfaction as well.

For crippled as they are, harassed as they may be, such people are not only creating the future, but living in it. They embody the interaction of art-and-science with technology—of generalist with specialist—and are the prototype of a future where everyone is at once artist and technician.

In the Bay Area, in Greater Boston, and elsewhere, people who embody the mentality of the protoculture and who were trained as personnel for the established economy but refuse to participate in it are creating a technology consistent with their beliefs. Informed by journals such as *The Co-Evolution Quarterly* (the child of *The Whole Earth Catalog*) and gathered together in associations such as The Farallones Institute they are uniting machinery and sophisticated instrumentation with protoculture specialists in all technical fields, backyard inventors, artists, millionaires, politicians, manufacturers, publicists, and lawyers in the making of a bohemian technology.

Economy, in its truest sense, is a central theme of the bohemian tradition. Bohemians have always used materials sparingly within a priority system established by art-for-art. Extrapolated, this trait is expressing itself in a new, soft, aesthetic technology combining art and science as equals. From this point of view, how well it looks is as important as how well it works.

Exemplary of all this is the development of Nitinol applications.[7]

Writing for *The Co-Evolution Quarterly*, Fred Gardner, formerly on the staff of *Scientific American* said:

"I first heard about the metal from Bob Trupin, an ex-physicist making his living as a carpenter in San Francisco. He was wildly enthusiastic, and hearing his story about a wire that contracted with great force when heated, I suspected he might have fallen for some Uri Geller bullshit. That would have been unlike Trupin, but the collapse of your society does funny things to people.

"In the kitchen he proceeded to demonstrate: dipped into a glass full of cool water a Nitinol wire bends easily in your fingers. Transferred to a glass of hot water it springs back to the straight position with remarkable force. It is an *amazing* phenomenon, and there is simply no conveying its impact."[8]

Nitinol, an alloy of nickel and titanium, goes through a solid-state transformation at a maximum temperature differential of eighty degrees Fahrenheit, one that causes it to shrink and straighten out with incredible force. This small differential exists in many places in nature and as waste heat in many industrial processes. Nitinol promises pumps, refrigerators, generators, air conditioners, motors, which run forever with no fuel at all save the low-grade heat differentials provided by sun and earth. Nitinol may make the deserts bloom, give free electricity to the mountaineer, heat the houses of the tundra, air-condition the houses of the tropics, and, as one project anticipates, by means of the earth's heat, supply all the electricity required by four city blocks of apartments—gratis!

Because the protoculture has come to see the get-rich-quick dream as the ultimate corrupter, it scorns riches and is permanently committed to bohemian values. Among the new-mentality types who have come into money or, as with the developers of Nitinol applications, may soon do so, are many who have no desire to get rich. Instead they are recycling or plan to recycle their profits into the romantic dreams of thousands of other cultural mutants who in true bohemian fashion are trying to realize alternative food, shelter, power, and cultural systems. These people in turn are expected to recycle *their* profits.

In this manner the protoculture is moving toward the center of events. It arose among youth and exists for youth; its bohemian antecedents began and developed in youth movements; and its traits are more commensurate with the nature of the adventurous young than with that of the middle-aged.

The protoculture has projected a sense of itself as alternative into bourgeois and embourgeoised mentalities everywhere, thus making people aware of an alternative to the grotesque and counterfeit security promised by the national-socialist program. In 1977, it appears that the protoculture has suffused from the Bay Area and other centers throughout the field of the general population, affecting first the young and then, through the young, their elders. It is common today for parents to tell their grown children: I'm beginning to realize you've been right all along. Studies indicate Americans are less inhibited, more tolerant and pessimistic than formerly and take, as one study says, "a much broader and deeper interest in the arts than previously believed."[9]

As symbol or as fact Haight/Berkeley and the other Haight/Berkeleys that soon appeared all over America—Boston, Los Angeles, Minneapolis, New York, Atlanta, Chicago, Albuquerque, Seattle, New Orleans, Boulder, Austin, Vancouver, Madison—served as the adolescence of the protoculture, an adolescence many of its carriers survived, rendering in them a cultural transformation that cannot be reversed. It is personified by the youth who, outraged at his father, ran the length of his living room straight through the picture window and kept on running until he got to the Haight; then, four years later, returned to talk to his father as an equal. It is embodied in Coyote, the hookers' organization started in Frisco by Margo St. James, a woman who is on top of all the contradictions. In 1975, this Dada labor union, this bundle of political and cultural dynamite which counts the county sheriff among the members of its board, held the Hookers' Ball in the Hyatt-Regency Hotel. The men and women of the Haight/Berkeleys, adults now, mellowed by experience and responsibility, compose a pool of post-traditional innovators, concentrating in California and Massachusetts but found everywhere, people who are introducing their innovations, refined and matured, into the cultural and economic mainstream.

These people have more in common with Thomas Edison than with their fathers and mothers. The Frisco pool is Wild West in that everyone is from somewhere else and is something of an outlaw, in that the walls of specialization have collapsed, everyone wears informal clothes and tries to live free, snobbery and social climbing are receding from sight, and practice is thought as important as theory. The pool contains every racial and ethnic background, the machinist is as respected as the physicist, the hooker as respected as the lawyer, the carpenter as the artist. Each member, by temperament, has a creative concentration. Joined together around the Nitinol pumps and engines, around Coyote, the New Games Festivals, the Faral-

"Dho Dho Dho" at the New Games Tournament. *Ted Streshinsky*

lones Institute, *The Co-Evolution Quarterly,* or some other center, the pieces compose a whole, a jazz band of innovators, each playing a different instrument, and together, in concert, capable of achieving a bloodless worldwide revolution by transforming politics and the economy and by setting technology free.

Seen together, all this appears as the American-Western theme of a New Beginning.

As orthodox relationships collapse and ancient institutions transmute, as the improbable becomes fact and the assured meets impeachment, it is increasingly clear that nothing is clear, that nothing is certain save uncertainty itself.

Abruptly mankind is realizing that change has become so rapid and fundamental that nothing can be predicted, that flexibility has become the most valuable character trait, that art, not dogma, should serve as guide, that the ultimate work of art is oneself, experienced in the right-now peak situation. It is fast becoming understood everywhere that we must prepare ourselves and each other for life in a world that does not yet exist and can scarcely be imagined. In the future we will think the unthinkable thought, conceive the inconceivable concept, and experience the inexperiencible experience.

Toughened by the trench war of his struggle for survival, the underground man of the protoculture, building the future in defiance of the present, is about to become overground man, building the future in conjunction with a transformed present.

This process is being accelerated by the Western drought and the energy shortage which are crowding everyone toward acceptance of more bohemian values.

In his old age, looking back over the revolution with which he was so intimately connected, John Adams concluded: "The Revolution was effected before the war commenced. The Revolution was in the minds and hearts of the people." This "radical change in the principles, opinions, sentiments, and affections of the people, was the real American Revolution."[10]

In 1786, three years after the Peace of Paris, Dr. Benjamin Rush of Philadelphia, another man closely associated with the patriot cause, declared that the American Revolution had just begun. "It remains yet to effect a revolution in our principles, opinions, and manners so as to accommodate them to the forms of government we have adopted."[11]

In their eighteenth-century way, both men are saying the American Revolution was not a war but a profound cultural change, one by no means completed.

As we enter the bicentennial of that war and for a moment become introspective about the general meaning of the succeeding eight generations of life—whether we look backward as are the people of the old East or look ahead as do the people of the new West —we see that the Americans, descendents of servants, slaves, outlaws, refugees, adventurers, Indians, and religious fanatics, initiated, not only for themselves but for all of Western culture, a transmutation in the principles, opinions, sentiments, affections, and manners of the people, one dedicated to liberty and the proposition that all men and women should have an equal right to enjoy that liberty.

The American Revolution, which started long before the war commenced, moves ahead with unabated energy, still an experiment, still the purview of the young, the bold, the idealistic,[12] still under the shadow of the question: can any nation so dedicated long endure?

Today, communist revolutions, fathered by authoritarian states with illiterate populations, mothered by the American dream, are sweeping the earth, bringing material well-being to the earth's millions in the context of authority, forming cultures rising directly out of rude peasant/worker values.

As the American Revolution moves on with this new generation of Americans, it limns the outlines of an alternative. If our romantic dream becomes real, in America, in the world, there will be neither arrogant rich nor desperate poor, but a classless society composed entirely of the middle classes. The American Revolution can bring material well-being to the earth's millions in the context not of authority but of liberty, forming cultures rising not directly out of rude worker/peasant values, but from the middle-class values refined from worker/peasant values through more than two centuries of living in America.

But these will not be the distorted middle-class values of the suburbs. They will be instead those of the bohemian artist transformed into the protoculture. The American Revolution is being decided today on a battlefield where Nazi and artist struggle for mastery, a battlefield not outside in some meadow or on some continent, but inside of each of us where a civil war rages between patterns of death and patterns of life.

Zooming the camera far back, seeing the long revolution whole, concentrating on the bohemian community developing into the protoculture, the details disappear and a larger form becomes apparent.

Since 1815, art has been leading the way toward a classless society because, relatively speaking, of all the people in transitional society, the Wild West excepted, artists are the only ones who stand outside of the class system.

After 1815, it truly seems as if every artist, every poet, every writer who is still remembered, came from the bourgeoisie yet loathed and detested the bourgeoisie as a deadly blight on all sensibility, all adventure, all truth, all romance, all humanity—as a deadly blight on life itself.

Would they then strangle their mothers and drown their fathers?

By no means.

In reality, this long story is not that of the most idealistic and sensitive offspring of the middle classes trying to destroy the middle classes but that of the most idealistic and sensitive offspring of the middle classes trying to refine the middle-class spirit so that it can become its promise.

Once that happens, the art-socialism of the American Revolution can confront the scientific-socialism of the Communist Revolution.

The liberty of the one and the community of the other can then combine into the world culture of the future.[13]

And just in time—for world civilization, the culmination of three and one-half billion years of terrestrial evolution, is now for the first time entering into cosmic significance—into the community of the one million advanced civilizations believed to be inhabiting our galaxy.[14]

Ivory J. Vaughn

Notes

† Joan Baez quoted in San Francisco *Chronicle*, 16 January 1973.

PREFACE   The Long Revolution

1. Walter E. Houghton, *The Victorian Frame of Mind, 1830–1870* (New Haven, 1957), says on p. 1: That they were living in "an age of transition" was "the basic and almost universal conception of the Victorian period." Here he quotes John Stuart Mill who in 1831 "found transition to be the leading characteristic of the time." As Mill put it, "mankind have outgrown old institutions and old doctrines, and have not yet acquired new ones," a fact he thought became apparent to the most perceptive only "a few years ago" but now (1831) had come to be generally recognized. In Mill's view, what had been outgrown was the Middle Ages. Frances Trollope in her *Paris and the Parisians in 1835* (New York, 1836) says on p. 396: " '*The country is in a state of transition*' is a phrase which I have often listened to." Houghton says, "never before had men thought of their own time as an era of change *from* the past *to* the future." See also pp. 13, 22–23. For an extended discussion of the beginning of the long revolution in its largest context see E. J. Hobsbawm, *The Age of Revolution, 1789–1848* (New York, 1962).

2. A truly traditional order would be one in which essence precedes existence without exception, a tribal society not yet in history like the Tasaday people recently discovered in the Philippines. To use the order of the High Middle Ages as the traditional norm is somewhat arbitrary, for it too was a time of change. A sense of what it was can be gained from Joseph R. Strayer, *Western Europe in the Middle Ages* (New York, 1955) and Will Durant,

The Age of Faith, A History of Medieval Civilization ... (New York, 1950). Robert L. Heilbroner in *The Making of Economic Society* (Englewood Cliffs, 1962), p. 45, says: "Tradition, changeless order—these were the key concepts of economic society in the Middle Ages." Durant gives the population figures on p. 642. The five cities are Douai, Lille, Ypres, Ghent, and Bruges. Constantinople had 800,000, Cordova and Palermo, 500,000 each.

Oscar Handlin in *The Uprooted, The Epic Story of the Great Migrations that Made the American People* (New York, 1951), pp. 7–36, 95–111, describes the nature and collapse of traditional "peasant society" in Europe. "From the westernmost regions of Europe, in Ireland, to Russia in the East, the peasant masses had maintained an imperturbable sameness; for fifteen centuries they were the backbone of a continent, unchanging while all about them radical changes again and again recast the civilization in which they lived" (p. 7). This peasant culture is the central referent of *traditional order* as used in this book. Margaret Mead in *Culture and Commitment, A Study of the Generation Gap* (Garden City, 1970), presents a similar cultural taxonomy: postfigurative, configurative, and prefigurative. Postfigurative culture, roughly equating with traditional culture as used here, is one in which the old provide the young with a complete model of what life is, where "children learn primarily from their forebears" (pp. 1, 2–31). She says (p. 31) "we have now arrived at a new stage of human culture."

3. That European civilization owes its character to this fact is the thesis of Guizot's lectures. In 1721, speaking of England where the balance remained even, Joseph-François de Montesquieu spoke of "liberty rising ceaselessly from the fires of discord and sedition, a prince constantly trembling on an unshakable throne." This quotation appears in J. H. Plumb, "The World Beyond America," in Richard M. Ketchum, ed., *The American Heritage Book of Revolution* (New York, 1958), p. 11.

4. Quoted in Will Durant, *The Story of Philosophy: The Lives and Opinions of the Great Philosophers* (Garden City, 1926), p. 233. Durant renders it, "Men ... till...."

PART ONE   The Romantic Resistance

* Gabriel Pélin, *Les Laideurs de Beau Paris, Histoire Morale, Critique et Philisophique des Industries, des Habitants et des Monuments de la Capitale* (Paris, 1861), p. 169.

1   Progress and Poverty

1. Henry George, Jr., *The Life of Henry George by His Son, Henry George, Jr.* (New York, 1900), p. 301. Henry George, *Prog-*

ress and Poverty, An Inquiry into the Causes of Industrial Depression and on Increase of Want with Increase of Wealth (New York, 1938—first in 1879) , p. 9.

2. For more of this see Kenneth Allsop, *Hard Travellin': The Hobo and His History* (New York, 1967) ; Jacob Riis, *How the Other Half Lives, Studies Among the Tenements of New York* (New York, 1890); Herbert Asbury, *The Gangs of New York . . .* (New York, 1928) ; Helen Campbell, Colonel Thomas W. Knox, and Superintendent Thomas Byrnes, *Darkness and Daylight, On Lights and Shadows of New York Life . . .* (Hartford, 1897) ; Stephen Crane, *Maggie, A Girl of the Streets* (New York, 1893) ; Henry Mayhew, *London Labour and the London Poor: Cyclopedia of the Conditions and Earnings,* in 4 Vols. (London, 1861–2; New York, 1968) ; Jack London, *The People of the Abyss* (New York, 1903) ; J. J. Tobias, *Crime and Industrial Society in the 19th Century* (New York, 1967). On p. 86 Tobias quotes an Ojibway Indian speaking for a party of Indians visiting London in the 1840's: "We see hundreds of little children with their naked feet in the snow and we pity them, for we know they are hungry." We think it would be better for your missionaries "all to stay home, and go to work right in your own streets," which is exactly the point Jack London makes sixty years later. When visiting cities, Sitting Bull often gave money to newsboys and shoeshine boys. He could not understand how the white man, with such an abundance of wealth, could let his own people—even children—suffer from hunger and want. See Don Russell, ʻ*The Wild West or a History of the Wild West Shows . . .* (Fort Worth, 1970) , p. 22. On p. 85 Tobias says: "Dr. Barnardo estimated in 1876 that about 30,000 neglected children under 16 years old slept out in the streets of London." Today, in New York City 15,000 children are living wild, some in ruined buildings in the Bronx: George Vesey, "For Young Urban Nomads, Home Is the Streets," New York *Times,* 1 June 1976.

3. Hobsbawm (*Revolution,* p. 137) says that after 1815 for a generation the supreme object of politics was to prevent a second French revolution or, worse, a European revolution on the French model. I think the nationalism and militarism this policy implied proved to be the most effective contrarevolutionary strategy and thus can be seen as an expression of this guilt/fear. Houghton (*Victorian,* p. 54) tells us that in 1869 Bertrand Russell's father heard a loud noise in the street and thought it heralded the revolution.

4. Gerhard Masur, *Prophets of Yesterday: Studies in European Culture, 1890–1914* (New York, 1961) , p. 36. A sense of Imperial Russian policy in action is imparted in Farley Mowat, *The Siberians* (Baltimore, 1972) .

In the denouement of the Rif Rebellion in Morocco in 1925,

Abd el Krim, the patriot leader, is reputed to have said on surrendering to the French, "You and your horrible civilization of iron call *me* barbarian because I am poorly armed."

5. For development of this, see Frantz Fanon (Constance Farrington, tr.), *The Wretched of the Earth* (New York, 1968); Frantz Fanon (C. L. Markmann, tr.), *Black Skin White Masks* (New York, 1967); and Jean-Paul Sartre, "Introduction, A Victory," in Henri Alleg, *The Question* (New York, 1958).

6. François Pierre Guillaume Guizot, *History of Civilization in Europe from the Fall of the Roman Empire to the French Revolution* (New York, 1885), p. 23.

7. George Bernard Shaw, "Preface to Major Barbara," *Six Plays By Bernard Shaw with Prefaces* (New York, 1947), p. 324. In fact, there is reason to believe that the pirate republic in the Dry Tortugas during the seventeenth century was outstanding in the West as a humane and just society. Pirates have always received a bad press, except when sailing as privateers for some established Christian state. The time has come for a sympathetic history of piracy in the West from Greco-Roman times to the present, of its cultural, social, and political institutions and their influence.

8. Quoted in Richard Hofstadter, William Miller, and Daniel Aaron, *The American Republic,* II (*Since 1865* [Englewood Cliffs, 1959]), p. 309.

9. Franklin Charles Palm discusses this question in *The Middle Classes Then and Now* (New York, 1936), p. 231. "Deadly blight" is Palm's phrase. This question is central in César Graña, *Bohemian Versus Bourgeois...* (New York, 1964), p. 60.

10. A recent study of the relation between revolution and romanticism is Howard Mumford Jones's *Revolution and Romanticism* (Cambridge, 1974). He says (p. 1) he wrote the book to demonstrate the interrelation of the two between 1763 and 1861, a time when the West was "shaken by two convulsions, one in the area of thought and art, and one in the area of politics": romanticism and revolution.

11. This sense in all its complexity is preserved in Henri Beyle (Stendhal), *Le Rouge et le Noir,* first published in 1828. The estimate of four million dead is in Philibert Audebrand, *Derniers Jours de la Bohème, Souvenirs de la Vie Littéraire* (Paris, 1905), p. 8.

12. Alexis de Tocqueville says that "eighteenth-century man had little of the craving for material well-being which leads the way to servitude." Alexis de Tocqueville (Stuart Gilbert, tr.), *The Old Regime and the French Revolution* (New York, 1955, first in 1856), p. 118.

13. Henri Bourrelier, *La Vie du Quartier Latin dès Origines à la Cité Universitaire* (Paris, 1936), p. 135. Bourrelier says here that the Revolution brought about a cultural change only in the

elite—that it took fifty years for the new conceptions to penetrate popular culure. Restoration youth, he says, went on to realize the conceptions of its elders. These young men fought in the street—and also on the field of art, morals, and literature (p. 156).

14. Gustave Flaubert, *Madame Bovary*, first in 1857.

15. Bohemia, the geographical term, derives from *Boihaemum*, Latin for "home of the Boii." The Boii, an early Celtic tribe, long ago lived in the region that now bears their name.

PART TWO   The First Bohemia

* Théophile Gautier, *Histoire de Romantisme Suivie de Notices Romantiques* ... (Paris, *c*. 1872), p. 2.

2   Victor Hugo's Romantic Army

1. Victor Hugo is a god in the Bao Dai sect in Vietnam and a god in the Western Heaven of Chinese folk Taoism. Closer to home, Jean-Paul Sartre remembers his grandfather as " a man of the nineteenth century who took himself for Victor Hugo, as did many others, including Victor Hugo himself." Jean-Paul Sartre, (Bernard Frechtman, tr.,), *The Words* (New York, 1964), p. 24. For a sense of the awesome influence of Victor Hugo in France, see André Maurois (Oliver Bernard, tr.), *Victor Hugo and His World* (London, 1966).

2. The information about Hugo comes from Matthew Josephson, *Victor Hugo, a Realistic Biography of the Great Romantic* (New York, 1942); André Maurois (Gerard Hopkins, tr.), *Olympio, the Life of Victor Hugo* (New York, 1956); Evelyn Geler, "Hugo, Victor Marie," in Stanley Kunitz and Veneta Colby, eds., *European Authors, 1000–1900, A Biographical Dictionary of European Authors* (New York, 1967); and Pierre-Georges Castex and Paul Surer, *Manuel des Études Littéraires Françaises, XIXe Siècle* (Paris, 1950).

3. Maurois, *Hugo*, p. 44.

4. Ibid., p. 65.

5. Ibid., p. 114.

6. Idem.

7. Josephson, *Hugo*, p. 125.

8. Maurois, *Hugo*, p. 124.

9. Josephson, *Hugo*, p. 132. He renders it: a "soul that dwells apart."

10. Ibid., p. 140.

11. Castex and Surer, *Études*, p. 44.

12. Bourrelier, *Quartier*, pp. 156–157.

13. Gautier, *Romantisme*, p. 53. John E. Matzke, "Introduction," Victor Hugo, *Hernani*. ... (Boston, 1891), p. xxvii. George

C. Williamson, ed., *Bryan's Dictionary of Painters and Engravers,* IV (Port Washington, 1964), p. 3. After a debilitating life spent making illustrations to earn the price of paint and canvas, Nanteuil ended his days as director of the Dijon Academy (of art). Philip Carr, *Days with the French Romantics in the Paris of 1830* (London, 1932), p. 89.

14. Evelyn Geler, "Nerval, Gérard de," in Kunitz & Colby, *Authors,* p. 677. Also Raymond Jean, ed., *Nerval par Lui-Même* (Paris, 1964).

15. Gautier, *Romantisme,* pp. 6–7. The information about Gautier is mainly from Seymour S. Weiner, "Gautier, (Pierre Jules) Théophile," in Kunitz & Colby, *Authors;* from René Jasinski, *Les Années Romantiques de Th. Gautier* (Paris, 1929); and Maxime du Camp, *Théophile Gautier* (Paris, 1890). Also Joanna Richardson, *Théophile Gautier, His Life and Times* (London, 1958). For a bibliography of Gautier and the other romantics: Charles Asselineau, *Bibliographie Romantique, Catalogue Anecdotique et Pittoresque des Éditions Originales des Oeuvres de Victor Hugo ... etc* (Paris, 1872).

16. Gautier, *Romantisme,* p. 21. A beard in 1830 constituted an outrage of public decency according to Orlo Williams, *Vie de Bohème, A Patch of Romantic Paris* (Boston, 1913). This is the first book in English if not in any language to tell the story of early Bohemian Paris. Williams discusses this question on p. 110. The other book in English—and not so good—is Joanna Richardson, *The Bohemians: La Vie de Bohème in Paris, 1830–1914* (London, 1969). Graña, *Bohemian;* Malcolm Eastland, *Artists and Writers in Paris: The Bohemian Idea, 1803–1867* (London, 1964); and Arthur Bartlett Maurice, *The Paris of the Novelists* (New York, 1919) treat the subject obliquely. The best book is Pierre Labracherie, *La Vie Quotidienne de la Bohème Littéraire au XIXe Siècle* (Paris, 1967).

17. Gautier, *Romantisme,* pp. 95–96.

18. Ibid., p. 96.

19. Armand Augustin Joseph Marie Ferrard, Comte de Pontmartin, *Mes Memoirs,* I (*Enfance et Jeunesse* [Paris, 1882]), p. 133.

20. Gautier, *Romantisme,* pp. 95–96.

21. Josephson, *Hugo,* p. 142; Gautier, *Romantisme,* pp. 63–64; Williams, *Bohème,* p. 134; and O'Neddy's biography by his lifelong friend, Ernest Havet ("Notice," *Poésies Posthumes de Philothée O'Neddy* [Paris, 1887], pp. 1–129). Du Camp, (*Gautier,* p. 27) says this exchange took place when Nerval first gave Gautier the tickets. Josephson (*Hugo,* pp. 141–142) says it happened when Nerval and the Gautier contingent were leaving Hugo's house. To me it seems most likely (if at all) it happened on the scene. On p. 27 n. 1., du Camp says someone told him this story in 1851 in the presence of Gautier and Hugo. Gautier's only response was to

say: "Those were the days." A propos the composition of the Hernanists du Camp says on p. 26: "The painters, the sculptors responded to the call with alacrity; the architects were slack and tardy; to the great doorway of Notre-Dame they preferred the colonnade of the Stock Exchange, but recently constructed; wishing however to utilize them, they [the leaders] mixed them with the other artists, who were charged with watching them and keeping them on the right road, be it by kicking their ankles." Williams (p. 136) says the army comprised many artists and art students.

22. Josephson, *Hugo*, p. 142.

23. Gautier, *Romantisme*, p. 101.

24. The only eyewitness accounts seem to be those of Gautier; Adèle Hugo (*Victor Hugo Raconté par un Témoin de Sa Vie* [Paris, first in 1868]); and Pontmartin, *Memoirs*. This is valuable for perspective, more than for information. The quotation is on pp. 137–8. The rest is from Gautier, *Romantisme*, pp. 102–107, and A. Hugo, *Hugo*, p. 236.

25. Gautier, *Romantisme*, pp. 90, 97; A. Hugo, *Hugo*, p. 260. Gautier (p. 104) called them "young Shakespearean barbarians."

26. Gautier, *Romantisme*, p. 115.

27. Most of the impressions, the quotations from Baron Taylor and Mlle. Mars (except for the last line: Josephson, *Hugo*, p. 143), and the piss story are from Adèle Hugo, *Hugo*, pp. 236–237. The young sculptor is from Gautier, *Romantisme*, p. 97.

28. Josephson, *Hugo*, pp. 143–144; Maurois, *Hugo*, p. 134; Bourrelier, *Quartier*, p. 156; Du Camp, *Gautier*, pp. 28–29.

29. Castex & Surer, *Etudes*, p. 69.

30. A. Hugo, *Hugo*, p. 239.

31. Ibid., p. 238; Augustin Challamel, *Souvenirs d' un Hugo-lâtre, La Génération de 1830* (Paris, 1885), p. 25.

32. Victor Hugo, *Journal, 1830–1848* (Paris, 1954), p. 9.

33. Bourrelier (*Quartier*, p. 106) says that from circa 1588 to 1830 the Latin Quarter was in lethargy, that *Hernani* served as the resurrection of its long-lost effervescence. Donald Drew Egbert in *Social Radicalism and the Arts: Western Europe* ... (New York, 1970) says on p. 149 that *Hernani* marked "the first clear application of the idea of revolution to the arts." No one really seems to know how many times *Hernani* was produced. Adèle says 45 times (p. 242) and adds that it was closed because Mlle. Mars went on vacation. The editor of Hugo's *Journal* (p. 354) says 39 times.

34. Leroy F. Aarons of the *Times-Post* Service in the San Francisco *Chronicle*, 7 August 1970.

35. I had the pleasure of participating.

36. Franklin J. Bardacke reported this in conversation on returning from Washington, D.C.

37. I had the pleasure of participating.

3 The First Bohemians

1. The Goliards are in a sense precursors of the Bohemians as they certainly are of the Wandervögel. About 1100, at the summit of the High Middle Ages, when the traditional order was loose and viable, student life found voice among the mendicant scholars and other clerical vagabonds pledged to the brotherhood of the mythical and profligate Saint Golias. Here was a quasi-religious order, a youth movement lasting 200 years, composed of vagrants who sang songs celebrating gentleness and drunkenness, gluttony and idleness, sex and sensuality.

From "The Confessions of Golias:"

Res est arduissima	Meum est propositum
vincere naturam,	in taberna mori:
legeum sequi duram,	vinum sit appositum
mentem esse puram;	morientis ori,
iuvenes non possumus	ut dicant cum venerint
legem sequi duram,	angelorum chori:
leviumque corporum	"Deus sit propitius
non habere curam.	huic potatori!"

All of which means something like this:

It's really awfully hard	My intention is you see
To overcome my nature,	To die in some saloon;
When a virgin comes along	Wine must be served to me
To keep my thinking pure;	To drink as I sink down,
Kids will never follow laws	So that the angel chorus
Or rigid forms of censure,	Will be saying as it comes:
Made quite without regard	"God shed his grace on thee
For sensual adventure.	You crazy drunken bum!"

The Latin verses come from George F. Whicher, *The Goliard Poets, Medieval Latin Songs and Satires* (New York, 1949), pp. 108, 110. The translation is mine.

2. Théophile Gautier, *Histoire de Romantisme Suivie de Notices Romantiques* ... (Paris, c. 1872), p. 99.

3. Orlo Williams, *Vie de Bohème, A Patch of Romantic Paris* (London, 1913), pp. 135–136.

4. This information is compiled from many sources. The other four members are Don José (Joseph Bouchardy), Alphonse Brot, Noël (Léon Clopet), Napoléon Thom (as).

5. For this and subsequent information about Borel: Gautier, *Romantisme*, pp. 21–22, 36; and Enid Starkie, *Pétrus Borel, the Lycanthrope: His Life and Times* (London, c. 1950). On p. 26 she says they called their group the Little Cenacle to distinguish it

from that conducted by Nodier. Certainly they called it such to distinguish it from the group conducted by Hugo and Sainte-Beuve. Pétrus Borel, "Preface," *Rhapsodies* (Paris 1832).

6. René Jasinski, *Les Années Romantiques de Th. Gautier* (Paris, 1890), p. 88.

7. Williams, *Bohème*, pp. 138–140.

8. Evelyn Geler, "Nerval, Gérard de," in Kunitz & Colby, *Authors*, p. 677. Gautier, *Romantisme*, p. 25. In a letter written 23 September 1862 and published in Marcel Hervier's "Introduction" to Philothée O'Neddy, *Feu et Flamme, Publié avec un Introduction des Notes par Marcel Hervier.* (Paris, 1926), p. xxiv, O'Neddy says that they only called themselves "Jeunes-France" and that such is what "we must be called." On p. 5, O'Neddy printed a poem of Borel's, beginning:

> "Bohémiens, sans toits, sans bancs,
> Sans existance engainée . . . ,"

which implies that in French *Bohemian* still meant *gypsy* or *vagabond*, that it had yet to be applied to the people it would soon denote. In "Robert Baldick: The First Bohemian . . . ," *The* (London) *Times Literary Supplement*, 19 May 1961, p. 307, an anonymous reviewer says that contrary to what some believe, Balzac did not use Bohemian in its current meaning as early as 1830; his novel, *Un Grand Homme de Province à Paris,* where it is so used, was published in 1839. In her novel *La Dernière Aldini* (Paris, 1837) George Sand has a character say, "Vive la bohème!" Labnachèrie, *La Vie Quotidienne*, p. 9, says this is the literary debut of the word in its new meaning.

9. Williams, *Bohème,* p. 56. Herb Caen (San Francisco *Chronicle,* 4 May 1958) wrote: "Novelist Jack 'On the Road' Kerouac, the voice of the Beatniks, will have a new one out in the fall, titled 'The Dharma Bums.' " The above O'Neddy letter (O'Neddy, *Feu et Flamme,* pp. xxiv–xxv) tells the bouzingo story and resolves all doubt as to the origin of this novel appellation.

10. Idem.

11. Gautier, *Romantisme,* pp. 48, 50–51.

12. Ibid., p. 31.

13. Jasinski, *Gautier,* p. 130. *Figaro,* 20 January 1832.

14. Smoking, says Williams (*Bohème,* p. 151) was a romantic duty, be it the Byronic cigar, the Faust-Hoffmann pipe of Germany and Flanders, or the cigarette of Spain. The smoke was the smoke of hell. O'Neddy declared that the Devil "is more artist than God." This is quoted by O'Neddy's lifelong friend and biographer: Ernest Havet, "Notice," *Poésies Posthumes de Philothée O'Neddy* (Paris, 1887), p. 20. Du Seigneur's studio, where this takes place, was embellished by sketches by Eugène and Achille Devéria and a copy of a Venetian painting by Louis Boulanger (Malcolm Easton, *Artists*

and Writers in Paris: The Bohemian Idea, 1803–1867 [London, 1964], p. 58). In *Feu et Flamme*, p. 5, O'Neddy says that "in the young studio of Jehan, the statuary/Hides in its magic and profound sanctuary."

15. O'Neddy is described by Gautier (*Romantisme*, pp. 63–64) and by Havet in *Poésies*, p. 11. O'Neddy, *Feu et Flamme*, pp. 8, 11, 13, 14, 16.

16. Williams, *Bohème*, p. 50.

17. Havet in *Poésies*, p. 5.

18. Charles Asselineau, *Bibliographie Romantique, Catalogue Anecdotique et Pittoresque des Editions Originales des Oeuvres de Victor Hugo....* (Paris, 1872), pp. 201, 215; Challamel, *Souvenirs*, p. 42; Maxime Du Camp, *Théophile Gautier* (Paris, 1890), p. 36.

19. The Bouchardie information is in Herbert Gorman, *The Incredible Marquis, Alexandre Dumas* (New York, 1929), p. 177. The quotation is in a letter written to Gautier and printed in Gautier, *Romantisme*, pp. 84–86.

20. Ibid., p. 87.

4 Doyenné: The Wealthy Model

1. In an article written in 1870 about Paul de Kock, Gautier described the Parisian type he remembered from childhood and youth (Williams, *Bohème*, p. 288). Honoré de Balzac, *La Femme aux Yeux d'Or* (Paris, 1835). Victor Hugo, *Les Misérables* (Paris, 1862). Emile Zola, *L'Assommoir* (Paris, 1867). For a modern study of the people, Louis Chevalier (Frank Jellinek, tr.), *Laboring Classes and Dangerous Classes in Paris During the First Half of the Nineteenth Century* (New York, 1973). For the architecture of old Paris, David H. Pinkney, *Napoleon III and the rebuilding of Paris* (Princeton, 1972). For its streets, Félix and Louis Lazarre, *Dictionnaire Administratif et Historique des Rues de Paris et Ses Monuments* (Paris, 1844).

2. This information is from Arsène Houssaye, *Les Confessions, Souvenirs d'un Demi-Siècle, 1830–1880*, I (Paris, 1885), pp. 87, 171–173, 182–196, 209, 292–296. Williams (*Bohème*, pp. 23–28) tells of the artistic/political split. Jasinski (*Gautier*, pp. 86–87) elaborates on this, describes the cholera epidemic and (p. 129) quotes Thiers. He ascribes the success of macabre literature to the epidemic. The Nerval quote is in Challamel, *Hugolâtre*, p. 20.

3. Gautier, *Romantisme*, pp. 71–74, and Houssaye, *Confessions*, pp. 314, 297.

4. Williams, *Bohème*, pp. 160–177; Houssaye, *Confessions*, p. 300.

5. The student information comes from Bourrelier, *Quartier*.

6. Williams, *Bohéme*, pp. 78–79, says that after the Revolution of 1830 many aristocrats resigned their commissions and,

careers shattered, devoted themselves entirely to the pursuit of pleasure on the boulevards.

7. Most of the Doyenné details come from Houssaye, *Confessions*, pp. 297–358.

8. Williams (*Bohème*, pp. 89–90) and Starkey (*Borel*, pp. 61–62 ff.) describe these festivals. Starkey tells of the epidemic and of the Mis-Carême the Parisians enjoyed while waiting for the cholera to cross over from England. This was the wildest public festival in memory. The romantics reveled in wild dancing, especially in the newly-introduced *can-can, chahut,* and *galop infernal.* Williams tells about them in *Bohème*, pp. 181–185, 274–281.

9. Maurice *Paris*, p. 109 says Murger visited Doyenné. This story is in Houssaye, *Confessions*, pp. 358–359.

5 Murger: The Poverty Models

1. This is from Henry Murger's "Preface" to his *Scènes de Bohème* (also *Scènes de la Vie de Bohème*), published in book form beginning in 1851 in a multitude of editions in many languages.

2. Henry Murger to Léon Noël, 23 May 1842, published in Adrien François Lelioux, Léon Noël, and Nadar, *Histoire de Murger Pour Servir à l'Histoire de la Vrai Bohème par Trois Buveurs d'Eau* (Paris, 1864), p. 125; Murger to Noël, 30 May 1842, Ibid., p. 126.

3. The general information about Murger in this chapter is from Robert Baldick, *The First Bohemian: the Life of Henry Murger* (London, 1961), and from Orlo Williams, *Vie de Bohème, A Patch of Romantic Paris* (Boston, 1913). A few items are from Arthur Moss and Evalyn Marvell, *The Legend of the Latin Quarter, Henry Murger and the Birth of Bohemia* (New York, 1946). Noël in Lelioux, *Murger*, p. 88. Lelioux, Ibid., pp. 58, 34.

4. Ibid., p. 19.

5. Noël in Ibid., p. 86.

6. Ibid., p. 94.

7. Ibid., p. 92.

8. Lelioux in Ibid., p. 53.

9. Baldick, *Murger*, p. 46.

10. Lelioux, *Murger*, pp. 59–61.

11. Murger, *Scènes de Bohème.*

12. Henry Murger, *Les Buveurs d'Eau* (Paris, 1870).

13. Noël in Lelioux, *Murger*, p. 108.

14. Nathan Adler, *The Underground Stream: New Life Styles and the Antinomian Personality* (New York, 1972), p. 1. Bruce Cook, *The Beat Generation, The Tumultuous '50's Movement and Its Impact on Today* (New York, 1971), p. 194. For the beer, Marius Boisson, *Les Compagnons de la Vie de Bohème...* (Paris, 1929), p. 60.

15. Williams (*Bohème*, pp. 208–209) says that at this juncture when journalism and illustration were beginning to pay, the art world was trisected into the well-paid, the ill-paid, and the not-paid. Consequently, equality vanished. Raymond Jean (Raymond Jean, ed., *Nerval par Lui-Même* [Paris, 1964], p. 30) says: At this time journalism became an outlet for writers without resources. But the journals owe their existence "to a public avid for a certain form of literary vulgarization to the demands of which authors spontaneously submit. The writer enters into a system which necessarily influences the nature of his production. It is then that l'oeuvre becomes merchandise that one must *place*, that literature degrades itself into the state of copy."

16. Baldick, *Murger*, pp. 65–66.

17. Henry Murger to Henry Mazuel, 3 January 1845, in Baldick, *Murger*, pp. 67–68.

18. Baldick, *Murger*, p. 69.

19. *Le Corsair* had lately been called *Le Corsair-Satan*.

20. Baldick, *Murger*, p. 126. Nadar (in Lelioux, *Murger*, pp. 239–241) recalls the opening night.

21. Murger, "Preface," *Bohème*.

22. Bourrelier, *Quartier*, p. 162 says *Scènes de Bohème* intoxicated a large proportion of the students, bringing them to use it for a life-style model.

23. Among the many examples of this influence are James Gibbon Huneker who tells us in his autobiography (*Steeplejack* [New York, 1922], p. 222) that on arriving in Paris as a youth in 1872 he modeled himself on Murger's characters, and the fact that James Abbott McNeill Whistler "knew Murger by heart" before he went to Paris: Stanley Weintraub, *Whistler, A Biography* (New York, 1974), p. 33.

24. Williams, *Bohème*, p. 251.

25. Boisson, *Compagnons*, p. 26.

6 The Real Bohemia

1. Quoted in the *Oxford English Dictionary*.

2. Ernest Havet, *Poésies Posthumes de Philothée O'Neddy* (Paris, 1887), p. 144: "Il est, depuis longtemps, avéré que nous sommes,/ Dans le siècle, environ dix mille jeunes hommes,/ Qui du démon de l'Art nous croyant tourmentés,/ Dépensons notre vie en excentricités;/ Qui, du fatal Byron copiant des allures,/ De solonnels manteaux drapons nos enclures./ ..." Orlo Williams, *Vie de Bohème, A Patch of Romantic Paris* (London, 1913), p. 130.

3. Ibid., p. 131.

4. When in 1843 Célestin Nanteuil was asked to recruit 300 young men to defend Hugo's play *Les Burgraves* as they had once defended *Hernani* he replied, "There are no more young men." Williams (*Bohème*, p. 251) quotes Théodore Pelloquet speaking over Murger's grave: "He belonged to a sorry generation, to a generation old before its time, and, in spite of its premature old age, without experience, without enthusiasm and without rage, having some vanity but no pride whatever, a foolish vanity, puerile, which manifested itself above all in the affectation of a pitiful irony, in the presence of all enthusiasms and all large causes; to a generation, in a word, which let die in its hands the magnificent heritage that had been left by the men of 1830."

5. Baldick, *Murger* (p. xi), cites for this " 'Notice Géographique, Historique, Politique et Littéraire Sur la Bohème.' *La Silhouette*, 1849." *La Silhouette, Journal des Caricatures*, began in 1829.

6. Théophile Gautier, *Histoire du Romantisme Suivie de Notices Romantiques.* . . . (Paris, *c.* 1872) , p. 150 says "Victor Hugo, if he were not a poet, would have been a painter of the first order."

7. Arsène Houssaye, *Les Cosfessions, Souvenirs d'un Demi-Siècle, 1830–1880*, I (Paris, 1885), p. 313 evokes this scene while explaining that bouzingo originated as bousin*goth*, a word invented during one of these chants. Williams (*Bohème*, p. 252) says this pose of jaded sophistication was common among adolescent romantics.

8. George Orwell, *Down and Out in Paris and London* (New York, 1933) ; Henry Miller, *Tropic of Cancer* (Paris, 1934) , and *Tropic of Capricorn* (Paris, 1938).

9. Gautier, *Romantisme*, p. 17.

10. Another facet of this is examined by Malcolm Easton in *Artists and Writers in Paris: The Bohemian Idea, 1803–1867* (London, 1964) , pp. 136–137. Here, he says, Murger's low-brow heroes were shocking to many as was the funky life they led. Some see this as the beginning of realism, an attitude Courbet, scorning both classicism and romanticism, carried over into painting. Certainly low-brow heroes living funky lives are a modality of the novel as far back as the Marquis de Sade's *Justine* (first in 1793) or, for that matter, Petronius' *Satyricon* (first in the 1st century A.D.) . Perhaps the advent of photography in 1839 should be regarded as the beginning of realism.

PART THREE   The Bohemian International

* Mabel Urmy Seares, "William Keith and His Times," in Anonymous, *Art in California.* . . . (San Francisco, 1916) , p. 105.

7 Bohemian Frisco

1. These are from a special U.S. census of California taken in 1852 and from *The Census of 1860*. In 1860 the enumerators found 52,866 whites; 1,176 free coloreds; 2,179 Asiatics; and 41 Indians—a total of 56,262. But the *Census* announces a grand total 56,802. Half of the enumerated were born in foreign countries. Frank Soulé, John H. Gihon, M.D., and James Nisbet, *The Annals of San Francisco* ... (Palo Alto, 1966, first in 1855), pp. 209, 446, 462, 493–494, 536, 685, 495–496, 494, 517, 509. More remarkable even than that the city's history was written during its sixth year of importance is that it already had enough history to fill a thick book. Doris Muscatine, *Old San Francisco, The Biography of a City, From Early Days to the Earthquake* (New York, 1975), pp. 164, 155, 108, 109, 125.

2. Ibid., p. 158.

3. The art association began in 1871, the school in 1874. It was the only art school west of Chicago. Harry Mulford, "Artists and Literary Men, A History of the San Francisco Art Institute," *San Francisco Art Institute Calendar of Events*, March, 1973.

4. Idwal Jones, *Ark of Empire, San Francisco's Montgomery Block: San Francisco's Unique Bohemia, 1853–1953* (New York, 1972), p. 27.

5. Henry George, Jr., *The Life of Henry George by His Son* ... (New York, 1900), pp. 69–70.

6. Soulé, *Annals*, pp. 506–507, 502, 504.

7. Jones's *Ark* is about Henry W. Halleck's Montgomery Block. The other men appear occasionally in its pages.

8. Bernard Taper, ed. & comp., *Mark Twain's San Francisco* (New York, 1963), pp. 54, xxi.

9. Albert Parry, *Garrets and Pretenders, A History of Bohemianism in America* (New York, 1933), pp. 212–213. Taper, *Twain*, p. 53.

10. Walton Bean, *California, An Interpretive History* (New York, 1968), p. 113.

8 Bohemians in the Bourgeois Empire

1. On 7 September 1830, Hugo wrote: "With us too it's a question of liberty; ours also is a revolution; she will march in solidarity with her sister, the political one. Revolutions, like wolves, do not devour each other (Matthew Josephson, *Victor Hugo, A Realistic Biography of the Great Romantic* [New York, 1942], p. 150)." J. L. Talmon in *Romanticism and Revolt: Europe 1815–1848* (New York, 1967) says on p. 9: "Up to the hour of trial—1848—it is reasonable to speak of a peoples' camp facing an alliance of kings." He believes that the force of revolution, intensified

by repression, propelled the age, first as a drive for revolutionary change, next as a swelling rebelliousness—rejection of divine authority—then of temporal.

2. The quotation is in D. W. Brogan, *The French Nation from Napoleon to Pétain, 1814–1940* (New York, 1963), p. 97. I translated it from Brogan's English into American. The cab is on p. 92.

3. Henri Bourrelier, *La Vie du Quartier Latin des Origines à la Cité Universitaire* (Paris, 1936), pp. 106, 153, 160.

4. C. W. Ceram, *Archaeology of the Cinema* (New York, c. 1970), p. 78.

5. The background of the Second Empire is mainly from Brogan, *French Nation;* Roger L. Williams, *Gaslight and Shadow, the World of Napoleon III* (New York, 1957); and Roger L. Williams, *The French Revolution of 1870–1871* (New York, 1969). None of these, however, refer to the Empire as a proto-fascist state.

6. David H. Pinkney, *Napoleon III and the Rebuilding of Paris* (Princeton, 1972).

7. George du Maurier, *Trilby, a Novel, with Illustrations by the Author* (New York, 1895), p. 105. Although written in the 1890's, *Trilby* is set in the fifties. J. G. Alger, *The New Paris Sketch Book: Manners, Men, Institutions* (London, 1889), p. 63. James D. McCabe, Jr., *Paris by Sunlight and Gaslight....* (Philadelphia, 1869), pp. 602, 75, 664.

8. André Zeller, *Les Hommes de la Commune* (Paris, 1969), p. 61. McCabe, *Paris,* p. 15.

9. *Ibid.,* pp. 231–244. Williams (*Revolution,* pp. 8–9) says the vigorous, militant opposition of the students derived mainly from their contempt for the *Genesis* cosmology sanctioned by the Empire. The Empire shows its transitional quality in its equivocation between science and traditional theology. The young (pp. 11–12), cool to the ideals of 1848, found inspiration in what they'd been trained to revere: science.

10. McCabe, *Paris,* p. 243.

11. McCabe (p. 258) tells of the police and (p. 564) says the French still conducted public executions. Jean Gimpel, *The Cult of Art, Against Art and Artists* (New York, 1969), p. 108.

12. Williams (*Napoleon III,* p. 103) says the object of licensing theaters through the Ministry of the Interior was censorship, primarily for the regime's security, secondarily to please the Catholic Church. On p. 5 of *Revolution* he says the strict censorship laws, enforcing political conformity and bourgeois morality, were odious to most writers. Labracherie, *Bohème,* pp. 117–118, says "There was no longer scarcely any place for the writer in this coarse and materialistic world." All this relaxed somewhat toward the end. *Hernani* and other Hugo plays, hitherto proscribed, were, in 1867,

reproduced with great success. A lucid and detailed discussion of censorship and its poisonous effects is in F. J. W. Hemmings, *Culture and Society in France, 1848–1898, Dissidents and Philistines* (New York, 1971), pp. 43–77, a book which examines the relation between art and power in France.

13. Williams, *Napoleon III*, p. 102. McCabe, *Paris*, pp. 708–713.

14. Gimpel, *Art*, pp. 103–104, discusses this.

15. This is all based on Labracherie, *Bohème*.

16. Alphonse Daudet (Laura Ensor, tr.), *Thirty Years of Paris and of My Literary Life* (London, 1893), p. 233.

17. Labracherie, *Bohème*. p. 123.

18. Ibid., p. 120. All of the information above and below is from this book excepting some Vallès information from Marie-Claire Banquart, *Jules Vallès* (Paris, 1971), p. 8 and elsewhere.

19. Labracherie, *Bohème*, p. 126.

20. Ibid., p. 130.

21. Ibid., pp. 146–147.

22. Ibid., p. 140.

9 The Bohemian Commune

1 . André Zeller, *Les Hommes de la Commune* (Paris, 1969), is the source of all this information and of most of what follows. Zeller's is an excellent book, one which should be available in English translation.

2. Hugo announced: "In view of present conditions in France, protest—absolute, inflexible, eternal protest—is my one duty. . . . I shall share to the end the exile of Liberty. *When Liberty returns, I shall return!*" (Matthew Josephon, *Victor Hugo, a Realistic Biography of the Great Romantic* [New York, 1942], pp. 435–436.)

3. Zeller, *Commune*, p. 95.

4. On 19 August 1839, François Arago told a joint meeting of the Academies of Science and of Fine Arts that Nicéphore Nièpce and Louis-Jacques-Mandé Daguerre had chemically fixed images captured by the camera obscura. Among other sensational implications at once understood was: Oil painting is dead! See Jean Gimpel, *The Cult of Art, Against Art and Artists* (New York, 1969), p. 111. Beaumont Newhall in his *The History of Photography from 1839 to the Present Day* (New York, 1949), on p. 63, says: "The more prominent portraitists had for the most part been young Romantics of the Latin Quarter, living the Vie de Bohème as second-rate painters, caricaturists and writers." Michel François Braive (David Britt, tr.), *The Photograph, a Social History* (New York, 1966), pp. 95, 121, 163, 180. Braive refers to photography as a "bourgeois art" (p. 163) and informs us that Nadar originated

photo-journalism (p. 220). When Nadar photographed Balzac, Balzac confided that all things are composed like an onion of a large number of layers he called "spectres." The act of photographing transfers one spectre from the object to the plate. Heinrich Schwarz, "Nadar," *The Encyclopedia of Photography*, XIII (New York, 1963), p. 2484.

5. Braive, *Photograph*, p. 238; *Collier's Encyclopedia*, XVI (New York, 1967), p. 142.

6. Zeller, *Commune*, p. 128.

7. Ibid., p. 167.

8. Josephson, *Hugo*, p. 480.

9. Zeller, *Commune*, p. 211.

10. André Maurois (Gerald Hopkins, tr.), *Olympio, The Life of Victor Hugo* (New York, 1956), p. 396.

11. The real ruler of France was the Council of the King (the high command of the bureaucracy) which during the Revolution changed its name but not its function and kept on ruling under various names until today. It's now called the Council of State. This is a leitmotif in de Tocqueville's *Ancien Régime* and is treated by Herbert Leuthy (a Swiss) in his *France Against Herself* (Eric Mossbacher, tr., New York, 1955), pp. 15–18. At this point in 1871, all of the government officials and functionaries, even the postmen, had either quit work or left town.

12. Maybe not smugly, as he was ill. See Joanna Richardson, *Théophile Gautier, His Life and Times* (London, 1958), pp. 258–262. Gautier wrote of "the sane part of Paris" being "terrorized by a few ruffians (p. 258)" and (p. 262): "The savages, tattooed with red and wearing rings in their noses, are dancing the scalp dance on the smoking ruins of Society."

13. Roger L. Williams, *The French Revolution of 1870–1871* (New York, 1969), p. 140. For the fine arts, Egbert, *Social Radicalism*, p. 203.

14. Ernest Alfred Viztelly (*My Adventures in the Commune, Paris, 1871* [London, 1914]), then a perceptive but snobbish and conservative English youth, gives an eyewitness account of these events. He tells of the American girl (p. 281) and says, "In those days the cult of Napoleon had no disciples in the United States."

15. Ibid., p. 279.

16. Viztelly (ibid., p. 316) writes of the bourgeoisie as that "hated class" known "to have no sympathy with the Commune." Like Gautier, most of the literati and journalists, of both the first and second rank, had no sympathy with the Commune, while most of the fine artists of both ranks ranged from sympathizer to participant. This is clearly demonstrated in the excellent collection of essays and documents gathered together by John Hicks and Robert Tucker in *Revolution and Reaction, The Paris Commune 1871* (Amherst, 1973). In his *The Civil War in France*, published in

London on 30 May 1871, Karl Marx says that the Paris of Thiers was "a phantom Paris," the Paris of the absconders, "the Paris of the boulevards, male and female—the rich, the capitalist, the gilded, the idle Paris, now thronging with its lackeys, its blacklegs, its literary *bohème,* and its *cocottes.* . . ."

There still are two Parises occupying one city: the international Paris of sensual luxury and the much larger Paris of the desperate and struggling poor.

17. Vizetelly reports this (*Commune,* p. 146).

18. Hicks and Tucker (*Commune*) follows the theme of meaning and background. One aspect is its examination of the Commune's influence on Marx, Lenin, the USSR, and the People's Republic of China.

19. Zeller, *Commune,* p. 274.

20. Ibid., p. 364.

21. Ibid., p. 48.

22. Ibid., p. 361. The quotation is from Marx's son-in-law Lefrançois.

23. D. W. Brogan in *The French Nation from Napoleon to Pétain, 1814–1940* (New York, 1963), p. 157, says Bloody Week "made final" the "alienation of the workers of Paris from the official organization of the French State," a schism opened in 1848.

24. Many of the prisoners had been transported to prison colonies like Devil's Island.

25. A controversy turns around the question: was Rimbaud a soldier of the Commune? or at least in Paris at that time? The translation of the poem is mine.

26. San Francisco *Good Times,* 30 April 1971.

10   The Bohemian International

1. This felicitous phrase is from Robert Baldick, *The First Bohemian: The Life of Henry Murger* (London, 1961), p. xii.

2. A story by Agence France-Presse in the San Francisco *Chronicle* of 21 May 1973 tells of an official study composed of interviews with 200 persons of "international standing" which concludes that the "dynamic elements" are leaving Paris, that Paris no longer stands as the cultural leader of the world, and that Paris plays but "a secondary role in international financial and economic relations" and is losing its political primacy in Europe.

3. The above information is mainly from Pierre Labracherie, *La Vie Quotidienne de la Bohème Littéraire au XIXe Siècle* (Paris, 1967), pp. 153–187. For a description of these readings, W. C. Morrow (from notes by Edouard Cucuel), *Bohemian Paris To-day* (London, 1899), pp. 190–191.

4. Labracherie, *Bohème,* p. 167.

5. In *La Vie du Quartier Latin dès Origines à la Cité Uni-*

versitaire (Paris, 1936) Henri Bourrelier says (pp. 18–56) in the twelfth and thirteenth centuries about 1,000 students lived in Paris, in the late fourteenth century, from 10,000 to 20,000. In 1200 (p. 65) there was a strike by students and professors.

6. Edmond Faral, *La Vie Quotidiènne au Temps de Saint Louis* (Paris, 1938), pp. 108, 18.

7. Bourrelier, *Quartier,* pp. 160–162.

8. Ibid., pp. 143–144.

9. Ibid., p. 145.

10. Ibid., pp. 152–154.

11. Ibid., pp. 69–70. He says these orgies peopled the dreams of the students.

12. Alexandre Privat d'Anglemont, *Paris Anecdote, Avec une Préface et des Notes par Charles Monselet...* (Paris, 1885), p. 157. This is the major primary source for Childebert (pp. 141–161).

13. Idem. See also Labracherie, *Bohème,* pp. 79–81; Orlo Williams, *Vie de Bohème, A Patch of Romantic Paris* (Boston, 1913), pp. 223–224; and Albert Dresden Vandam, *An Englishman in Paris ... I (Reign of Louis-Philippe* [London, 1892]), pp. 9–25.

14. Williams, *Bohème,* pp. 221–222.

15. William Makepeace Thackeray, *The Paris Sketch Book* (London, 1870), pp. 57–60, 75. Thackeray mentions a French novel in which a wild student turns into a dignified and conventional government official. The man explains: "You know that what is permitted to a student is not very becoming to a magistrate (p. 141)." Arsène Houssaye, in a letter from London to the *Revue de Paris* (May 1836), tells us that "artists are no better than laborers in the eyes of high society." When admitted to this august company they were given chores like painting portraits of dogs. Among the artists themselves "there is a whole palette of social distinctions, a whole comedy of social reverberations. That is why there are no artistic friendships, no groups, no schools in England." Quoted in Henry Kneppler (ed. & tr.), *Man About Paris...* (New York, 1970), p. 85.

16. This system also served to deliver control of the arts to the state. It was developed by the Bourbon monarchy before the Revolution. For more on Beaux Arts see R. B. A. Shirley-Fox, *An Art Student Reminisces of Paris in the Eighties* (London, 1909), pp. 95–121. Jean Gimpel, *The Cult of Art, Against Art and Artists* (New York, 1969), pp. 64–81.

17. Morrow (Cucuel), *Paris,* pp. 41–49.

18. Ibid., p. 59. Bourrelier, *Quartier,* pp. 207–208. Ralph Nevill, *Days and Nights in Montmartre and the Latin Quarter* (New York, 1927), pp. 308–313.

19. Morrow (Cucuel), *Paris,* p. 40.

20. Ibid., pp. 79–108.

11. The Last Bohemia

1. This is the subject of Frederick Lewis Allen, *The Big Change, America Transforms Itself* (New York, 1952).

2. Quoted in Wyatt Blassingame, *The French Foreign Legion* (New York, 1955), p. 78.

3. Jean Roman (James Emmons, tr.), *Paris, Fin de Siècle* (New York, 1960), pp. 5, 7–8, 34–35. An amazing pictorial record of the romance of machines is contained in Richard Avedon, ed., *Diary of a Century, Jacques-Henri Lartigue* (New York, 1970) and Jacques-Henri Lartigue, *Boyhood Photographs of J.-H. Lartigue, The Family Album of a Gilded Age* (Switzerland, 1966).

4. Roman, *Paris,* p. 97.

5. For Montparnasse, Labracherie, *Bohème,* pp. 185–187. For Lenin, Labracherie, p. 186, and Robert Wilson, *Paris on Parade* (Indianapolis, 1924), p. 212.

6. Jean Emile-Bayard (Ralph Annington and Tudor Davies, trs.), *Montmartre Past and Present with Reminiscences by Well Known Artists and Writers* (New York, c. 1925), pp. 48, 42–43. On p. x, Emile-Bayard says that the Chat Noir owed its clientele of artists and poets "to the decadence of the Quartier Latin which had become a bourgeois suburb." The Chat Noir closed in 1897.

7. *Ibid.,* pp. 60–61.

8. *Ibid.,* pp. 78–84. E.-B. senses (p. 85) that the bourgeois killed Montmartre to get even with its scornful artists and their girl friends. For the quote: Francis Carco, *Montmartre à Vingt Ans* (Paris, 1938), p. 47.

9. For the Lapin Agile and its clients also see Labracherie, *Bohème,* pp. 213–221, and Francis Carco (Madelaine Boyd, tr.), *From Montmartre to the Latin Quarter (The Last Bohemia)* (London, c. 1920), pp. 4–163. On p. 38, Carco writes: "We were enthusiastic about Bohemia, adventure, Negroes, Cubism and travelers' tales," and: "we had a certain presentiment of the events which were later to upset the world." On p. 35 he declares that to Picasso's "stolen" black art "our generation owes its freedom, for the most part, from aimless fantasy, sarcasm and facetiousness."

10. *Ibid.,* p. 67.

11. Seymour S. Weiner, *Francis Carco, The Career of a Literary Bohemian* (New York, 1952), p. 30. Labracherie, *Bohème,* p. 228.

12. Ph. Huisman and M. G. Dortu (Corinne Bellow, ed. & tr.), *Lautrec by Lautrec* (New York, 1964), pp. 68–69. On pp. 129–131 they say brothels were a significant part of bourgeois society in the nineteenth century, that they served as a bulwark of the family and of bourgeois morality. See also Steven Marcus, *The Other Victorians, A Study of Sexuality and Pornography in Mid-Nineteenth-Century England* (New York, 1964).

13. Huisman and Dortu, *Lautrec,* pp. 71, 120, 147–148.
14. Morrow (Cucueil), *Paris,* p. 163.
15. Weiner, *Carco,* p. 70.

PART FOUR The Bourgeois Bohemia

* Quoted from Ernst Jünger, *Diary,* 21 September 1929, in Amos Elon (Michael Roloff, tr.), *Journey Through a Haunted Land, The New Germany* (New York, 1967), p. 233.

12. Bourgeois Bohemia

1. Henry James, for one, wrote (to Rhoda Broughton, 10 August 1914): "You and I, the ornaments of our generation, should have been spared this wreck of our belief that through the long years we had seen civilization grow and the worst become impossible. The tide that bore us along was then all the while moving to *this* as its grand Niagara—yet what a blessing we didn't know it." Hilton Kramer, "The Grand Niagara," *Arts Magazine,* XXXVIII (September 1964), p. 15.
2. Barbara Tuchman in *Guns of August* (New York, 1962) best tells the story of the opening of the war. The pickpockets are in Carco, *Montmartre,* p. 270. Herbert Leuthy (Eric Mossbacher, tr.), *France Against Herself...* (New York, 1955), p. 47, reports that in 1914 the respectable centrist press demanded more arms, more troops, full support for the forces, yet at the same time fought imposition of the necessary taxes.
3. Stefan Zweig, *The World of Yesterday, An Autobiography by Stefan Zweig* (New York, 1943), pp. 223–232.
4. William Hermanns, *The Holocaust, From a Survivor of Verdun* (New York, 1972), pp. 4, 1. James W. Gerard, U.S. Ambassador to Germany from 1913 to 1917, believed that the German establishment, particularly the Prussian, aspired to world conquest and brought on the war because the German people were showing a new spirit of resistance to militarism and autocracy. "This is no new trick" for autocracies "have always turned to war as the best antidote to the spirit of democracy." James W. Gerard, *My Four Years in Germany* (New York, 1917), p. 103. Not everyone was swept away. See Hermann Hesse (Ralph Manheim, tr.), *If the War Goes on...Reflections on War and Politics* (New York, 1970).
5. Zweig, *Zweig,* pp. 255–256.
6. For example, 8 million French served, about 4 million fought, and 1.3 million died. Jacques Meyer, *La Vie Quotidienne des Soldats Pendant la Grande Guerre* (Paris, 1966), p. 23.
7. Erich Fromm, *Beyond the Chains of Illusion, My Encounter with Marx and Freud* (New York, 1962), pp. 6, 85. To this

Friedrich Meinecke (Sidney B. Fay, tr.), *The German Catastrophe, Reflections and Recollections* (Boston, 1950), p. 89, adds: until 1914 there was still "a common Occidental Christian atmosphere."

8. His name is really Remarque. He decends from refugees from the French Revolution. The story that "Remarque" is Kramer spelled backward is probably one of the canards the Nazis circulated about him. In Germany alone, *All Quiet on the Western Front* sold 1.2 million copies within a year after publication. Both as book and film it was anathema to the Nazis.

9. Erich Maria Remarque (A. W. Wheen, tr.), *All Quiet on the Western Front* (Boston, 1929), p. 20.

10. J. Péricard and Charles Delvert, *Verdun, La Grande Bataille de Verdun, Le Drame de Douaumont (J. Péricard), La Défense de R¹ (Ch. Delvert), L'Enfer de Verdun* (Paris, *c.* 1945), p. 120. In the third section, this book presents short statements by a number of other participants.

11. Remarque, *Front,* p. 72.

12. Philip Gibbs, *Now It Can Be Told* (New York, 1920), p. 170.

13. Remarque, *Front,* p. 114.

14. Péricard-Delvert, *Verdun,* p. 91.

15. Remarque, *Front,* pp. 115–116.

16. Gibbs, *Told,* p. 253.

17. Remarque, *Front,* p. 135.

18. Péricard-Delvert, *Verdun,* p. 121.

19. Remarque, *Front,* p. 10. Zweig, (*Zweig,* p. 248) concurs.

20. Péricard-Delvert, *Verdun,* p. 111.

21. Remarque, *Front,* p. 107.

22. Gibbs, *Told,* p. 319.

23. Remarque, *Front,* p. 133.

24. Gibbs, *Told,* p. 365.

25. Remarque, *Front,* p. 105.

26. Gibbs, *Told,* p. 169.

27. Remarque, *Front,* p. 112.

28. Gibbs, *Told,* p. 172.

29. Remarque, *Front,* p. 25.

30. Péricard-Delvert, *Verdun,* p. 102.

31. Hitler's exact words are: "If I weren't myself hardened by this experience, I would have been incapable of undertaking this Cyclopian task which the building of an Empire means for a single man." Adolf Hitler, *Hitler's Secret Conversations, 1914–1944, With an Introductory Essay by H. Trevor-Roper* (New York, 1953), p. 69.

32. Péricard-Delvert, *Verdun,* p. 87.

33. Remarque, *Front,* p. 139.

34. Gibbs, *Told,* p. 461.

35. Remarque, *Front,* p. 139.

36. Gibbs, *Told,* p. 352.

37. *The Encyclopedia Americana*, XXIV (New York, 1932), pp. 529–530.

38. This marching song says: Long live death! Long live war! Long live the Foreign Legion!

39. Malcolm Cowley, *A Second Flowering, Works and Days of the Lost Generation* (New York, 1973), pp. 4, 7.

40. Remarque, *Front*, p. 11.

41. For a sense of this see Gibbs, *Told*, pp. 444–446. Writing in 1918–1919, Gibbs says (p. 444): "Modern civilization was wrecked on those fire-blasted fields, though they led to what we called 'Victory.' More died there than the flower of our youth and German manhood. The Old Order of the world died there, because many men who came alive out of that conflict were changed, and vowed not to tolerate a system of thought which had led us to such a monstrous massacre of human beings. . . ." Others accommodated their thought to the massacre: Ernst Jünger (Basil Creighton, tr.), *The Storm of Steel, From the Diary of a German Storm-Troop Officer on the Western Front* (London, 1929).

To set the effects of the war in proportion the terrible effects of the war experience on children must be examined. See Peter Loewenberg, "The Psychohistorical Origins of the Nazi Youth Cohort," *American Historical Review*, LXXVI (1971), pp. 1457–1502.

13   Bohemia and the War

1. Seymour S. Weiner, *Francis Carco: The Career of a Literary Bohemian* (New York, 1952), p. 97, says many of the most promising bohemians died in 1914–1918. Among them is Guillaume Apollinaire (de Kostrowitsky) whom Pierre Labracherie (*La Vie Quotidienne de la Bohème Littéraire au XIXᵉ Siècle* [Paris, 1967], p. 233) calls the greatest poet of that generation.

2. Hans Richter (David Britt, tr.), *Dada: Art or Anti-Art?* (London, 1965), p. 183. This admirable book by one of the men central to the movement is the base for most of what is said here about Dada. Stefan Zweig (*The World of Yesterday, An Autobiography by Stefan Zweig* [New York, 1943], p. 273 ff.) says during the war Zurich was the center of European life, of intellect and intrigue.

3. Richter, *Dada*, p. 13.

4. Ibid., p. 25.

5. Idem.

6. This is still a matter of personal experience for millions. For a view of how it came about for the British, see Gibbs, *Told*, pp. 65–148, especially pp. 110–111.

7. Erich Maria Remarque (A. H. Wheen, tr.), *The Road Back* (Boston, 1931). Meyer, *Soldats*, pp. 361–365.

8. "Democracy of death" is Gerhard Masur's phrase (*Prophets of Yesterday*... [New York, 1961], p. 415. Hans Kohn, "The Crisis in European Thought and Culture," in Jack J. Roth, ed., *World War I, a Turning Point in Modern History* (New York, 1967), p. 36. David Schoenbaum, *Hitler's Social Revolution: Class and Status in Nazi Germany* (New York, 1967), p. 66.

9. For this see Remarque, *Front*, and his *Road Back*.

10. Robert W. Service, who in his *Ballads of a Bohemian* (New York, 1921), in the poem "The Three Tommies," pp. 182–184, tells of a painter, a musician and a writer who talked in the trenches of after the war when

"... each would be true to his part,
Upbuilding a Palace of Beauty to the wonder and
glory of Art...",

shows in terrible detail how each was killed. This book, written in the first person, begins with the sentimental and romantic image of a Murger-inspired impoverished poet on the Boul' Mich' just before August 1914, and then—despite its sometimes ludicrous doggerel—crushes down with the awful reality concealed behind the romance of war.

PART FIVE   Bohemians in Arms

* Quoted in Werner Heisenberg (Arnold J. Pomerans, tr.), *Physics and Beyond, Encounters and Conversations* (New York, 1971), p. 167.

14   Bohemians Manqués

1. Howard Becker, *German Youth, Bond or Free* (New York, 1946), p. 51.

2. This most significant movement seems almost unknown in English-speaking countries. I have found it treated in some detail in only five books and three unpublished doctoral dissertations: Becker, *Youth;* Walter Z. Laqueur, *Young Germany, A History of the German Youth Movement* (New York, 1962); Gerhard Masur, *Prophets of Yesterday, Studies in European Culture, 1890–1914* (New York, 1961); George L. Mosse, *The Crisis of German Ideology: Intellectual Origins of the Third Reich* (New York, 1964); Robert G. L. Waite, *Vanguard of Nazism: The Free Corps Movement in Postwar Germany, 1918–1923* (Cambridge, 1952); Mario Domandi, "The German Youth Movement," Columbia University, 1960; Joseph Held, "Embattled Youth: the Independent German Youth Movements in the Twentieth Century," Rutgers University, 1968; Robert Karl Schmid, "German Youth Movements, a Typological Study," University of Wisconsin, 1941. The information presented here comes mainly from Domandi, Held, Laqueur, and

Mosse. In his *Politics of Cultural Despair* (Berkeley, 1963), p. 176, Fritz Stern writes: "in a country that was still strictly authoritarian, the very act of organizing brought the young to the brink of revolt, because student organizations in school or out were forbidden by law."

Certainly, this revolt of youth was absolutely justified by what the conventional behavior of its elders produced in 1914–1918, for who can seriously argue that the life style of the Wandervögel was not better for youth than the Western Front?

For the story in German, see Hans Blüher, *Wandervogel, Geschichte einer Jugendbewegung* (Prien, 1922—first in 1912).

3. These quotations are from Becker, *Youth*, p. 54; Laqueur, *Youth*, p. 22; Schmid, "Youth," p. 88.

4. Domandi, "Youth," p. 46.

5. Ibid., p. 101.

6. Ibid., p. 82. Gustav Wynecken, a prominent liberal educator and mentor of the movement, coined "Jugendkultur" (Waite, *Free Corps*, p. 18). Mosse (*Crisis*, p. 177) tells us that Wandervogel journals relied on paintings by Karl Höppner (Fidus) to illustrate the ideal Nordic type, the physical standard of the movement.

7. Domandi, "Youth," p. 9. In 1912 Hans Blüher, a veteran führer and close friend of Fischer, published the first history of the movement. The first two volumes were followed a few months later by a third: *The German Wandervogel as an Erotic Phenomenon*. Blüher, who was familiar with Freudian theory and had his own unorthodox interpretation of it, asserted (as Domandi puts it in "Youth," pp. 117–118) "that homosexual love, inborn in all men but repressed by society, was now expressing itself in the intimate friendship and the general atmosphere of male camaraderie that prevailed in the youth movement." Blüher contended that the movement recreated the primitive male league, a concept he drew from anthropology. Built around Eros, excluding women totally as by nature incapable of being "spiritual," these leagues, to him, were the ideal form of youthful association, for they perfectly fit the true nature of youth and directed its erotic energy from futile dissipation in the pursuit of women to constructive ends (pp. 119–124). The leagues (Bünde) "must bring forth the new nobility" (p. 124). Further: "a woman 'the equal of man' is simply the creation of a man who is really trying to find another man in his female partner" (p. 121, n. 2). All this is referred to Blüher's books, mainly to *Die deutsche Wandervogelbewegung als erotisches Phaenomen* (Berlin, 1912).

8. Gustav Wynecken, quoted in Waite, *Free Corps*, p. 20, cited to Blüher whose italics these are (*Führer und Volk in der Jugendbewegung* [Jena, 1924]).

9. Becker, *Youth,* p. 59.
10. Ibid., p. 97.
11. Domandi, "Youth," pp. 154–155.
12. Remarque, *Road,* p. 337.
13. Schmid, "Youth," pp. 151, 53. Laqueur, *Youth,* pp. 134–135; for quotation from Reich, p. 65, n. 2.
14. Hans Friedrich Blunck, Nazi chief of the German writers' organization, said: "The German revolution began in the youth movement, and was carried on by National Socialism to victory." This is quoted in Laqueur, *Youth,* p. 209. The atomic physicist Werner Heisenberg was in the Wandervögel just after the war. His group had much the same ethos as the pre-war Wandervögel. Heisenberg was horrified by what the movement became in the hands of Hitler Youth (Heisenberg, *Physics,* pp. 52–55, 146).
15. The information given here about the storm troopers and the Free Corps comes from Waite, *Free Corps.* A vivid memoir is Ernst Jünger (Basil Creighton, tr.), *The Storm of Steel, From the Diary of a German Storm-Troop Officer on the Western Front* (London, 1929), pp. 195–204, 227–237, 245–278.
16. The conventional interpretation of the 1918–1919 revolution needs revision accommodating what Ben Hecht (*A Child of the Century* [New York, 1954], pp. 280–299) learned in Germany while covering these events as a journalist. He presents evidence that the German General Staff was the prime mover of the revolution.
17. This posttraditional attitude should be seen in contrast to the traditional and transitional attitudes characteristic of (but not unanimous in) the regular officer corps. For this, the revolutions, and the Free Corps, see Walter Goerlitz (Brian Battershaw, tr.), *History of the German General Staff, 1657–1945* (New York, 1962), pp. 204–239. Albert Speer (Richard and Clara Winston, trs.) in *Spandau, The Secret Diaries* (New York, 1976) says on p. 194 of the Spandau prisoners "Except for Neurath, none of us is a real conservative." We are "technologists, military men, youth movementers, careerists."
18. Friedrich William Heinz quoted in Waite, *Free Corps,* p. 42.
19. Ernst von Salomon (Ian F. D. Morrow, tr.), *The Outlaws* (London, 1931), pp. 62–63. Waite (*Free Corps,* p. 56, n. 66) says all the writers agree that von Salomon "is the most reliable spokesman of the Free Corps."
20. Ibid., pp. 140–141, 141 n. 1. The tune is that of "Goodbye My Bluebell."
21. Ibid., p. 213.
22. Ibid., p. 209.
23. Erich Balla quoted in Ibid., p. 108.

24. Salomon quoted in Ibid., p. 56.

25. Ibid., p. 267.

26. Gerhard Loose, *Ernst Jünger* (New York, 1974). Ernst Jünger (Stuart Hood, tr.), *On the Marble Cliffs, A Novel by Ernst Juenger* (New York, 1947), for his eventual mental state. For his mentality before and throughout the war, Ernst Jünger (Stuart Hood, tr.), *African Diversions* (London, 1954) and his *Storm of Steel*.

27. Waite, *Free Corps*, p. 51.

28. This comparison is Zweig's (*Zweig*, p. 294).

29. Ibid., pp. 295.

30. For the exchange rate: New York *Times*, 10 November 1923. Notwithstanding minor defects, an excellent book on the Putsch and the situation leading to it is Richard Hanser, *Putsch! How Hitler Made Revolution* (New York, 1970). Writing from an Austrian/ South-German point-of-view, following the career of Adolf Hitler, Hanser gives a sense of the emotional factors underlying the Putsch and Hitler's rise to power. For the Weimar spirit: Otto Friedrich, *Before the Deluge, A Portrait of Berlin in the 1920's* (New York, 1972); Walter Laqueur, *Weimar, A Cultural History, 1918–1933* (New York, 1974); and August Sander (with an introduction by Gunther Sander and foreword by Golo Mann), *Men Without Masks, Faces of Germany, 1910–1938* (Greenwich, 1973).

31. Hitler, *Conversations*, p. 40.

32. Of all those who write or have written in German, Karl May is said to be the most widely read. Albert Einstein as well as Hitler read him as a boy. Young people in Germany, Sweden, and other countries read him today. Every summer a Karl May festival at Espe, West Germany, draws thousands of fans who watch his stories dramatized. May wrote adventures set for the most part among the Indians of the American West or the Bedouin of North Africa and Arabia. The stories are embedded in what the Austrian Minister of Education in 1954 called "substantial geographical and ethnographic information."

The protagonist, called Old Shatterhand, is a sincere Christian, a charming romantic, and a gentle misogynist who usually travels in the company of some Winnetou. Although the stories are melodramatic, violent, bloody, Shatterhand never kills people. He prefers to stun them with a karate chop he developed in the Wild West by combining American and Japanese fighting styles. From it he derives his nickname. By using brains instead of deadly force to overcome his enemies and by subsequently showing them magnanimity he demonstrates to his companions the superiority of Christ's teaching about love, to him, the theme of the Christian religion.

In *Conversations* pp. 306–307, Hitler says—and this in 1942!—:

"I've just been reading a very fine article on Karl May. I found it delightful. It would be nice if his work were republished. I owe him my first notions of geography, and the fact that he opened my eyes on the world. I used to read him by candle-light, or by moonlight with the help of a huge magnifying-glass. The first thing I read of that kind was *The Last of the Mohicans*. But Fritz Seidl told me at once: 'Fenimore Cooper is nothing; you must read Karl May.' " "In Germany, besides Karl May, Jules Verne and Félix Dohn are essential." As Chancellor, Hitler kept seven feet of May books on his shelf. Speer (*Spandau*, p. 347) thinks May was probably "the greatest dilettante of all" and says that "Hitler would lean on Karl May as proof for everything imaginable."

See Karl May (C. A. Willoughby, tr.) *In the Desert* (Bamberg, 1955) ; Hanser, *Putsch*, pp. 16, 18; Shawn Cristoph, "Cowboys und Indianer," San Francisco *Examiner*, 18 August 1974. The Germans and Slavs are in Herzstein, *Adolf Hitler*, pp. 2–3.

33. Hitler and the Third Reich are discussed at length in Chapter Seventeen and notes, *infra*. In Munich in the late 1920's and early 1930's Stefan Lornat often saw Hitler with the dog whip (San Francisco *Chronicle*, 10 July 1975). The syphilis is reported in an interview with Ernst Hanfstaengl, a fallen-away friend of Hitler's who served as his press officer (San Francisco *Chronicle*, 12 June 1972). This also tells of Hitler's bizarre relation with women.

34. Hermann Rauschning, *The Voice of Destruction* (New York, 1940), p. 256. On p. 235 of this book, based on conversations with Hitler, Rauschning says Hitler believed "man exists in some magic association with the universe."

35. Trevor Ravenscourt, *The Spear of Destiny* ... (New York, 1973), p. 246.

36. Hans Bernd Gisevius (Richard and Clara Winston, trs.), *To the Bitter End* (Boston, 1947), pp. 93, 43, 59. This account of men and events at the center of Nazi Germany by a police official who resisted the Nazis throughout a career leading from an early association with the Gestapo through the 1944 bomb plot affords a close view of the personal character of high officials and functionaries. The strong similarity between these Nazis and Nixon's entourage is, in my opinion, more than coincidental.

37. Albert Speer (Richard and Clara Winston, trs.), *Inside the Third Reich, Memoirs of Albert Speer* (New York, 1970), p. 51.

38. Kurt Ludecke quoted in T. L. Jarman, *The Rise and Fall of Nazi Germany* (London, 1955), p. 107.

39. Hermann Rauschning, *The Revolution of Nihilism, Warning to the West* (New York, 1939), pp. 63–64.

40. For the Bauhaus movement in historical context, Raymond J. Sontag, *A Broken World, 1919–1939* (New York, 1971), particularly pp. 212–213.

15   Henry Mencken's Romantic Army

1.   Hans Richter (David Britt, tr.), *Dada: Art and Anti-Art* (London, 1965), p. 133. For an account of the festival by a guest: Ben Hecht, *Letters from Bohemia* (Garden City, 1964), pp. 142–144. This is part of his memoir of the artist George Grosz who (p. 150) depicted "Authority crucifying a bewildered and helpless century." John F. Carter, Jr., " 'Those Wild Young People' by One of Them," *The Atlantic Monthly*, CXXVI (September 1920), p. 302.

2.   Ben Hecht, *A Child of the Century* (New York, 1954), p. 175.

3.   Alistaire Cooke, ed., *The Vintage Mencken* (New York, 1956), p. 25.

4.   Frederick Lewis Allen, *Only Yesterday, An Informal History of the Nineteen Twenties* (New York, 1931), p. 164.

5.   Cooke, *Mencken*, p. 22.

6.   Ibid., pp. 132, 136, 131–132, 130, 129.

7.   Ibid., p. 136.

8.   Ibid., p. vi.

9.   Allen, *Twenties*, p. 168.

10.   Quoted in William Manchester, *Disturber of the Peace, The Life of H. L. Mencken* (New York, 1950), p. 185.

11.   For Bohemia in the East and Midwest, see Albert Parry, *Garrets and Pretenders, A History of Bohemianism in America* (New York, 1933) and Emily Hahn, *Romantic Rebels, An Informal History of Bohemianism in America* (Boston, 1967). These books show that in New York and elsewhere Bohemia was modeled on Murger and derivative of Paris. Orlo Williams (*Vie de Bohème, A Patch of Romantic Paris* [Boston, 1913], pp. 6–7) shows how as of 1913 Bohemia could not have existed in London. The social and mental anatomy of Greenwich Village is presented by Caroline F. Ware in her classic sociological study, *Greenwich Village, 1920–1930, A Comment on American Civilization in the Post-War Years* (Boston, 1935).

12.   Parry (*Bohemianism*, p. 191) says the anti-Red hysteria of 1919–1920 scared the Village out of politics. Allen (*Twenties*, pp. 7–57) says short hair on women, like long hair on men, associated with free love and red revolution. Submerged by the radio craze, hysteria about the red menace transmuted into hysteria about the youth menace.

13.   André Maurois (Ella d'Arcy, tr.), *Ariel, The Life of Shelley* (New York, 1924), p. 56.

14.   Ibid., p. 199.

15.   Henri Bourrelier, *La Vie du Quartier Latin Dès Origines à la Cité Universitaire* (Paris, 1936), p. 162.

16.   Henri Guillemin, *Victor Hugo par Lui-Même* (Paris,

1951), p. 51. Hugo, on his honeymoon night, 12–13 October 1822 —as Guillemin puts it—boasted in old age that he had "possessed" Adèle "nine times."

17. Hahn, *Bohemianism*, p. 108, says this is true of the nineteenth century and, with few exceptions, of much of this one. We might even except the exceptions. She says here that they all followed Murger. For a sense of this, and also of life in the Village, see Maxwell Bodenheim, *My Life and Loves in Greenwich Village* (New York, 1954).

18. Harry Carr in *The* Los Angeles *Times,* 28 February 1908.

19. Stefan Zweig, *The World of Yesterday, An Autobiography by Stefan Zweig* (New York, 1943), pp. 67–91, in a chapter called "Eros Matutinus," and on pp. 193–196, gives a classic discussion of these matters. For a general treatment: Richard Lewinsohn, M.D. (Alexander Mayce, tr.), *A History of Sexual Customs* (New York, 1958). Remi Nadeau in *California, the New Society* (New York, 1963) describes how California has led the way in returning the human body to the pagan sensuality of the sun. Laurence Wylie in "Youth in France and the United States" in Erik Erikson, ed., *Youth: Change and Challenge* (New York, 1963), tells of the rearing of young men in France. Steven Marcus, *The Other Victorians, A Study of Sexuality and Pornography in Mid-Nineteenth-Century England* (New York, 1964), pp. 284–285. Of special interest is Judge Ben B. Lindsay and W. Evans, *The Revolt of Modern Youth* (New York, 1925). This book, based on the close relationship of Lindsay, the nation's pioneer juvenile court judge, and thousands of young Denverites, gives a sense of the intensity and scope of the youth revolt of the twenties, particularly à propos sexual behavior. On p. 54, he says, "Not only is this revolt from old standards of conduct taking place, but it is unlike any revolt that has ever taken place before." He then says that youth has always been rebellious, but without effect. This time, however, the external restraints, both economic and "Fear of Hell Fire," once so potent, have lost their power.

20. Zweig, *Zweig,* p. 195. He also says (pp. 188–189) that, culturally, New York was far behind Europe and did not yet have a truly distinctive character.

21. Lindsay, *Youth,* pp. 66–68.

22. Malcolm Cowley, *Exile's Return, A Narrative of Ideas* (New York, 1934), pp. 62–75. This book is a classic discussion of the mentality of the Lost Generation and the origin thereof—which Cowley identifies as a continuous and cumulative deracination (pp. 15–56).

23. Vincent Sheean, *Personal History* (New York, 1925), p. 311.

16   Interwar Bohemia

1. For one of these banquets (1925), see Roger Shattuck, *The Banquet Years, The Origins of the Avant Garde in France, 1885–World War I* (New York, 1955), pp. 359–360. For Americans: Albert Parry, *Garrets and Pretenders, A History of Bohemianism in America* (New York, 1933), pp. 331–334; Robert Forest Wilson, *Paris on Parade* (Indianapolis, 1924), p. 197; George Wharton Edwards, *Paris* (Philadelphia, 1924), p. 93.

2. Wilson, *Paris*, p. 26. Gertrude Stein, *Paris France* (London, 1940), p. 21. Edwards (*Paris*, p. 154) says: "The Art of America is due to the tuition, given free, mind you, to our men, who have for years studied in the Beaux-Arts School." George Wickes (*Americans in Paris* [Garden City, 1969]) says (p. 5): Chiefly the Americans "felt the all-pervasive classical spirit of France." Under "this influence they became more conscious of form, style, language, or medium than any previous generation of Americans." From 1874 to 1917, the art school in San Francisco was called The California School of Design; from 1917 to 1961, The California School of Fine Arts. Since 1961, it has been The College of the San Francisco Art Institute.

3. Edwards, *Paris*, pp. 10–13; Wilson, *Paris*, p. 287.

4. Arthur Bartlett Maurice, *The Paris of the Novelists* (New York, 1919), p. 183. Edwards, *Paris*, pp. 13–16, 401.

5. Ibid., pp. 317, 341.

6. Wilson, *Paris*, pp. 274–275

7. Idem. On pp. 203–204 Wilson says the American colony detested ku-kluxery, prohibition, and the other stupidities of home.

8. Edwards, *Paris*, p. 396; Wilson, *Paris*, pp. 212–218; Parry *Bohemianism*, p. 341.

9. Cowley, *Exile*, pp. 173–179. Cowley gives a valuable account of the American expatriots both here and in his *A Second Flowering, Works and Days of the Lost Generation* (New York, 1973). For the writers see Ernest Hemingway, *A Moveable Feast* (New York, 1964). For the political orientations of American writers in the first three decades of the century: Daniel Aaron, *Writers on the Left* (New York, 1961).

10. Parry, *Bohemianism*, discusses this on pp. 329–345; Wilson, *Paris*, on pp. 243–247.

11. Ibid., pp. 193–195.

12. Elliot Paul in *The Last Time I Saw Paris* (Garden City, 1943) affords a deeply human sense of the changing climate of feeling over the 1920's and 1930's by telling the story of his neighborhood, la rue de la Huchette—a short street connecting rue Saint-Jacques and place Saint-Michel. Here he writes (pp. 291–

292) : "No matter how many Frenchmen voted, the same predatory combination ran the country for the benefit of large employers and speculators."

13. Romain Gary (J. M. Beach, tr.), *Promise at Dawn* (New York, 1961), pp. 178–185.

14. Henry Miller, *Tropic of Cancer* (Paris, 1934), p. 295.

15. For W.P.A., Robert Bendiner, *Just Around the Corner, A Highly Selective History of the Thirties* (New York, 1967), pp. 179–185. and Francis V. O'Connor, ed., *Art for the Millions: Essays from the 1930's by Artists and Administrators of the WPA Federal Arts Project* (Greenwich, Connecticut, 1973). For general background, Frederick Lewis Allen, *Since Yesterday, The Nineteen-Thirties in America* (New York, 1940), pp. 129–143, 252–262, *passim*. For the Village, Parry, *Bohemianism*, pp. 350–359. For the morale of the bohemians there, Loker Raley, "The World Is Too Much with Us," *The* Woodstock *Aquarian* (1971), p. 31.

16. New York *Times*, 27 July 1935. Conversations with William Jameson, 1949.

17 The SS State

1. That I cannot find anything primarily concerned with this question may be because among historians such questions are only now coming into fashion. The current condition of historical thinking about Nazi Germany is reviewed by Geoffrey Barraclough in "Mandarins and Nazis: Part I"; "The Liberals and German History: Part II," and "A New View of German History: Part III," *The New York Review of Books*, 19 October, 2 and 16 November 1972, respectively.

2. For the classic discussion of this point, Milovan Djilas, *The New Class, An Analysis of the Communist System* (New York, 1957).

3. The best insight into Hitler's thinking is provided by H. R. Trevor-Roper, ed., *Hitler's Secret Conversations, 1941–1944* (New York, 1953), in German: H. Picker, *Hitlers Tischgespräche in Führerhauptquartier* (Stuttgart, 1965). Here Hitler confides that "if there hadn't been the danger of the Red peril's overwhelming Europe, I'd not have interfered in the revolution in Spain." Why? "The clergy would have been exterminated." (p. 310) Elsewhere (p. 567) : "If I had not decided in 1936 to send him the first of our Junker aircraft, Franco would never have survived. To-day, his salvation is attributed to Saint Isabella! ... the greatest harlot in history." For an early discussion of the unique character of the Nazi revolution, Hermann Rauschning, *The Revolution of Nihilism, Warning to the West* (New York, 1939). This excellent book, by a genuine conservative, the one-time Nazi mayor of Danzig, contains an understanding of the irrational quality of the Nazi revolu-

tion, one which most students of the Nazis seem unable to conceive, even today. For an excellent recent discussion, Ernst Nolte (Leila Vennewitz, tr.), *Three Faces of Fascism: Action Française, Italian Fascism, National Socialism* (New York, 1966). Nolte speaks of Italian Fascism being "born of bourgeois resistance to the attempted communist revolution (p. 388)." Rauschning writes (pp. 18–42) that the Nazis had no program but the intensification and expansion of power.

4. See David Schoenbaum, *Hitler's Social Revolution: Class and Status in Nazi Germany* (New York, 1967), p. 154.

5. Hitler's hatred of and determination to destroy the middle classes are unbounded. Ironically, as historian Karl Dietrich Bracher puts it (quoted in Barraclough, "Part I," p. 41), the hard core of Hitler's following was "the lower middle class of town and countryside." August Kubizek, Hitler's boyhood friend, said: "He just didn't fit into any bourgeois order" (Quoted in George H. Stein, ed., *Great Lives Observed: Hitler* [New York, 1968], p. 95). For Hitler on the bourgeoisie, Adolf Hitler (Ralph Manheim, tr.), *Mein Kampf* (Boston, 1943), pp. 59, 130, 611–612, and Hitler, *Conversations*, pp. 48, 150. To Hitler, the bourgeois way of life derives from the Jewish way of life, which is to say from anathema. In his *Hitler, A Study in Tyranny* (New York, 1958), p. 415, Alan Bullock concludes that Hitler's mission was to destroy the European "liberal bourgeois order" of 1789–1939.

6. For a sense of the energy that made the Nazi revolution see Hans Bernd Gisevius (Richard and Clara Winston, trs.), *To the Bitter End* (Boston, 1947), and Konrad Heiden (Ralph Manheim, tr.), *Der Führer, Hitler's Rise to Power* (Boston, 1944). Heiden, who began fighting the Nazis in 1923, regards the early Nazis essentially as "armed bohemians" whose home was war. For an excellent general discussion of the energy and mentality of the Nazis, Peter Viereck, *Metapolitics, The Roots of the Nazi Mind* (New York, 1961). The Mussolini quote is in Ernst Hanfstaengl, *Unheard Witness* (Philadelphia, 1957), p. 257. Göring is quoted in Robert G. L. Waite, *Vanguard of Nazism: The Free Corps Movement in Postwar Germany, 1918–1923* (Cambridge, Massachusetts, 1952), p. 276. For the dual state—SS and traditional—and the law see Karl Dietrich Bracher (Jean Steinberg, tr.), *The German Dictatorship: The Origins, Structure, and Effects of National Socialism* (New York, 1970), pp. 363, 232, and Hans Buchheim (Richard Barry, tr.), "The SS—Instrument of Domination," in Elizabeth Wiskemann, ed., *Anatomy of the SS State* (New York, 1968), p. 142. For the SS armed force, George H. Stein, *The Waffen SS, Hitler's Elite Guard at War, 1939–1945* (Ithaca, 1966). For a general discussion, Richard Grunberger, *Hitler's SS* (New York, 1970), pp. 76, 87.

7. Dr. Hans Frank, the Law Leader, is quoted in William L. Shirer, *The Rise and Fall of the Third Reich, A History of Nazi*

Germany (New York, 1960), p. 268. An excellent discussion of Hitler and conscience—and of Nazi Germany as the advent of post-Christian times—is in Friedrich Meinecke (Sydney R. Fay, tr.), *The German Catastrophe, Reflections and Recollections* (Boston, 1950), pp. 82-85. Walter Langer in his psychoanalytical study of Hitler, completed in 1943 for use in psychological warfare, *The Mind of Adolf Hitler, The Secret Wartime Report* (New York, 1972), p. 190, speaks of Hitler calling conscience "dirty and degrading," "a Jewish invention," and "a blemish like circumcision." A recent psychoanalytical study of Hitler by Erich Fromm appears in his *The Anatomy of Human Destructiveness* (New York, 1973) in a chapter called "Malignant Aggression: Adolf Hitler, a Clinical Case of Necrophila," pp. 369–433. Fromm also presents a study of Heinrich Himmler under the title of "Heinrich Himmler: A Clinical Case of Anal-Hoarding Sadism," pp. 299–324. Göring is quoted in Eugen Kogon (Heinz Norden, tr.), *The Theory and Practice of Hell: The German Concentration Camps and the System Behind Them* (New York, 1950), p. 21.

8. Ibid., p. 42; Bracher, *Dictatorship*, p. 361; Martin Broszat (Marian Jackson, tr.), "The Concentration Camps 1933–1945," in Wiskemann, *SS State*, pp. 450–455.

9. Kogan, *Camps*, p. 14, n. 1; Schoenbaum, *Nazi Germany*, p. 292.

10. Barraclough ("Part II," p. 35) speaks of the "psychological blockage liberal historians experience when confronted by anything as alien to their mentality as Nazism." Historians shy from the kind of information furnished by men like Hermann Rauschning in *The Voice of Destruction* (conversations with Hitler), (New York, 1940), Louis Pauwels and Jacques Bergier (Rollo May, tr.), *The Morning of the Magicians* (New York, 1968), or Trevor Ravenscourt, *The Spear of Destiny, The Occult Power Behind the Spear Which Pierced the Side of Christ* (New York, 1973), a book which examines Hitler's connection with black magic, diabolism, and the occult. In *Conversations* (p. 251) Hitler says, "I'm quite well inclined to accept the cosmic theories of Hörbiger." On p. 313, he compares Hörbiger's contribution to cosmology to that of Copernicus. Despite this, Hitler's views on cosmology are missing from most books about Nazi Germany. As described by Pauwels and Bergier, Hans Hörbiger's cosmology posits that the dynamic of history is the struggle between fire and ice (*Magicians*, pp. 204–298). Hörbiger regarded the universe as a living being of neo-Platonic quality. Not only does the liberal historian have to open to all this, to magic, to the occult, to secret knowledge and secret masters, but, in Hitler's case, to a man who wiped his ass on his high-school certificate (*Conversations*, p. 202), a man whose ultimate sexual gratification seems to have derived from women squatting over him and shitting and pissing

on him (Langer, *Hitler*, p. 134). For more on the occult and Hörbiger, note 40, *infra*.

11. Colonel Rudolf Franz Höss, commander of Auschwitz, told of the hair and the gold while on the stand at Nuremberg. See G. M. Gilbert, Ph.D., *Nuremberg Diary* (New York, 1947), p. 264. Gilbert was prison psychologist at the trials. Speer (*Spandau*, p. 202) says Gilbert "reproduces the atmosphere with amazing objectivity." I doubt if any other book affords the insight into Hitler's deputies that this one does. Gilbert relates the day-to-day behavior of the defendants on the stand as they are forced to confront the evidence of what they have done. He describes the content of private interviews with them and gives the results of the I.Q. tests they each took. Excepting Albert Speer, they all show themselves as contemptible human beings. Most if not all are posttraditional types exemplifying what might be called technological man. I suspect that under similar circumstances the high officials of Lyndon Johnson and Richard Nixon would have proved to be of much the same composition as these Nazis, an observation sustained in part by the Watergate hearings and trials.

12. An acquaintance who has seen gold bars in Swiss banks says some bear the impression of the swastika.

13. Hermann Rauschning, one-time mayor of the free city of Danzig and a quondam Nazi, refers to this as the "suicide of the old order," *Nihilism*, p. 98. He was later proscribed by Hitler. For the proscription list prepared for the conquest of England (reminiscent of Nixon's "enemies list"), Shirer, *Third Reich*, p. 784.

14. See Shirer, p. 942; Bracher, *Dictatorship*, p. 406; Albert Speer (Richard and Clara Winston, trs.), *Inside the Third Reich* (New York, 1970), pp. 70, 181–182, 523; Speer, *Spandau*, pp. 153, 47–49; Nolte, *Fascism*, p. 395; Hitler, *Conversations*, pp. 385, 582. Obliquely, this is the subject of Norman Rich, *Hitler's War Aims*, I (*Ideology, The Nazi State and the Course of Expansion* [New York, 1973]).

15. Pauwels and Bergier (*Magicians*, p. 291) quote Heinrich Himmler on this subject.

16. See Peter Fleming, *Operation Sea Lion, The Projected Invasion of England in 1940* . . . (New York, 1957), p. 261; Shirer, *Third Reich*, pp. 782–784. Franz Neumann, *Behemoth, The Structure and Practice of National Socialism* (New York, 1942), p. 557.

17. Quoted in Shirer, *Third Reich*, pp. 937–938.

18. Hitler, *Conversations*, p. 92. As a boy Hitler used to read James Fenimore Cooper and Karl May, the German Wild-West writer. For Hitler's youth see Werner Maser (Peter and Betty Ross, trs.), *Hitler* (London, 1973, and Bradley F. Smith, *Adolf Hitler: His Family, Childhood and Youth* (Stanford, 1967).

19. This is compiled mainly from Hans-Adolf Jacobsen (Doro-

thy Lang, tr.), "The Kommissarbefehl and Mass Executions of Soviet Russian Prisoners of War," in Wiskemann, *SS State*, pp. 509–512; *Atlas, World Press Review*, August 1971, p. 62; Shirer, *Third Reich*, pp. 937, 942; Gilbert, *Nuremberg*, pp. 272, 339; Nolte, *Fascism*, pp. 336, 410–414; Hitler, *Conversations*, p. 44, and, for his plans for the East, *passim*. For the 120 years, J. H. Brennan, *The Occult Reich* (New York, 1974), p. 124. Although an ex-prisoner of the Germans told me about the Anglo-American Free Corps, I have never seen it mentioned in print except as the "Free American Corps" in Kurt Vonnegut, Jr., "A Fourth-Generation German-American Now Living in Easy Circumstances on Cape Cod..., *Slaughterhouse-Five, or, The Children's Crusade...* (New York, 1969), pp. 139–142, and in the film *Slaughterhouse Five*. Vonnegut was a prisoner of war and he survived the fire-bombing of Dresden.

20. Speer (*Third Reich*, pp. 226–229) says the Germans could have had atomic warheads by 1947. The story of German atomic research is told in David Irving, *The German Atomic Bomb, The History of Nuclear Research in Nazi Germany* (New York, 1967). See also Rauschning, *Voice*, pp. 64–65.

21. Hitler, *Conversations*. See Nolte's discussion of this matter in *Fascism*, particularly p. 418.

22. For Hitler, Otto Dietrich (Richard and Clara Winston, trs.), *The Hitler I Knew* (London, 1957), p. 112. Rauschning, *Voice*, p. 31, for R. Walther Darré, Minister of Agriculture. For the Olympics, William Johnson, "The Taking Part," *Sports Illustrated*, 10 July 1972, pp. 36–44. For babies: Karl Schmidt-Polex, "Hitler's Godchildren, An Investigation of the Nazi Baby-Breeding Program," *Atlas World Press Review*, January 1976, pp. 52–53.

23. For Hitler quotes: *Conversations*, pp. 461, 462. For feudal quality, Theodore Abel, *Why Hitler Came Into Power, An Answer Based on the Original Life Stories of Six Hundred of His Followers* (New York, 1938), p. 231. For "people's community," Bracher, *Dictatorship*, pp. 337–338, *passim*. For Ley, Nolte, *Fascism*, p. 385.

24. For the VW, Shirer, *Third Reich*, pp. 266–267, and Schoenbaum, *Nazi Germany*, p. 110.

25. Hitler, *Conversations*, p. 494.

26. The Nazis were determined to freeze women into subservient, traditional, domestic roles (See Bracher, *Dictatorship*, p. 338). Schoenbaum (*Nazi Germany*, p. 187) says: "Anti-feminism functioned as a kind of secondary racism." Hitler was ill at ease with women and often said he would never marry because Germany was his bride (*Time*, 2 October 1972, p. 50). Shirer tells us (*Third Reich*, p. 1087) that for ideological reasons until the end of the war Hitler kept women out of factories. Speer thought it more efficient to employ women than foreign and slave labor but could not win this point with Hitler. The factories employed many more women in World War I than in World War II (Speer, *Third Reich*,

pp. 220–221, 320) . Despite all this, Schoenbaum concludes (p. 201) "the pressures of the totalitarian state combined with those of an industrializing and industrial society to produce for women, as they had for labor in general, a new status of relative if unconventional equality."

27. Schoenbaum, *Nazi Germany*, pp. 164–165, 137–138. Shirer, *Third Reich*, pp. 257–258, 261–262. On p. 262 Shirer says, "Laws decreed in October 1937 simply dissolved all corporations with a capital under $40,000 and forbade the establishment of new ones with a capital of less than $200,000. This quickly disposed of one fifth of all small business firms."

28. Hans Schemm, the Minister of Culture, is quoted by Bracher, *Dictatorship*, p. 268. The Führers Show is in Shirer, *Third Reich*, pp. 242–243, the Führer's show on pp. 243–244. For Hitler as an artist and for some of his art, Maser, *Hitler*, pp. 39–69. For Nazi art: Rudolph Chelminski, "West Germans Screw Up Courage to Show Nazi Art," *Smithsonian*, V (February 1975) , pp. 70–78. Of the efficacy of propaganda, Shirer noted that despite his continuous access to the foreign press and his "inherent distrust" of Nazi sources, Nazi propaganda "made a certain impression on one's mind and often misled it" (pp. 247–248) .

29. Rauschning, *Voice*, pp. 251–252.

30. Eric Norden, "Playboy Interview: Albert Speer . . . ," *Playboy*, June 1971, p. 72. In *Nihilism* on p. 145 Rauschning says "reality in Germany is already a different thing from reality in the rest of Europe." Speer, *Spandau*, p. 370.

31. Rauschning, *Voice*, pp. 251–262.

32. Ibid., pp. 245–246, for the quotations. Also, Hitler, *Conversations*, pp. 48, 233.

33. For social democracy in the army see Neumann, *Behemoth*, pp. 473–474, and Richard Grunberger, *The 12-Year Reich, A Social History of Nazi Germany, 1933–1945* (New York, 1971) , pp. 139–140.

34. Rauschning (*Voice*, p. 40) tells of the Masonic model and then shows us Hitler banging the table and saying of the Party: "An Order, that's what is has to be—an Order, the hierarchial Order of a secular priesthood!" For the schools, Bracher, *Dictatorship*, pp. 263–265; Shirer, *Third Reich*, p. 185; Schoenbaum, *Nazi Germany*, p. 281; Pauwels & Bergier, *Magicians*, pp. 290–292. The quote from *Das Schwarze Korps* of 26 November 1942, is at p. 290. For an empirical sense of what this means see Kogon's quotation of an SS officer, *Concentration Camps*, pp. 13–14. Speer (*Third Reich*, p. 123) says the top Nazis held these schools in such contempt that they never sent their own children to them. An exception was Martin Bormann who sent a son to an Adolf Hitler school as punishment.

35. Kogon, *Concentration Camps*, pp. 28–30. Hitler's *Conversations* tells how the war "hardened" him. "It was with feelings of

pure idealism that I set out for the front in 1914. Then I saw men falling around me in the thousands. Thus I learnt that life is a cruel struggle, and has no other object but the preservation of the species. The individual can disappear provided there are other men to replace him." Pp. 69–70.

I think it would be difficult to exaggerate the influence of World War I on the subsequent career of the Europeans. It created the Hitler we know. The epitome of the war experience is the Western Front where millions of young men were sent by their elders to engage in endless mutual extermination in an air of rotting flesh on an erupting lunar surface. The essence of that experience is preserved in Erich Maria Remarque's *All Quiet on the Western Front,* in Ernst Jünger's *Storm of Steel,* and in William Hermanns, *The Holocaust, From a Survivor of Verdun* (New York, 1972). Hermanns published this book, in ms. since 1922, on the urging of his students at The California State University of San Jose as part of the anti-war movement. For naval service and the mutiny, Theodor Plivier (Margaret Green, tr.), *The Kaiser's Coolies* (New York, 1931).

36. Hans Buchheim (Richard Barry, tr.), "Command and Compliance," in Wiskemann, *SS State,* pp. 320–338. Shirer, *Third Reich,* p. 248. Quote is in Gilbert, *Nuremberg,* p. 260.

37. For the quotations, Rauschning, *Voice,* p. 243, and Kogon, *Concentration Camps,* p. 16.

38. Rauschning, *Voice,* p. 252.

39. Ibid., p. 248.

40. Pauwels and Bergier (*Magicians,* pp. 274–295) believe that behind the façade of National Socialism existed a community of Initiates, The Thule Society, the real vortex of the Nazi movement. The initiates were in communion with the invisible, had concluded a pact with hidden forces and, true to Occultism, had both a master magician and a medium—Karl Haushofer and Hitler. The New Man would not have to be an earthly creature nor, in the living cosmos, would there be any limit to his energy. Hans Hörbiger's fire-and-ice theory originally appeared in 1913 in a 790-page book called *Glazial-Kosmogonie.* For a discussion of this theory, Martin Gardner, *In the Name of Science* (New York, 1952), pp. 37–41, and Colin Wilson, *The Occult, A History* (New York, 1971), pp. 158–162. See also Brennan, *Occult.* Dietrich, *Hitler,* on p. 153, says Hitler was "a passionate adherent of Hoerbiger's Universal Ice Theory." For more on this, note 10, *supra.* Langer in *Hitler* (p. 120) diagnoses Hitler as a "neurotic psychopath bordering on schizophrenia" who, as the *Time* review (2 October 1972, p. 48) put it, spent his whole life in an unsuccessful attempt to compensate for feelings of helplessness and inferiority. Erich Fromm (*Destruction,* pp. 431, 413) says Hitler was sane, as evidenced by the fact he always had himself under control, but was "a withdrawn, extremely narcissistic,

unrelated, undisciplined, sadomasochistic, and necrophilous person."
It seems to Fromm (pp. 430–431) as if Hitler were a man of such
destructiveness that, unconsciously, he sought his own destruction,
the catastrophe he finally achieved—that he never really tried to
win at all!

41. This astute observation is made by Bradley F. Smith (*Hitler*, p. 59). Erich Kahler (*The Germans* [Princeton, 1974], p. 32),
says basic to the Germanic character is "a powerful drive for independence combined with an equally strong need for submission to
a sanctified authority. German history is characterized by the interaction of these two motivations." But is this peculiarly German?

42. Albert Speer (*Spandau*, p. 25), says the "absolute domination of utilitarian ends, such as I pursued as minister of armaments,
is nothing but a form of inhumanity." Bracher (*Dictatorship*, p. 25)
refers to the SS elite as "fanatically trained technicians of authority."
In *The Green Berets* (New York, 1965) Robin Moore presents a
Germanic prototype of posttraditional man. One suspects that Robin
Moore with his fatuous enthusiasm for "unconventional warfare"
and for "the almost unknown marvellous undercover work of our
Special Forces in Vietnam and countries around the world (p. 1)"
is another. A leading protagonist in Moore's roman à clef and an
honored exemplar of the Special Forces is Captain Sven Kornie,
onetime Nazi soldier, who leads a hand-picked "Germanic-Viking"
A-team. Most of the Berets in the book do their job (in Rauschning's
phrase) regardless of any moral or human considerations, thus occasionally coming into conflict with more conventional soldiers who
feel certain traditional moral and human restraints about how and
whom to kill. See especially pp. 18–19, 23, 29, 38–42, 50. A similar
mentality is that of the commanding generals of the Wehrmacht.
To them, the whole world is a field for their game and everything
on that field, a piece. This is clearly implicit in B. H. Liddell Hart,
The German Generals Talk (New York, 1948). Officer-corps mentality, as it developed throughout Western culture, is the proto-
mentality of technological man. As it moves from the Middle Ages
to the present, the mentality becomes more and more itself. Rauschning (*Nihilism*, pp. 123–125) quotes war minister Field Marshal
Werner von Blomberg as having once said "It was a point of honor
with the Prussian officer to be correct; it is a duty of the German
officer to be crafty," and goes on from this to contrast the traditional
officers who regard war as the last resort with the new officers who
conceive of war as the single purpose and organizing principle of
the state. See also William H. Whyte, *The Organization Man* (New
York, 1956). For Skinner, B. F. Skinner, *About Behaviorism* (New
York, 1974).

43. Speer tells the story (*Third Reich*, pp. 443–470).

44. Idem.

45. Rauschning (*Voice*, p. 41) reports that in the new world

planned by Adolf Hitler there was to be a new middle class of technicians—above this, a Führer class (the high aristocracy) and a Herren class composed of party members arranged in a hierarchy. Below, would be a servile class and below that a slave class of subjected alien races. This would seem to be a traditional hereditary aristocracy recast into a populistic and international mode. Implied in all this is an ultimate future in which every human being on earth would be of the Nordic type, the other types having been exterminated.

The inverse of technological man—Hitler's new middle class—is, I think, aesthetic man. The return of Willi Brandt to office in the elections of 1972 symbolizes the advent of a new epoch for the Germans. This approval by the majority of the voters of a man who, by Third Reich standards, was a traitor, and of his peace policy along with its cost—a permanently divided Germany—is an appropriate epitaph for Adolf Hitler, one probably written by young voters.

Amos Elon (Michael Roloff, tr.) in *Journey Through a Haunted Land, The New Germany* (New York, 1967), pp. 194–212, in a chapter called "Fathers and Sons," describes the repudiation by German youth of its fathers and their Third Reich.

PART SIX   Bohemia Now

* Gertrude Stein, *The Autobiography of Alice B. Toklas* (New York, 1933), p. 78.

18   The Black Bohemia

1. For background on this, see Robert July, *A History of the African People* (New York, 1970), and Roger Bastide (Peter Green, tr.), *African Civilization in the New World* (New York, 1971).

2. The story of black music in America is presented by Eileen Southern, *The Music of Black Americans, A History* (New York, 1971); LeRoi Jones (Imamu Amiri Baraka), *Blues People, Negro Music in White America* (New York, 1963); and Elliot Paul, *That Crazy American Music* (Indianapolis, 1957). Jazz in New Orleans is treated in the above and in Martin Williams, *Jazz Masters of New Orleans* (New York, 1967); Ann Fairbairn (Dorothy Tate), *Call Him George* (New York, 1969); Robert Goffin, *La Nouvelle-Orléans, Capitale du Jazz* (New York, 1946); and by some of the participants: Sidney Bechet, *Treat It Gentle, An Autobiography* (New York, 1960); Louis Armstrong, *Satchmo, My Life in New Orleans* (Englewood Cliffs, 1954); Ferdinand Morton (Alan Lomax, ed.), *Mr. Jelly Roll* (New York, 1956); Warren Dodds (as told to Larry Gara), *The Baby Dodds Story* (Los Angeles, 1959); and George Murphy Foster (as told to Tom Stoddard), inter-

chapters by Ross Russell, *Pops Foster, The Autobiography of a New Orleans Jazzman* (Berkeley, 1971).

3. The quotation is in Fairbairn, *George*, p. 23. For many years, Dorothy Tate a.k.a. Anne Fairbairn managed George Lewis and thus came to know many of the early jazz musicians personally. On p. 24, she says the music has always been a language, so improvisations are natural.

4. Bechet, *Gentle*, p. 50.

5. Ibid., p. 48.

6. Janheinz Jahn (Marjorie Green, tr.), *Muntu, An Outline of the New African Culture* (New York, 1961).

7. Bechet, *Gentle*, p. 50.

8. Williams, *Jazz*, p. 10.

9. Ross Russell in Foster, *Foster*, pp. 70–71.

10. Bechet, *Gentle*, p. 52.

11. Ibid., pp. 61–63, 217.

12. Fairbairn, *George*, p. 44.

13. Bechet, *Gentle*, pp. 63–64.

14. Ibid., pp. 67–68.

15. Ibid., p. 68.

16. Paul, *Music*, p. 166. Goffin's *Nouvelle-Orleans,* a book which seems to have been ignored by historians of jazz, possibly because it's in French, is based on interviews with many of the early New Orleans musicians and contains much information about those obscure times. Goffin follows the theme of Buddy Bolden and argues that Bolden was an accordian player who only began to play the cornet in 1900. He says Bolden began jazz in 1900.

17. Williams, *Jazz*, p. 2.

18. Ibid., p. 12; Foster, *Foster*, pp. 26–37; Bechet, *Gentle*, pp. 62, 83–84; Williams, *Jazz*, p. 14.

19. Paul, *Music*, p. 177. Williams (*Jazz*, p. 1) quotes Wallace Collins as saying, "They had lots of band fellows could play like that after Bolden gave them the idea," and Paul Dominguez: "Bolden cause all that.... He cause these younger Creoles, men like Bechet and Keppard, to have a different style from old heads like Tio and Perez."

20. Foster, *Foster*, pp. 65, 47. Ramsey, *Jazzmen*, p. 24.

21. Bechet, *Gentle*, pp. 111–116, 131–132.

22. Associated Press story in the Longview (Washington) *Daily News*, 6 July 1971.

23. Walter Blum, "Turk Murhpy, Living Legend," *California Living* (San Francisco *Sunday Examiner & Chronicle*), 27 June 1976, p. 25. The quote from Dave Walker is on p. 24. Sid Moody in Longview (Washington) *Daily News*, 6 July 1971.

24. Walter Laqueur, *Weimar, A Cultural iistory 1918–1933* (New York, 1974), pp. 252, 161.

25. Milton "Mezz" Mezzrow and Bernard Wolfe, *Really the*

Blues (New York, 1946), p. 326. Jones, *Blues,* p. 231.
   26. Ramsey, *Jazzmen,* p. 212, for these lyrics.

19   The Mobile Bohemia

   1. For Jules Verne, see Franz Born (Juliana Bird, tr.), *The Man Who Invented the Future: Jules Verne* (New York, 1963), pp. 110–111.
   2. For the Wild West image, Don Russell, *The Wild West or, A History of the Wild West Shows* ... (Fort Worth, 1970) and Henry Nash Smith, *Virgin Land, The American West as Symbol and Myth* (Cambridge, 1950). For Francis Bret Harte, Bernard Taper, ed. and comp., *Mark Twain's San Francisco* (New York, 1963), p. xxii. Harte's "Luck of Roaring Camp" appeared in *Overland Monthly* 2, July 1868. *Overland Monthly,* published in San Francisco between 1868 and 1875, was the equal of any other magazine published in America.
   3. H. S. Smith, ed., *Story of the Wild West and, by Buffalo Bill, (Hon. W. F. Cody), A Full and Complete History of the Pioneer Quartette* ... (Richmond, 1888), pp. 735–737.
   4. Both Albert Parry (*Garrets and Pretenders, A History of Bohemianism in America* (New York, 1933) p. 244 and Emily Hahn (*Romantic Rebels, An Informal History of Bohemianism in America* (Boston, 1967), pp. 219–220 credit Carmel with this distinction. Isobel Field, R.L.S.'s daughter-in-law writes that Joseph Strong, a painter and her husband-to-be, warned: Monterey is "the most beautiful town in California. But don't tell anybody about it. If it's ever discovered by fashionable people, they'll tear it down to build expensive hotels and fine shops (*This Life I've Loved* [New York, 1937], pp. 116–117)." She also writes about bohemian life in San Francisco.
   5. Herbert Asbury, *The Barbary Coast, An Informal History of the San Francisco Underworld* (New York, 1933).
   6. Oscar Lewis, *Bay Window Bohemia, An Account of the Brilliant Artistic World of Gaslit San Francisco* (New York, 1956), pp. 19, 231.
   7. Asbury, *Barbary,* p. 116.
   8. Two recent books about the Bohemian Club are: G. William Domhoff, *The Bohemian Grove and Other Retreats: A Study in Ruling-Class Cohesiveness* (New York, 1974) and John van der Zee, *The Greatest Men's Party on Earth: Inside the Bohemian Grove* (New York, 1974). The quotations are from Edward Bosqui, *Memoirs of Edward Bosqui* (Oakland, 1952), p. 126.
   9. Aspects of Frisco's Bohemia are treated in Lewis, *Bohemia;* Kevin Starr, *Americans and the California Dream* (New York, 1973), pp. 239–287; Warren Unna, *The Coppa Murals, A Pageant of Bohemian Life in San Francisco at the Turn of the Century* (San

Francisco, 1932); Parry, *Bohemianism* (p. 235 for street-car Bohemia); Richard O'Connor, *Ambrose Bierce, A Biography* (Boston, 1967), and Idwal Jones, *Ark of Empire, San Francisco's Montgomery Block; San Francisco's Unique Bohemia, 1853–1953* (New York, 1951). Jones calls the Montgomery Block "the Montparnasse of the Western World." For San Francisco and Carmel, Arnold Genthe, *As I Remember, With One Hundred and Twelve Photographic Illustrations by the Author* (New York, 1936), pp. 32–119.

Before 1900 people in Frisco were saying "outa sight" as is evinced by Marius' frequent use of the term in Frank Norris' *McTeague, A Story of San Francisco*, first published in 1899. This book gives an intimate sense of ordinary life in Frisco in the early 1890's. For the arts, Seares and Walter in Anonymous, *Art in California*. For *The Lark* and *Le Petit Journal des Refusées*: Gelett Burgess, *Bayside Bohemia* (San Francisco, 1954) and its "Introduction" by James D. Hart. Hart on p. ix quotes Burgess as saying: "One finds in San Francisco whatever one looks for. I was young and ardent. I found Romance. I found Adventure. I found Bohemia." For a painter, central to all this, George W. Neubert, *Xavier Martinez (1869–1943)* (Oakland, 1974).

10. The best account of Carmel is Franklin Walker, *The Seacoast of Bohemia, An Account of Early Carmel* (San Francisco, 1966). For the history of Carmel and the Monterey Peninsula, Augusta Fink, *Monterey, the Presence of the Past* (San Francisco, 1972). Also Parry, *Bohemianism*, pp. 148, 239–247; Lewis, *Bohemia*; Hahn, *Bohemianism*, pp. 216–219; and Charles S. Brooks, *A Western Wind* (New York, 1935), pp. 27–33. For London and Sterling, Joseph Noel, *Footloose in Arcadia, A Personal Record of Jack London, George Sterling, Ambrose Bierce* (New York, 1940), pp. 87–94. For Big Sur, Henry Miller, *Big Sur and the Oranges of Hieronymus Bosch* (New York, 1957).

11. Parry, *Bohemianism*, p. 238.

12. Walker, *Bohemia*, pp. 15, 14.

13. Their favorite dish was "Thackeray Stew:" Ibid., p. 19. "The Abalone Song" was doubtless inspired by Thackeray's "Bouillabaise Song." "The Abalone Song" is a folk song in that the verses keep changing and people keep inventing new ones. The "God" verse is one that I've heard.

14. Bierce called Carmel "a nest of anarchists:" Lewis, *Bohemia*, p. 180. Rémi Nadeau in *California: the New Society* (New York, 1953), pp. 139, 146, *passim*, writes at length about the liberating force of California sun living and its influence elsewhere.

15. For the racists, Langston Hughes, *I Wonder as I Wander, An Autobiographical Journey* (New York, 1956), p. 285. In "Interesting Facts About Carmel," *The Monterey Peninsula Review* (August 9–15, 1973), published the platform:

"Believing that what 9,999 towns of 10,000 want is just what

Carmel shouldn't have, I am a candidate for trustee on the platform, DON'T BOOST. I am making a spirited campaign to win by asking those who disagree with me to vote against me.

"Don't vote for Perry Newberry.

"If you hope to see Carmel become a city.

"If you want its growth boosted.

"If you desire its commercial success.

"If street lamps on its corners mean happiness to you.

"If concrete street pavements represent your civic ambitions.

"If you think that a glass factory is of greater value than a sand dune, or a millionaire than an artist, or a mansion than a little brown cottage.

"If you truly want Carmel to become a boosting, hustling, wide-awake lively metropolis.

"DON'T VOTE FOR PERRY NEWBERRY."

In San Francisco, Newberry had been a bohemian associate of Burgess's.

16. John Steinbeck, *Travels with Charley, In Search of America* (New York, 1962), p. 182.

17. For the atom in Berkeley; Nuel Pharr Davis, *Lawrence and Oppenheimer* (New York, 1968). For the San Francisco renaissance: Robert E. Johnson, ed., *Rolling Renaissance: San Francisco Underground Art in Celebration: 1945–1968* (San Francisco, 1975).

18. Jack London, *The Road* (New York, 1970—first in 1907), p. 173. The "pit" quotation, cited to a 1905 issue of *The Comrade,* is on p. 203 of Kenneth Allsop, *Hard Travellin', The Hobo and His History* (New York, 1967). A prototype is Harry Kemp, *Tramping on Life, An Autobiographical Narrative* (Garden City, 1922). For Joe Hill, Gibbs M. Smith, *Joe Hill* (Salt Lake City, 1969).

19. Allsop, *Hobo,* p. 312.

20. Ibid., pp. 181–185. Although not discussed here, another class of people sharing bohemian/hobo traits is the early professional baseball player.

21. For Kerouac, Ann Charters, *Kerouac, A Biography* (San Francisco, 1973). This, by a longtime friend of Kerouac's, is the best on the subject.

22. For an intimate sense of life among (as he estimates it) Frisco's 500 "hard-core" beatniks, Jerry Kamstra, *The Frisco Kid* (New York, 1975). This is a roman à clef based on experience. See also Jack Kerouac, *The Subterraneans* (New York, 1958), a book written from a different romantic viewpoint. A good contemporary study is Francis J. Rigney and L. Douglas Smith, *The Real Bohemia, A Sociological and Psychological Study of the "Beats"* (New York, 1961); Another is, Kenneth Rexroth, "Rexroth Has Found S.F. Has Gone to the Cats," *This World,* San Francisco *Sunday Chronicle,* 29 November 1959. For an overview of beat writers,

Thomas Parkinson, ed., *A Casebook on the Beat* (New York, 1961).
See also Lawrence Lipton, *The Holy Barbarians* (New York, 1959).

23. Bruce Cook, *The Beat Generation, The Tumultuous '50's Movement and Its Impact on Today* (New York, 1971), pp. 74–75. That all of this emerged on the paper with absolute spontaneity is the image Kerouac liked to present and seems to be true—symbolically. For the facts, Charters, *Kerouac*.

24. This is from an interview Cook had with Kerouac shortly before Kerouac's death (Cook, *Beat*, p. 89). Jerry Kamstra (*Weed, Adventures of a Dope Smuggler* [New York, 1974]) compares the beatnik and hippie styles as he tells the story of the marijuana business, from source to consumer, and of its changes through the years. This book, based on personal experience, affords a perspective of primary importance to those who would understand what the changing youth culture is all about.

25. The complexity of the facts of this matter is evident in Donald Drew Egbert and Stow Persons, eds., *Socialism and American Life*, II (*Bibliography: Descriptive and Critical* [Princeton, 1952]), pp. 492–497.

26. Conversations with Pete Seeger, Beacon, New York, 1953. Of the banjo, he said: "The banjo was brought to America by the slaves." Banjos were "thought vulgar and no white person would touch one. But, then, a white teenager, a sharecropper's son named Joel Walker Sweeney, learned how to play a banjo and in twenty years it was the most popular instrument in America." This was before the Civil War.

27. Perambulations with Bob (Samuel R.) Gibson, Putnam County, New York, 1950.

28. During the conversation Pete Seeger said: "Guitar and banjo pickers began sitting around in Washington Square, more came, now it's an institution." This, the origin of its first institution, suggests the total informality of the folk-song movement, especially at the beginning.

29. For a sense of the repertoire and the spirit, Alan Lomax, ed., *The 111 Best American Ballads, Folk Song U.S.A.* (New York, 1947); Woody Guthrie, *Bound for Glory* (New York, 1943) and Woody Guthrie (Robert Shelton, ed.), *Born to Win* (New York, 1965). For the movement in embryo and more repertoire, John A. Lomax, *Adventures of a Ballad Hunter* (New York, 1947) and Carl Sandburg, *The American Songbag* (New York, 1927). Before the movement, the songs seem to have been regarded as old curiosities at best. German folk songs, too, were in currency long before the Wandervögel collected them. H. L. Mencken along with other pupils enrolled in Friedrich Knapp's Institute in Baltimore, beginning in 1886, used to sing German "Volks-lieder" at the beginning of most school days: Isaac Goldberg, *The Man Mencken, A Biographical and Critical Study* (New York, 1925), pp. 69–70.

30. © Stormking Music, New York.

31. Louis Adamic, *A Nation of Nations* (New York, 1945), pp. 6–13.

32. "Rye Whiskey," a folk song and a Seeger favorite.

33. Pete Seeger to Richard Miller, 18 April 1975.

34. Pete Seeger, "More Praise for the Non-Traveller," *Sing Out! The Folk-Song Magazine*, XXII (1974), p. 31.

20 Bohemia in Transformation

1. For the Harlem Renaissance, Langston Hughes, *The Big Sea, an Autobiography by Langston Hughes* (New York, 1940); Milton "Mezz" Mezzrow and Bernard Wolfe, *Really the Blues* (New York, 1946); Carl Van Vechten, *Nigger Heaven* (New York, 1926); and, more formally, Nathan Irvin Huggins, *Harlem Renaissance* (New York, 1971).

2. Hughes, *Sea*, p. 238.

3. Mezzrow, *Blues*, pp. 201–202.

4. Ibid., pp. 220–222.

5. Ibid., p. 222

6. Ibid., p. 108.

7. Malcolm X with Alex Haley, *The Autobiography of Malcolm X* (New York, 1964), p. 94.

8. Langston Hughes, *The Panther and the Lash, Poems of Our Times* (New York, 1967), p. vii.

9. This is from my experience. The motorcycle police, in crash helmets, were the ones who clubbed students. In most cases, the blue-uniformed police watched or helped people up who had slipped on the wet marble. Neither students nor police had ever experienced anything like this before. They had neither precedent nor instructions to guide their behavior. Both groups, save some of the motorcycle police and the sergeant of police intelligence who ordered the fire hoses turned on, acted with admirable restraint. The extreme emotional intensity of the situation and the slippery condition of the floors and steps meant that any general loss of self-control would have resulted in many injuries and, possibly deaths. A good account of these and subsequent events, and of the mentality of youth at the time, is Albert T. Anderson and Bernice Prince Biggs, eds. and comps., *A Focus on Rebellion* (San Francisco, 1962).

10. This is from my experience. Jean-François Revel (J. F. Bernard, tr.), in *Without Marx or Jesus, The New American Revolution Has Begun* (New York, 1970), says on p. 6: "In 1964–65, at Berkeley, occurred the first of these student revolts which are a wholly new phenomenon," a "prototype" which went to Europe and the Third World. The meaning of these revolts is powerfully

presented in Kaye Boyle's memoir about the San Francisco State College strike of 1968: *The Long Walk at San Francisco State and Other Essays* (New York, 1970).

11. Max Scherr is the founder of the *Barb*. The story of the early Haight is told by David E. Smith, M.D., and John Luce in *Love Needs Care, a History of San Francisco's Haight-Ashbury Free Medical Clinic. . . .* (Boston, 1971), pp. 75–77. Smith refers to these artistically oriented young whites as "bohemians (p. 77)." He adds (p. 83) "their universal hero was the American Negro."

12. Michael Harrington in "We Few, We Happy Few, We Bohemians, A Memoir of the Culture Before the Counterculture," *Esquire*, August 1972, pp. 93–103, 162–164, laments that what once belonged to a small group—the bohemian style—has now suffused the millions.

13. The Mime Troop was established and conducted by Ronald G. Davis. In *Ringolevio, A Life Played for Keeps* (Boston, 1972), on p. 363, Emmett Grogan, a New Yorker and founder of the Diggers, says it happened in Frisco first.

14. Revel, *Revolution*. William S. Burroughs, *The Job, Interviews with William S. Burroughs by Daniel Odier . . .* (New York, 1974), p. 78.

15. Luria Castell, quoted in Ralph J. Gleason, *The Jefferson Airplane and the San Francisco Sound* (New York, 1969), p. 3.

16. This is from personal experience.

17. Gleason (*Airplane*) gives the best account of all this. He was the jazz critic of the *Chronicle* and he tells most of the story from personal experience. See also Johnathan Eisen, ed., *The Age of Rock: Sounds of the American Cultural Revolution* (New York, 1969); Charles Perry, "From Eternity to Here: What a Long Strange Trip It's Been," *Rolling Stone*, 26 February 1976, pp. 38–54; and Ben Fong-Torres, "Love Is Just a Song We Sing But a Contract Is Something Else . . . , *Rolling Stone*, 26 February 1976, pp. 58–65, 82–87.

18. Mark Messer in "Running Out of Era: Some Nonpharmacological Notes on the Psychadelic Revolution," in David E. Smith, ed., *The New Social Drug: Cultural, Medical, and Legal Perspectives on Marijuana* (Englewood Cliffs, 1970), on p. 157, says youth's "historical location is in the center of a storm of cultural forces, which has already altered their consciousness, and which the drugs augment and make lucid. In short, a mind-altering drug *shows* them where they're at; it does not *put* them there." Messer seems to be one of those few men who understand what's going on while it's going on.

19. Norman Mailer, "The White Negro, Superficial Reflections on the Hipster," *Dissent*, IV (Summer 1957), p. 282.

21 The Acid Bohemians

1. This is all in Tom Wolfe, *Electric Kool-Aid Acid Test* (New York, 1968). This is quality journalism, true to the spirit and much more accurate to the details than could be expected of a man who was not present at most of the events he reports.

2. From experience and conversations with Ken Kesey and some of the Pranksters.

3. Reported in conversation with Lee Quarnstrom who shared this ride with Kesey.

4. Ralph J. Gleason, *The Jefferson Airplane and the San Francisco Sound* (New York, 1969), p. 36.

5. Wolfe, *Acid*, p. 232 ff., and Gleason, *Airplane*, pp. 18–22.

6. This is also discussed in Leonard Wolf, ed., *Voice from the Love Generation* (Boston, 1968).

7. David E. Smith, M.D. and John Luce, *Love Needs Care* (Boston, 1971), pp. 109, 116, 151. For the generally accepted estimate of 100,000 and for the effect on the Diggers—a specimen institution—see Emmett Grogan, *Ringolevio, A Life Played for Keeps* (Boston, 1972); Malcolm X with Alex Haley, *The Autobiography of Malcolm X* (New York, 1964), p. 92.

8. From conversations with David Getz, drummer for Big Brother and the Holding Company.

9. Three M.D.'s, J. Fred E. Shick, David E. Smith and Frederick H. Meyers ("Use of Marijuana in the Haight-Ashbury Subculture," David E. Smith, *The New Social Drug* [Englewood Cliffs, 1970], pp. 43–44) tell us of a study they made in the summer and fall of 1967 showing that of 413 respondents, the mean age was 20.5 years $+/-$ 1.5 and that only 16.2% had been reared in the San Francisco Bay Area while 44% came to the Haight directly from another state.

10. For this and more, see Nicholas von Hoffman, *We Are the People Our Parents Warned Us Against* (Chicago, 1968), p. 261 ff. Von Hoffman, an outstanding journalist of national reputation, spent several months in and about the Haight.

11. The first is from conversation with a hitchhiking playwright from New York whose name I never learned. The second: Carol Taylor, "Like an Extravagant Love Affair that Ended Savagely," *Rolling Stone*, 26 February 1976, p. 70.

12. "Acid casualty" is a term Lee Quarnstrom applies to some of his quondam colleagues among the Pranksters.

13. Conversations with Ernest Alcorn, San Francisco, 1972.

14. Margaret Meade, *Culture and Commitment, a Study of the Generation Gap* (New York, 1970). Recent suggestions as to the worldwide influence of the protoculture appear in *Atlas World Press Review*, April 1975, p. 6, summarizing a report of Olivia Wendt of the *Deutsche Zeitung* saying that young people in North Vietnam "yearn for the long hair and blue jeans they see in East

European movies," and in the account in the San Francisco *Chronicle* of 13 May 1975, of the visit to Boston of the first Soviet warship arriving in the U.S.A. since World War II which says the sailors were "eager to find out about 'the mood of American youth' and 'the ordinary working man.'"

22 The Protoculture

1. For discussion of the protoculture in its original form see Von Hoffman, *Parents,* p. 266 ff; David E. Smith, M.D. and John Luce, *Love Needs Care* (Boston, 1971); Mark Messer, "Running Out of Era: Some Nonpharmacological Notes on the Psychedelic Revolution." in David Smith, ed. *The New Social Drug* (Englewood Cliffs, 1970); and for autobiographical presentations based in California see William J. Craddock, *Be Not Content* (Garden City, 1970); John S. Simon, *The Sign of the Fool, Memoirs of the Haight-Ashbury, 1965–1968* (New York, 1971) and Wolf, *Voice.* For an East-coast view, Robert Mungo, *Total Loss Farm, A Year in the Life* (New York, 1970) and, more generally, Paul Krassner, *How a Satirical Editor Became a Yippie Conspirator in Ten Easy Years* (New York, *c.* 1971).

For variant contexts, see Jerry Farber, *The Student as Nigger, Essays and Stories by Jerry Farber* (New York, 1969) and Keith Melville, *Communes in the Counter Culture, Origins, Theories, Styles of Life* (New York, 1972). For the dark side of its dark side, William J. Craddock, *Twilight Candelabra, An Absurdly Disrespectful Horror Story and Tight Pornographic Allegory* (Garden City, New York, 1972).

For discussion of the protoculture in deeper context see Philip E. Slater, *The Pursuit of Loneliness, American Culture at the Breaking Point* (Boston, 1970), p. 100, *passim;* Margaret Mead, *Culture and Commitment, A Study of the Generation Gap* (Garden City, 1970); Henry Malcolm, *Generation of Narcissus* (Boston, 1971); Charles Reich, *The Greening of America* (New York, 1970); and Mark Gerzon, *The Whole World Is Watching, A Young Man Looks at Youth's Dissent* (New York, 1969).

At least two books try with some success to place the cultural transformation in the field of a sophisticated philosophy and social-psychology: Thomas Hanna, *Bodies in Revolt: The Evolution-Revolution of 20th Century Man Toward the Somatic Culture of the 21st Century* (New York, 1970) and George B. Leonard, *The Transformation, A Guide to the Inevitable Changes in Humankind* (New York, 1972).

There are other books on these subjects, many of which have received more attention than they deserve.

2. For the concept of apparency/transparency, and for careful editing and fundamental criticism which along with other proportions and concepts have been of primary importance to this book,

I am indebted to Anders Edvard Smiltens. George Leonard (*Transformation*) conceives of the ultimate reality as "vibrancy."

3. This insight comes from Jean Genêt (Bernard Frechtman, tr.), *The Thief's Journal* (New York, 1964).

4. For a discussion of the personality type represented by Nixon and his close political associates see Michael Davis, "British View of the White House: The 'Orange County' Spirit," San Francisco *Chronicle*, 28 April 1973, and Kilpatrick Sale, "The World Behind Watergate," *New York Review of Books*, 3 May 1973, pp. 9–16. These men exemplify the post-traditional functionary herein called technological man or the bureaucratic Nazi, a type displayed in several manifestations by G. M. Gilbert in *Nuremberg Diary* (New York, 1947); Hans Bernd Gisevius (Richard and Clara Winston, trs.), *To the Bitter End* (Boston, 1947); and Bob Woodward and Carl Bernstein in *All the President's Men* (New York, 1974).

5. The rearing of this generation of Americans was guided through early childhood by Dr. Benjamin Spock's *Common Sense Book of Baby and Child Care* (New York, 1946).
For *Mad* and *Zap*, Jacob Brackman, "The International Comix Conspiracy," *Playboy* (December 1970), pp. 195–199, 328–334.

6. Diane Fredericks in a paper, February 1972.

7. Richter, *Dada*, p. 139: "Schwitters was a totally free spirit; he was ruled by Nature."

8. Sigmund Freud (James Strachey, ed. and tr.), *Civilization and Its Discontents* (New York, 1961), first published in 1930.

9. Abraham H. Maslow, *Toward a Psychology of Being* (New York, 1962), p. 29.

10. This question is discussed in Jeremy Bernstein, "When the Computer Procreates," *The New York Times Magazine*, 15 February 1976, pp. 9, 34–38. He thinks the development of such a machine possible but not probable. The subject of genetic control is just now broaching in the media. See, for example, Robert C. Cowan, "Should Biologists Redesign Organic Life?" *The Christian Science Monitor* (Boston), 3 February 1977.

11. Dr. Frank Barnaby, "Precision Warfare," *New Scientist*, 8 May 1975, p. 304. United Press International, "Another CIA Plot: Cuba Crops, San Francisco *Sunday Examiner & Chronicle*, 27 June 1976. Jack Anderson, "CIA Germ Warfare," Monterey (California) *Peninsula Herald*, 18 January 1977. Jack Anderson, "U.S. Ready With Nuclear Weapons," San Francisco *Chronicle*, 8 July 1975.

12. Anders Edvard Smiltens to Richard Miller, 5 July 1976.

23 Current Transformation

1. This is a central theme of Erich Fromm's *Escape from Freedom* (New York, 1941) and of his *Man for Himself, An In-*

quiry Into the Psychology of Ethics (New York, 1947). For his current view, see *The Anatomy of Human Destructiveness* (New York, 1973), pp. 34–342, *passim.* Here he quotes the result of a study of the relation between the necrophilous personality and sociopolitical attitudes made by Michael Maccoby and himself ("Emotional Attitudes and Political Choices," *Politics and Society,* II [Winter 1972], pp. 209–239), quotation on p. 223:

"In all of the samples, we found that anti-life tendencies were significantly correlated to the political positions that supported increased military power and favored repression against dissenters. The following priorities were considered most important by individuals who have dominant anti-life tendencies: tighter control of rioters, tighter enforcement of anti-drug laws, winning the war in Vietnam, controlling subversive groups, strengthening the police, and fighting Communism throughout the world."

Fromm's book then goes on to discuss "The Connection Between Necrophilia and the Worship of Technique."

American Nazis can be seen and heard in the film "Hearts and Minds," Warner Brothers, *c.* 1972.

2. Most of this information has been in the news media at one time or another, albeit buried deeply and distorted, *e.g.,* New York *Times,* 7 December 1960 p. 72. For Air Marshal Slemon's noble part, Drew Pearson, San Francisco *Chronicle,* 16 May 1961. An excellent summary article is Lloyd J. Dumas, "National Insecurity in the Nuclear Age," *The Bulletin of the Atomic Scientists,* XXXII (May 1976), pp. 24–35. On page 27 he says the North Carolina bombs were rated at 24 megatons each and the four Spanish bombs at 20 to 25. He then says that between 1950 and 1973 "there have been at least 63 serious accidents publicly reported involving major mass destruction weapons carrier systems" and (p. 29) there have been "*many*" false alarms. Gail Sheehy, "California's Impossible Nuclear Decision: A Reporter's Personal Search for an Answer," *New West,* 7 June 1976, p. 51, says General Electric is building four nuclear power plants in Taiwan.

3. There is a vast literature on the built-in defects of the system, *e.g.,* Geoffrey Barraclough, "The Great World Crisis, I," *New York Review of Books,* 23 January 1975, pp. 20–30. A sense of the peril built into all applications of atomic energy can be gained by reading through recent issues of *The Bulletin of the Atomic Scientists.* For example, Bernard T. Field's editorial "Making the World Safe for Plutonium," XXXI (May 1975), pp. 5–6; Gerald Wald's editorial "Arise, Ye Prisoners," XXX (December 1974), pp. 4–6; David Krieger's "Terrorists and Nuclear Technology," XXXI (June 1975), pp. 28–34; and Barry M. Caspar's "Laser Enrichment: A New Path to Proliferation?" XXXIII (January, 1977), 28–41.

Wald says (p. 4) "I am one of those scientists who does not

see how to bring the human race much past the year 2000." We make three hydrogen warheads a day. "We are told that our security (strange thought) lies in Mutual Assured Destruction—MAD." And (p. 6): "The only thing that can save us now is political power—for the peoples of the world to take that power away from their present masters."

The subhead on Krieger's article about nuclear terrorism declares "The danger is great; the question is not whether the worst will happen, but where and how." He then tells us (pp. 28–29) that 22 nations in addition to India can make bombs out of the plutonium manufactured in their power plants. Twenty pounds of plutonium will make a bomb (p. 29). In 1971 (p. 32) 13 tons of plutonium were produced by the world's power plants—leading to an estimated 750 tons yearly by the turn of the century. He quotes from a Ford Foundation study (p. 30): "The widespread use of nuclear energy requires the rapid development of near perfect social and political institutions" and says (p. 34) "One may well ask what repressions a government and its police forces will be capable of when confronted by nuclear terror, blackmail or extortion."

In his newsletter of April 1975, Senator Alan Cranston tells us that "South Korea very nearly got a nuclear powerplant capable of producing enough plutonium for 16 nuclear bombs a year—compliments of the United States."

The atomic establishment has trained the public to believe that uranium 235 and plutonium 239 can be concentrated with no possibility of a chain-reaction event until reaching a quantity called "critical mass." This is questionable. At less than critical mass the probability of an event is low but real. To concentrate these materials for any reason at all is a crime against man and nature and renders an unwanted event certain, not because of political and psychological considerations, but because of the nature of the metals themselves and the cumulative character of probability (conversations with Charles Raymond, Marshall, California, 1974).

After studying the pros and cons, Gail Sheehy ("Nuclear," p. 51) concluded "that commercial nuclear power is more a menace than a promise." Kevin Howe, in reporting a missile systems conference at the Naval Postgraduate School ("Physicist Predicts Nuclear Arms Use in Anger Before End of This Century," Monterey Peninsula Herald, 17 January 1976), says "At present there are 35 countries with sufficient materials within their borders to make one or two nuclear weapons a year ... and another 50 with an announced policy of acquiring nuclear power generating technology."

One awaits the Ugandan A-bomb.

4. Roger Rapoport, The Great American Bomb Machine (New York, 1971).

5. I heard a radio report on this, but do not have the reference. As yet, computers can play chess no better than middle-range,

tournament amateur chess players, (*Scientific American*, CCXXXV [July 1976], p. 66).

6. Hans Magnus Enzensberger, "The Industrialization of the Mind," *Partisan Review*, XXXVI (1969), pp. 100–111. For a discussion of art and the protoculture: Herbert Marcuse, *An Essay on Liberation* (Boston, 1969) or the forthcoming book of S. P. R. Charter.

7. "Nitinol" is an acronym of *NIckel-Titanium-Naval-Ordnance-Laboratory* where, for a different purpose, the alloy was first developed.

8. Fred Gardner, "Nitinol, The Torque of the Town," *The Co-Evolution Quarterly*, Spring 1975, pp. 68–72.

9. Quotation is from a United Press report (San Francisco *Chronicle*, 14 June 1973) showing the results of a study of cultural attitudes in New York State. Musicians ranked fourth in public esteem—behind scientists, doctors, lawyers—poets shared sixth place with businessmen, and painters ranked seventh. Tolerance and pessimism is from a study reported on television, December 1973.' See also Robert Commandy, "California Support of the Arts," *This World*, San Francisco *Sunday Examiner & Chronicle*, 20 April 1975. This reports a study showing among other things that in California the arts do not have an elitist image. A page-one feature in the Cleveland *Plain Dealer* of 11 August 1975 (Louis Harris, "New Life Styles"), says: "as much as their elders complain about the different ways of the young, a whole society appears to have been changed in its tastes and habits by the life styles of the younger generation."

10. John Adams to H. Niles, 13 February 1818, in Charles Francis Adams, ed., *The Works of John Adams . . .*, X (Boston, 1856), pp. 282, 283.

11. Benjamin Rush to Richard Price, 25 May 1786, in L. H. Butterfield, ed., *Letters of Benjamin Rush*, I (*1761–1792* [Princeton, 1951]), p. 386.

12. John Franklin Jameson, *The American Revolution Considered as a Social Movement* (Princeton, 1926). Jameson estimates that ⅓ of the colonists were patriots, ⅓ loyalists, and ⅓ indifferents. The patriots tended to be young and bold, the loyalists, settled and timid. See also Frederick B. Tolles, "The American Revolution Considered as a Social Movement: A Re-Evaluation," *The American Historical Review*, LX (October 1954), pp. 1–12.

13. Anthropologist Francis L. K. Hsu in his *Americans and Chinese, Reflections on Two Cultures and Their People* (New York, 1970) clearly demonstrates the Americans' defective sense of community—and the Chinese's defective sense of individuality.

14. Carl Sagan and Frank Drake, "The Search for Extraterrestrial Intelligence," *Scientific American*, CCXXXI (May 1975), pp. 80–89.

Bibliography

FRANCE

Alger, J. G. *The New Paris Sketch Book: Manners, Men, Institutions.* London, 1889.

Allem, Maurice. *La Vie Quotidienne Sous le Second Empire.* Paris, 1948.

Anglemont, Alexandre Privat d'. *Paris Anecdote, Avec Une Préface et des Notes par Charles Monselet....* Paris, 1885.

Anonymous. "Robert Baldick: The First Bohemian." *The* (London) *Times Literary Supplement.* 19 May 1961. P. 307.

Asselineau, Charles. *Bibliographie Romantique, Catalogue Anecdotique et Pittoresque des Editions Originales des Oeuvres de Victor Hugo....* Paris, 1872.

Audebrand, Philibert. *Derniers Jours de la Bohème, Souvenirs de la Vie Littéraire.* Paris, 1905.

Avedon, Richard, ed. *Diary of a Century, Jacques-Henri Lartigue.* New York, 1970.

Babeau, Albert. *Paris en 1789.* Paris, 1891.

Baldick, Robert. *The First Bohemian: The Life of Henry Murger.* London, 1961.

Baldwin, Carl. W. "Courbet and the Column." *Art News.* LXX (May 1971). Pp. 36, 38.

Balzac, Honoré de. *La Femme aux Yeux d'Or.* Paris, 1835.

_____. *Un Grand Homme de Province à Paris.* Paris, 1839.

Banquart, Marie-Claire, ed. *Jules Vallès, Un Tableau Synoptique de la Vie et des Oeuvres....* Paris, 1971.

Biré, Edmond. *Victor Hugo Avant 1830.* Paris, 1902.

Blassingame, Wyatt. *The French Foreign Legion*. New York, 1955.

Boisson, Marius. *Les Compagnons de la Vie de Bohème, Mimi, Musette, Murger, Baudelaire, Schaunard, Champfleury.* . . . Paris, 1929.

Borel, Pétrus. *Rhapsodies*. Paris, 1832.

Born, Franz (Juliana Biro, tr.). *The Man Who Invented the Future: Jules Verne*. New York, 1963.

Bourrelier, Henri. *La Vie du Quartier Latin dès Origines à la Cité Universitaire*. Paris, 1936.

Brogan, D. W. *The French Nation from Napoleon to Pétain, 1814–1940*. New York, 1963.

Burnand, Robert. *La Vie Quotidienne en France de 1870 à 1900*. Paris, 1947.

Carco, Francis (Madeleine Boyd, tr.). *From Montmartre to the Latin Quarter (The Last Bohemia)*. London, c. 1920.

————. *Montmartre à Vingt Ans*. Paris, 1938.

————. *Nostalgie de Paris Suivi de Ombres Vivantes*. Paris, 1952.

Carr, Philip. *Days with the French Romantics in the Paris of 1830*. London, 1932.

Castex, Pierre-Georges and Paul Surer. *Manuel des Etudes Littéraires Françaises, XIXᵉ Siècle*. Paris, 1950.

Challamel, Augustin. *Souvenirs d'un Hugolâtre, La Génération de 1830*. Paris, 1885.

Chevalier, Louis (Frank Jellinek, tr.). *Laboring Classes and Dangerous Classes in Paris During the First Half of the Nineteenth Century*. New York, 1973.

Cohn-Bendit, Daniel and Gabriel Cohn-Bendit. *Le Gauchisme, Remède à la Maladie Sénile du Communisme*. Paris, 1968. (Also the variant English language edition, Arnold Pomerans, tr., *Obsolete Communism, The Left-Wing Alternative*. New York, 1968).

Cowley, Malcolm. *Exile's Return, A Narrative of Ideas*. New York, 1934.

————. *A Second Flowering, Works and Days of the Lost Generation*. New York, 1973.

Daudet, Alphonse (Laura Ensor, tr.). *Thirty Years of Paris and of My Literary Life*. London, 1893.

Du Camp, Maxime. *Théophile Gautier*. Paris, 1890.

Dumas, Alexandre. *Mes Mémoires*. Nouveau Edition. Paris, 1883.

Du Maurier, George. *Trilby, A Novel with Illustrations by the Author*. New York, 1895.

Dunbar, Ernest. *The Black Expatriates, A Study of American Negroes in Exile*. New York, 1968.

Dupeaux, Georges. *La Société Française*. Paris, 1964.

Easton, Malcolm. *Artists and Writers in Paris: The Bohemian Idea, 1803–1867*. London, 1964.

Edwards, George Wharton. *Paris*. Philadelphia, 1924.

Egbert, Donald D. "The Idea of 'Avant-Garde' in Art and Politics." *The American Historical Review.* LXXIII (1967), pp. 339–366.

Emile-Bayard, Jean. (Ralph Anningson and Tudor Davies, trs.). *Montmartre Past and Present with Reminiscences by Well-Known Artists and Writers*. New York, c. 1925.

Engels, Friedrich. "Introduction to *Excerpts from The Civil War in France*." Lewis S. Feueur, ed. *Basic Writings on Politics and Philosophy, Karl Marx and Friedrich Engels*. New York, 1959. pp. 349–362.

Faral, Edmond. *La Vie Quotidienne au Temps de Saint Louis*. Paris, 1938.

Figaro. Paris, 20 January; 9, 18, 26, 27, 28 February; 5, 6, 16, 19, 20, 23, 25 March; 1, 4 April; 20 October 1832.

Flaubert, Gustave. *Madame Bovary*. New York, 1965.

Ford, Hugh, ed. *The Left Bank Revisited: Selections from the Paris Tribune, 1917–1934*. University Park, Pennsylvania, 1972.

Gary, Romain (John Markham Beach, tr.). *Promise at Dawn*. New York, 1961.

Gautier, Théophile. *Histoire du Romantisme Suivie de Notices Romantiques....* Paris, c. 1872.

————. *Les Jeunes-France*. Paris, 1833.

————. *Mademoiselle de Maupin and "A Note by the Author."* New York, 1930. First published in 1836.

Geler, Evelyn. "Hugo, Victor Marie," and "Nerval, Gérard de." Stanley J. Kunitz and Vineta Colby, eds. *European Authors, 1000–1900, A Biographical Dictionary of European Authors*. New York, 1967. pp. 426–430; 676–679.

Genêt, Jean. (Bernard Frechtman, tr.). *The Thief's Journal*. New York, 1964.

Gerbod, Paul. *La Vie Quotidienne dans les Lycées et Collèges au XIXᵉ Siècle*. Paris, 1968.

Gorman, Herbert. *The Incredible Marquis, Alexandre Dumas*. New York, 1929.

Graña, César. *Bohemian Versus Bourgeois: French Society and the French Man of Letters in the Nineteenth Century*. New York, 1964.

Guillemin, Henri. *Victor Hugo par Lui-Même*. Paris, 1951.

Hare, Augustus J. C. *Walks in Paris*. London, 1888.

Harris, Frank. *My Lives and Loves*. I. Paris, c. 1923.

Havet, Ernest. "Notice." *Poésies Posthumes de Philothée O'Neddy*. Paris, 1877. pp. 1–129.

Hemingway, Ernest. *A Moveable Feast*. New York, 1964.

————. *The Sun Also Rises*. New York, 1926.

Hemmings, F. W. J. *Culture and Society in France, 1848–1898, Dissidents and Philistines.* New York, 1971.

Hicks, John and Robert Tucker, eds. *Revolution and Reaction, The Paris Commune 1871.* Amherst, 1973.

Houssaye, Arsène. *Les Confessions, Souvenirs d'un Demi-Siècle, 1830–1880.* I. Paris, 1885.

————. *Souvenirs de Jeunesse, 1850–1870.* Paris, c. 1880.

Huddleston, Sisley. *Paris Salons, Cafés, Studios, Being Social Artistic and Literary Memoirs.* Philadelphia, 1928.

Hugo, Adèle. *Victor Hugo Raconté par un Témoin de Sa Vie.* Paris, c. 1868.

Hugo, Victor. *Hernani, Edited with Introduction and Critical and Explanatory Notes by John E. Matzke, Ph.D. . . .* Boston, 1891.

————. *Journal, 1830–1848.* Paris, 1954.

————. (Charles E. Wilbour, tr.). *Les Misérables.* New York, 1964.

————. *Les Orientales.* Paris, 1882.

Huisman, Ph. and M. G. Dortu (Corinne Bellow, tr. and ed.). *Lautrec by Lautrec.* New York, 1964.

Huneker, James Gibbon. *Steeplejack.* New York, 1922.

Jasinski, René. *Les Années Romantiques de Th. Gautier.* Paris, 1929.

Jean, Raymond. ed. *Nerval par Lui-Même,* Paris, 1964.

Jones, James. *The Merry Month of May.* New York, 1970.

Josephson, Matthew. *Victor Hugo, A Realistic Biography of the Great Romantic.* New York, 1970.

Kneppler, Henry, tr. and ed. *Man about Paris, The Confessions of Arsène Houssaye.* New York, 1970.

Labracherie, Pierre. *La Vie Quotidienne de la Bohème Littéraire au XIXᵉ Siècle.* Paris, 1967.

Lartigue, Jacques-Henri. *Boyhood Photographs of J.-H. Lartigue, The Family Album of a Gilded Age.* Switzerland, 1966.

Lazarre, Félix and Louis Lazarre. *Dictionnaire Administratif et Historique des Rues de Paris et Ses Monuments.* Paris, 1844.

Lelioux, Adrien François, Léon Noël, and Nadar. *Histoire de Murger Pour Servir à la Histoire de la Vrai Bohème par Trois Buveurs d'Eau.* Paris, 1864.

Leuthy, Herbert (Eric Mosbacher, tr.). *France Against Herself, The Past Politics and Crises of Modern France.* New York, 1955.

Lissagaray, Prosper-Olivier. (Eleanor Marx Aveling, tr.). *History of the Commune of 1871.* New York, 1898.

McCabe, James D., Jr. *Paris by Sunlight and Gaslight, A Work Descriptive of the Mysteries and Miseries, the Virtues, the Vices, the Splendors, and the Crimes of the City of Paris.* Philadelphia, 1869.

Marx, Karl. "Excerpts from The Civil War in France." Lewis S.

Feueur, ed. *Basic Writings on Politics and Philosophy, Karl Marx and Friedrich Engels.* New York, 1959. pp. 362–391.

Maurice, Arthur Bartlett. *The Paris of the Novelists.* New York, thor. New York, 1895.

Maurois, André (Gerard Hopkins, tr.). *Olympio, The Life of Victor Hugo.* New York, 1956.

——————. (Oliver Bernard, tr.). *Victor Hugo and His World.* London, 1966.

Meyer, Jacques. *La Vie Quotidienne des Soldats Pendant la Grande Guerre.* Paris, 1966.

Miller, Henry. *Tropic of Cancer.* Paris, 1934.

——————. *Tropic of Capricorn.* Paris, 1938.

Morrow, W. C., from notes by Edouard Cucuel. *Bohemian Paris To-day.* London, 1899.

Moss, Arthur and Evalyn Marvel. *The Legend of the Latin Quarter, Henry Murger and the Birth of Bohemia.* New York, 1946.

Murger, Henry. *Les Buveurs d'Eau.* Paris, 1870. First published in 1856.

——————. *Scènes de la Vie de Bohème.* Paris, 1874.

Nevill, Ralph. *Days and Nights in Montmartre and the Latin Quarter.* New York, 1927.

Nohain, Jean and F. Cardec (Warren Tute, tr.). *Le Petomane, 1857–1945.* Los Angeles, 1967.

O'Neddy, Philothée. *Feu et Flamme, Publié avec un Introduction des Notes par Marcel Hervier.* Paris, 1926.

——————. Havet, Ernest, ed. *Poésies Posthumes de Philothée O'Neddy.* Paris, 1877.

Orwell, George. *Down and Out in Paris and London.* New York, 1933.

Paul, Elliot. *The Last Time I Saw Paris.* Garden City, 1943.

Pélin, Gabriel. *Les Laideurs du Beau Paris, Histoire Morale, Critique et Philisophique des Industries, des Habitants et des Monuments de la Capitale.* Paris, 1861.

Péricard, J. and Charles Delvert. *Verdun, La Grande Bataille de Verdun, le Drame de Douaumont (J. Péricard), la Défense de R' (Ch. Delvert), l'Enfer de Verdun.* Paris, c. 1945.

Pinkney, David H. *Napoleon III and the Rebuilding of Paris.* Princeton, 1972.

Pontmartin, Armand Augustin Joseph Marie Ferrard, Comte de. *Mes Mémories. I (Souvenirs de l' Enfrance et de la Jeaunesse)* Paris, 1882.

Rheims, Maurice. *The Flowering of Art Nouveau.* New York, c. 1966.

Richardson, Joanna. *The Bohemians: La Vie de Bohéme in Paris, 1830–1914.* London, 1969.

——————. *Théophile Gautier, His Life and Times.* London, 1958.

Rimbaud, Arthur. *Rimbaud, Introduced and Edited by Oliver Bernard, With Plain Prose Translations of Each Poem.* Baltimore, 1962.

Robiquet, Jean. *La Vie Quotidienne au Temps de Napoléon.* Paris, 1942.

Roman, Jean (James Emmons, tr.). *Paris, Fin de Siècle.* New York, 1960.

Romains, Jules (Gerard Hopkins, tr.). *The Prelude, The Battle—Verdun.* New York, 1939.

Sachs, Maurice (G. M. Sachs, tr.). *The Decade of Illusion, Paris 1918–1928.* New York, 1933.

Sade, Marquis de. *Justine.* New York, 1964. First published in 1791.

San Francisco *Good Times.* 30 April 1971.

Sand, George. *La Dernière Aldini.* Paris, 1837.

Sartre, Jean-Paul (Bernard Frechtman, tr.). *The Words.* New York, 1964.

Schwarz, Heinrich. "Nadar." *The Encyclopedia of Photography.* XIII. New York, 1963. pp. 2484–2485.

Scott, John. *Paris Revisited in 1815, By Way of Brussels: Including a Walk Over the Field of Battle at Waterloo.* London, 1816.

Service, Robert W. *Ballads of a Bohemian.* New York, 1921.

Shattuck, Roger. *The Banquet Years, The Origins of the Avant Garde in France, 1885 to World War I.* New York, 1955.

Shirley-Fox, R. B. A. *An Art Student Reminisces of Paris in the Eighties.* London, 1909.

Smith, F. Berkeley. *The Real Latin Quarter.* New York, 1901.

Sprigge, Elizabeth. *Gertrude Stein, Her Life and Work.* New York, 1957.

Starkie, Enid. *Pétrus Borel, The Lycanthrope: His Life and Times.* London, c. 1950.

Stein, Gertrude. *The Autobiography of Alice B. Toklas.* New York, 1933.

————. *Paris France.* London, 1940.

Swart, Koenraad W. *The Sense of Decadence in Nineteenth-Century France,* The Hague, 1964.

Thackeray, William Makepeace. *The Paris Sketch Book.* London, 1870.

Tocqueville, Alexis de (Stuart Gilbert, tr.). *The Old Regime and the French Revolution.* New York, 1955.

Trollope, Frances. *Paris and the Parisians in 1835.* New York, 1836.

Vandam, Albert Dresden. *An Englishman in Paris (Notes and Recollections)* I *(Reign of Louis-Philippe).* London, 1892.

Villon, François. *Poésies. Préface de Ch. M. des Granges, Charles d'Orléans Choix de Poésies.* Paris, c. 1945.

Vizetelly, Ernest Alfred. *My Adventures in the Commune, Paris, 1871.* London, 1914.

Waters, Harold A. *Paul Claudel*. New York, 1970.

Weiner, Seymour S. *Francis Carco: The Career of a Literary Bohemian*. New York, 1952.

————. "Gautier (Pierre Jules), Théophile." Stanley J. Kunitz and Vineta Colby, eds. *European Authors, 1000–1900, A Biographical Dictionary of European Authors*. New York, 1967. pp. 317–319.

Wickes, George. *Americans in Paris*. Garden City, 1969.

Williams, Orlo. *Vie de Bohème, A Patch of Romantic Paris*. Boston, 1913.

Williams, Roger L., ed. *The Commune of Paris, 1871*. New York, 1969.

————. *The French Revolution of 1870–1871*. New York, 1969.

————. *Gaslight and Shadow, The World of Napoleon III, 1851–1870*. New York, 1957.

Williamson, George C., ed. *Bryan's Dictionary of Painters and Engravers*. IV (Port Washington, 1964).

Wilson, Robert Forest. *Paris on Parade*. Indianapolis, 1924.

Verne, Jules. *Around the World in Eighty Days*. New York, 1926.

Zeller, André. *Les Hommes de la Commune*. Paris, 1969.

Zola, Emile. *L'Assommoir*. Paris, 1877.

CALIFORNIA AND THE WEST

Anderson, Albert T. and Bernice Prince Biggs, eds. and comps. *A Focus on Rebellion, Materials for Analysis*. San Francisco, 1962.

Anonymous. "Interesting Facts about Carmel." The Monterery Peninsula *Review*. 9–15 August 1973.

Asbury, Herbert. *The Barbary Coast, An Informal History of the San Francisco Underworld*. New York, 1933.

Bartlett, Richard A. *A Social History of the American Frontier, 1776–1890*. New York, 1974.

Bean, Walton. *Boss Reuf's San Francisco*. Berkeley, 1952.

————. *California, An Interpretive History*. New York, 1968.

Becker, Howard S., ed. *Culture and Civility in San Francisco*. Chicago, 1971.

Blum, Walter. "Turk Murphy, Living Legend." *California Living Magazine*, San Francisco *Sunday Examiner & Chronicle*. 27 June 1976.

Bosqui, Edward. *Memoirs of Edward Bosqui*. Oakland, 1952.

Boyle, Kay. *The Long Walk at San Francisco State and Other Essays*. New York, 1970.

Brooks, Charles S. *A Western Wind*. New York, 1935.

Burgess, Gelett. *Bayside Bohemia*. San Francisco, 1954.

Caen, Herb. San Francisco *Chronicle*. 4 May 1958.

Commanday, Robert. "California Supports the Arts." *This World,* San Francisco *Sunday Examiner & Chronicle.* 20 April 1975.

Craddock, William J. *Be Not Content.* Garden City, 1970.

_____. *Twilight Candelabra, An Absurdly Disrespectful Horror Story and Tight Pornographic Allegory.* Garden City, 1972.

Dobie, Charles Caldwell. *San Francisco, A Pageant.* New York, 1934.

Domhoff, G. William. *The Bohemian Grove and Other Retreats: A Study in Ruling-Class Cohesiveness.* New York, 1974.

Field, Isobel. *This Life I've Loved.* New York, 1937.

Fink, Augusta. *Monterey, The Presence of the Past.* San Francisco, 1972.

Fong-Torres, Ben. "Love Is Just a Song We Sing But a Contract Is Something Else: A Dischordant History of the San Francisco Sound." *Rolling Stone.* 26 February 1976.

Gleason, Ralph J. *The Jefferson Airplane and the San Francisco Sound.* New York, 1969.

Hart James D. "Introduction." Gelett Burgess. *Bayside Bohemia.* San Francisco, 1954.

Hoffman, Nicholas von. *We Are the People Our Parents Warned Us Against.* Chicago, 1968.

Hollon, W. Eugene. *Frontier Violence, Another Look.* New York, 1974.

Johnson, Robert E., ed. *Rolling Renaissance: San Francisco Underground Art in Celebration: 1945–1968.* San Francisco, 1975.

Jones, Idwal. *Ark of Empire, San Francisco's Montgomery Block: San Francisco's Unique Bohemia, 1853–1953.* New York, 1972.

Kamstra, Jerry. *The Frisco Kid.* New York, 1975.

Kerouac, Jack. *The Subterraneans.* New York, 1958.

Lewis, Oscar. *Bay Window Bohemia: An Account of the Brilliant Artistic World of Gaslit San Francisco.* New York, 1956.

Lipton, Lawrence. *The Holy Barbarians.* New York, 1959.

Longstreet, Stephen. *The Wilder Shore, A Gala History of San Francisco's Sinners and Spenders, 1849–1906.* New York, 1968.

Messer, Mark. "Running Out of Era: Some Nonpharmacological Notes on the Psychedelic Revolution." David Smith, ed. *The New Social Drug: Cultural, Medical, and Legal Perspectives on Marijuana.* Englewood Cliff, 1970. pp. 157–167.

Miller, Henry. *Big Sur and the Oranges of Hieronymous Bosch.* New York, 1957.

Mulford, Harry. "Artistic and Literary Men, A History of the San Francisco Art Institute." *San Francisco Art Institute Calendar of Events.* March 1973.

Muscatine, Doris. *Old San Francisco, The Biography of a City from Early Days to the Earthquake.* New York, 1975.

Nadeau, Rémi. *California, The New Society.* New York, 1963.

Neubert, George W. *Xavier Martinez (1869–1943).* Oakland, 1974.

Noel, Joseph. *Footloose in Arcadia, A Personal Record of Jack*

London, George Sterling, Ambrose Bierce. New York, 1940.

Norris, Frank. *McTeague, A Story of San Francisco.* New York, 1960.

Parkinson, Thomas, ed. *A Casebook on the Beat.* New York, 1961.

Perry, Charles. "From Eternity to Here: What a Long, Strange Trip It's Been." *Rolling Stone.* 26 February 1976.

Rexroth, Kenneth. "Rexroth Has Found S.F. Has Gone to the Cats." *This World.* San Francisco *Sunday Chronicle.* 29 November 1959.

Rigney, Francis J. and L. Douglas Smith. *The Real Bohemia, A Sociological and Psychological Study of the "Beat."* New York, 1961.

Russell, Don. *The Wild West or, A History of the Wild West Shows, . . . , Which Created a Wonderfully Imaginative and Unrealistic Image of the American West.* Fort Worth, 1970.

Seares, Mabel Urmy. "William Keith and His Times." Anonymous. *Art in California.* . . . San Francisco, 1916. pp. 105–110.

Simon, John S. *The Sign of the Fool, Memoirs from the Haight-Ashbury, 1965–68.* New York, 1971.

Smith, David E., M.D., and John Luce. *Love Needs Care, A History of San Francisco's Haight-Ashbury Free Medical Clinic and Its Pioneer Role in Treating Drug-Abuse Problems.* Boston, 1971.

Smith, Henry Nash. *Virgin Land, The American West as Symbol and Myth.* Cambridge, Massachusetts, 1950.

Smith, H. S., ed. *Story of the Wild West and, By Buffalo Bill,* (Hon. W. F. Cody), *A Full and Complete History of the Pioneer Quartette.* . . . Richmond, 1888.

Soulé, Frank, John H. Gihon, M.D., and James Nisbet. *The Annals of San Francisco.* . . . Palo Alto, 1966. First published in 1855.

Starr, Kevin. *Americans and the California Dream.* New York, 1973.

Taper, Bernard, ed. and comp. *Mark Twain's San Francisco.* New York, 1963.

Taylor, Carol. "Like an Extravagant Love Affair That Ended Savagely." *Rolling Stone.* 22 February 1976.

Unna, Warren. *The Coppa Murals, A Pageant of Bohemian Life in San Francisco at the Turn of the Century.* San Francisco, 1932.

Walker, Franklin. *The Seacoast of Bohemia, An Account of Early Carmel.* San Francisco, 1966.

Walter, John I. "The San Francisco Art Association." Anonymous. *Art in California.* . . . San Francisco, 1916. pp. 97–101.

Wilentz, Elias, ed. *The Beat Scene.* New York, 1960.

Wolf, Leonard, ed. *Voice from the Love Generation.* Boston, 1968.

Wolfe, Tom. *The Electric Kool-Aid Acid Test.* New York, 1968.

Zee, John van der. *The Greatest Men's Party on Earth: Inside the Bohemian Grove.* New York, 1974.

YOUTH AND BOHEMIA

Adler, Nathan. *The Underground Stream: New Life Styles and the Antinomian Personality.* New York, 1972.

Aldridge, John W. *In the Country of the Young.* New York, 1969.

Bodenheim, Maxwell. *My Life and Loves in Greenwich Village.* New York, 1954.

Carter, John F., Jr. " 'These Wild Young People' by One of Them." *The Atlantic Monthly.* CXXVI (September 1920). pp. 301–304.

Carey, James T., Ph. D. "Marijuana Use Among the New Bohemians." David E. Smith, ed. *The New Social Drug.* . . . Englewood Cliffs, 1970.

Charters, Ann. *Kerouac, A Biography.* San Francisco, 1973.

Conant, Jane Eshleman. "Youth Living at 'The End of Time.' " San Francisco *Examiner.* 15 September 1969.

Cook, Bruce. *The Beat Generation, The Tumultuous '50's Movement and Its Impact on Today.* New York, 1971.

Crane, Stephen. *Maggie, A Girl of the Streets.* New York, 1893.

Eisen, Jonothan, ed. *The Age of Rock: Sounds of the American Cultural Revolution.* New York, 1969.

Farber, Jerry. *The Student As Nigger, Essays and Stories by Jerry Farber.* New York, 1969.

Fast, Julius. *The Beatles, The Real Story.* New York, 1968.

Feldman, Gene and Max Gartenberg, eds. *The Beat Generation and the Angry Young Men.* New York, 1958.

Gerzon, Mark. *The Whole World Is Watching: A Young Man Looks at Youth's Dissent.* New York, 1970.

Gillis, John R. *Youth and History: Tradition and Change in European Age-Relations 1770—Present.* New York, 1974.

Grogan, Emmett. *Ringolevio, A Life Played for Keeps.* Boston, 1972.

Gruen, John. *The New Bohemia, The Combine Generation.* New York, 1966.

Guthrie, Woody (Robert Shelton, ed.). *Born to Win.* New York, 1965.

———. *Bound for Glory.* New York, 1943.

Hahn, Emily. *Romantic Rebels, An Informal History of Bohemianism in America.* Boston, 1967.

Harrington, Michael. "We Few, We Happy Few, We Bohemians, A Memoir of the Culture Before the Counterculture." *Esquire* August 1972. pp. 99–103, 162–164.

Harris, Louis. "New Life Styles." Cleveland *Plain Dealer.* 11 August 1975.

Hecht, Ben. *Letters from Bohemia.* New York, 1964.

Hoffman, Frederick J., ed. *Marginal Manners, The Variants of Bohemia.* Evanston, 1962.

Josephson, Matthew. *Edison, A Biography.* New York, 1959.

Kamstra, Jerry. *Weed: Adventures of a Dope Smuggler.* New York, 1974.

Kemp, Harry. *Tramping on Life, An Autobiographical Narrative.* Garden City, 1922.

Kerouac, Jack. *On the Road.* New York, 1957.

Kohn, Hans. "Youth Movements." *Encyclopedia of the Social Sciences.* XV. pp. 516–520.

Krassner, Paul. *How a Satirical Editor Became a Yippie Conspirator in Ten Easy Years.* New York, c. 1971.

Leonard, George B. *The Transformation, A Guide to the Inevitable Changes in Humankind.* New York, 1972.

Lindsey, Judge Ben B. and W. Evans. *The Revolt of Modern Youth.* New York, 1925.

Mailer, Norman. "The White Negro, Superficial Reflections on the Hipster." *Dissent.* IV (Summer 1957). pp. 276–293.

Malcolm, Henry. *Generation of Narcissus with an Introduction by R. Buckminster Fuller.* Boston, 1971.

Maurois, André. *Ariel, The Life of Shelley.* New York, 1924.

Meade, Margaret. *Culture and Commitment, A Study of the Generation Gap.* Garden City, 1970.

Melville, Keith. *Communes in the Counter Culture: Origins, Theories, Styles of Life.* New York, 1972.

Mungo, Raymond. *Total Loss Farm, A Year in the Life.* New York, 1970.

Parry, Albert. *Garrets and Pretenders, A History of Bohemianism in America.* New York, 1933.

Pennebaker, D. A. *Bob Dylan: Don't Look Back.* New York, 1968.

Raley, Loker. "The World Is Too Much with Us." *The* Woodstock *Aquarian.* 1971. p. 31.

Revel, Jean-François (J. F. Bernard, tr.). *Without Marx or Jesus, The New American Revolution Has Begun, With an Afterword by Mary McCarthy.* New York, 1970.

Richter, Hans (David Britt, tr.). *Dada: Art and Anti-Art.* London, 1965.

Roszak, Theodore. *The Making of a Counter Culture.* New York, 1969.

Smith, David E., ed. *The New Social Drug, Cultural, Medical, and Legal Perspectives on Marijuana.* Englewood Cliffs, 1970.

Stevenson, Elizabeth. *Babbitts and Bohemians, The American 1920's.* New York, 1967.

Tate, Alfred O. *Edison's Open Door: The Life Story of Thomas A. Edison, a Great Individualist.* New York, 1938.

Vesey, George. "For Young Urban Nomads, Home Is the Streets." New York *Times.* 1 June 1976.

Wylie, Laurence. "Youth in France and the United States." Erik H. Erikson, ed. *Youth, Change and Challenge.* New York, 1963.

Young, Allen. "Allen Ginsberg: 'Your Own Heart Is Your Guru'—an Interview." Berkeley *Barb*. April 6–12, 13–19, 20–26, 1973. Reprinted from *Gay Sunshine* # 16.

GERMANY

Abel, Theodore. *Why Hitler Came Into Power, An Answer Based on the Original Life Stories of Six Hundred of His Followers*. New York, 1938.

Allen, William Sheridan. *The Nazi Seizure of Power, The Experience of a Single German Town, 1930–1935*. Chicago, 1965.

Anonymous. "A Bizarre Tale of Hitler's Loves." (An interview with Ernst Hanfstaengl.) San Francisco *Chronicle*. 12 June 1972.

_____. "The Two Hitlers." *Time*. 2 October 1972. pp. 48–49.

Barraclough, Geoffrey. "Mandarins and Nazis: Part I," "The Liberals and German History: Part III," "A New View of German History: Part III." *The New York Review of Books*. 19 October, 2, 16 November 1972. pp. 37–44, 32–37, 25–31.

Becker, Howard. *German Youth: Bond or Free?* New York, 1946.

Binion, Rudolf. *Hitler Among the Germans*. New York, 1976.

Blüher, Hans. *Die Deutsche Wandervogelbewegung als Erotisches Phaenomen*. Berlin, 1912.

_____. *Führer und Volk in der Jugundbewegung*. Jena, 1924.

_____. *Wandervogel, Geschichte Eine Jugundbewegung*. Prien, 1922.

Bowra, C. M. *Memoirs, 1898–1939*. Cambridge, Massachusetts, 1967.

Bracher, Karl Dietrich (Jean Steinberg, tr.). *The German Dictatorship: The Origins, Structure, and Effects of National Socialism*. New York, 1970.

Brennan, J. H. *The Occult Reich*. New York, 1974.

Bullock, Alan. *Hitler: A Study in Tyranny*. New York, 1958.

Carsten, F. L. *The Reichwehr and Politics, 1918 to 1933*. New York, 1966.

Chelminski, Rudolph. "West Germans Screw Up Courage to Show Nazi Art." *Smithsonian*. V (February 1975). pp. 70–78.

Christoph, Shawn. "...Cowboys und Indianer...the Range in Wild West Germany." San Francisco *Sunday Examiner & Chronicle*. 18 August 1974.

Conway, J. S. *The Nazi Persecution of the Churches, 1933–1945*. New York, 1968.

Domandi, Mario. "The German Youth Movement." Unpublished Doctoral Dissertation. Columbia University. 1960.

Dietrich, Otto (Richard and Clara Winston, trs.). *The Hitler I Knew*. London, 1957.

Elon, Amos (Michael Roloff, tr.). *Journey Through a Haunted Land, The New Germany*. New York, 1967.

Fleming, Alice. "Heinrich Böll, Germany Restored." *Intellectual Digest*. May 1973. pp. 64–65.

Fleming, Peter. *Operation Sea Lion, The Projected Invasion of England in 1940—An Account of the German Preparation and the British Countermeasures*. New York, 1957.

Friedrich, Otto. *Before the Deluge, A Portrait of Berlin in the 1920's*. New York, 1972.

Gay, Peter. *Weimar Culture: The Outsider as Insider*. New York, 1968.

Gerard, James W., Late Ambassador to the German Imperial Court. *My Four Years in Germany*. New York, 1917.

Gilbert, G. M., Ph.D. Formerly prison psychiatrist at the Nuremberg Trial of the Nazi war criminals. *Nuremberg Diary*. New York, 1947.

Gisevius, Hans Bernd (Richard and Clara Winston, trs.). *To the Bitter End*. Boston, 1947.

Goebbels, Joseph (Louis P. Lochner, tr.). *The Goebbels Diaries*. New York, 1971.

Goerlitz, Walter (Brian Battershaw, tr.). *History of the German General Staff, 1657–1945*. New York, 1953.

Grunberger, Richard. *Hitler's SS*. New York, 1970.

————. *The 12-Year Reich, A Social History of Nazi Germany, 1933–1945*. New York, 1971.

Hanfstaengl, Ernst. *Unheard Witness*. Philadelphia, 1957.

Hanser, Richard. *Putsch! How Hitler Made Revolution*. New York, 1970.

Hart, B. H. Liddell. *The German Generals Talk*. New York, 1948.

Heiden, Konrad (Ralph Manheim, tr.). *Der Fuehrer, Hitler's Rise to Power*. Boston, 1944.

Heisenberg, Werner (Arnold J. Pomerans, tr.). *Physics and Beyond, Encounters and Conversations*. New York, 1971.

Held, Joseph. "Embattled Youth, The Independent German Youth Movements in the Twentieth Century." Unpublished Doctoral Dissertation. Rutgers University. 1968.

Hermanns, William. *The Holocaust, From a Survivor of Verdun*. New York, 1972.

Herzstein, Robert E. *Adolf Hitler and the German Trauma, 1913–1945: An Interpretation of the Nazi Phenomenon*. New York, 1974.

Hesse, Hermann (Ralph Manheim, tr.). *If the War Goes On . . . Reflections on War and Politics*. New York, 1970.

Hitler, Adolf. *Hitler's Secret Conversations, 1941–1944, With an Introductory Essay by H. R. Trevor-Roper*. New York, 1953.

————. (Ralph Manheim, tr.). *Mein Kampf*. Boston, 1943.

Irving, David. *The German Atomic Bomb, The History of Nuclear Research in Nazi Germany*. New York, 1967.

Johnson, William. "The Taking Part." *Sports Illustrated*. 10 July 1972. pp. 36–44.

Jünger, Ernst (Stuart Hood, tr.). *African Diversions*. London, 1954.

————. *On the Marble Cliffs, A Novel by Ernst Juenger*. New York, 1947.

————. (Basil Creighton, tr.). *The Storm of Steel, From the Diary of a German Storm-Troop Officer on the Western Front*. London, 1929.

Kahler, Erich. *The Germans*. Princeton, 1974.

Koenigsberg, Richard A. *Hitler's Ideology, A Study in Psychoanalytic Sociology*. New York, 1975.

Kogon, Eugen (Heinz Norden, tr.). *The Theory and Practice of Hell, The German Concentration Camps and the System Behind Them*. New York, 1950.

Kubizek, August (E. V. Anderson, tr.). *The Young Hitler I Knew*. New York, 1955.

Langer, Walter. *The Mind of Adolf Hitler, The Secret Wartime Report, Foreword by William L. Langer, Afterword by Robert G. L. Waite*. New York, 1972.

Laqueur, Walter Z. *Weimar, A Cultural History, 1918–1933*. New York, 1974.

————. *Young Germany, A History of the German Youth Movement*. New York, 1962.

Loewenberg, Peter. "The Psychohistorical Origins of the Nazi Youth Cohort." *The American Historical Review*. LXXVI (1971). pp. 1457–1502.

Loose, Gerhard. *Ernst Jünger*. New York, 1974.

Lorant, Stefan (James Cleugh, tr.). *I Was Hitler's Prisoner, Leaves from a Prison Diary*. Harmondsworth, 1935.

Maser, Werner (Peter and Betty Ross, trs.). *Hitler*. London, 1973.

Masur, Gerhard. *Prophets of Yesterday, Studies in European Culture, 1890–1914*. New York, 1961.

Meinecke, Friederich (Sidney B. Fay, tr.). *The German Catastrophe*. Cambridge, Massachusetts, c. 1960.

Mosse, George L. *The Crisis of German Ideology, Intellectual Origins of the Third Reich*. New York, 1964.

Neumann, Franz, *Behemoth, The Structure and Practice of National Socialism*. New York, 1942.

New York *Times* 10 November 1923.

Nolte, Ernst (Leila Vennewitz, tr.). *Three Faces of Fascism*. New York, 1966.

Norden, Eric. "Playboy Interview: Albert Speer. . . ." *Playboy*, June 1971.

Orlow, Dietrich. "The Conversion of Myths into Political Power, The Case of the Nazi Party, 1925–1926." *The American Historical Review*. LXXII (1967). pp. 908–924.

————. "The Organizational History and Structure of the NSDAP,

1919–1923." *The Journal of Modern History.* XXXVII (March, 1965). pp. 208–226.

Plivier, Theodore (Margaret Green, tr.). *The Kaiser's Coolies.* New York, 1932.

Rauschning, Hermann. *Men of Chaos.* New York, 1942.

————. *The Revolution of Nihilism, Warning to the West.* New York, 1939.

————. *The Voice of Destruction.* (Conversations with Hitler). New York, 1940.

Ravenscroft, Trevor. *The Spear of Destiny, The Occult Power Behind the Spear Which Pierced the Side of Christ.* New York, 1973.

Reitlinger, Gerald. *The SS, Alibi of a Nation.* New York, 1957.

Remarque, Erich Maria (A. W. Wheen, tr.). *All Quiet on the Western Front.* Boston, 1929.

————. *The Road Back.* Boston, 1931.

Rich, Norman. *Hitler's War Aims.* I (*Ideology, The Nazi State, and the Course of Expansion*). New York, 1973.

Riefenstahl, Leni. *Triumph of the Will.* A film. Berlin, 1934.

Salomon, Ernst von (Ian F. D. Morrow, tr.). *The Outlaws.* London, 1931.

Sander, August (With an introduction by Gunther Sander and a foreword by Golo Mann). *Men Without Masks, Faces of Germany 1910–1938.* Greenwich, Connecticut, 1973.

Schmid, Robert Karl. "German Youth Movements, A Typological Study." Unpublished Doctoral Dissertation. The University of Wisconsin. 1941.

Schmidt-Polex, Karl. "Hitler's Godchildren, An Investigation of the Nazi Baby-Breeding Program." *Atlas World Press Review.* January 1976. pp. 52–53.

Schoenbaum, David. *Hitler's Social Revolution, Class and Status in Nazi Germany.* New York, 1966.

Shirer, William L. *The End of a Berlin Diary.* New York, 1947.

————. *The Rise and Fall of the Third Reich, A History of Nazi Germany.* New York, 1960.

Smith, Bradley F. *Adolf Hitler, His Family, Childhood and Youth.* Stanford, 1967.

Speer, Albert (Richard and Clara Winston, trs.). *Inside the Third Reich, Memoirs by Albert Speer.* New York, 1970.

————. *Spandau, The Secret Diaries.* New York, 1976.

Stein, George H., ed. *Great Lives Observed: Hitler.* Englewood Cliffs, 1968.

————. *The Waffen SS, Hitler's Elite Body Guard at War, 1939–1945.* Ithaca, 1966.

Steiner, Jean-François (Helen Weaver, tr.). *Treblinka.* New York, 1967.

Stern, Fritz. *The Politics of Cultural Despair.* Berkeley, 1963.

Toland, John. *Adolf Hitler*. Garden City, 1976.

Viereck, Peter. *Metapolitics, The Roots of the Nazi Mind*. New York, 1961.

Vonnegut, Kurt, Jr., A Fourth-Generation German-American . . . , Who . . . Witnessed the Fire-Bombing of Dresden, Germany. . . . *Slaughterhouse-Five: Or, The Children's Crusade, A Duty-Dance with Death*. New York, 1969.

Waite, Robert G. L. *Vanguard of Nazism, The Free Corps Movement in Postwar Germany, 1918–1923*. Cambridge, Massachusetts, 1952.

Whicher, George F., ed and tr. *The Goliard Poets: Medieval Latin Songs and Satires*. New York, 1949.

Winterbotham, F. W. *The Ultra Secret*. New York, 1974.

Wiskemann, Elizabeth, ed., Helmut Krausnick, Hans Buccheim, Martin Broszat, and Hans-Adolf Jacobsen. *Anatomy of the SS State*. New York, 1968.

AMERICA

Aaron, Daniel. *Writers on the Left*. New York, 1965.

Adamic, Louis. *Dynamite: The Story of Class Violence in America*. New York, 1931.

————. *A Nation of Nations*. New York, 1945.

Adams, John. "John Adams to H. Niles." Quincy, 13 February 1818. Charles Francis Adams, ed. *The Works of John Adams*. . . . X (Boston, 1856). pp. 282–283.

Allen, Frederick Lewis. *The Big Change, America Transforms Itself, 1900–1950*. New York, 1952.

————. *Only Yesterday, An Informal History of the Nineteen-Twenties*. New York, 1931.

————. *Since Yesterday, The Nineteen-Thirties In America*. New York, 1940.

Allsop, Kenneth. *Hard Travellin', The Hobo and His History*. New York, 1967.

Armstrong, Louis. *Satchmo: My Life in New Orleans*. New York, 1954.

Asbury, Herbert. *The French Quarter, An Informal History of the New Orleans Underworld*. New York, 1936.

————. *The Gangs of New York, An Informal History of the Underworld*. New York, 1928.

Bechet, Sidney. *Treat It Gentle, An Autobiography*. New York, 1960.

Bendiner, Robert. *Just Around the Corner, A Highly Selective History of the Thirties*. New York, 1967.

Bernstein, Carl and Bob Woodward. *All the President's Men*. New York, 1974.

Brackman, Jacob. "The International Comix Conspiracy." *Playboy.* December 1970. pp. 195–199, 328–334.

Campbell, Helen, Col. Thomas W. Knox, and Superintendent Thomas Byrnes, *Darkness and Daylight; or, Lights and Shadows of New York Life. A Pictorial Record of Personal Experiences by Day and Night in the Great Metropolis.* . . . Hartford, 1897.

Cochran, Thomas C. and William Miller. *The Age of Enterprise, A Social History of Industrial America.* New York, 1961.

Cooke, Alistair, ed. *The Vintage Mencken.* New York, 1956.

Cranston, Alan. *U.S. Senator Alan Cranston Reports to Californians.* April 1975.

Davie, Michael. "British View of the White House: The 'Orange County' Spirit." San Francisco *Chronicle.* 28 April 1973.

Davis, Nuel Pharr. *Lawrence and Oppenheimer.* New York, 1968.

de Mille, Anna George (Don C. Shoemaker, ed.). *Henry George, Citizen of the World.* Chapel Hill, 1950.

Dexter, Dave, Jr. *The Jazz Story, from the '90's to the '60's, with a Foreword by Woody Herman.* Englewood Cliffs, 1964.

Dodds, Warren (as told to Larry Gara). *The Baby Dodds Story.* Los Angeles, 1959.

Egbert, Donald Drew and Stow Persons, eds. *Socialism and American Life.* II *(Bibliography, Descriptive and Critical).* Princeton, 1952.

Fairbairn, Ann. *Call Him George.* New York, 1969.

Ferguson, Blanche E. *Countee Cullen and the Negro Renaissance.* New York, 1966.

Foster, George Murphy (as told to Tom Stoddard), interchapters by Ross Russell. *Pops Foster, The Autobiography of a New Orleans Jazzman.* Berkeley, 1971.

George, Henry, Jr. *The Life of Henry George by His Son, Henry George, Jr.* New York, 1900.

Goffin, Robert. *La Nouvelle-Orléans, Capitale du Jazz.* New York, 1946.

Goldberg, Isaac. *The Man Mencken, A Biographical and Critical Study.* New York, 1925.

Handlin, Oscar. *The Uprooted: The Epic Story of the Great Migrations That Made the American People.* New York, 1951.

Hofstadter, Richard, William Miller and Daniel Aaron. *The American Republic.* II *(Since 1865).* Englewood Cliffs, 1959.

Hsu, Francis L. K. *Americans and Chinese, Reflections on Two Cultures and Their People.* New York, 1970.

Huggins, Nathan Irvin. *Harlem Renaissance.* New York, 1971.

Hughes, Langston. *The Big Sea, An Autobiography by Langston Hughes.* New York, 1940.

————. *The Panther and the Lash, Poems of Our Times.* New York, 1967.

————. *I Wonder as I Wander, An Autobiographical Journey.* New York, 1956.

Jameson, John Franklin. *The American Revolution Considered as a Social Movement.* Princeton, 1926.

Jones, LeRoi (Imamu Amiri Baraka), *Blues People: Negro Music in White America.* New York, 1963.

Kesey, Ken. *One Flew Over the Cuckoo's Nest.* New York, 1962.

Kunitz, Stanley and Colby, Veneta, eds. *European Authors, 1000– 1900, A Biographical Dictionary of European Authors.* New York, 1967.

Lomax, Allen, ed. *The 111 Best American Ballads, Folk Song USA.* New York, 1947.

Lomax, John A. *Adventures of a Ballad Hunter.* New York, 1947.

London, Jack. *The Road.* New York, 1970.

Longview (Washington) *Daily News,* 6 July 1971.

Malcolm X with Alex Haley. *The Autobiography of Malcolm X.* New York, 1964.

Manchester, William. *Disturber of the Peace, The Life of H. L. Mencken.* New York, 1950.

Mezzrow, Milton "Mezz," with Bernard Wolfe. *Really the Blues.* New York, 1946.

Mills, C. Wright. *The Power Elite.* New York, 1959.

Moody, Sid. "The King Is Dead, There Is No Prince." Longview (Washington) *Daily News.* 6 July 1965.

Moore, Robin. *The Green Berets.* New York, 1965.

Morton, Ferdinand (Allen Lomax, ed.). *Mr. Jelly Roll.* New York, 1956.

New York *Times.* 27 July 1935.

O'Connor, Francis V., ed. *Art for the Millions: Essays from the 1930's by Artists and Administrators of the WPA Federal Art Project.* Greenwich, Connecticut, 1973.

Paul, Elliot. *That Crazy American Music.* Indianapolis, 1957.

Pearson, Drew. San Francisco *Chronicle.* 16 May 1961.

Ramsey, Frederic, Jr., and Charles Edward Smith, eds. *Jazzmen.* New York, 1939.

Rapoport, Roger. *The Great American Bomb Machine.* New York, 1971.

Rush, Benjamin. "Benjamin Rush to Richard Price." Philadelphia, 25 May 1786. L. H. Butterfield, ed. *Letters of Benjamin Rush.* I *(1761–1792).* Princeton, 1951.

Sale, Kilpatrick. "The World Behind Watergate." *The New York Review of Books.* 3 May 1973. pp. 9–16.

Sandburg, Carl. *The American Songbag.* New York, 1927.

Seeger, Pete. *The Incompleat* [sic] *Folksinger.* New York, 1972.

————. "More Praise for the Non-Traveller." *Sing Out! The Folk Song Magazine.* XXII (1974). p. 31.

Shapiro, Nat and Nat Hentoff, eds. *The Jazz Makers*. New York, 1957.

Slater, Philip E. *The Pursuit of Loneliness, American Culture at the Breaking Point*. Boston, 1970.

Smith, Gibbs M. *Joe Hill*. Salt Lake·City, 1969.

Southern, Eileen. *The Music of Black Americans, A History*. New York, 1971.

Steinbeck, John. *Travels with Charley, In Search of America*. New York, 1962.

Tolles, Frederick B. "The American Revolution Considered as a Social Movement: A Re-Evaluation." *The American Historical Review*. LX (1954). pp. 1–12.

United Press International. "Another CIA Plot: Cuba Crops." San Francisco *Sunday Examiner & Chronicle*. 27 June 1976.

Van Vechten, Carl. *Nigger Heaven*. New York, 1926.

Ware, Caroline F. *Greenwich Village, 1920–1930, A Comment on American Civilization in the Post-War Years*. Boston, 1935.

Warner Brothers Studios. *Hearts and Minds*. A Film. Los Angeles, 1974.

Whyte, William W. *The Organization Man*. New York, 1956.

Williams, Martin. *Jazz Masters of New Orleans*. New York, 1967.

Wittke, Carl. *We Who Built America: The Saga of the Immigrant*. New York, 1945.

GENERAL

Anderson, Jack. "CIA Germ Warfare." Monterey (California) *Peninsula Herald*. 18 January 1977.

————. "U.S. Ready with Neuclear Weapons." San Francisco *Chronicle*. 8 July 1975.

Barnaby, Dr. Frank. "Precision Warfare." *New Scientist*. 8 May 1975. pp. 304–307.

Barraclough, Geoffrey. "The Great World Crisis." *The New York Review of Books*. Part I. 23 January 1975. pp. 20–30.

Bastide, Roger (Peter Green, tr.). *African Civilization in the New World*. New York, 1971.

Bernstein, Jeremy. "When the Computer Procreates." *The* New York *Times Magazine*. 15 February 1976. pp. 9, 34–38.

Boulding, Kenneth E. *The Image*. Ann Arbor, 1961.

Braive, Michel François (David Britt, tr.). *The Photograph, A Social History*. New York, 1966.

Carsten, F. L. *The Rise of Fascism*. Berkeley, 1967.

Casper, Barry M. "Laser Enrichment: A New Path to Proliferation?" *The Bulletin of the Atomic Scientists*. XXXIII (January, 1977). pp. 28–41.

Ceram, C. W. *Archaeology of the Cinema*. New York, c. 1970.

Cowen, Robert C. "Should Biologists Redesign Organic Life?" *The Christian Science Monitor* (Boston). 3 February 1977.

Djilas, Milovan. *The New Class, An Analysis of the Communist System*. New York, 1957.

Dumas, Lloyd J. "National Insecurity in the Nuclear Age." *The Bulletin of the Atomic Scientists*. XXXII (May 1976). pp. 24–35.

Durant, Will. *The Age of Faith, A History of Medieval Civilization—Christian, Islamic, and Judaic—from Constantine to Dante: A.D. 325–1300*. New York, 1950.

————. *The Story of Philosophy: The Lives and Opinions of the Great Philosophers*. Garden City, 1926.

Egbert, Donald Drew. *Social Radicalism and the Arts: Western Europe, A Cultural History from the French Revolution to 1968*. New York, 1970.

Enzenberger, Hans Magnus. "The Industrialization of the Mind." *The Partisan Review*. XXXVI (1969). pp. 100–111.

Fanon, Frantz (Constance Farrington, tr.). *The Wretched of the Earth, Preface by Jean-Paul Sartre*. New York, 1968.

Feld, Bernard T. "Making the World Safe for Plutonium." *The Bulletin of the Atomic Scientists*. XXXI (May 1975). pp. 5–6.

Fleming, William. *Arts and Ideas*. New York, 1963.

Frank, Dr. Barnaby. "The Weapons in Our Future." *Atlas, World Press Review*. July 1975. pp. 20–22.

Freud, Sigmund (James Strachey, ed. and tr.). *Civilization and Its Discontents*. New York, 1961. First published in 1930.

Fromm, Erich. *The Anatomy of Human Destructiveness*. New York, 1973.

————. *Beyond the Chains of Illusion, My Encounter with Marx and Freud*. New York, 1962.

————. *Escape from Freedom*. New York, 1941.

————. *Man for Himself, An Inquiry Into the Psychology of Ethics*. New York, 1947.

Fuller, R. Buckminster. *Operating Manual for Spaceship Earth*. Carbondale, Illinois, 1969.

Gardner, Fred. "Nitinol: Torque of the Town." *The Co-Evolution Quarterly*. Spring 1975. pp. 68–72.

Gardner, Martin. *In the Name of Science*. New York, 1952.

George, Henry. *Progress and Poverty, An Inquiry into the Cause of Industrial Depression and of Increase of Want with Increase of Wealth*. New York, 1938.

Gibbs, Sir Philip. *Now It Can Be Told*. New York, 1920.

Gimpel, Jean. *The Cult of Art, Against Art and Artists*. New York, 1969.

Guizot, François Pierre Guillaume. *History of Civilization in Europe, The Fall of the Roman Empire to the French Revolution*. New York, 1885.

Hanna, Thomas. *Bodies in Revolt: The Evolution-Revolution of*

20th Century Man Toward the Somatic Culture of the 21st Century. New York, 1970.

Hecht, Ben. *A Child of the Century.* New York, 1954.

Heilbroner, Robert L. *The Making of Economic Society.* Englewood Cliffs, 1962.

Hobsbawm, E. J. *The Age of Revolution, 1789–1848.* New York, 1962.

Houghton, Walter E. *The Victorian Frame of Mind, 1830–1870.* New Haven, 1957.

Howe, Kevin. "Physicist Predicts Nuclear Arms Use in Anger Before End of This Century." Monterey (California) *Peninsula Herald.* 17 January 1976.

Jahn, Janheinz (Marjorie Green, tr.). *Muntu, An Outline of the New African Culture.* New York, 1961.

Jones, Howard Mumford. *Revolution and Romanticism.* Cambridge, Massachusetts, 1974.

July, Robert W. *A History of the African People.* New York, 1970.

Kohn, Hans. "The Crisis in European Thought and Culture." Jack J. Roth, ed. *World War I: A Turning Point in Modern History.* New York, 1967. pp. 25–46.

Kramer, Hilton. "The Grand Niagara." *Arts Magazine.* XXXVIII (September 1964). p. 15.

Krieger, David. "Terrorism and Nuclear Technology." *The Bulletin of the Atomic Scientists.* XXXI (1975). pp. 28–34.

Lewinsohn, Richard, M.D. (Alexander Mayce, tr.). *A History of Sexual Customs.* New York, 1958.

London, Jack. *The People of the Abyss.* New York, 1903.

Maccoby, Michael. "Emotional Attitudes and Political Choices." *Politics and Society.* Winter 1972. pp. 209–239.

McManners, John. *Lectures on European History, 1789–1914: Men, Machines and Freedom.* New York, 1967.

Marcus, Steven. *The Other Victorians, A Study of Sexuality and Pornography in Mid-Nineteenth-Century England.* New York, 1964.

Marcuse, Herbert. *An Essay on Liberation.* Boston, 1969.

Maslow, Abraham H. *Toward a Psychology of Being.* Princeton, 1962.

May, Karl (C. A. Willoughby, tr.). *In the Desert.* Bamberg, 1955.

Mayhew, Henry. *London Labour and the London Poor: Cyclopedia of the Condition and Earnings.* 4 Vols. London, 1861–1862 (New York, 1968).

Mowat, Farley. *The Sieberians.* Baltimore, 1972.

Nance, John. *The Gentle Tasaday, A Stone Age People in the Philippine Rain Forest, Foreword by Charles A. Lindbergh.* New York, 1975.

Newhall, Beaumont. *The History of Photography from 1839 to the Present Day.* New York, 1949.

Oates, Joyce Carol. "New Heaven and Earth." *Saturday Review/The Arts.* 4 November 1972.

Palm, Charles Franklin. *The Middle Classes, Then and Now.* New York, 1936.

Pauwels, Louis and Jacques Bergier (Rollo Myers, tr.). *The Morning of the Magicians.* New York, 1968.

Plumb, J. H. "The World Beyond America." Richard M. Ketchum, ed. *The American Heritage Book of the Revolution.* New York, 1968.

Pollack, Peter. *The Picture History of Photography from the Earliest Beginnings to the Present Day.* New York, 1969.

Reich, Wilhelm (Vincent R. Carfagno, tr.). *The Mass Psychology of Fascism.* New York, 1970.

Sarti, Roland. "Fascist Modernization in Italy: Traditional or Revolutionary?" *The American Historical Review.* LXXXV (1970). pp. 1029–1045.

Sartre, Jean-Paul. "Introduction, 'A Victory.'" Henri Alleg. *The Question.* New York, 1958. pp. 13–36.

Sagan, Carl, and Frank Drake. "The Search for Extraterrestrial Intelligence." *The Scientific American.* CCXXXII (1975). pp. 80–89.

Schumaker, E. F. *Small Is Beautiful: Economics as if People Mattered.* London, 1973.

Shaw, George Bernard. "Preface to Major Barbara." *Six Plays by Bernard Shaw with Prefaces.* New York, 1947.

Sheean, Vincent. *Personal History.* New York, 1936.

Sheehy, Gail. "California's Impossible Nuclear Decision: A Reporter's Search for an Answer." *New West.* 7 June 1976. pp. 51–58.

Skinner, B. F. *About Behaviorism.* New York, 1974.

Sontag, Raymond J. *A Broken World, 1919–1939.* New York, 1971.

Spock, Benjamin, Dr. *Common Sense Book of Baby and Child Care.* New York, 1946.

Strayer, Joseph R. *Western Europe in the Middle Ages, A Short History.* New York, 1955.

Talmon, J. L. *Romanticism and Revolt: Europe 1815–1848.* New York, 1967.

Tannenbaum, Edward R. "The Goals of Italian Fascism." *The American Historical Review.* LXXIV (1969). pp. 1183–1204.

Taylor, A. J. P. *English History, 1914–1945.* New York, 1965.

Tobias, J. J. *Crime and Industrial Society in the 19th Century.* New York, 1967.

Tuchman, Barbara. *The Guns of August.* New York, 1962.

Wald, Gerald. "Arise, Ye Prisoners." *The Bulletin of the Atomic Scientists,* XXX (December 1974). pp. 4–6.

Weintraub, Stanley. *Whistler, A Biography.* New York, 1974.

Williamson, George C., ed. *Bryan's Dictionary of Painters and Engravers*. IV. Port Washington, 1964.

Wilson, Colin. *The Occult, A History*. New York, 1971.

Wilson, Edmund. *To the Finland Station, A Study in the Writing and Acting of History*. New York, 1940.

Zweig, Stefan. *The World of Yesterday, An Autobiography by Stefan Zweig*. New York, 1943.

Index

George Bernard Shaw - <u>Major Barbara</u>
Victor Hugo - <u>Cromwell</u>, <u>Orientales</u>, Castilian Honor
Theophile Gautier - painter
"pour tout peindre, il Faut tout sentir"
——→ "to portray all, one must sense all"